**The Soviet
Union: The
Seventies and
Beyond**

The Soviet Union: The Seventies and Beyond

Edited by

Bernard W. Eissenstat
Oklahoma State University

Lexington Books

D.C. Heath and Company
Lexington, Massachusetts
Toronto   London

Library of Congress Cataloging in Publication Data

Eissenstat, Bernard W.
   The Soviet Union: the seventies and beyond.

   Includes index.
   1. Russia—History—1953-   2. Russia—Foreign relations—
1953-   . I. Title.
DK274.E37   914.7'03'85   74-310
ISBN 0-669-92718-x

Published simultaneously in Canada.

Printed in the United States of America.

International Standard Book Number: 0-669-92718-x

Library of Congress Catalog Card Number: 74-310

Contents

List of Tables

**The Soviet
Union: The
Seventies and
Beyond**

Introduction

Bernard W. Eissenstat

Among the major problems confronting the general well-being of the nations of the world is that of the economic, political, and military relations between the United States and the Soviet Union. The answers to the questions of peaceful coexistence, detente, convergence, or conflict—whether economic, political, cultural or military—are basic not only to the well-being and security of both the United States and the Soviet Union, but to the rest of the world as well.

In these times, with a significant change in the relations between the USSR and the USA, and a visionary but myopic view of detente, there is a pressing need to focus on the interests and needs of the seventies and beyond with scholarly objectivity. Consequently, this volume explores the motivations, intentions, underlying attitudes, tactics, strategy, and national interests of the Soviet Union in world affairs. Furthermore, the book attempts to put the external policies of the Soviet Union into historical continuity and ideological perspective, and to illuminate and bring into focus the patterns of traditional Russian behavior and permanent national interests, as well as the Soviet patterns and ideology that have been superimposed over them.

While the chapters in this volume are, in part, based on papers presented at the Twelfth Annual Meeting of the Central Slavic Conference, hosted by the Department of History at Oklahoma State University, scholars of competency and reputation other than those participating in the conference have been carefully chosen to contribute chapters, in order to bring harmony within the major theme of the book and to fill in with depth the gaps in topics and in areas not substantially discussed at the conference. In addition, the conference papers have been substantially revised and reworked to focus on a single topic: The Soviet Union in the Seventies and Beyond.

This book has four purposes: to give some depth to Western, and especially US, policy-makers in their foreign policy relations with the Soviet Union; to serve as a guide for the business community, both those interested in the buying and selling of natural resources, or the exploration, discovery, and exploitation of such resources and those looking for trade in finished products; to provide information on cultural, religious, and political attitudes and motivations within the Soviet Union; and to serve as a textbook or as collateral reading at both the graduate and undergraduate level, not necessarily exclusively for those students concentrating their efforts in the specific area of the external policies of the USSR, but perhaps even more so for those who have a general interest in the

3

entire area of world national activities, in particular those students who are looking not for a single and superficial history of Soviet foreign policy, but for a
number of studies in depth—economic, political, religious, and cultural—written
by professional scholars.

The single most decisive factor in popular opinion about the Soviet Union
is the widespread popularity and belief in the myth of the Communist monolith.
The devil thesis of history—the paranoid belief in a single cause of all the world's
problems—with its dogmatic and simplistic faith that the world's political problems could be solved quickly and equitably by the eradication of the Communist
monolith (or, from the Communist point of view, by the eradication of the
capitalist socioeconomic formation, and the formation of the progressive and
higher stage of socialism) dominated the world's energies and dictated national
policies for over a quarter of a century. The concept of the Communist monolith
of nation-states, with the Soviet Union, the most powerful and earliest of the
states to achieve a socialist society, as the leader of the conspiracy to make the
world safe for socialism, was, from its very inception, nonsense. The belief in
the Soviet monolith was not based on hard concrete historical evidence, but on
the fears and anxieties of people and politicians who mistook the myth for the
reality, who fallaciously took the strident and repetitious intoning of the party
line as evidence of a unified, single-minded conspiracy of Communist states.

Since the Great October Revolution of 1917, it is true, most Communist
parties, no matter what their national origin, have sworn allegiance and paid
homage to Moscow. But during this early period no other Communist country
existed. Where else could the national parties seek succor and support for their
sometimes illegal group? In the very period when the Communist monolith
seemingly reached its greatest growth and strength, it had within it, as Karl
Marx was wont to say, the seeds of its successor. I make reference to the period
between the close of World War II and 1957, when Togliatti coined his famous
word "polycentricism" to describe the new period of Communist fraternal relations.

The persistence of the idea of the monolith continued in the West until very
recently. (This is not to argue that there is no cooperation among the various
countries espousing communism; Vietnam disproves that. It is to argue, rather,
that the cooperation is based on what the cooperating country conceives to be
its national interest). Certainly, long before Western politicians, Soviet political
leaders recognized that the cement that held the monolith together was the
strength and actions of the Soviet military forces rather than the ideological
bindings of dialectical materialism. The problems implicit in governing an
empire plagued the Communist party of the Soviet Union. After 1945, however,
with the imperialistic attempts to impose Russian sovereignty upon other
countries under the guise of humanitarian scientific socialism and the rationale of dialectic materialism, compounded by the rapidly intensifying revolutionary movements in underdeveloped areas, it became evident that the Soviet
commissars met with many of the same problems as their tsarist predecessors.

While there were states that might join Moscow on the basis of "fraternal brotherhood" and "equality of nations," the evidence today is very clear that most were themselves too nationalistic to subject themselves to the dictates of Soviet nationalism. The refusal of Tito to subject himself to Stalin in 1948, the victory of Mao Tse-tung in China in 1949 (largely through his own efforts), the establishment of the Truman Doctrine of 1948-49, the fact that the Russians had to deal with revolution in areas under their control, as well as a number of other factors, all in concert motivated a substantial change in party line.

The essence of class struggle, for example, was contorted in the strangest way and came to be based on nations rather than classes, with the term "struggle of peoples" (*borba narodov*) coming to dominate; later, every nation was to find its own path to socialism. The revolutions in Poland and Hungary (1956) accelerated this pattern, and the still later attempt by China to split the movement along racial lines, as well as its challenge to Soviet leadership, seemed to stabilize it. Therefore, in an attempt to control a deteriorating situation the CPSU decreed, "in emphasizing the need for class analysis as a major criterion for the Marxist historian, we must speak out decisively against all attempts to discard nationality traditions and differences."

By the early 1950s, the CPSU began to recognize the threat that the "relative independence of the superstructure" posed to its own interests, and attempts were made to control the political voluntarism that Stalin's particular brand of creative Marxism had brought about. During this same period the Western powers, under the leadership of the United States, were not lax. A policy of containment was implemented by the Truman Doctrine, Marshall Plan, NATO, and other means to thwart Soviet expansion into Europe. The policy of containment was perhaps the most successful of the long range foreign policies of the United States. It did everything that it was designed to do. In fact, it was so successful that it was applied with few changes to Southeast Asia—where it was a notorious failure. So long as Vietnam, and all that term implies, hangs like an albatross around the neck of United States foreign policy, it inhibits decisive changes in that policy.

Perhaps the distinguishing characteristic of our times is our concentration on absolutes, on polarization, on seeing things as a struggle between good and evil with few areas in between for toleration or compromise, and then covering this entire, perhaps unexpressed attitude with a veneer of understanding and a cry for toleration and compromise. Consequently, it is really very difficult to realize that national policy should be dictated by national interests. No nation has permanent friends or permanent enemies, but *every* nation has permanent interests, and perhaps this is why detente seems possible at a time when the interests of the major nuclear powers seem to be less abrasive than they have been for a quarter of a century.

In the simplest terms, detente is defined as an agreed diplomatic framework within which agreement is reached to seek solutions to problems without using the threat of nuclear war as a bargaining counter—it simply provides, in the nuclear age, a less dangerous framework for international life. Every nation, however, has certain national interests that oftentimes go far beyond her own borders, and oftentimes these national interests, or what a nation conceives of as her national interests, conflict with those of other nations. It cannot be emphasized too strongly that Russia has certain permanent national interests that it would undertake to implement regardless of its political system or the ideology of its rulers. While today these interests may be concealed in the rhetoric of the internationalism of communism, they are in fact basic Russian interests.

Basic Russian interests are at times implemented, enhanced, and disguised in the rhetoric of the dialectic, but the attempt at detente with the United States that implies military and economic cooperation has created a dilemma for the Soviet Union, compounded by the fact that the Soviet Union has become a major industrialized nation and has great hope of progressing even more rapidly in this area with Western technological help. Consequently, the Soviet dilemma is to find a way so as not to be so divorced from the third world that Moscow is forced to accept the responsibility for the sins of the industrialized nations. In addition, while the Soviet Union has rapidly expanded its influence throughout the non-Communist world, and over a quarter of a century has elapsed since the United States lost its nuclear monopoly, and despite the fact that the United States has found no quick and easy solutions to what seem to be complex foreign problems and intractable domestic problems—there is little question that the United States still has more diplomatic influence than any other country in the world. An outstanding example of this is the conflict between American and Russian interests in the Middle East. The fact is that the Soviet navy has not been invited to participate in the clearing of mines from the Suez Canal; it is the American and British navies that have been asked to undertake this task. However, it is the Soviet navy that will benefit most from the reopening of the canal, as its ships based at Black Sea ports will have a much shorter access route to the Indian Ocean. Thus, it is as essential to Russian national interests as it is to American to retain a presence in this area. The need of the Western world for Arab oil and the enormous advantage the Soviet Union would have if it could control the Arab oil spigot, whether by its naval power or by its tremendous influence in this area, is too apparent to need emphasis here.

The Soviet Union is inhibited in the role it wants to play in the Middle East by having real influence only with the Arabs. On the one hand, it has considerably less influence with Israel, although this may change in the next few years, depending on how the leaders of the USSR conceive the best way to implement its national interests. On the other hand, the United States has a near patron influence with Israel and is being relied upon not only by the Israelis but also by the Arabs to bring about an acceptable settlement; consequently, there is clear conflict of interests in this area between the USA and the USSR.

At this time the USA is attempting to stabilize Arab-Israeli relations in the Middle East. In addition to stabilizing the area, the United States also hopes to increase her influence with the Arab countries and thus further decrease Soviet influence. While the Soviet Union may desire a settlement in the Middle East, it doesn't want it at the price of excluding her influence; consequently, as both countries pursue their national interests, collision is inevitable.

It is clear that even though US policy has a number of vociferous critics in the Middle East, the US is more present and more wanted in the Middle East than is the Soviet Union, not to mention China. Parenthetically, this is true also for Latin America. At this point, and for some time in the seventies and beyond, we may look for a continuing conflict of interests in these areas.

East of Suez there is a similar pattern—albeit in food, not arms. For a long time Moscow has courted India and supplied her with arms, but as famine threatens India, her prime minister, Indira Gandhi, is turning not to the Soviet Union but to the US because, here, as in related areas, only the US can deliver.

Also, in recent years American diplomacy has not been conducted as though this really is a multipolar, multipower world. Consequently, there is a fear in the chancelleries of Western Europe of the two great nuclear giants settling international affairs between themselves with the United States providing a balance of power with the Soviet Union by a continuing flirtation with China. (And when Mao and the old leadership of the Chinese Communist party are gone, will their successors continue this relationship?) All of this appears dangerous to the Western European nations, and they believe that they may possibly be the first victims if war breaks out. These fears have been compounded by the fact that cracks have begun to appear in NATO, both in unified purpose and in the question of how to share the defense costs, as well as in the question of whether the United States wants to, and in fact is, exerting dominance in this organization over its European allies.

Still, if detente were ot materialize, it could at one and the same time prove mutually profitable and lessen the pressures on NATO, and at this time there seems to be little question that the Soviet Union wants and needs economic, if not military, detente.

One of the major reasons why the Russians need detente is the many weaknesses in the Soviet economy. The Russian people, as people everywhere, are concerned with higher standards of living and with more consumer goods. But long lines for the purchase of many goods, shabby buildings, and a general scarcity of goods indicate that the rate of growth in the economy is far behind the projections in the current five-year plan. Especially behind is the output of livestock, which would mean more meat for the Russians. Despite this continued scarcity— perhaps more properly because of it—the Soviet leaders have revealed some extremely ambitious plans. Early in March 1974, in a speech given in the Central

Asian capital of Alma-Ata, Brezhnev projected development of a multimillion-ruble scheme to reclaim and develop millions of hectares of new land in the central and northern regions, an area perhaps as large as the entire American Midwest. Thirty-five billion rubles is projected for the first five years of the program. In the context of detente these plans will require enormous input from outside Soviet borders. In the face of growing population, both in the Soviet Union and worldwide, the party leaders cannot count on another massive wheat transfusion with the US. Consequently, the development of this area will in large part depend on inputs from both Russia's allies and from the West as well.

Obviously, these plans are not only economically important but also strategically important—especially for those areas bordering on the People's Republic of China. If the Russians are to move ahead in such huge development, detente with the West is essential, not only for strategic security but also because they need Western technology, capital investment, and goods to insure the success of this enterprise.

Trade between the USA and the USSR has steadily increased, with American grain exports accounting for almost 80 percent of the 1973 total of $1.4 billion in American exports to the Soviet Union. Currently, the amount of export-import credits authorized or pending for deals with the Soviet Union totals more than $485 million, and at this time it seems this figure will substantially be increased. Perhaps it is by increasing trade that detente between the US and the USSR can be reached and a disastrous military confrontation can be avoided.

Still, if detente is to come, it is being slowed by both the Soviet military and by the failure to substantially implement the intentions underlying the Strategic Arms Limitations Talks (SALT). There seems little question that the Soviet military forces in the person of its major political spokesman, Defense Minister Andrei Grechko, is playing a major role on the political front and seems to be slowing the possible progress of detente (although the present secretary of state, Henry Kissinger, has asserted that both the US and the USSR military are deliberately slowing the progress of the SALT talks). Grechko's influence has grown steadily during the past two years, especially since he was made a full member of the Politburo during the October 1973 Middle Eastern war.

Perhaps, if there is a key to the Soviet military's thinking on detente and the possible limitations on the Soviet Union's strategic nuclear weapons arsenal, it can be found in Grechko's article "Lenin and the Armed Forces of the Soviet State," which recently appeared in *Kommunist,* the political and ideological journal of the Central Committee of the Communist Party of the Soviet Union. Grechko argued that there were efforts by "strong circles of imperialism to poison the atmosphere and to push the world back into cold war." Of great import also is the fact that he quoted First Secretary Brezhnev to the effect that "the material preparations for a Third World War have already begun," and he concluded, "This heightens the responsibility of the Soviet armed forces which are aware that, despite a certain degree of detente, the danger of war is not yet removed."

Perhaps the successes, or more accurately, nonsuccesses, of the SALT talks provide a relatively reliable barometer of the problems involved in military detente. Secretary of State Kissinger's trip to Moscow in early 1974, followed by former President Nixon's, were attempts, at the best, to revive the then largely dormant SALT II talks that had begun in November 1972. The failure to gain substantial agreement should concurrently be looked at with a sense of relief and with a sense of discouragement, because negotiations of such world importance should not be conducted in haste to meet arbitrary deadlines, and also, it must be said, because of the gray fog of Watergate, which debilitated the US internally and made it vulnerable in foreign policy.

Certainly SALT I was affected by President Nixon's eagerness for success on his trip to the Soviet Union in 1972, and consequently a five-year "interim agreement" was reached. By this agreement the USSR was allowed about 40 percent more submarine missiles and ICBMs than the United States. Both countries were left free to install MIRVs (multiple independently targeted warheads), and in this latter category the US seemed to have a five-year lead, although there is now evidence that the Soviet Union has drastically cut this lead time.

The United States has continued its program to install MIRVs on about half of its Minutemen and three-quarters of its missile submarines, and concurrently the Soviet Union has developed some strategic missiles, at least three of which have four to six MIRVs and with a much larger payload than US missiles. When these missiles are operational, the total payload of the Soviet ICBM force will be doubled and will jeopardize the US land-based Minutemen.

More specifically, in the current nuclear balance the USSR edges the USA 1560 ICBMs to 1054 ICBMs, and in submarine-launched ballistic missiles the Soviet Union has now pulled to within about 100 of the total of 656 belonging to the United States. The Soviet Union is also currently testing four new ICBMs, three of them with MIRVs, and all could be ready in a relatively short time. A number of these missiles have two or three times the throw weight anticipated, and this means that the missiles can hurl more nuclear warheads with more power. In addition, Russian missile testing has also disclosed a greater missile accuracy than hitherto disclosed.

The US Department of Defense also believes that the Soviets are using an improved pop-up launching technique for land-based ICBMs. A missile is expelled from its silo by compressed air and gas before its engines are lit. This "cold launch" permits firing larger missiles from existing silos and allows faster silo reloading. The Soviet military have also developed and installed a new 4200-mile-range missile in the advanced Delta-class submarines, a missile that reaches 1300 miles farther than the US submarine-launched Poseidon.

On the other hand, the United States has plans to build a force of new

Trident submarines carrying a 6500-mile-range missile in the 1980s, and in addition, the US arsenal of strategic nuclear warheads outstrip those of the Soviet Union by about 6800 to 2200. In the 1980s, however, the USSR could deploy about 7000 warheads on their ICBM force alone.

During the early months of 1974, the US secretary of defense, James R. Schlesinger, made several public statements concerning the position of US strategic nuclear forces vis-à-vis those of the Soviet Union. Perhaps the most important point he made has to do with "essential equivalence." He said, in reference to strategic nuclear policy, "Our objective is to obtain . . . essential equivalence. . . . We are prepared to reduce, stay level, or if need be increase our level of strategic arms, and that level will be determined by the policies, the decisions of the Soviet Union." Perhaps this is what will dictate American nuclear policy in the seventies and beyond. Certainly, with the recent addition of India to the nuclear club and the probability of several more members in the relatively near future, both the USA and the USSR are showing remarkable aplomb at living in a greatly expanded, polypolared nuclear world. Perhaps the development of a new and qualitatively different weapons system such as the laser is what gives both nations their sense of quiet confidence.

In conventional forces, the USSR has about four million men under arms, in contrast to the US's two million. The ground forces of the Soviet Union are much superior in armor and gunpower, with four times as many tanks and three times as many artillery pieces.

In sea forces the Russian navy outnumbers that of the US in major warships and submarines, but the US has undertaken a modernization program in an attempt to equalize this discrepancy. In the air each side is rated about equal, with about 4800 fighters and bombers, and in antisubmarine warfare the US is rated ahead of the USSR, and is also rated superior in tactical support of ground troops. To compensate for this gap, the Soviet Union has a superiority in ship-to-ship missiles, and here the United States navy is trying to catch up. Soviet artillery also has a much longer range than that of the US. It must be conceded, in short, that the Soviet Union has a decided edge in conventional forces over those of the United States.

Another major impediment to the coming of detente is the fact that the Soviet Union is a totalitarian dictatorial society, with all the ramifications of internal repression and censorship that is implied in such a society. Let me concede at the outset that the reign of Stalin may have been at best a social aberration, and at the worst an intensification or exacerbation of tendencies in Russian internal policies of rule utilized by the tsars and enhanced by the commissars. Since the death of Stalin in March 1953, repression in the Soviet Union, generally, has let up. The skillful, smooth, and diplomatic maneuver of expelling the brilliant and perceptive Alexander Solzhenitsyn, and the subsequent release of his family and his papers, demonstrate a strategem of unusual delicacy for the ordinarily heavy-handed Soviet regime. The treatment of Soviet citizens involved in dissent and accused of anti-Soviet agitation has gradually become milder, and censorship, which had become more stringent after Nikita Khrushchev lost his position as first secretary, has gradually become looser. While party officials and official organs still warn against alien ideas and denounce "bourgeois deviations" and "cosmopolitanism," the cultural opposition, in practice, get away with statements and expressions unthinkable a few years ago.

Still, the American people have a suspicious and wary attitude toward the government in the USSR, and it should be noted that this attitude is reciprocated in kind. On the other hand there is a great affection between the two peoples, and this relationship, in existence long before the advent of the Soviet to power, is once again overbalanced to the side of suspicion. The exile of Alexander Solzhenitsyn from the Soviet Union in February 1974 is a reminder to the American people that the Soviet Union is a tyrannical dictatorship that cannot tolerate prolonged or intense dissent among its own people. (Parenthetically, however, the American people should continually be reminded that the courage to oppose Soviet tyranny from within does not make a dissenter a Western liberal. Indeed, the spectrum of dissent in the Soviet Union probably ranges from what people see as pure Leninism to theocracy.)

The expulsion of Solzhenitsyn, along with the question of free emigration of the Jews and other religious factions in the Soviet Union, combined with the nationality problems, have raised questions among the people in the United States as to the wisdom of the easing of military tensions and enhancing of trade that is called detente. This is not the first generation of Americans to be disturbed and oftentimes revolted by the way the Russian people are treated by their own government, as this is not the first generation of Russians to look with suspicion on what they perceive to be the unbridled and permissive democracy they perceive in the United States. Since the decline of the *vieche* in Kievan Rus, Russia has been an authoritarian state. But this doesn't mean that the United States should shun it or refuse to do business with it, provided the business is mutually profitable and useful.

Generally, as the seventies and beyond unfold, we may anticipate a stronger and more viable Soviet Union, a Soviet Union that will grow faster with Western trade and technological assistance, but will grow whether it has this help or not. The problem of detente, in fact, revolves around two basic questions, those of political and military intentions, and economic needs. There is little question that the Soviet Union needs Western technological assistance in certain areas such as computers, but what does the West need from the Soviet Union? Perhaps some of its natural resources, but are the Soviets willing to give part of these up for trade and assistance? If not natural resources, what else does the Soviet Union have to trade of equal value to what they will receive? In the May-June 1974 *US-USSR Report*, the fact that the Soviet Union is now selling tractors in the United States is noted with equal degrees of approbation, pride, and optimism. It is not that the Soviet Union is selling so many tractors in the United States, but that they are selling them at all which evokes surprise from the average citizen. Still, these tractors seem to be sturdy and durable, and certainly cheaper than a similar tractor of American manufacture. As the *US-USSR Report* put it:

> The growing tractor imports . . . are part of an effort to rectify a lop-sided balance of trade between the Russians and the Americans. Last year the US sold six times more than it bought from the Soviet Union and had a balance of $1 billion in its favor . . . by Soviet accounting, two-way trade with the US totaled $1.56 billion in 1973.

It could be increased substantially in the future, with the status of most-favored-nation.

What are the intentions of the Soviet Union for the decade of the seventies and beyond? Unfortunately, the answer remains ambiguous. The history of at least the last quarter of a century should provide some evidence that would enable us to answer this question, and two interesting attempts are made to do so in the final part of this volume, where Bertram D. Wolfe and Alfred G. Meyer interpret the evidence of these years completely differently and still manage to adduce similar conclusions.

It should also be kept in mind that in the Soviet Union the government is not the supreme political arbiter, but the party, and that the party resolutions still reflect the same general goals as they did in October 1917. One cannot deny that the Soviet Union has conclusively demonstrated by recent actions that it is desirous of at least some aspects of detente, but on the other hand, the West should realize some mutual benefits from these agreements. Detente should not be confined solely to those areas of sole advantage of the Soviet Union. In all probability if detente does come, it will come step by step. Certainly there are far greater advantages to both the Soviet Union and the United States and the West in agreement, where agreement can be reached without sacrifice of basic national interests, but we should not mistake our desires and wishes for agreement for the reality of detente. Scholars are, of course, not prophets. But on the basis of the hard concrete evidence and interpretations given in this volume, the prospects for the seventies and beyond show great promise for both internal development and international understanding and agreement.

Part I

The Ideological Background

1

Problems of Marxism and Relations Between the East and the West

Karl A. Wittfogel

I. Toward a Sociohistorical Interpretation of "East" and "West"

A. Disquieting Problems–disquieting Approaches

The present global crisis appears as a political crisis, and it must be faced as such. But it is also, and ultimately, a crisis of ideas and values. It involves a crisis in our attitude toward the Communist forces with which we, the citizens of modern open ("democratic") societies, have to live.

What is the Soviet Union that emerged from the Communist breakthrough revolution actually like? What is its institutional essence? And what is it that makes Marxism seem an appropriate means for discussing these questions, not only within, but also outside, the Communist world?

How do the problems of Marxism relate to the great problems of our time? The *Communist Manifesto,* is widely read and even more widely quoted. Marx's *Capital* is less widely read, but not a few of those who read it take it very seriously. Max Weber rejected the *Manifesto* as obsolete and "primitive," though he called it "a work of genius."[1] He ranked *Capital* with some of the greatest "ideal value objects" of his world—with Goethe's *Faust* and some of Goethe's letters, with the Orestes tragedies of classical Greece, and with Michelangelo's fresco on the ceiling of the Sistine Chapel.[2]

Was Marx indeed as supreme in the analysis of society and history as Weber suggested?[3] Whatever we answer, we do well to view Marxism not only as an important means of intellectual communication but also as an effective device for arousing political passions (which it has been since the *Manifesto*) and as a powerful analytic tool (which it has been at least since *Capital*). As such it has produced an economic theory that seems today rather obvious and doctrinaire. However, Marxism as a whole presents a wealth of challenging, if inconsistent, views—some important scientifically, some important politically, and some disquieting, not only for the contented non-Marxists,

The ideas incorporated in this inquiry have been briefly presented before the Twelfth Annual Central Slavic Conference at Oklahoma State University on November 2, 1973. They are part of a comprehensive study of Anarchism and Marxism which I have pursued for a number of years, and which in its recent phase is being supported by a grant from the National Endowment for the Humanities.

but, most decidedly, for the Communists and their friends. Outstanding
among these views are Marx's concepts of development (and lack of development), his concepts of Asiatic despotism and political slavery, his conclusion
that tsarist Russia was Orientally despotic. Lenin's interpretation of Russia,
which he derived from Marx, has explosive implications for the evaluation of
the Communist revolution in Russia (and in China).

B. The Concept of Political Slavery and the Comparative Approach to Asiatic Despotism

1. Classical beginnings. As a social and historical fact, political slavery, like
personal slavery, is easy to discern. Its identification requires comparison of
differently structured societies. Thus, the outsider is as well-conditioned as the
insider to recognize its peculiarity.[4] And in certain cases he is freer to recognize
the human tragedy involved.

The folklore and mythology of ancient Mesopotamia and Egypt depicted the
phenomenon of political slavery long before the emergence of classical Greece.[5]
But its underlying principles were first identified by comparison-oriented and
analytically sensitive thinkers of classical antiquity: Herodotus, Xenophon,
Hippocrates, Plato, and Aristotle. Deriving some of their categories from the
conditions of personal slavery, which they knew well, they designated the
supreme power-holder under conditions of political slavery as "master" (*despotes*).
And they found that such conditions prevailed conspicuously in the world to the
east of them, in Asia. In India and China, recognition of despotic power has a
long endogenous history.[6] But again the observations made by insiders gained a
new reality when they were supplemented by the observations of interested outsiders employing tested scientific methods of sociohistorical comparison.

a. Aristotle. Aristotle's treatment of tyranny complemented his concept
of depotism. Tyranny, as he defined it, was one of the six major political orders
("constitutions"), three of which he considered "good" and three "bad."
Tyranny (usurped power) was always arbitrary. It was likely to be cruel, because
it repressed the forces of inner-motivated change (the society's "self-developmental" energies, as Marx called them in 1853).[7] But it resembled the five other
orders in that, in one form or another, it preserved these energies, thus giving the
citizens the possibility of changing it into another order.[8] Despotism lacked
these energies. It was an order distinct from the others; it did not change.
According to Aristotle, its subjects acquiesced in their fate because the hot
climate in which they lived made them slavishly submissive.[9]

Aristotle's idea of political slavery under despotism is generally noted and
widely accepted as consistent with the philosopher's simple ecological premise.
Rarely noticed, and not consistent with this premise, is Aristotle's description

of the devious methods that the masters of the despotic order developed to keep the population fragmented and politically impotent.[10]   For obvious reasons, these methods greatly attracted Greek tyrants.[11]   The very existence of these methods implied that the despotic rulers were not certain whether their subjects were indeed "slaves by nature" as Aristotle postulated.[12]

b. *Thomas Aquinas.*   Thomas Aquinas perceptively reproduced and commented on Aristotle's *Politics.* This work, which contains the philosopher's basic views about Asia's unchanging despotism and the changeability of the other orders, jibed well with the multiple trends in the unfolding feudal West. But it created difficulties for the ideologues of East Rome and Byzantium;[13] not to speak of the negative reception it received in the Arab world: except for the *Dialogues,* the *Politics* was "the only major Aristotelian treatise . . . which was never translated into Arabic."[14]   Aquinas's awareness of contemporary forms of Orientally despotic power in the Moslem-dominated parts of the Mediterranean world possibly stimulated his willingness to accept Aristotle's view of Asiatic depotism[15] and to declare constitutional monarchy the best of all types of government.[16]

2. **Widening Horizons.**   After the Middle Ages the heirs of the classical tradition greatly extended the image of the world. In this process they developed a new comparative attitude toward European and non-European countries. And they differentiated the concepts with which the classical macroanalysts had approached "Asia."

a. *Machiavelli.*   Machiavelli found Asiatically despotic statecraft not only in the Persia of the classical Greeks, but also in the Roman Empire and in contemporary Turkey.[17]   Officially concerned with international relations between his Italian homeland and various types of foreign lands, he was struck by the different chances for penetration from without in such countries as feudal France and despotic Turkey. In loosely coordinated France, he noted, dissenting elements could easily assert themselves, and outsiders (today we might say, fifth columinsts) could easily establish contact with them and possibly bring about the fall of the existing regime. But in Turkey, where "all are slaves and dependent, it will be difficult to corrupt them." Not only that: "Even if they were corrupted, little effect could be hoped for, as they would not be able to carry the people with them for the reasons mentioned."[18]

Machiavelli was aware that also in the West more centralized patterns amounted to a new system of power—"absolute power" (*potenza assoluta*).[19] Obviously convinced that this system did not resemble the Eastern type of total power, he referred to it as an "absolute power, such as the ancient writers called a tyranny."[20]

b. Bodin. Machiavelli's Italian experiences, including his association with
Cesare Borgia, explain why he saw this new Western power structure as a variant
of a Greek tyranny. Bodin, who watched the growth of this system throughout
Europe, analyzed it systematically, as did Hobbes in the next century. But
Bodin showed considerable concern for the Eastern system of total power, which
Hobbes did not. Hence it is through Bodin, rather than Hobbes, that the com-
parative study of society and history advanced from the classical pioneers and
Machiavelli to Montesquieu and Montesquieu's successors.

In his main work, *The Six Books of the Republic,* Bodin, taking the problem
of sovereignty as his starting point, discussed three types of absolute monarchy:
the "lordly," the "royal," and the "tyrannical." In a "lordly" (*seigneurial*)
monarchy, the sovereign was "lord of all."[21] He was "lord of the goods and
persons of his subjects . . . governing them as the master of a family does his
'slaves.' "[22] This was Bodin's way of outlining the system of total ("absolute")
power under which the subjects were enslaved and the ruler figured as "seigneur"
or "master" (the Latin word for "master" is, of course, *dominus,* the Greek,
despotes). Evidently Bodin envisaged here a modernized version of what the
Greeks called despotism, and which they found mainly in Asia. The Bible,
Bodin declared, called the subjects of "the kings of Asia and Egypt . . . always
slaves." And the Greeks did likewise: "They always term themselves free, and
the barbarians slaves: meaning by the barbarians the people of Asia and
Egypt."[23] There were, Bodin asserted, "many" lordly monarchs "in Asia and
Africa": those of "the Assyrians, the Medes, Persians, and Egyptians, and at
this present [time] that of Aethiopia (the most ancient Monarch of all Asia
and Africa)."[24] Looking for "lordly" monarchies in Europe, he found "none,"
except "the princes of the Turks and Moscovites."[25]

Europe was the home of the second type of absolute power: the "royal"
or "lawful" monarchy.[26] Under this system the subjects are "free-born and
lords of their own goods."[27] How can this be so, if "absolute power" means
that the ruler is not bound by the laws of his country?[28] Because the ruler,
who is "absolved" from these laws, is bound by "the laws of nature" and by
his fear of God.[29]

Bodin did not explain fully the difference between the metaphysical-
religious conditions distinguishing the "lordly" and the "royal" types of
monarchies. But he indicated what he had in mind. While under the first
system the ruler is likely to be worshiped as the image of God,[30] under the
second he follows his inner ("natural") laws: being "as obedient under the
laws of nature as he desires his subjects to be toward himself, leaving unto every
man his natural liberty and the property of his own goods."[31] According to
this argument, Western absolutism grants its subjects safety of person and property; Eastern absolutism does not.

The third type of absolute power is less clearly defined than that of the
first two types, probably because Bodin's lack of socioeconomic interest made

him miss the institutional reasons for the ephemeral character of tyranny. Nevertheless, as the classical analysts had done, he recognized the third system's lack of staying power.[32] Royal monarchies endured longer than tyrannies; and the "lordly" (despotic) monarchies endured much longer. Why? Because they were more "majestic." Majestic in what way? The subjects of this type of absolute power were, in Bodin's opinion, subdued by "just war." Having lost control over their "lives, goods and liberties," they became totally submissive: "The slave acknowledging his condition, becomes humble, abject and having as they say a base and servile heart."[33]

3. **Diverse developments.** The deficiencies in Bodin's comparative study of total power are obvious, but its accomplishments are seminal. He classified Russia as a "lordly" absolutism, initiating an interpretation that was perpetuated by Montesquieu and that finally came into its own through Marx and, derivatively, through Lenin. Bodin foreshadowed an idea Marx formulated in 1877 by suggesting that, in order to understand the peculiarities of the Western order it is necessary to understand the peculiarities of the non-Western—especially the Oriental—order.[34] He demonstrated what he meant by discussing, in the framework of his institutional insights, the non-Western order prior to that of the West, devoting as much space to the former as to the latter and making it clear that, according to his criteria, "tyranny" differed from both orders.[35]

a. *Hobbes, Locke, and the Founding Fathers of The American Republic.* An English translation of Bodin's magnum opus appeared in London in 1606 under the title *The Six Bookes of a Commonweale.* But Hobbes's arguments indicate that he was either unaware of, or unmoved by, Bodin's comparative approach to absolutism. In his *Leviathan* (1651), Hobbes did refer to the "Western part of the world" as different from the East ("Constantinople, etc")[36] but his vindication of "absolute power"[37] reflected essentially the Western, particularly the English, aspect of the problem.

Locke knew Bodin's work, but his argumentation shows him more concerned with vindicating the Glorious Revolution than with the institutional differences between Western and non-Western absolutism that were central to Bodin's position. In his two treatises, *Of Civil Government* (1690), Locke admonished his country men to preserve their gloriously won liberties, but he bulwarked his warning against a possible reestablishment of total power by depicting absolutism as involving the destruction of man's personal liberty and property,[38] and by referring to the subject of an absolute prince as his "slave,"[39] that is by blurring the distinction between "royal" and "lordly" absolutism. Both of his examples—the "Czar" (of Muscovy) and the "Grand Signor"[40] (the Turkish Sultan)—fit the "lordly" (despotic) type of ruler. Manifestly, the target of the English revolution of 1688 (and, in fact, of Cromwell's revolution) was not a variant of Eastern, but of Western absolutism.

The Founding Fathers of the American republic were intensely aware that
Locke had written a philosophical justification of England's revolution against
absolutism, when, in the Declaration of Independence, they leaned heavily on
ideas offered in the treatise *Of Civil Government*.[41] The American colonists
responded to their peculiar situation by concentrating on the overthrow of
the "absolute despotism," the "absolute tyranny" they considered their lot.[42]
This orientation permitted the fighting pioneers to establish a constitution
that went beyond the English in its stress on popular control, and that served
their successors well in their daring advance from the Atlantic to the Pacific.
This same orientation permitted them to draw on Montesquieu's new political
thoughts, which had aroused Europe. But they took from him only what
would help them realize their glorious Western dream. They saw the outside
world essentially in terms of their rivalry with Europe. Exclaimed *The Federalist* in 1787: "Let the thirteen States, bound together in a strict and indis-
soluble Union, concur in creating one great American system, superior to the
control of all transatlantic force or influence, and able to dictate the terms of
the connection between the old and the new world."[43]

   b. Montesquieu. It would be intriguing to compare the Founding Fathers'
image of Montesquieu[44] with the real dimension and intent of his work. But
this cannot be our task here. In this context it must suffice to say, that although
the joint authors of *The Federalist* were trying to do justice to "that great
man," to "the oracle who is always consulted and cited on this subject [of the
separation of the three great departments of government] . . . the celebrated
Montesquieu . . . this great political critic,"[45] they showed little concern for
the macrohistorical view that was the core of Montesquieu's position. Having
fought the remnants of a Western variant of absolutism, the American Founding
Fathers were not really aware of the difference between this type of power
(which, according to Montesquieu, included the "moderate" governments of
Europe) and the despotic type of power.[46]
   For a variety of reasons, Montesquieu was intensely aware of these differences, and he early showed his concern for the underlying issue. Already in
his *Persian Letters* (1721) he had wrestled with the problem of "despotism."[47]
In his *Greatness and Decline of the Romans* (1743) he called the phenomenon
under consideration "Asiatic despotism."[48] And in *The Spirit of the Laws*
(1748) he used this term interchangeably with "Eastern" despotism,[49] thus
adjusting himself to the designation "Oriental despotism," which since 1704
had spread among the intellectuals of France and other countries of Europe.[50]
   The laws whose "nature" Montesquieu discussed in his magnum opus
are not those of the judicial system, but those concerned with the relations
of the "political" and "civil institutions" of society. "These relations," wrote
Montesquieu, "I shall examine since they all together constitute what I call
the 'Spirit of Laws.' "[51] The "fundamental" laws on which the institutions

of government and society rest are not those determining the separation of the powers of government but those concerned with, and indeed established by, the differences between Montesquieu's three major types of government: the "republican," most fully developed in the republics of ancient Greece and Rome; the "monarchical," related to Bodin's "lawful" European monarchies; and the "despotic."[52]

The decisive societal distinction between these three types of government is the existence or absence of what Montesquieu called the "intermediate" powers. In contemporary Europe, these intermediate powers consisted of three privileged social strata: the nobility, the clergy, and "the cities" (the urban middle class), plus a "depository of 'the laws' "—in courts.[53] These pluralistic forces constituted "the fundamental laws" of modern moderate governments.[54] Montesquieu found an early form of such an arrangement at the dawn of the European Middle Ages. In his opinion there existed at that time "a harmony between the civil liberty of the people, the privileges of the nobility and clergy, and the prince's prerogative," which he considered perfect. He called it "the best species of a constitution that could possibly be imagined by man."[55] In his opinion the pluralistic arrangements in modern moderate European monarchies were not as harmonious, but were also conducive to political liberty.[56]

Montesquieu declared that the lack of this kind of a sociopolitical balance endangered the basic freedom of countries that possessed great formal freedom. In ancient Greece, he asserted, "all lucrative arts and professions," including agriculture, were "unworthy of a freeman."[57] And in republican Rome the destruction of essential elements of the sociopolitical balance broke "the chain of the constitution"[58] and transformed Rome's republican officials into "bashaws,"[59] that is, into bureaucratic tools of despotic power.

According to the author of *The Spirit of the Laws,* the ancient Greeks and Romans never possessed a fully developed system of balancing forces, and they lost whatever elements of such a system they had. Under despotism this system never existed.[60] We do well to keep these key theses of Montesquieu's position in mind when we examine his ideas concerning the peculiarities of despotism that separated the Eastern from the two major non-Eastern types of government and society. Some of these peculiarities are easily defined. Some require a fuller explanation, especially those pertaining to Montesquieu's treatment of China (as a complex variant of despotism), of Russia (as a variant of despotism whose rulers deliberately, but vainly, tried to abandon the fundamental "laws" of that sociopolitical order), and of contemporary England (as a country with a highly advanced system of political liberty and, for this very reason, especially threatened by a shift to political slavery).

Negative equality. Under despotism "all men are equal," because all are "nothing."[61] Montesquieu's entire concept of despotism can be subsumed under this heading.

Political slavery. The subjects of the despot live in a condition of "political slavery."[62] Without the designation, this idea had existed since the days of classical Greece, but Montesquieu conceptualized it and devoted a whole book to the difference between private and "political" slavery.

Motivation. The "principle" that motivates the subjects of despotism is not "virtue" (civic-mindedness), as in republics, and not "honor," as in monarchies, but fear.[63] Their obedience is not the self-perpetuating obedience to the law, as in "modern and moderate states," but "extreme obedience," "blind" submission—the heritage of instinct and fear of punishment that man shares "with the beasts."[64]

Education under despotism. Under despotism, education "must necessarily be servile."[65] Montesquieu wrote this, although he knew that in such countries as China there existed quite a literature and that great efforts were made to study it.[66] But there is no doubt that Montesquieu badly oversimplified a very subtle problem: What kind of science, art, and literature is compatible with, stimulated by, or bearable under the despotic power structure?[67] However, there can be no doubt either that he put his finger on a deep reality of Asiatic soviety, when, citing Aristotle's political slavery proposition and raising the issue of education for good citizenship, he concluded: "Here in a certain way education is zero."[68]

The immutabilité of despotism. Corruption and disorder do not change the principle of despotic government. Speaking of "other [types of] governments," Montesquieu declared that they "are destroyed by particular accidents, which do violence to the principles of each constitution." But despotic government "is ruined by its own intrinsic imperfections." Ruined, but not destroyed! It maintains itself, if "circumstances drawn from the climate, religion, situation or the genius of the people oblige it to conform to order and to admit of some rule." But these circumstances force the "nature" of the despotic system "without changing it; its ferocity remains; it is tamed only for a while."[69]

In another context, Montesquieu found the mind of the "people of the Orient" characterized by the "unchangeability" (*l'immutabilité*) of their "religion, manners, customs and laws."[70] According to his concept of the fundamental "laws," this meant the "*immutabilité*" of despotism as a cultural and institutional order.

Political ecology. Montesquieu, as noted above, included climate among the circumstances that oblige a government "to conform to order and to admit of some rule." In fact, he insisted that "the empire of climate is the first, the most powerful of all empires."[71] Thus, he showed himself eager to preserve the climatological core of the classical geohistorical concept.

However, Montesquieu's attempts to give the old concept a new flexibility reveal his awareness of its deficiency. His search for a new ecological interpretation remained inconclusive, but it took him to the threshold of a new geoeconomic insight. A contemporary of the physiocrats, Montesquieu tried to evaluate man not only as a passive inhabitant of hot, cold, and temperate climates, but also as an active producer of fertility and wealth. New socioeconomic practices went hand-in-hand with new socioeconomic ideas. The state-directed "labor of man" improved the earth through "industry" and "good laws." It made "rivers flow where there had been lakes and marshes."[72]

China and other hydraulic countries. Montesquieu found China complex and fraught with great contradictions; and his view of that country reflects this. In stressing China's ancient agrohydraulic tradition, he described the starting point of its economic and political strength as situated not in the subtropical ("hot") south, but in the north (approximately in the same latitude as the coastal zone of the northern Mediterranean, which gave birth to the republican city-states of classical Greece and Rome). In China, the struggle for subsistence "required a mild and moderate government" as it did in two other similarly conditioned countries. Power was "necessarily moderated in that country, as it was formerly in Egypt, as it is now in Holland."[73]

With these arguments, Montesquieu suggested that the Chinese government's management of flood control, drainage, and agricultural fertility did not promote, but countered, the despotism that was generally produced by a hot climate—and also by the "excessive size of an empire."[74] Failing to explain why in Holland the hydraulic factor led to the development of a republic similar to that of Switzerland (which he suggested in another context),[75] he included Persia, along with China, Egypt, and Holland, in his list of hydraulic countries. He noted that the Persians, while they were "Masters of Asia," bestowed special comforts upon "those who conveyed springs to any place which had not been irrigated before" and that they "spared no expense in directing the course of a number of streams that flowed from Mount Taurus." In an unexplained way, these benefits were still to be found "in the fields and gardens" of Persia.[76]

But these activities did not, in Montesquieu's opinion, prevent the governments in question from being despotic. He did not, as it first appears, mean that vital state-directed hydraulic activities generally created nondespotic and lawful governments.

About ancient Egypt, Montesquieu said very little; but he did specify the political character of China and Persia. Although he stressed the "moderating" circumstances in China to the point of misinterpreting the effect of the government's hydraulic functions, he declared "servile obedience" the climatologically conditioned attitude of the Chinese people,[77] and "fear" (the fear of being beaten into submission) the outstanding "principle."[78] He summarized his final verdict about China (and Persia) as follows: "China is a despotic state whose principle is fear."[79] "The Persian Empire was a despotic state"[80] which "has always considered its subjects as slaves."[81]

Russia. Montesquieu's evaluation of Russia also contained strong contradictions. In accordance with the climatological interpretation of history, which he was unwilling to abandon, he suggested that Russia was really too cold for despotism.[82] But as in the cases of China and Persia, he did not close his eyes to the evidence before him.

Conquest had introduced a servile spirit into Russia.[83] Montesquieu did

not expressly name the Tatar conquest, but it was this event that had initiated
the tsarist regime in Muscovy; and his view of the effect of the Tatar conquest,
as juxtaposed to the conquest of the Roman Empire by the Goths, made it
clear that it was this conquest he had in mind. Coming from "the north" and
being a free people, the Goths had introduced "monarchy and freedom."[84] The
Tatars, who had adopted slavery in the "south" of Asia, carried with them "the
spirit of servitude which they had acquired in the climate of slavery"; thus, they
had introduced "slavery and despotic power."[85] The sociopolitical order that
conquest introduced into Russia precluded the development of a middle class.[86]
This order was a hierarchy of enslaved people. "All subjects of the empire are
slaves." And "the people are composed of those who are attached to the land
and those who are called clerics or gentlemen."[87]

The rulers of Russia, Montesquieu remarked, tried to modernize their
government and "to temper its arbitrary power," but they failed, due to "particular" causes, among which he specified "religion,"[88] and "general" causes,
which he did not specify, but which were obviously the sociopolitical effects
of the conquest. His pessimistic conclusion: "Russia would have liked to abandon despotism, but could not do it."[89]

England and beyond. Montesquieu's evaluation of China, Russia, and other
despotic countries was based on the complexity of their conditions, but his
evaluation of England went far beyond that country's conditions. For this reason, a narrow approach to Montesquieu's treatment of England is likely to miss
the actual socio-historical setting in which he placed it.

The Founding Fathers of the American republic strongly criticized the
oppressive features of England's policy during their struggle for independence;
but they also strongly emphasized the freedom-promoting character of England's
constitution when they established their republic. They emphasized the need for
the separation of the three main powers of government, expressly dwelling on
Montesquieu's praise of this principle of the English constitution. *The Federalist*
cited Montesquieu's dictum that without the separation of the three powers "there
can be no liberty."[90] Madison indicated that "other passages" in Montesquieu's
Spirit of the Laws "more fully" explained this matter.[91] But he did not explain
that some of these passages connected the problem of the English constitution
with the peculiarities of England's sociopolitical position and with corresponding
(and contrasting) conditions elsewhere.

In the decisive first part of his discussion "Of the Constitution of England,"
Montesquieu examined the relation of the separation of powers to the three major
types of government: (1) the system Montesquieu called "a popular state" (he
did not name England, but the chapter heading and the context confirm what
Madison assumed, that he was thinking primarily of England); (2) the kingdoms
of Europe that have "a moderate government" (in this case, too, Montesquieu
gave no example, but he was obviously thinking of France); and (3) "the despotic
powers of the Eastern princes" (fully represented by Turkey, incompletely by
many European republics, especially Venice.)[92]

Under "monarchical governments," as Montesquieu saw them, "the single person governs by fundamental laws," which "necessarily" included the existence of the "intermediate" channels "through which the power flows."[93] It is precisely at this point that Montesquieu's idea concerning the separation of the powers of society interlocks with his idea of the separation of the branches of government. In "most kingdoms of Europe . . . the prince, who is invested with the two first powers, leaves the exercise of the third to his subjects." Hence these kingdoms have "a moderate government."[94] This argument gives a deeper meaning to the statement Montesquieu made in a preparatory chapter: "Political liberty is to be found only in moderate governments."[95]

Did the author of *The Spirit of the Laws* consider the government of England "moderate"? Obviously not! The English, who in the seventeenth century had violently and unsuccessfully struggled for "democracy," had abolished all the "intermediate" powers. They were now in a very glorious, but also very dangerous position. According to Montesquieu, the absence of these "intermediate" powers would soon produce either "a popular state or else a despotic government."[96] Hence, the English had "every reason to be jealous of their liberty. If they should happen to lose it, they would be one of the most enslaved people on earth."[97]

In Montesquieu's terms, political slavery meant despotism. And his thesis that the absence of the "intermediate powers" must either lead to a "popular" or "despotic" government shows that this is what he had in mind when he declared that the English, who had abolished these powers, were faced with the danger of political slavery. Having created a new constitutional situation by abolishing the powers that kept "moderate" governments in balance, they needed new means to preserve their glorious freedom. In dealing with these means, Madison failed to notice the alternative that Montesquieu had clearly indicated. Madison thus missed the opportunity to identify the deficiency in Montesquieu's argument concerning the "intermediate" power. Montesquieu did not say that, by depriving these powers of their constitutional privileges, the English had not eliminated their societal significance.[98] Madison spoke only of the situation in which the unification of the legislative and executive powers "in the same person or in the same body of magistrates" would destroy liberty. He failed to familiarize the readers of *The Federalist* with the passages in Montesquieu that suggested that the removal of the "intermediate" powers would go beyond the absence of liberty and lead to the establishment of political slavery: despotism.

Montesquieu's effort to document carefully his exposition did not protect him from committing serious errors. The student of society and history is duty-bound to identify and, if possible, correct them. But he is also duty-bound to acknowledge that these errors occurred mainly on the micro- and meso-analytic levels of Montesquieu's inquiry; that even on these levels he also made pioneering advances and that on the macro-analytic level Montesquieu made seminal accomplishments.

Montesquieu's idea of the dehumanizing effect of political slavery assumes new significance at a time when a new interest in the phenomenon of social alienation has emerged. The modern endeavors to determine the formative role of ecology (and Communist-Marxist attempts to obscure this role) underline the fact that in the comparative study of total power and freedom, Montesquieu's macrocomparative approach touched upon geohistorical insights that Hobbes, Locke, Madison, and other mesocomparative students of state and society neglected. The foremost foreign commentator on American democracy, Alexis de Tocqueville, failed to learn from the classical heritage what Montesquieu continued and built upon. Tocqueville's mesoanalytic accomplishments are impressive, but the impact of his greatest sociohistorical vision was blunted because it lacked the macroanalytic depth that alone could make it meaningful.

II. Democracy and the Ultimate Alternative: Tocqueville

A. A Parochial "Democratic" Approach to International Relations

Tocqueville found that democracy favored the effective handling of domestic affairs—"the growth of internal resources," the development of the "public spirit," and the strengthening of "respect for law in the various classes." In all these fields "practical everyday wisdom" and "common sense" tended to produce positive results. "In a nation whose education has been completed, democratic liberty applied to the state's internal affairs brings blessing greater than the ills resulting from a democratic government's mistakes."

But, the author of *Democracy in America* continued: "This is not always true for relations between nation and nation." In the handling of these affairs "a democratic government does appear decidedly inferior to others."[99] "Others" meant countries dominated by aristocratic or monarchical forces (he considered aristocracy particularly apt to take a "firm and enlightened" attitude toward foreign affairs).[100] A democracy, Tocqueville argued, "finds it difficult to coordinate the details of a great undertaking. . . . It has little capacity for continuing measures in secret and waiting patiently for the results." In the realm of foreign relations, "feeling rather than calculations" and "the desire to satisfy a momentary passion" dominate.[101]

It has been widely recognized that the great French student of democracy found in the United States little interest in the thorough and systematic analysis of international conditions. Modern political scientists have pointed to the restless and shifting attitude of the contemporary Americans in these matters (not in technology and organization),[102] calling it the continuation of a trend that "troubled European observers from de Tocqueville to the writers of the present day."[103]

It has been much less widely recognized that Tocqueville, in a sophisticated way, shared important elements of this attitude when in 1835 he published the two first volumes of his famous work and, in 1840, its two last volumes. Although he spoke very respectfully of Montesquieu,[104] and although he adopted some of his significant ideas (e.g., with regard to despotic countries and political slavery),[105] Tocqueville was not fully aware of the dimension of Montesquieu's macroanalytic comparative approach when he engaged in his profound mesoanalytic comparative analysis of democracy. Hence his lack of concern for the nondemocratic countries of the world harmonized well with the attitude taken in this respect by his American contemporaries, who were too busy spreading their kind of democracy throughout the vast expanses of their subcontinent to pay much attention to the peculiarities of the "Asiatic" world in general and to "Asiatic" Russia in particular.

To be sure, lack of scholarly occupation with Russia was not limited to the United States. It existed until the beginning of the twentieth century also in such technically nondemocratic European countries as Germany. In the academies of that country some stray scholars did occupy themselves with Russian history and institutions, but the general principle was: *Russica non leguntur.* Things Russian were not part of the regular academic curriculum. The few scholars who studied Russia did not as a rule do so with recourse to the classical interpretations of Asiatic society and with concern for the Marxist version of this interpretation. Until the end of World War I, the indifference toward Russian studies in virtually all Western countries was supplemented by a similar lack of interest in the study of Marxism. If the academic leaders had dignified this suspect matter with a Latin formula, they probably would have said: *Marxistica non leguntur.*

B. After 1917: The USA, Raised to the Summit of a New International Situation, Encounters It by Means of the Old "Democratic" Approach

All this changed after 1917, when a new Communist power structure originated in Russia. After a few years of civil war, this force covered one-sixth of the globe; and after 1949, as the result of a derivative Communist revolution in China,[106] it covered a third of the globe. In the course of this development Marxism emerged as the ruling ideology in the Communist World and as a lingua franca (and idea franca) in many intellectual strata outside it.

The spread of the Communist world interlocked antagonistically with a profound transformation of the position of the US in the realm of international politics. After originally avoiding involvement in it, the country reluctantly entered into the tangle of international relations, rising during World War I to participation in world affairs and ascending to the rank of global prominence during World War II.

Thus situated, Tocqueville's great democracy could no longer uphold the intellectual attitude toward international problems it had assumed in 1835 and 1840, just as it could no longer uphold the social attitude toward internal conditions it had taken then. Now the country's intellectual and political leaders had to familiarize themselves with the many foreign countries that were part of their new sphere of political activity. While this happened, the country's studies had to assume a new dimension. They had to cover not only democratic and quasi-democratic countries of the kind Tocqueville endeavored to understand, but also countries of a blatantly nondemocratic kind.

C. America, Russia and the "Destiny" of the World

I am not saying that modern social scientists in general, and modern political scientists in particular, are unaware of Tocqueville's perception of the impending polarization of the world around two centers: Russia and the United States ("America"). The passage that contains this perspective belongs to the most frequently cited parts of *Democracy in America.* Tocqueville's vision of future developments sharply refuted the "blind" hope of in-between solutions, such as the monarchy of Henry IV or Louis XIV. "For my part," he asserted, "I am led to believe that there will be soon no room except for either democratic freedom or the tyranny of the Cesars."[107]

The word "soon" gives Tocqueville's prediction an urgency, which was obviously meant to stir his reader's imagination and resolution. In one part of this world, that of democratic freedom, "all" would be free. All would have "equal rights," with all that this implies: "The will of a democracy is changeable, its agents rough, its laws imperfect." But realizing this, we may "let ourselves be drawn by freedom" and reach "a state of complete [democratic] equality."[108]

In the other part of the world, the people would live under a "despot," under "the tyranny of the Cesars." To realize what this means, we must remember

the terrible centuries of Roman tyranny, when mores had been corrupted, memoirs obliterated, customs destroyed; when opinions became changeable and freedom, driven out from the laws, was uncertain where it could find asylum, when nothing protected the citizens and when the citizens no longer protected themselves: when man made sport of human nature and princes exhausted heaven's mercy before their subjects' patience.

Whenever the world would come to this, "there will be no independence left for anybody, neither for the middle classes nor for the nobility, neither for the poor nor for the rich, but only an equal tyranny for all."[109]

Tocqueville's great perspective singled out America as the outstanding case of a decidedly democratic country. Once geography and choice had protected this country from the fate of Europe, whose nations, in varying degrees, combined democratic with aristocratic and monarchial features, but whose citizens could and should be led to "the gradual development of democratic institutions."[110] In this context, Tocqueville did not say what, in his opinion, was the outstanding representative of the modern form of "Roman tyranny," but he did not leave it at that. In the conclusion of the first section of his magnum opus, he became specific about the tyrannical counterpart to the democratic world. He predicted that America was incontestably moving toward supreme leadership in the democratic part of the world. Russia was moving toward the same prominence in the other part of the world. "All other peoples seem to have nearly reached their natural limits . . . but [the Americans and the Russians] are growing. All the others halted or advanced only through great exertion; they alone went easily and quickly forward along the path whose end no eye can yet see."

The American advances by fighting against "natural obstacles" ("the wilderness and barbarians"), the Russian by fighting "men" (he combats "civilization"); the former advances in his way by relying on "personal interest and by giving free scope to the unspoiled strength and common sense of individuals," the latter by concentrating "the whole power of society in one man." The two forces represent two fundamentally different attitudes toward the human condition: "One has freedom as the principal means of action, the other has servitude." They have different points of departure and more along different paths. But "each seems called by some secret design of Providence one day to hold in its hands the destiny of half the world."[111]

D. An Apocalyptic Perspective Blurred

These were apocalyptic visions. They did much to make the serious citizen of the West conscious of the democratic potential of his world. They intensified the concern for responsible democratic thought and actions. And they nourished the feeling that tsarist Russia was an autocratic colossus that must be distrusted.

But Tocqueville's perspective, in which Russia loomed as a supreme threat, remained intellectually and practically inconsequential. Although Tocqueville, as J.P. Mayer states, had "many affinities" with Montesquieu,[112] he was more interested in comparing the democratic way of government and life in America with the corresponding conditions in other parts of the modern West, particularly in France, than in comparing the entire modern West with the sociopolitical structures of republican Greece and Rome and with the institutional pecularities of the contemporary "tyrannies," whose possible advance he considered terrifying.

Tocqueville's furtive treatment of Montesquieu's concept of the unchangeability of Oriental despotism[113] does justice neither to his own religious interpretation of this phenomenon, nor to Montesquieu's sociopolitical interpretation.
He did not bother to test his religious thesis empirically as he tested his views about
the religious and secular conditions of democracy. Nor did he bother to familiarize his readers with the sociopolitical reasons Montesquieu had given to
explain the self-perpetuation of Oriental despotism. Failing to concern himself
with the differences between self-perpetuating systems of total power (Aristotle's
"despotism") and temporary systems of such power (Aristotle's "tyrannies"),
he confused these terms and obscured the underlying institutional diversities.
Indifferent to the classical concept of Asiatic society elaborated by Machiavelli,
Bodin, and Montesquieu and thereafter by the English classical economists
(especially Smith) and the German classical philosophers (especially Hegel),
Tocqueville did not give his vision of the final alternative between freedom and
"tyranny" a shape that enabled his adherents to recognize the meaning of Marx's
Asiatic interpretation of Russia and Lenin's interpretation of the Russian revolu-
tion.

Hence, his remarks about the final open historical situation, in which men
must "come to choose between all being free or all slaves, all having equal rights
or all being deprived of them,"[114] was a great but ineffective gesture of good will.
It did not provide a key to the sociohistorical reality, which Marx (largely with
classical arguments) identified and which Lenin (largely with Marxist arguments)
ambivalently promoted.

III. The Discovery of "Asiatic Society": Marx

A. Marx "and" Engels

In this context I shall speak primarily of Marx's role without forgetting the
many ways in which he profited from his cooperation with Engels. And I shall
speak of Marx's and Engels's advance toward a concept of the Asiatic state without forgetting that, in the summer of 1844 when they first entered into a political and theoretical alliance, they had not yet formulated their version of "scientific" socialism (communism), which later became known as Marxism; and that,
after they had reached this point, they did not immediately recognize the peculiarity of Asiatic society.

Marx and Engels first presented their "materialist" interpretation of history,
with its primary emphasis on man's economic action and its natural setting, in
1845/46, in a large manuscript, *The German Ideology,* which was submitted to
several publishers, but remained unpublished until the 1920s.[115] And they con-
cisely formulated their new position with primary emphasis on its political consequences, while they were working on drafts of a program for the Communist League

which, in its final form and under the title *The Manifesto of the Communist Party*, was published in 1848.

Unlike 1853, when the key features of the theory of Asiatic society were published in the *New York Daily Tribune* in two articles on India that carried Marx's signature alone, both the *German Ideology* and the *Manifesto* named Marx and Engels as coauthors. This fact underlines the closeness of their cooperation, but it tells us nothing of the division of labor they set for themselves. In January 1851, Engels pointed to his "well-known laziness in theoretical matters."[116] His statement does not do justice to his intellectual drive or his analytical and conceptual creativity, but it does imply that, when it came to major theoretical issues, he felt he could not match Marx. In November 1851 he saw his intellectual achievement as insignificant compared with Marx's "heavy artillery."[117] And in 1853, Marx, on his side, indicated his understanding of their individual contributions when he wrote that Engels would deal with geographical and military problems, while he would be responsible for "the general point of view."[118]

Marx's advance toward the materialist concept of history can be discerned in the changes that occurred in his philosophical position from the spring to the fall of 1844 in his writings, from his "alienation" manuscripts to *The Holy Family*. Engels's development is not as readily discerned, perhaps because in his writings during this time he dwelt less than Marx on the big, macroanalytical issues.[119] In 1885, Engels recalled that prior to 1845 he had been moving in the same direction as Marx, but that when he came to Brussels in that year, Marx had already established the "new theory in its main features."[120] Three years later he was more specific. The basic idea of the materialist interpretation of history "belongs to Marx. . . . When I met Marx again in Brussels in 1845, he had it fully worked out and put it before me in terms almost as clear as those in which I have stated it here."[121]

In the case of the *Manifesto* there is contemporary evidence concerning Engels's position when the leaders of the Communist League decided that their organization should have a serious theoretical and political program. Engels wrote his draft of the "credo," as he called it, in Paris between October 23 and 29, 1847. He entitled it *Principles of Communism* and used the form of a catechism: "Question 1: What is Communism? . . . Q[uestion] 2: What is the proletariat? . . ."[122] Engels himself described his draft as "simply narrative, but miserably put together, in terrible haste."[123] It was in fact more than a narrative. But while it contained important elements of the emerging Marxist position, it was schoolmasterish in style, loose in construction, and limited in vision.

On November 23, 1847, while he was still in Paris, Engels had written Marx that he ought to take a look at the "credo," which, he suggested, might be called *"Communist Manifesto."*[124] And he brought his draft with him to show Marx in London at the Second Congress of the League, which was meeting from

November 29 to December 8. According to an "urgent resolution" passed by
the Central Authority of the League in London on January 24, 1848, Marx had
consented "at the last congress" to write the *Manifesto*. And this he did, after
he returned to Brussels on December 14. Engels, in all probability, had discussed
the problems of the program with Marx during their stay in London, and he
certainly did so from December 17 to 27 in Brussels when they were together
again. But we need not rely on the conclusion of the editors of the "historical-
critical" *Gesamtausgabe* of Marx's and Engels's writings that "the final version
of the Manifesto"—the manuscript completed by the end of January in Brussels
and printed in London in February 1848—"apparently stems from Marx."[125]
For better or worse, it was the "heavy artillery" of the *Manifesto* that, years
later, was to shake the world. This "heavy artillery," with its challenging prop-
ositions, was clearly the brainchild of Marx.

Marx's and Engels's cooperation in achieving an understanding of the
character of the Asiatic state followed a similar pattern. From the spring of
1852 to the early months of 1853, Engels had been adding significantly to his
knowledge of Russia,[126] Turkey,[127] and the Orient as a whole.[128] He had
mustered many new facts and had formulated new and stimulating concepts.
But his analytical framework was limited. In the end, it was Marx who, drawing
on Engels's new ideas but going far beyond them, laid the sociohistorical foundation for a new structural analysis of "Asia" in general and tsarist Russia in
particular.

B. The Concept of "Asiatic Society"

What did Marx—and following him, Engels—discover in 1853 about Asiatic
society? Having described this aspect of their development in various of my
writings during the last twenty-five years, I would be happy to leave the answer
to one or another of the many individuals who have recently professed an
extraordinary interest in this matter. The recent eagerness to engage in a
debate, the so-called great debate, on Marx's view of the "Asiatic mode of production" is as significant as it is problematic. The Communist Marxists and their
friends, who have been in the forefront of this endeavor, have distorted rather
than clarified the issue.[129] And even such a seemingly independent theoretician
of the New Left as the economist Ernest Mandel (who, unlike the participants in
the "great debate," praises what I have been saying about Marx's and Engels's
views of Asiatic society) still cripples Marx's and Engels's (and Lenin's) Asiatic
interpretation of tsarist Russia.[130]

Thus, I feel obligated to reproduce once again, and with particular attention
to the favored targets of "Marxist" censorship, the hard core of Marx's and Engels's
concept of Asiatic society, including Russia. In this connection I draw primarily
on Engels's letter to Marx dated June 5, 1853, in which he noted crucial features

of Asiatic society, and on the two articles Marx wrote for the *New York Daily Tribune* on June 10 and July 22, 1853, respectively, "British Rule in India" and "The Future Results of British Rule in India" in which, on the basis of statements made by Engels and other perceptive authors, he offered his new view on Asiatic society and Oriental despotism.

My concept of Asiatic (or Oriental or hydraulic) society is much more differentiated than that of Marx, but I do owe much to him. Those who attack my hydraulic arguments as simplistic are in fact often attacking Marx. It is well to remember that most pioneering ventures post factum seem simplistic; but it is well to remember also that, by their very nature, they are often singularly productive.

As early as 1923, I recognized the existence of Marx's concept of the Asiatic mode of production. Throughout the twenties, I explored various aspects of its economic, social, political, and historical meaning within the context of Marxism as I then understood it. In 1931 I elaborated Marx's views on Asia in a detailed analysis of China as "a great Asiatic agrarian society." And since the 1950s, I have supplemented my study of the Asiatic core structure (Marx's "completely" Asiatic society) by the study of "marginal" Asiatic society, a type exemplified by tsarist Russia (Marx's "semi-"Asiatic society).

I do not fault the Communist critics who comment superficially on the concept of Asiatic society presented by me (whom they treat with hostility), since they also comment superficially on "Asiatic" ideas of Marx (whom they treat with reverence). But it seems fair—in fact, imperative—to establish the theoretical starting point as accurately as possible by citing relevant formulations Marx offered in the two articles in June and July 1853 and elsewhere during this same period.

Marx did not develop these ideas systematically or fully. Moreover, he wrote them in English, a language he first began to use in print in January 1853.[131] But the New York editors had too much respect for "Dr. Karl Marx" to alter his style or his vocabulary, and his Yankee readers took both in their stride.[132] For these, as well as other reasons, I reproduce below key elements of Marx's arguments, when possible in his own words, confident that their obvious intent will be clear and that their deeper meaning and political consequence will be clarified in the course of my presentation.

1. **Ecological peculiarity.** "Climate and territorial conditions, especially the vast tracts of desert, extending from the Sahara, through Arabia, Persia, India, and Tartary, to the most elevated Asiatic highlands."[133] Marx took this passage verbatim from the letter Engels wrote him on June 6, four days before Marx wrote the first of his articles on British rule.[134] A fuller statement of this point can be found in *An Essay on the Distribution of Wealth,* written by the classical economist Richard Jones and published in 1831. Here Jones includes the northwestern part of North Africa, areas between Persia and Tartary, and

the northern edge of China.[135] Engels does not mention these areas. But he reproduces the core of Jones's statement, in part verbatim.

2. **General human response.** "An economical and common use of water" became a "prime necessity."[136] Such a use could be accomplished only by "the formation of tanks where ground is required for embankment, and by the conveyance of water along different lines."[137]

3. **Macro-institutional consequences.** Where "private enterprise," "voluntary association, as in Flanders and Italy," was inadequate, an agency to handle the water had to be established through "the interference of the centralizing power of the Government. Hence an economical function developed upon all Asiatic governments, the function of providing public works."[138] In fact, "great public works" became "the prime condition of agriculture and commerce."[139]

4. **Socioeconomic correlations.** The mass of the producers were "dispersed . . . over the surface of the country, and agglomerated in small centres by the domestic union of agricultural and manufacturing pursuits."[140] These small communities "were based on domestic industry, in that peculiar combination of hand-weaving, hand-spinning and hand-tilling agriculture, which gave them self-supporting power."[141]

5. **Sociopsychological consequences.** "These idyllic village communities . . . had always been the solid foundation of Oriental despotism . . . they transformed a self-developing social state into never-changing destiny."[142] Prior to the British conquest of India, Asia knew no social revolution: "English interference . . . dissolved these small semi-barbarian, semi-civilized communities, by blowing up their economical basis," and thus "produced the greatest, and to speak the truth, the only *social* revolution ever heard of in Asia."[143]

6. **Summary with special reference to India (the "two circumstances").** On June 14, 1853, four days after writing his first article on India for the *New York Herald Tribune,* Marx, in a letter to Engels, recapitulated with small changes the major points he had made in it. After having given his "only-social-revolution" thesis, he continued:

> The stationary character of this part of Asia [India], despite all purposeless movement on the political surface, is fully explained by 2 circumstances that mutually support each other: 1. The public works the task of the central government. 2. By its side the whole Empire, except for a few large cities, dissolved in *villages* that had a completely distinct organization and formed a small world of their own."[144]

In the article itself Marx had indicated that these criteria were valid for the Orient as a whole:

> These two circumstances—the Hindoo, on the one hand, leaving,
> like all Oriental peoples, to the central government the care of the
> great public works, the prime conditions of his agriculture and
> commerce, dispersed, on the other hand over the surface of the
> country, and agglomorated in small centres by the domestic union
> of agricultural and manufacturing pursuits.[145]

7. **China.** Since Engels, his mentor on matters of geography, did not include China in the "vast tracts of desert" that "can be made fruitful only through irrigation" (Jones), Marx did not include it in his geohydraulic list. But his subsequent behavior shows that he had no doubts as to China's socio-historical position. A German with Marx's education who became interested in China's waterworks would quite likely recall the relevant comments of such eminent philosophers of history as Herder and Hegel, and such an eminent geographer as Karl Ritter. All three of these scholars acknowledged the importance of government-managed waterworks in China. Ritter spoke of China's "water economy" (*Wasserwirtschaft*). But whether Marx, who knew Herder's views on world literature, was familiar with the remarks on China's waterworks Herder had made is not clear.[146] He was possibly aware of Ritter's pertinent idea: in 1838 he registered for Ritter's course on General Geography.[147] And he may have gotten from Ritter the terms *orography* and *hydrography*, which he used in *German Ideology*.[148] He certainly knew Hegel's *Philosophy of History*, and he knew it well. While Hegel's discussion of waterworks in China probably seemed irrelevant to Marx during his *Communist Manifesto* period, it may well have become meaningful to him when he was developing his new views on Asia.

As to his second circumstance, Marx emphasized in his two India articles the union of small agriculture and handicraft and the absence of private ownership of land as making the villages self-supporting and stationary. In 1853, he had no reason to doubt that such a union existed in China—nor did he question its presence later, when he learned that there the communal land system had yielded to private landownership.[149]

The image of China that emerged from Marx's new "Asiatic" insights was no longer the one he had had in 1850, when he (and Engels) felt that the popular attack on the emperor and his mandarins then under way might lead to an enormously important "social revolution" and a crude Chinese socialism, whose slogan ("*Republique chinoise. Liberté, Égalité, Fraternité*") might frighten the European reactionaries.[150] In 1853, Marx no longer viewed China's mass uprising as progressive. In "British Rule in India" he asserted that Asiatic society could only unleash "wild, aimless, unbounded forces of destruction."

In an article completed on July 19, 1853 (twenty-nine days after he had written "British Rule in India," with his "two circumstances" criterion), he referred to the "disorders in China" as "completely Eastern."[151]

8. **Russia.** In the same sentence in which Marx thus classified China as "Eastern," he spoke of tsarist Russia's impact on Europe's international policy as "half Eastern."[152] Marx, of course, was aware that Russia's agriculture did not require large-scale waterworks for purposes of irrigation. But he was also aware of the enduring character of the Russian village communities. These communities had been brought to his attention no later than the winter of 1852/53 through his reading of Herzen's *Development of Revolutionary Ideas in Russia.*[153] Thus, while tsarist Russia lacked Marx's first circumstance of Asiatic society, it exhibited the second, the progress-stifling village communities that "had always been the solid foundation of Oriental despotism."

From 1853, Marx (and Engels) applied the designation "semi-Asiatic" to tsarist Russia, not just in a geographical but also in an institutional sense. In the later part of 1853, in his articles on Palmerston, Marx pointed to the Tatars as having been responsible for the Orientally despotic order that now prevailed in Russia.[154] Taken together, these views indicate that, in Marx's opinion, the first of the two circumstances was essential for the *genesis* of the Orientally despotic order, the second was sufficient for its *perpetuation.*

C. Multiple Consequences: Disquieting Questions

Marx made these discoveries after he and Engels had withdrawn from active politics. On November 17, 1852, Marx had dissolved the Communist League, because it was "no longer timely."[155] The continental phase of his and Engels' revolutionary activities, which had culminated ideologically in the *Communist Manifesto*, and operationally in their participation in the 1848/49 revolution, had come to an end.

In this situation, Marx turned to the basic economic analysis of the Western bourgeois world, whose final doom he predicted. At the same time, he (and Engels) began to view the world as a whole. Practically speaking, this was necessitated by the fact that Marx had to write bread-and-butter articles for the *New York Daily Tribune*, whose readers liked to be informed not only about Europe but also about Asia: India, China, Russia, and all the rest. Theoretically, Marx was ready to raise all sorts of new problems that transcended the interests of most of his Yankee readers. But they bore with Marx's theoretical asides, because he presented his ideas in a dramatic and richly documented way.

Even though in 1853 Marx wrote his India articles to sustain himself and his family, he eagerly concentrated on his systematic analysis of capitalism.

And it is significant that, stimulated by Engels, he discovered Asiatic society for no special political reason. It is also significant that, having structured his new Asiatic ideas in accordance with his socioeconomic approach to past and present conditions, he did not follow them up with a systematic study of the relation between the East and the West. Quite possibly, he did not at first notice the full implications of his Asiatic discoveries for the understanding of Western economy and society and for the image of the world which, in a visionary way, he had portrayed in the *Communist Manifesto*.

But these implications were inherent in his discoveries. And the theoretical and political changes in Marx's behavior after 1853 show him at least dimly aware of them. What is clear in the thoughts of both Marx and Engels is that the problem of India became less significant as the problem of Russia became increasingly complex and urgent. And in the widening world of East-and-West relations in which Marx and Engels found their place—analytically, and eventually politically—the Russian revolutionaries also found their place.

Initially, the Russian revolutionaries appeared in the main as recipients of Marx's and Engels's ideas, but eventually they became revolutionaries in their own right: as authentically orthodox Marxists (up to a point, Plekhanov, and as supposedly orthodox Marxists (Lenin and his supporters). Diverted by Lenin, the Bolsheviks advanced toward an extremist revolution that purportedly established "socialism" in Marx's terms, but which, according to Plekhanov (and Lenin), ran the risk of evolving an entirely different system of economy and government.

1. Key tenets of the *Communist Manifesto* abandoned. Marx certainly did not envisage this alternative when in 1853 he included Russia in the Asiatic world he had newly discovered. And for a long time thereafter he did not take into account what effect his new discovery would have on the core tenets of the *Manifesto*.

a. Historical "materialism"? At the height of Max Weber's admiration for Marx, he suggested that this "great thinker",[156] as he called him, would better have spoken of an economic rather than a materialistic interpretation of history.[157] Weber's rejection of the *Manifesto* and his praise of *Capital* was in part motivated by this judgment.[158] He was unaware of certain of Marx's posthumously published manuscripts, especially *German Ideology* (which systematically elaborated Marx's and Engels's early "historical materialism"), and the *Grundrisse* (which elaborated Marx's advance toward a different position from the one he had taken in the *Manifesto*).

In *German Ideology* and other works of this period, Marx and Engels rejected the thesis (postulated by Adam Smith) that organization and division of labor was the decisive agent of economic change. Instead, they singled out the materialistic sector of the powers of production—man-made tools—as the decisive formative agent.[159] The discoveries of 1853 did not refute the validity of this correlation for the West; but they opened up the vast "Asiatic" world of human activity in which labor, especially the organization of large numbers of toilers for hydraulic and other "public works," was socioeconomically decisive.

The evidence of the Oriental world exposed the fallacy of the materialistic generalization that Marx and Engels had earlier drawn from spatially and chronologically limited facts. But during the years thereafter they did not speak of a hydraulic revolution or of an organizational revolution; both concepts emerged considerably later.[160] They did, however, recognize the crucial significance of "cooperation" in Asiatic soviety, as they had since 1845 inconclusively recognized it in the first period of industrial ("manufacturing") capitalism.[161] Moreover, they now conceptualized it as having introduced a new "power of production."[162]

b.   *Was centralized statist control over labor and the means of production conducive to human freedom?* Did Marx realize after 1853 that the Communist revolution he had predicted in the *Manifesto* was something like an organizational revolution? Did he realize that this operational revolution involved a corresponding proprietary revolution? The revolutionary state that was supposed to organize the toilers in state-controlled enterprises and industrial (agricultural etc.) "armies"[163] was supposed also to centralize the material means of production in its hands.[164] Did this twofold concentration of power in the only case in which it was realized—in Asiatic society—give the producers freedom, human dignity, and control over their fate? Certainly not. It gave them political slavery and despotism.

What about the socialist society of the future? The author of the *Manifesto* assured his readers that such a centralization of power would lead to democracy, because the state that was meant to accomplish this centralization was "the proletariat organized as a ruling class."[165] Did Marx continue to believe this after 1853? To be sure, as late as 1872 he declared: "The general principles that have been laid down in this *Manifesto* are, on the whole, as correct as ever."[166] But what were these general principles? Marx answered this question only indirectly. In 1871 he extolled the Paris Commune as a model of the Communist society of the future, but he did not repeat his request for a centralized system of state-controlled property and production. In *State and Revolution* Lenin tried to give the impression that Marx had adhered to this request until the end. When presenting the idea of centralized statist production and property he did not, however, invoke as his authority Marx's Commune pamphlet, *Civil War in France,* but the *Communist Manifesto.*[167]

Did Marx remember what he had asserted in 1853, that in order to escape from the total power of the functional state *any* form of private property was preferable to its state-imposed absence?[168] Whatever the case may be, the central government of Marx's commune society was meant to preserve only a few important features to assure national unity. The revolutionary producers should take over the means of production; and as members of local self-governing communes they should, according to a plan, use them "cooperatively," as "tools of free and associated labor."[169]

The difficulties of this idea are obvious. But this much is certain. If Marx wanted his future society to rest on the principle of free association and self-government (the basic principle of all genuine cooperatives), then he had indeed abandoned the centralized state socialism that was the operational core of the *Manifesto*.

The change was profound, but was it entirely accidental? Did Marx, who in 1867, in the first volume of *Capital*, starkly depicted the social horrors of Asiatic despotism, totally forget them in 1871? Was he likely to forget that this system left no room for self-developing action—and no room either for class struggle, because, under its rule, all persons were politically enslaved?[170] Was he likely to forget, what he had envisaged during the early phases of his career, that of all forms of alienation the one imposed by pseudocommunism was the worst?[171]

Max Weber, who was eager to learn from Marx's *Capital* but who had no vested political interest in revolutionary myths, rejected the *Manifesto*. And although he deeply sympathized with the spirit of dedication that he found in the modern socialist labor movement, he unequivocally rejected state-socialism as "reactionary."[172] Marx, very much in contrast to the pertinent tenets of the *Manifesto*, had recognized in 1864 and 1867 the ameliorative potential inherent in modern private-property based (capitalist) economy.[173] Why then did he fail to speak clearly about the general principles on which his changing attitude toward capitalism and socialism were based?

2. A strong rejection of the unilinear ("universal") concept of historical development withheld. Why did Marx also hesitate to speak clearly about his rejection of the concept of unilinear development, which is the core of the *Manifesto*'s scheme of historical change? In the present inquiry, this issue, like several others, can be treated only briefly. But it must be mentioned, because it involves the core problem of the relation between the East and the West, a problem that has profoundly aroused Russian Marxists since Plekhanov adopted Marx's Asiatic interpretation of Russia in the 1880s and since Lenin did likewise in the 1890s and during the prewar period of the twentieth century.

The most spectacular manifestation of Marx's ambivalence in this matter is the letter he wrote to the editor of the radical Petersburg journal *Otechest-venniye Zapiski*, in 1877. This letter is significant not only for Marx's and Engels's attitude toward it, which determined the letter's early fate, but also for the role it played in Lenin's first Marxist publication: *What the "Friends of the People" are and How They Fight the Social Democrats.* It was incorrectly reproduced in the last "Marxist consideration" Lenin formulated on January 16, 1923 in "Our Revolution," the third to the last article he wrote.

Marx drafted his *Zapiski* letter as a comment on the controversy that had been waged among Russian Marxists concerning his view of the relation between the development of Russia and the West. From the standpoint of the present inquiry, it is sufficient to say that this controversy constituted the background for Marx's statement about the developmental position of Russia and the value (or lack of value) of a universal concept of historical development.

Marx opened his substantive remarks with the declaration that he was "not fond of leaving 'something to be guessed.'" But that is precisely what he did when he presented his views on "the economic development of Russia." By speaking only of the road Russia had embarked upon "since 1861," he deprived his views of their sociohistorical depth. Marx had indicated that since 1861 Russia's agrarian order had made great strides toward the establishment of "a capitalist regime," thus interrupting the country's "own historically given preconditions."[174] What were these historically given preconditions?

Marx and Engels had declared since 1853 that, according to their new sociohistorical frame of reference, traditional Russia was an Asiatic (or semi-Asiatic) society dominated by an unqualified despotism, and they argued along this line in a number of Western newspapers and journals.[175] How generally aware were the Russian radicals of these remarks, and specifically of Marx's articles on the Tatarization of Russia?[176] They certainly knew Engels's 1875 article in *Der Volksstaat* in which he stated that Oriental despotism was the "social formation" (*Gesellschaftsform*) that, on the basis of self-contained village communities, prevailed "from India to Russia."[177] Engels repeated this idea almost with the same words in the part of his *Anti-Düring* that appeared in *Vorwärts* just prior to the writing of Marx's *Zapiski* letter.[178]

Marx obviously assumed that his prospective readers could follow him when, in connection with the problem of Western and non-Western developments, he drew their attention to his pertinent remarks in *Capital*. His statement that the account of the original accumulation of capital he had given in the first volume was valid only for the society of Western Europe with its feudal past, implied that Russia's historically given preconditions were different. In his endeavor to avoid involvement in the Russian debate, he refused to commit himself concerning the Russian perspective. But his formulation indicated his hope that, by utilizing the collectivist elements inherent in the traditional village community, Russia could advance directly to socialism, avoiding the "fatal vicissitudes of the capitalist regime."[179] While he did not specify Russia's non-Western past, he indicated his conviction that before 1861 Russia had been an Orientally despotic order. As such, it had involved not self-developmental progress, but stagnation.

Marx did specify that although ancient Rome was first a society of free peasants and that although it had become one of large-landed estates and big-money capital, it had not advanced to a modern industrial order based on wage labor but had ended with a mode of production based on slave labor.[180] Already in the middle of his letter, he emphatically warned his prospective readers against interpreting his account of the origin of capitalism in Western Europe as implying "a historical-philosophical theory of a general course of development as proscribed by fate to every people, whatever the historical circumstances may be." After having outlined the retrogressive development of ancient Rome, he returned to this point again:

> Thus events of a strikingly analogous character which occur in a different historical setting, led to entirely different results. By studying each of these developments separately and then comparing them, one will easily find the key to this phenomenon, but one will never arrive there with the universal key of a historical-philosophical theory, whose supreme value is to be supra-historical.[181]

The clarity and force of this statement left no doubt as to Marx's meaning and intent. By calling the universalist approach to world history "supra-historical," Marx condemned it as unscientific. This judgment was crucial for the Russian Marxists. It confirmed what they had been taught since the beginning of their movement, that tsarist Russia was not the result of a general development, but of special conditions. These conditions necessitated a policy that was eventually supposed to merge with their Western comrades' struggle for socialism, but which, for the time being, had special aims and required special methods. In this respect, Marx's view of the Russian version of the difference between the East and the West was politically vital. It goes far to explain the debates of the Russian Social Democrats, (particularly those that took place at the Congresses of 1903 and 1906) about their party program.

Marx's judgment affected the doctrine of all Marxist Social Democratic parties, but it was particularly meaningful to the Russian Marxists, who were extremely sensitive to ideological problems. The Marxist socialists called themselves "scientific" because of their "economic" or "materialistic" approach; and they considered history the core of their scientific position: they were "historical" materialists. By declaring the universalist approach to the history of mankind unscientific, Marx underlined the distinction between the Marxist (the rational political) and non-Marxist (the speculative or sentimental) forms of socialism. When, in 1894, Lenin associated himself with Marx's *Zapiski* letter, he condemned, as Marx had, the "general" and "abstract" approach to history as "metaphysical."[182] And in 1895, when Plekhanov identified himself with this same letter, he condemned the universalist approach to history as "mystical."[183]

But what about the *Communist Manifesto*? Did not Marx's antiuniversalist pronouncement of 1877 refute the developmental core of the *Manifesto*? The

Russian Marxists avoided this question, following the highest authority they had—the example set by Marx and Engels.

Marx, who since 1853 had withdrawn from the universalist thesis of the *Manifesto*, failed for a long time to conceptualize the multilinear position inherent in his new discoveries. Only the Russian controversy stimulated him, in the fall of 1877, to compose the *Zapiski* letter, which elliptically, but unmistakably, presented his new position. But after having written this letter, he never dispatched it.

Engels found Marx's letter among his deceased friend's manuscripts. On March 6, 1884 he sent a copy of it to Vera Zassulich, a member of the Russian-Marxist group in Geneva. Obviously attempting to justify the cautious form of Marx's presentation, he declared in an accompanying note, that Marx had written this letter with an eye to its publication in Russia. He added that Marx had never "sent it to Petersburg, because his very name might endanger the existence of the journal which would publish his answer."[184] Marx quite likely had various possibilities to publish his antiuniversalist statement outside of Russia. But he chose to forego them.

Engels's declaration attempts to explain why Marx finally resolved not to send this letter to Russia; it fails completely to explain its theoretical significance. And this is a remarkable omission! In the realm of socialism, a pronouncement by Marx correcting faulty views of historical development was certainly worth making known. But Engels obviously did not ascribe particular significance to Marx's antiuniversalist statement. He did not dwell on this point when he sent Marx's letter to Vera Zasulich. Nor did he do so on two subsequent occasions. In 1893, in a conversation with a Russian visitor, he acknowledged that virtually all Russians who came to see him inquired about the meaning of Marx's letter, but he could not understand what was unclear about it.[185] And while he commented in this context on some problems of the Russian and Western revolutions, he said nothing about the basic sociohistorical thesis Marx had presented in his letter. Engels remained equally uninterested in 1894 in a postscript to his article "Social Conditions in Russia." Although he again spoke of Marx's 1877 letter and again acknowledged the significance the Russian Marxists ascribed to it, he again avoided referring to the crucial developmental statement.[186]

Obviously, Marx and Engels were willing to recognize the special conditions of Russia's historical position, but not willing to present the underlying theoretical issue in a form that would have smashed the key developmental thesis of the *Communist Manifesto*. But Lenin was willing to give Marx's and Engels's concept of Russia's special (Asiatic) development a bold turn, indeed so bold that his argument raised the most disquieting ideas about Russia's revolutionary development and about the risk he and his followers might run: the risk of an abysmal (Asiatic) restoration.

IV. The Specter of an "Asiatic Restoration" in Russia: Lenin

After 1853, Marx spoke of India, China, and Russia as three major variants of Asiatic society. He first concentrated on India in his discussion of the transformation of an Asiatic into a non-Asiatic society. Subsequently, he and Engels made brief, but suggestive, remarks about the retardation of this process in China.[187] They turned increasingly to Russia as a particularly instructive—and politically relevant—case of the disintegration of an Orientally despotic social formation.

A number of these ideas survived in Marx's and Engels's writings and unpublished manuscripts and letters; some in personal communications of Engels, who, of course, outlived Marx by more than a dozen years. Engels readily discussed with friends and comrades his and Marx's views of Russia. He helped the leading young orthodox Marxists, Karl Kautsky and George Plekhanov, to familiarize themselves with this part of the Marxist heritage. They, in turn, elaborated on it in *Die Neue Zeit* and elsewhere during the last years of Engels's life.[188] Plekhanov handed on this heritage to the next generation of Russian Marxists, which included Lenin. In 1910, Lenin asserted that Plekhanov had "helped to educate a whole generation of Russian Marxists."[189]

As soon as Plekhanov had established himself as an orthodox Marxist (a Russian Social Democrat), he admonished his associates not to advocate an impatient and voluntaristic revolutionary policy, as the Narodniki, the heirs of revolutionary anarchism, were doing. He made this point briefly in 1883 in his pamphlet *Socialism and the Political Struggle*[190] and more fully in 1884 in his first Marxist book, *Our Differences*. In this book, which Lenin in 1894 (at the start of his career as a Marxist Social Democrat) cited as authoritative,[191] Plekhanov insisted that such a policy would be self-defeating. Instead of leading to a people's government and eventually to democratic socialism, it would create "a political monster similar to the ancient Chinese or Peruvian Empires, i.e., to the restoration of Tsarist despotism with a communist cover."[192]

A. The Specter

Did Plekhanov in 1884 recognize the full meaning of the type of restoration he was warning against? Probably not. But while his understanding of this nightmarish perspective was limited, he was more perceptive than other orthodox Marxists, Engels included, who, on the basis of the Asiatic interpretation of Russia, engaged in predicting that country's future. In 1906, Plekhanov again did not exhaust the sociopolitical possibilities of his restoration agrument. But he was apparently more perceptive than other orthodox Marxists.

After 1905 ideas for shortcuts in revolutionary strategy were advanced by
a number of Marxists, outstanding among them Parvus, Trotsky, and Lenin.
Parvus, whose Marxist reasoning Lenin found much more convincing than that
of Trotsky,[193] ascribed the weakness of the Russian bourgeoisie to the Asiatic
pattern of Russia's cities. These cities were closer to "the Chinese than the
European model." They were "administrative centers of a purely governmental
character." Hence, the Russian workers could by-pass the poorly developed
bourgeoisie, become the leaders in the revolution, and advance to a "workers'
democracy."[194] Trotsky, who acknowledged his debt to Parvus's Asiatic interpretation of Russia's middle class, was going beyond him when he proposed
that, in view of the weakness of the Russian bourgeoisie, the Russian proletariat
could move straight ahead to a socialist revolution. But the resulting regime,
Trotsky argued, could preserve its socialist intent only with outside assistance,
only "with the forces of the socialist proletariat of Western Europe." Here we
have the germ of Trotsky's concept of the socialist revolution in Russia and its
necessary relation to the Western revolution.

Plekhanov in his 1906 polemics was not addressing his warning to Parvus,
who was free but not a member of the Russian Socialist party, or to Trotsky,
who was a member of that party but not free. He was addressing it to Lenin,
who was free and the head of a large sector of the party.

1. 1906: The Fourth Party Congress at Stockholm and thereafter. Lenin
was not unaware of Russia's capitalistic development. In the late 1890s he rated
it highly, but when the 1905 revolution exposed the feebleness of the Russian
bourgeoisie he down-graded it notably. Pointing to the strength of the Western,
and especially the English, bourgeoisie, he stated that Russia's capitalism was
crippled, that, in fact, it was "Asiatic."[195] Building on his version of the Asiatic
interpretation of Russia, he began to reshape his and his followers' attitude
toward the peasantry.

Lenin now maintained that the small Russian proletariat, led by "its" party,
could seize power if it gained the support of the discontented peasants. At first
he envisaged a brittle alliance with the villagers, but from the winter of 1905/06
he sought their full and continuing cooperation. The nationalization of the land,
which he now advocated, would abolish the payment of rent.[196] It would
encourage the rural masses to give rein to their (bourgeois) economic energies
until a breakthrough to the socialist revolution was possible.

Plekhanov used Lenin's nationalization program to connect the agrarian
issue and the dangers inherent in Russia's (semi-) Asiatic background. By
nationalizing all land the revolutionary state would gain as much power over
the peasants as had the state of Muscovy. To be sure, as long as the toilers
were in control of the state, such an arrangement would be no threat to them;
but if they lost control, they would be doomed. Plekhanov labelled Lenin's
program for a successful revolution "Utopian," derisively citing Napoleon's

statement that any general was a "bad" general who based his plans on the assumption that all conditions would be favorable. They never were. If Lenin's blueprint failed—and, in agreement with Napoleon's statement, Plekhanov predicted this was inevitable—then the nationalization of the land would leave "the survivals of the old semi-Asiatic order untouched." In fact it would facilitate its "restoration." As a guarantee against such a development Plekhanov proposed that the land should be held by self-governing regional bodies, "municipalities."

In rejecting Plekhanov's plan Lenin employed seemingly realistic arguments.[197] Such a plan, he maintained, could not prevent the catastrophic development that Plekhanov feared, a development that Lenin referred to interchangeably as "the semi-Asiatic restoration." "the restoration of the semi-Asiatic order," "the return to the *Aziatchina* [the Asiatic system]," or Russia's "Asiatic restoration." In some of his arguments he categorically denied the danger of such a development; in others he admitted that, despite the 1905 revolution, the shell of the old Asiatic order was still intact and, indeed, quite strong. But he held that the nationalization of the land would "far more radically" than municipalization "eliminate the economic foundation of the *Aziatchina*."[198]

2. **Reluctant and inconsistent admissions.** Lenin insisted that the dreaded restoration could be avoided only if one absolute, external guarantee was fulfilled: "A socialist revolution in the West is the only absolute guarantee against restoration in Russia." Internal measures could provide "relative guarantees." The revolutionary government must be radically democratic: it must have no bureaucracy and no standing army.

Lenin mentioned these two "relative" guarantees in 1906/07 while discussing the Asiatic restoration with Plekhanov. As the crisis deepened during World War I he shied away from the Asiatic interpretation of Russia and the possibility of an Asiatic restoration. But on the eve of the October Revolution and immediately thereafter, he repeatedly asserted that the socialist revolution in the West was necessary for the protection of Russia's advancing revolution. And in his pamphlet *State and Revolution,* which he wrote in August and September of 1917, he insisted that the revolutionary dictatorship he had in mind must be controlled by the people. Consistent with Marx's interpretation of the Paris Commune, and elaborating on his own 1906/07 formulation, Lenin now proclaimed that the victorious revolution could consolidate its accomplishments only if the new "commune" state operated without an independent bureaucracy, without a standing army, and without a professional police.[199] He did not in this context mention the Asiatic restoration, but he elaborated on his 1906/07 formulation and added a third relative guarantee (no police) to those he had originally specified.

3. **A discoverer in spite of himself.** The student of modern radical thought will not be impressed by Lenin's way of dealing with the problem of

an Asiatic restoration. Neither in the passages cited nor elsewhere did he
develop this problem fully or systematically. Why not? He was, we know,
well able to engage in scientific researches when it suited his purpose; and
his agrarian studies show that he could present his findings with precision when
he wanted to. But this was obviously not his aim when he spoke of the relation between Marx's Asiatic argument and the course a successful extremist
Russian revolution might take.

In 1905, Lenin introduced his new and very radical revolutionary program
without referring to Plekhanov's early warnings concerning the possibility of
something like a Chinese or Peruvian restoration. In 1906/07 his views on
this issue were forced from him by Plekhanov's frontal attack on his new
"tactics." His subsequent comments on it, including those after 1917, were
also forced from him by attacks on his perspectives and policies.[200]

Manifestly, Lenin's views on the danger of an Asiatic restoration in post-
revolution Russia constituted no well-formulated concept. But were they,
for this reason, irrelevant? This question brings to mind a remark Churchill
is said to have made. Democracy, he allegedly noted, was the worst of all forms
of government—except for all the others. Lenin argued his concept of an Asiatic
restoration unevenly, and it could well be considered the worst of all such concepts—except for all the others. Like Columbus, Lenin discovered the contours
of a new truth (he envisaged developmental problems not foreseen by Toqueville,
Marx, or Max Weber). Like Columbus, he discovered the wrong continent. But
his continent, like Columbus's, provided a priceless key to the understanding of
a new world that, for better or worse, has become an essential part of our present-
day reality.

B.   The Reality

Lenin's reality was, of course, the Russian revolution. But it was more than
that. His interpretation of tsarist Russia interlocked with the interpretation
of a complex the Marxists called "Asia." And his perspective for a successful
Russian revolution recognized the need for a socialist revolution in the capitalist
West.

How well did Lenin understand the Russian workers and peasants on whose
combined support his plan for revolution was based? In his early analyses he
had misjudged the condition of the Russian peasantry and the class-conscious-
ness of the Russian workers. Beginning in 1905 he saw things differently.[201]
In his early statements on Russia's "Asiatic" background he accepted important
elements of Marx's concept of Asiatic society, but unlike Marx,[202] he classed
the rich peasants as capitalists and crassly overrated the development of capitalism in contemporary Russia.[203] In 1905 he corrected his evaluation of the
peasants, but not his evaluation of the rich peasants and the workers. As

stated above, he now termed Russia's capitalism "Asiatic,"[204] and this obviously because he had become conscious that Russia's capitalist development was being crippled by an Asiatic system of power and society.

And then there was the Western labor movement. Prior to the outbreak of the World War, Lenin had rated its revolutionary potential, especially that of its vital German sector, very highly. This judgment he revised sharply at the beginning of the war, when the major socialist parties of the West instead of, as anticipated, attacking their respective governments, supported them. In 1916 in a pamphlet, *Imperialism, the Highest Stage of Capitalism,* he asserted that the leading elements in the Western labor movement were not revolutionaries, but reformists, because they benefited from their country's "imperialism." In this pamphlet Lenin gives many illuminating details, but in terms of his own definition, his basic argument is faulty. His thesis that imperial rule ultimately rests on colonial possessions poorly fitted the case of the foremost capitalist country of Europe: Germany. Like the USA, Germany had almost no colonies.[205] And like leading strata of the American workers, their German counterparts were not propelled into a nonrevolutionary mood because of "extra profits" derived from a colonial empire.

Thus, Lenin's understanding of the international situation was not very realistic when he based his plans for a Bolshevist revolution on the likelihood of a Western socialist revolution. And his understanding of Russia's internal situation was not entirely realistic either. This being so, how effective could the guarantees be that for years he had been viewing as the necessary defense against an Asiatic restoration in Russia?

1. **The fate of two of Lenin's relative (internal) guarantees.** Lenin's relative internal guarantees were put to the test first at the time of the October Revolution,[206] when the workers of the West were still at war. Because of exigencies arising from the revolution, the second and third of his relative guarantees (no police and no standing army) were put to the test before the weakness of his first relative guarantee (no bureaucracy) became fully apparent.

    a. No police. When the Bolsheviks seized power, they declared that "the armed people," "the armed workers," would enforce order.[207] But they quickly realized that this arrangement could not adequately assure the stability of their regime. Hence, on December 20, 1917, one month after the October Revolution, the Soviet government set up a special political police, the Cheka.[208]

    b. No standing army. On December 29, 1917, the new regime abolished military ranks, and in the following month it announced that the army would be controlled "from below." A half year later conscription for army service was introduced. In September 1918 a Revolutionary War Council was created, and soon thereafter a small but permanent staff of officers.[209] All this occurred less than a year after the October Revolution.

2. **The fate of the decisive relative (internal) guarantee: no bureaucracy.**
With the war ending, Lenin was understandably euphoric. But his conviction
"that the uprisings in central Europe were the first major step in a proletarian
socialist revolution" was illusionary. And his conviction that the Soviet revolution had eliminated the danger of an omnipotent bureaucracy was equally so.
In November 1918 in a pamphlet directed against "the renegade Kautsky,"
he declared that in Russia "the bureaucratic machine has been completely
smashed, razed to the ground." Indeed, the Soviets of workers and peasants

> have replaced the bureaucrats, or *their* Soviets have been put in
> control of the bureaucrats. This fact alone is enough for all the
> oppressed classes to recognize that Soviet power, i.e., the present
> form of the dictatorship of the proletariat, is a million times more
> democratic than the most democratic bourgois republic.[210]

a. *"Sliding down"–to what? (January 1919).* Lenin was engaging in
wishful thinking when he asserted that a proletarian revolution in the West was
in the making. Although the German and Austrian workers were not al all dis-
pleased when the Bolshevik revolution put an end to Russia's participation in
the war, and although many of them sympathized with the Bolshevik drive
toward socialism, they were no Communists. Small groups of Communists
(Spartacists) in Berlin and other radical elements in central Europe were
attempting to establish a dictatorship of the proletariat, but they learned
quickly and painfully that they constituted no effective revolutionary vanguard, since they had no revolutionary mass movement behind them. The
assassination of Karl Liebknecht and Rosa Luxemburg on January 15, 1919
demonstrated the determination of the German anti-Communists to block
the Communist advance and the lack of interest in such an advance among
the majority of the German workers, who, despite their sympathy with the
Bolshevik experiment, wanted to rebuild their country in a non-Communist
way.

Lenin's response to the murders of Liebknecht and Luxemburg shows
him intensely aware of their meaning for the Soviet future. In a speech made
before the Second All-Russian Trade Union Congress five days later, he stated
that these violent actions were proof of "the way the problems of the present-
day struggle are presented by the various trends of political thought and in
the various theoretical systems of today."[211]

In this speech Lenin did not refer directly to the danger of an Asiatic
restoration in Soviet Russia or to the guarantees he considered necessary to
avert it. Nor did he repeat his 1905 judgment that in the twentieth century
Russia's capitalism was still hampered by its "Asiatic" heritage. But he now
said that the Russian workers were poorly qualified for revolutionary action:
Russia being "one of the weakest and least prepared of countries,"[212] "we"

could not think of making a socialist revolution in Russia, but only of "holding on as best we could until the West-European proletariat came to life."

Comparing the Bolshevik and "the great French Revolution," he noted that, although the French revolutionaries had been ousted one year after they had seized power, they had done much to advance the bourgeois cause. "In about the same time," he continued, the Bolsheviks had done much more to advance the proletarian cause. By this juxtaposition Lenin was suggesting a parallel between the Jacobin and Bolshevik revolutions. After just one year the Russian revolution was also being endangered by adverse external events. To underline his point, he added: "We have now arrived at the decisive moment of the struggle internationally."[214]

Lenin did not say openly that the Bolshevik revolution might go down to defeat. Nor did he refer openly to the possibility that the failure of his absolute external guarantee would result in a reversion to Russia's "Asiatic" past. But he did say that Russia's socialist revolution could "only be lasting" if a certain "condition," a certain "guarantee," was fulfilled. What condition? What guarantee? Lenin here was conspicuously elliptic, but those familiar with his and Plekhanov's 1906 debate could not fail to understand his message. The events of January 15 had nullified his single absolute external guarantee, and the establishment of a professional police and a standing army had nullified two of his three original relative internal guarantees. Now only one of these last remained to stem the regressive tide—the toilers' control over the state apparatus and its bureaucracy. The working people would "adapt themselves easily" to the job of "governing the state" and "establishing law and order."[215] And the trade unions would be their teachers: they must show millions and tens of millions "how to run the state and industry."[216]

In this context, Lenin did not say, as he had done prior to and immediately after the October Revolution, that the armed workers must be in charge of the country's defense. But he insisted that his two other relative guarantees (no standing army and no bureaucracy) be enforced. And in concluding his statement on the danger that threatened the Soviet regime, he now declared that the workers' control over the state and industry constituted "the only sure guarantee that the cause of socialism will completely triumph, precluding any chance of a reversion (bosbrata) to the past."[217]

Lenin now also avoided the word "absolute," but his phrasing demonstrated his hope that after the manifest crumbling of his only absolute guarantee—the Western revolution—the reactivization of two of his original relative guarantees might provide complete protection from the danger that now was threatening the Bolshevik revolution. In subsequent statements, he again indicated his full recognition of this danger. But in his January 1919 speech he spoke only of "a reversion to the past."

What form did Lenin believe this reversion to the past would take? Would the radical core of the Soviet regime be destroyed by foreign intervention?

His reference to the fate of the Jacobin revolution shows him aware that such
an eventuality could by no means be excluded. His argument shows him also
aware that an external military attack on a revolutionary regime had, not
infrequently, led to the regime's overthrow by internal forces, as had been
the case in France during the Thermidor. In fact, in 1905, Lenin had predicted that if Russia's revolutionary socialists, following his blueprint, should
seize power, their main political enemy would be the "petty bourgeoisie,"
particularly the peasantry. It was this class he again envisaged as the main
threat when, after the October Revolution, his absolute and relative guarantees
were being eroded. In an unusually revealing remark made after Kronstadt,
Lenin pointed to "the petty-bourgeois-anarchist elements" as the main enemy
that had to be beaten: "If we do not [beat them], we shall slide down as the
French Revolution did."[218]

How did the French Revolution "slide down"? How did the Jacobins
"slide down"? For an understanding of Lenin's behavior these questions are
not unimportant. Lenin certainly remembered that in 1794 the Jacobin leaders
were destroyed not only politically, but physically. I do not doubt that Lenin
and many of his followers were ready to die for their cause; but I do not doubt
either that when Lenin envisaged the danger of a restoration, he viewed it not
only as a doctrinal abstraction but, also and pre-eminently, as a physical threat.

After the German assassinations in January 1919, the writing on the wall
was clear. It explains why in March 1919, prematurely according to not a few
of his friends, Lenin forced the founding of the Communist International.
It explains why Moscow urged the speedy organization of Communist parties
and the splitting away from Socialist parties, even though in the long run a
slower pace might have better served the cause of the Communist revolution.
It explains why Moscow, in the spring of 1919, went out of its way to support
the crudely non-Leninist Hungarian Soviet Republic, and why, in the summer
of 1920, Lenin, obviously in the hope of establishing direct contact with the
revolutionary forces in Germany,[219] abandoned his defensive tactics to engage
in an aggressive and ill-conceived adventure. (Subsequently, he acknowledged
that "during the Polish war we advanced too far.")[220] It explains why, in
March 1921, at the time of the Kronstadt uprising, the Lenin-directed Comintern
was willing to have Bela Kun et al. direct a Putsch-like uprising in central Germany.
(Lenin's *post-festum* criticism of this so-called "March action" was a poor effort
to obscure his role in initiating this disastrous enterprise.) Subsequently, he
still defended "the theory of the revolutionary offensive." But while praising
the German workers for their brave fight, he asserted that the application of
this theory "to the March action in Germany in 1921 was incorrect"[221] and
must "not be repeated."[222]

Certainly, when his original relative guarantees were being invalidated in
large part or altogether, Lenin tried to develop new relative internal guarantees.
After he and his aides had established a professional police and a standing army,

they imposed on the workers and peasants an allegedly Communist economic policy that Lenin eventually designated as "war communism." But this policy, instead of enabling the workers to exert control over the bureaucracy, increased the power of the bureaucracy to exert control over the workers. And it completely aliented the peasants.

Lenin's international policy after January 1919 showed him eager to activate the revolutionary forces in the West, but his efforts were of little avail. In the summer of 1920 he was still stressing the "ever-growing" revolutionary ferment in the West, but he was no longer sure of its strength. Now he felt that an anticolonial revolution in the East must remove the obstacles that were impeding the Western revolution. And in order to underline the difficulties his regime was facing, he repeated, in that fateful March of 1921, some of his previous proposals for averting a restoration. "Two conditions," he now asserted, were necessary for the continuing success of Russia's socialist revolution. The first (external) condition was the "timely" support by a socialist revolution in one or several advanced countries. He added that the Communists had "done much" to bring this about—but far from enough to make it a reality.[223] The (internal) second condition, "war communism" (a fourth relative guarantee, as it were) was collapsing. The peasants, he noted, had hated the measures taken by the Soviet regime to enforce "a direct transition to communism."[224] Lenin did not now reinvoke his 1918 image of the workers and peasants as the political masters of the state and industry, and this for obvious reasons. That image certainly did not jibe with his March 1921 statement in which he admitted that the peasants felt they were being victimized by the state-imposed communism. And it certainly did not jibe with the obvious and spectacular growth of the new Soviet bureaucracy.

Had Lenin been guilty of self-deception when he spoke as he did in 1918? Or had the bureaucracy become terrifyingly strong only in 1919 and 1920? However this may be, when Lenin, in the spring of March 1921, spoke of the new bureaucracy, he could hardly have forgotten what he had said about Russia's Orientally despotic tradition to Rosa Luxemburg on the eve of the World War in the course of a debate about the right of self-determination. Here Lenin, in apparent agreement with "our Rosa," judged the state system of contemporary Russia in terms of its "economic, political and sociological characteristics and everyday life—a totality of features, which taken together, produce the concept of 'Asiatic' despotism." And he added: "It is generally known that this kind of state system possesses great stability whenever completely patriarchal and precapitalist features predominate in the economic system and where commodity production and class differention are scarcely developed."[225]

b. Return to the Orientally despotic bureaucracy (1921). Did Lenin, while debating with Rosa Luxemburg, remember Marx's sketch of Asiatic

society made in his letter to Engels on June 14, 1853, which Lenin had certainly
read in 1913 when he was studying the Marx-Engels *Correspondence* so intensely.[226] It seems legitimate to believe that he did. Returning in the spring of
1921 to the problems of Russia's post-October period, he referred to the dispersed and atomized condition of the small producer, a feature Marx had
specified in his letter of 1853 as the circumstance responsible for the stationary
character of Oriental despotism.[227] And, as he had done in 1914, Lenin again
saw in Russia an exemplification of a special type of primitive economy; and
now with particular stress on its special type of bureaucracy he juxtaposed
the society correlated with this bureaucracy to socialism and capitalism. A
month later, elaborating on the ideas he had presented in March 1921, he
declared in his watershed pamphlet *The Tax in Kind*:

> A developed *bourgeoisie* needs a bureaucratic apparatus, primarily
> a military apparatus, and then a judiciary, etc., to use against the
> revolutionary movement of the workers (and partly of the peasants).
> *That is something we have not.* . . . In our country bureaucratic
> practices have different economic roots, namely the *atomized and
> scattered state of the small producer* with his poverty, illiteracy,
> lack of culture, the absence of roads and *exchange* between agricul-
> ture and industry, the absence of connection and interaction be-
> tween them.[228]

He added that what was happening in the Soviet Union had been caused "largely"
by the Civil War. "Largely," but not entirely: there was a "medieval" root.
In 1914, Lenin had identified this root as Russia's Asiatically despotic system.
In his post-Kronstadt pamphlet, he justaposed various systems of government:
"Socialism," he wrote now, "is better than capitalism." But "capitalism,"
he went on to say, "is better than medievalism, small production and a bureaucracy connected with the dispersed character of the small producers."[229] That
is, according to Marx's concept, upheld by Lenin from 1894 to 1914, it is
better than Oriental despotism. Taken as a whole, Lenin's argument shows
that, in his opinion, the Soviet bureaucracy was indeed old and Orientally
despotic.

    The third of Lenin's relative guarantees had withered away as had the
other two. His new relative guarantee, "war communism," had failed abysmally,
and his single absolute guarantee against an Asiatic restoration—the Western
revolution—"had not become a reality." Lenin had acknowledged this on
March 15, 1921, when the Bolsheviks were preparing for their final assault
on Kronstadt.[230] He repeated it after the Soviet regime had crushed the
Kronstadt uprising and when he hoped to appease the peasants by announcing
his New Economic Policy. On July 5, 1921, at the Third Congress of the
Communist International, Lenin predicted that "sooner or later" colonial

revolutions might "quite possibly change the unstable international 'equilibrium'" between "the international bourgeoisie as a whole and Soviet Russia." But as of now, despite the progress the revolutionary movement had made, he admitted that "the development of the international revolution this year has not proceeded along as straight a line as we had expected."[231]

3. **The fate of Lenin's absolute international guarantee: the socialist revolution in the West.** Comparing the Soviet Union, which was trying to assure the victory of the proletarian revolution, and the "international revolution" in "the capitalistically more developed countries," Lenin explained to the Comintern Congress why the Bolsheviks were so intensely concerned with the international revolution:

> When we started the international revolution, we did so, not because we were convinced that we could forestall its development, but because a number of circumstances compelled us to start it. We thought: either the international revolution comes to our assistance, and in that case our victory will be fully assured, or we shall do our modest revolutionary work in the conviction that even in the event of *defeat* we shall have served the cause of the revolution and that our experience will benefit other revolutions.

This statement was consistent with the restoration thesis Lenin had presented on January 20, 1919, and it was also consistent with his subsequent argument:

> It was clear to us that without the support of the international world revolution the victory of the [Russian] proletarian revolution was *impossible*. Before the revolution, and even after it, we thought: either revolution breaks out in the other countries, in the capitalistically more developed countries, immediately or at least very quickly, or we must perish.[232]

In his July 1921 speech Lenin was acknowledging with unusual frankness that the Bolsheviks had engaged in the international revolution because "a number of circumstances" forced them to do so. This speech reveals that the circumstances that determined his policy were those he had discussed with Plekhanov in 1906/07: in particular, the need of a revolution in the major countries of the West to assure the success of the Russian revolution. In March 1921 he had declared it must be "*timely*." Now he added to his 1906/07 arguments that the Western revolution must come fast, that it must come "*immediately or at least very quickly or we must perish*." In this July statement he also admitted that the last years had brought an unexpected international development toward an "equilibrium," which deprived the

Soviet Union of the support of the Western socialist revolution—that is, of the only absolute guarantee against the restoration.

a. The raw fact. Did this international development come to a halt during the last phase of Lenin's career? It did not! In his last article, dated March 2, 1923, seven days before a third stroke incapacitated him altogether, Lenin once more expressed his hope that at some future time a revolution in the "East" would bring about a world revolution. But he asserted more strongly than in 1921 that the Socialist Western revolution was not coming. It was not coming because Germany had lost its freedom of action and the victor states ("a number of states, the oldest states of the West") had found ways of retarding the revolutionary movement by making concessions to "their oppressed classes." Lenin called these concessions "insignificant", and measured by his revolutionary standards, they certainly were. But measured by the response of the Western workers, the concessions were not at all insignificant. Lenin himself admitted that they were seriously weakening the class struggle. In fact they were producing something like a "class truce."[233]

b. The blurred response. The only absolute (external) guarantee against an Asiatic restoration that Lenin had proclaimed prior to and again after the October Revolution had failed. And the new (internal) guarantees that he had proclaimed after the October Revolution (when his original relative guarantees were failing) proved to be equally ineffective. As already stated, they included the policy of war communism, which Lenin abandoned in 1921, and several other policies he increasingly emphasized during the last years of his career: universal cooperation,[234] a cultural revolution,[235] electrification,[236] and attempts to reorganize (cleanse) the Soviet bureaucracy.

After 1921, Lenin was convinced that the Soviet regime was neither socialist nor bourgeois but bureaucratic in the sense of Russia's old Orientally despotic order. No wonder then that he spoke of the Soviet state apparatus not as something new in Russian history, but as something the Bolsheviks "took over in its entirety from the preceding epoch[237] and that their anti-bureaucratic measures had barely touched. To be sure, the Soviet apparatus was not exactly like the old one—it was "painted over on the surface." But this only "slightly." Substantially, it was still "our old state apparatus."[238]

Would the mass of the toilers, when encouraged to set up cooperatives everywhere, be able to develop genuinely self-governing organizations, if the basic means of production and the credit system[239] were in the hands of an Orientally despotic bureaucracy? Would the masters of such an apparatus carry out the tasks of the new economic policy—which stressed "cultured" (rational) trading—in a cultured manner, if they and the masses were accustomed to trading "in an Asiatic manner?"[240] Would the masters of such an apparatus, in pursuing their "cultural revolution," not only increase literacy but permit the workers and peasants to use their newly acquired skill to promote a planned economy that would be really socialistic, because it was controlled by the producers? Would the masters of such an apparatus be willing to relinquish the advantages they derived from their position, even if, contrary to all historical experience, the masters of this apparatus should be willing to abandon their power? According to Lenin's final evaluation, the Soviet Union's "new culture" was neither proletarian nor bourgeois. It was, in fact, "a cruder type of pre-bourgeois culture." It was a "bureaucratic culture," a "bondage" (*krepostnich-eskoi*) culture[241] rooted in "semi-Asiatic ignorance."[242] In this connection it is well to remember that in specifying the Asiatic, nonfeudal type of serfdom (which he distinguished from the Western feudal type), Lenin referred to the former system as "bondage."[243]

Would this type of "semi-Asiatic ignorance" (literate in form and ignorant in substance) be conducive to the unleashing of the "self-developing" energies that, according to Marx, the Orientally despotic system of power paralyzed? Would government-controlled electrification and government-controlled large-scale industry combined with government-supervised cooperatization[244] liquidate the power of a semi-Asiatic bureaucracy? Would the state apparatus, which in tsarist Russia had bureaucratically controlled the growth of capitalism, become less despotic in the wake of a widespread electrification and state-promoted cooperatization? Or would it advance further on the road to total managerial power?

In his final directives Lenin raised all these questions, while he wishfully repeated the key slogan of the victorious October Revolution, "Political power is in the hands of the working class,"[245] and while he wishfully expressed the hope that a new (state-appointed) Workers' and Peasants' Inspection would solve the problems he had been unable to solve in the preceding "five years" and which the utopians among the beneficiaries of Oriental despotism had been unable to solve in thousands of years.

In the last paragraph of Lenin's last article he expressed this hope, this "dream," as he called it.[246] His final thought, that the Soviet state apparatus would be cured of its evils if the new Inspection Committee were raised to the level of the Central Committee and if the Central Committee were amalgamated with "an ordinary People's Commissariat"[247] symbolizes Lenin's pathetic efforts to find ever-new bureaucratic devices to reverse the growth of the "Asiatic" system in whose restoration he himself had played the decisive role.

Conclusion

Is this the end of the story? Of course not! In 1894, and with reference to Marx's *Zapiski* letter, Lenin had rejected the idea of a general ("universalist") pattern of historical development. Since 1916 he had referred to world history

in formulations that suggested the universalist image of development given
by the Marx of the *Manifesto* period,[248] but not the antiuniversalist image
of development given by Marx in his writings after 1853 and particularly
in his letter of 1877. In "Our Revolution," the third-to-the-last article Lenin
wrote, on January 16, 1923, he went beyond the factual abandonment of his
own early position and stated expressly that the difference between the West
European and the Russian (Oriental) developments was "quite insignificant
from the standpoint of the general development of world history."[249] By
calling these developmental diversities insignificant, Lenin rejected his own
earlier view that these diversities were profoundly significant. By using
elements of Marx's 1877 letter and by referring to the underlying "purely
theoretical point of view" as involving "Marxist considerations," he indicated
that he was still haunted by the specter of the *Zapiski* letter, which in 1894
he had called the only scientific one. In "Our Revolution" Lenin did not
say that in 1894 he had rejected the generalist view of history as "metaphysical."

A. Max Weber's Idea of the "Central Problem" of World History

On the level of political theory and action, Lenin did not do justice to the
reality of society and history, even when he openly spoke of the danger of a
degeneration of his kind of a Russian revolution as an "Asiatic restoration. In
this case, as in the case of the developmental argument, he could have learned
from his German contemporary, the social scientist Max Weber, who, like Lenin,
was deeply concerned with the developmental problems of history and who also
in 1906 tried to determine the character of the to-be-expected next Russian
revolution. The sociohistorically sensitive reader will remember that Weber
who ascended to the height of his creativity, after a severe crisis, in 1902 and
who, in 1904, extolled the "singular" truth-finding power of Marx's developmental constructs,[250] insisted since *The Protestant Ethic and the Spirit of
Capitalism* (1904/05) on the fundamental difference between the development
of the Western and the non-Western (especially the Oriental) world. In 1913,
Weber called this issue "the central problem" of the economic and cultural
history of mankind,[251] and he repeated this thesis in 1919/20, at the very end
of his life.[252]

In his analysis of the Russian revolution, Weber did not do justice to the
developmental peculiarities of Western "high capitalism." And he certainly
did not do justice to the peculiarity of a Leninist-style Jacobin revolution as
an organizational revolution.[253] But he recognized what neither Lenin nor,
for that matter, Plekhanov did—that on the basis of the elements of "high
capitalism" introduced into Russia at the beginning of the twentieth century[254]

the ruling bureaucracy of the new Jacobin power was unlikely to be a replica of the old Orientally despotic tsarist order. Different from the old "centralist police-bureaucratic" system (which more accurately may be called "semi-managerial"), the Jacobin-socialist system would have a new economic and bureaucratic dimension, the dimension of a potentially total managerial system.[255]

B. No Reason Why We Should Heed Max Weber's and Tocqueville's (and Lenin's) Warning—Except the Will to Survive

There is, of course, no reason why Lenin, who disregarded many of Marx's ideas about world history and the peculiarities of Oriental despotism, should have paid any attention to the ideas of Max Weber, even though Weber accepted the developmental constructs of the author of *Capital*. And there is, of course, no reason, except perhaps the will to survive, why the opinion-makers and policy-makers of the open societies of today should pay any attention to Marx's Asiatic interpretation of old Russia, to Lenin's specter of an "Asiatic" restoration of that order, or to what Weber called "the central problem" of world history.

The power system that emerged from this development has given a new quality of relations between the East and the West. This quality involves new institutional features, to which the study of Oriental despotism provides not the entire explanation, but the only experience-rooted partial explanation we have. And it involves a new type of organizational and operational power that makes ample allowance for all sorts of intermediate arrangements (peaceful coexistence, detente, and even temporary alliances), but which pursues a policy of expansion all of its own. It can draw on the support of fifth columnists, which, as Machiavelli noted for the East-and-West relations of his time, multi-centered societies can not do. This power can avail itself of diplomatic ruses which, as Marx grimly noted concerning the East-West relations of his time, pokes fun at the "foolish credulity" of a Palmerston or a Metternich.[256] And it feels entitled, indeed it is obliged, to unleash directly or by proxy wars and warlike forces of total destruction, which include holocausts: ethnic holocausts (that may devour millions of people), continential holocausts (that may devour tens of millions of people) and if need be a global holocaust.

The world of democracy, as Tocqueville envisaged it, is possibly in great danger—the danger Tocqueville predicted—if we continue to take an impressionistic approach to international relations. The world of democracy is certainly in great danger if we refuse to heed the lessons that can be learned from our friends—and our enemies.

Notes

1. Max Weber, *Gesammelte Aufsaetze zur Wissenschaftslehre* (Tuebingen: 1922), p. 167. Hereafter cited as Weber 1922.
2. Ibid., p. 249.
3. Ibid., p. 205.
4. See Robert K. Merton, "Insider and Outsider: A Chapter in the Sociology of Knowledge," *American Journal of Sociology* 72 (July 1972): 9 passim.
5. Karl A. Wittfogel, *Oriental Despotism. A Comparative Study of Total Power* (New Haven: 1957), pp. 138. Hereafter cited as OD.
6. Ibid., pp. 150.
7. See below.
8. Aristotle *Politics,* 1279 a and b; 1295 a; 1316 a.
9. Ibid., 1285 a and b; 1327 b.
10. Ibid., 1314 a.
11. Ibid., 1313 a and b.
12. Ibid., 1285 a.
13. Ernest Barker, *From Alexander to Constantine* (Oxford: 1959), pp. 304 ff., 359; idem., *Social and Political Thought in Byzantium,* (Oxford: 1961), pp. 139.
14. Richard Walzer, *Greek into Arabic* (Cambridge, Mass.: 1962), p. 243.
15. *S. Thomas Aquinatis In Libros Politicorum Aristotelis Expositio* (Rome: 1951), pp. 168, 361 f., 168.
16. Dino Bigongiari, *The Political Ideas of St. Thomas Aquinas* (New York: 1963), pp. xxix.
17. Niccolo Machiavelli, *The Prince and the Discourses* (New York: 1940), pp. 15.
18. Ibid., p. 16.
19. Ibid., p. 183. See *Opere di N. Machiavelli* (Italy: 1913), vol. 3, p. 87.
20. Ibid.
21. Jean Bodin, *The Six Bookes of a Commonweale* (Cambridge: 1962), fascimile reproduction of Richard Knolles's English translation (London: 1606), p. 199. Hereafter cited as Bodin 1606.
22. Ibid., pp. 200.
23. Ibid.
24. Ibid., p. 204.
25. Ibid., p. 201.
26. Ibid., pp. 200 and 205.
27. Ibid., p. 204.
28. Ibid., pp. 84 and 91.
29. Ibid., pp. 204.
30. Ibid., p. 201.
31. Ibid., p. 204.

32. Ibid., pp. 210.

33. Ibid., p. 204.

34. Karl Marx—Friedrich Engels, *Werke* (1957-1966), vol. 19, pp. 111. Here-after cited as MEW.

35. Bodin 1606, pp. 197-204 and 210.

36. Thomas Hobbes, *Leviathan* (London: 1943), p. 113.

37. Ibid., pp. 101, 107, 118.

38. John Locke, *Of Civil Government* (London: 1924), pp. 158, 180, 188.

39. Ibid., p. 161.

40. Ibid.

41. Carl L. Becker, *The Declaration of Independence* (New York: 1924), pp. 27.

42. Charles Callan Tansil, *The Making of the American Republic: The Great Documents, 1774-1789* (New Rochelle, N.Y.: n.d.), pp. 22. In these two key formulations the word "absolute" is the common denominator. In the Declaration of Independence the word "despotism" occurs once, "tyranny" and "tyrant(s)" four times. In the Preamble and Resolution of the Virginia Convention, May 15, 1776, the Virginians directed their rebellious manifesto against the "overbearing tyrants" of the British Crown (ibid., p. 19).

43. *The Federalist* (London: Everyman's Library, n.d.) no. 11, p. 54. This paper, written by "Publius" (Madison), is undated; it probably originated in November 1787.

44. Ibid., pp. 38 and 245.

45. Ibid.

46. See the letter Jefferson wrote to Thomas Mann Randolph on 20 May 1970, long after the publication of Helvetius's posthumous last work, *De l'Homme*. In this letter the great Virginian called "Locke's little book on Government . . . perfect as far as it goes." His evaluation of Montesquieu was far more reserved. With reference to a recently published letter of Helvetius, which "gives us a solution for the mixture of truth and error found in this book," he wrote that *The Spirit of the Laws* contained "a great number of heresies." He identified himself with the young Helvetius's dubious compliment of praising the author of *The Spirit of the Laws* for his "ingenuity" in "reconciling the contradictory facts it presents." Montesquieu's "contradictory" presentation pointed to basic problems of an equalitarian democracy that Helvetius did not recognize. Helvetius's last work blurred the very facts on which Montesquieu had based his apocalyptic warnings. Jefferson was obviously not bothered by the perversions of the despotism argument that Helvetius committed in *De l'Homme*. (See my forthcoming book, *Anarchism, Marxism and the Nihilist Revolution*.)

47. Montesquieu, *Oeuvres Complétes* (Paris, 1958), Vol. I, pp. 281 and 327. Hereafter cited as O.C.

48. Montesquieu, *O.C.*, II, p. 119.

49. Ibid., p. 250. passim.

50. Franco Venturi, "Despotism Orientale," in *Revista Storia Italiana* 72, no. 1 (1960): 118. According to recent studies that Prof. Venturi surveyed, the term "Oriental despotism" was probably first used by Pierre Bayle in 1704.

51. Montesquieu OC 2, p. 238. As far as possible I have followed the translation by Thomas Nugent (New York: 1949). Professor Franz Neumann declared that " a new translation is necessary, but it is not desirable before a critical edition of the *Esprit des Lois* had been made" (ibid., p. vii).

52. Ibid., p. 239.

53. Ibid., pp. 247.

54. Ibid. For an earlier version of the idea of "moderated monarchies and well-framed governments," see Locke 1924, p. 199.

55. Montesquieu OC 2, p. 409.

56. Ibid., p. 271.

57. Ibid.

58. Ibid., p. 426.

59. Ibid., p. 428. *Bashaw* is an early Western transcription of the Turkish word *pasha*.

60. Ibid., pp. 247.

61. Ibid., p. 311.

62. Ibid., pp. 490.

63. Ibid., p. 258.

64. Ibid., p. 260.

65. Ibid., p. 265.

66. Ibid., pp. 567.

67. See Wittfogel, "Ideas and the Power Structure," in *Approaches to Asian Civilizations*, ed. by Wm. Theodore de Bary and Ainslee T. Embree (New York and London: 1964), pp. 89.

68. Montesquieu OC 2, pp. 265. Nugent's: translation of *nulle* as "needless' hardly does justice to the harshness of Montesquieu's dictum.

69. Montesquieu OC 2, pp. 357.

70. Ibid., p. 479.

71. Ibid., p. 565.

72. Ibid., p. 535.

73. Ibid.

74. Ibid.

75. Ibid., p. 371.

76. Ibid., p. 535.

77. Ibid.

78. Ibid., p. 368.

79. Ibid.

80. Ibid., pp. 409.

81. Ibid., pp. 457.

82. Ibid., p. 565.

83. Ibid.

84. Ibid., p. 528.

85. Ibid., pp. 527.

86. Ibid., p. 671.

87. Ibid.

88. Ibid., p. 294.

89. Ibid., p. 671.

90. *The Federalist*, no. 47, pp. 246. Cf. Montesquieu OC 2. p. 397.

91. *The Federalist*, no. 47, p. 247.

92. Montesquieu, OC 2, pp. 397.

93. Ibid., p. 247.

94. Ibid., p. 397.

95. Ibid., p. 395.

96. Ibid., p. 247.

97. Ibid., p. 248.

98. See Wittfogel OD, pp. 78, 103, and 417.

99. Alexis de Tocqueville, *Democracy in America*, ed. J.P. Mayer and Max Lerner (New York: 1966), p. 211. Hereafter cited as Tocqueville 1966.

100. Ibid., p. 212.

101. Ibid., p. 211.

102. Gabriel A. Almond, *The American People and Foreign Policy* (New York: 1960), p. 51; See also pp. 73, 76 and 80. For incisive remarks on the traditional American dislike of systematic and persistent studies in this field, see Daniel J. Boorstein, *The Americans. The Colonial Experience* (New York: 1958), pp. 155., 209, 235, 243.

103. Almond, pp. 30 and 42.

104. Tocqueville 1966, p. 773.

105. Ibid., pp. 82, 285, 411, 423, 635, 775.

106. For this concept, see Wittfogel, "The Chinese and Russian Revolutions: A Socio-historical Comparison," *The Year Book of World Affairs* (London: 1961), vol. 15, p. 42.

107. Tocqueville 1966, p. 289.

108. Ibid.

109. Ibid.

110. Ibid.

111. Ibid., pp. 378.

112. Ibid., p. xxi.

113. Ibid., p. 88.

114. Ibid., p. 289.

115. See MEW 27, pp. 32, 47, 58, 67, 71, 75, 79. In view of the numerous efforts Marx and Engels made to get their voluminous opus published, it

is slightly amusing to read the statement Marx made in 1859 that they had written this manuscript—"two large octavo volumes"—mainly for "self-clarification," and that, having failed to get it printed in Westphalia, they "readily abandoned it to the gnawing criticism of the mice" (MEW 13, p. 10).

116. MEW 27, p. 170.
117. Ibid., p. 375.
118. MEW 28, p. 222.
119. For a statement on the different dimensions of a conceptual approach see Wittfogel OD (1963 ed.) pp. iii.
120. MEW 8, p. 582.
121. MEW 4, p. 581.
122. MEW 4, p. 363.
123. MEW 27, p. 107.
124. Ibid.
125. Karl Marx, Friedrich Engels, *Historisch-Kritische Gesamtausgabe,* section I, 6 (Berlin: 1932), pp. 582. Hereafter cited as MEGA.
126. MEW 28, p. 40.
127. MEW 9, pp. 22 and 35.
128. MEW 28, pp. 252 and 259. (Dated "June 6, evening".)
129. Cf. G.L. Ulmen, *The Science of Society: Toward an Understanding of the Life and Work of Karl August Wittfogel,* chapter 17 (to appear in 1975).
130. See Ernest Mandel, *The Formation of the Economic Thought of Karl Marx* (New York and London: 1971), p. 118 passim.
131. MEW 28, pp. 209, 223, 225, 249, and 251.
132. Ibid., p. 275.
133. NYDT, June 25, 1853, Cf. *Karl Marx and Friedrich Engels. Selected Works* (Moscow: 1951) 1, p. 314. Hereafter cited as MESW.
134. MEW 28, p. 259.
135. Richard Jones, *An Essay on the Distribution of Wealth and on the Source of Taxation* (London: 1831), pp. 119 f. This is how Jones described the desert zone (which interested him especially with regard to Persia), whose soil, he asserted, "can be made fruitful only by irrigation":

> One of the most remarkable geological features of the old World is that great tract of sandy desert which extends across its whole breadth, and imposes a peculiar character on the tribes which roam over its surface, or inhibit its borders. It forms the shores of the Atlantic on the western coast of Africa, and constitutes the Zahara or great sandy desert, which has contributed to conceal so long the central regions of that quarter of the globe from European curiosity. It forms next the surface of Egypt with the exception of the valley of the Nile; stretches across the Arabian wastes to Syria,

> Persia, and upper India; and turning from Persia northwards, threads between Mushed and Herat, the Elburz and Parapomisan mountains, parts of the Caucasian or Himalayan chain; runs north-eastward through Tartary, and rounding the northern extremity of China, sinks finally, it is supposed, beneath the waves of the Pacific.

136. MESW 1, p. 314.
137. Ibid., p. 321.
138. Ibid., p. 314.
139. Ibid., 315.
140. Ibid.
141. Ibid., pp. 316.
142. Ibid., p. 317.
143. Ibid.
144. MEW 28, p. 267.
145. MESW 1, p. 315.
146. For pertinent references, see Wittfogel, "Geopolitik, Geographischer Materialismus und Marxismus," in *Unter dem Banner des Marxismus,* vol. 3 (1929), fasc. 4, pp. 495.
147. MEGA I, 1, 2, p. 248.
148. A footnote in *German Ideology,* written by Marx and attached to a sentence stressing man's natural needs, reads: *"Hegel.* Geological, hydrographical etc. conditions. The human bodies. Need, labor" (MEW 3, p. 28). The note underlines an idea expressed earlier in the text regarding "man's physical constitution and natural conditions in which man finds himself, the geological, orohydrographical, climatic and others" (ibid., p. 21). Hegel did indeed consider mountains and water part of man's natural setting; but to my knowledge he did not use the terms "orography" and "hydrography," whereas Ritter did (see Karl Ritter, *Die Erdkunde im Verhältniss zur Natur und zur Geschichte des Menschen, oder allgemeine vergleichende Geographie* (Berlin: 1817), part I pp. 65.
149. MEW 25, p. 346.
150. MEW 7, p. 222.
151. NYDT August 5, 1853; MEW 9, p. 216.
152. Ibid.
153. MEW 28, pp. 207, 211, 220, 244. Herzen discussed the commune in the epilogue to his *Du Développment des Idées Révolutionaires en Russie,* par A. Iscander [pseudonym for Alexander Herzen] (Paris: 1851), pp. 162.
154. MEW 9, pp. 396 and 407. See also above.
155. MEW 28, p. 195.
156. Weber 1922, p. 204.
157. Ibid., pp. 165, 240, 299.
158. Ibid., p. 167.

159. MEW 3, pp. 21 and 65 f; 4, p. 119. See also Marx's letter to Engels of July 7, 1866, in which he referred to the history of warfare as "splendidly" confirming "our theory of the determination of the organization of labor through the means of production" (MEW 31, p. 234).

160. For the thesis that the hydraulic revolution was essentially (certain technical elements notwithstanding) an organizational revolution, see Wittfogel, "Developmental Aspects of Hydraulic Societies," in *Irrigation Civilizations: A Comparative Study* (Washington, D.C.: 1955), pp. 43; idem, "Chinese Society: A Historical Survey," *The Journal of Asian Studies* 1957, pp. 345; and OD, pp. 49 passim.

161. MEW 3, p. 54; 4, p. 152.

162. MEW 23, p. 341.

163. MEW 4, p. 481.

164. Ibid.

165. Ibid.

166. Ibid., p. 573.

167. V.I. Lenin, *Collected Works* (Moscow: 1963-   ), 25, p. 402. Hereafter cited as Lenin CW.

168. MESW 1, pp. 320.

169. MEW 17, pp. 342.

170. For the development of this argument, see Wittfogel OD, pp. 328.

171. MEW, Supplement 1, pp. 534.

172. See Marianne Weber, *Max Weber, Ein Lebensbild* (Tuebingen: 1926), p. 284. Hereafter cited as Weber 1926; and Max Weber, "Zur Lage der buergerlichen Demokratie in Russland," *Archiv fuer Sozialwissenschaft und Sozialpolitik* 22 (1906): 346.

173. See MEW 16, pp. 10; 23, p. 312.

174. MEW 19, p. 108.

175. MEW 9, pp. 396, 407; 10, pp. 164, 470, 592; 11, p. 197; 12, pp. 128, 670, 682, passim.

176. Marx, "Revelations of the Diplomatic History of the Eighteenth Century," in *The Free Press* (1857), pp. 203, 218, 226, 265.

177. MEW 18, p. 563.

178. MEW 20, p. 168. For the dates of the publication of this part of the *Anti-Düring,* see p. 624.

179. MEW 19, p. 108.

180. Ibid., pp. 111.

181. Ibid., p. 112.

182. Lenin CW 1, pp. 143.

183. G. Plekhanov, Selected Philosophical Works (Moscow: n.d.), 1, p. 759. Hereafter cited as Plekhanov SPW.

184. MEW 36, p. 121.

185. A. Voden, "Talks with Engels," in *Reminiscences of Marx and Engels* (Moscow: n.d.), p. 329.

186. MEW 22, p. 430.
187. See Wittfogel, "Social Revolution in China," in *A World in Revolution?* The Australian National University Lectures 1970, ed. by Eugene Kamenka (Canberra: 1970), pp. 39 *passim.*
188. See Wittfogel, "The Marxist View of China" in *China Quarterly,* no. 11 (1962): 10. Hereafter cited as Wittfogel 1962.
189. Lenin CW, 16, p. 269.
190. Plekhanov SPW, p. 114.
191. Lenin CW, 1, p. 193.
192. Plekhanov SPW 1, p. 347. For the original text, to which I returned when the meaning was in doubt, see the Russian edition of this volume (Moscow: 1956), p. 347.
193. Lenin CW 8, p. 289. See also CW 4, p. 488; CW 8, pp. 168, 170, 289n.
194. For documentary evidence for this and the subsequent statements of Trotsky and Lenin, see Wittfogel, "The Marxist View of Russian Society and Revolution" in *World Politics* 12, no. 4 (1960): 501; see also Wittfogel OD, pp. 403.
195. Lenin CW 9, p. 48.
196. For documentary evidence on subsequent section, in addition to the two above-cited publications, see Wittfogel, "The Peasants," in *Handbook of Communism,* ed. Joseph M. Bochenski and Gerhart Niemeyer (New York: 1962), p. 354. Hereafter cited as HC.
197. Wittfogel OD., p. 393.
198. Lenin CW 13, p. 329.
199. Lenin CW 25, pp. 419, 434, 451.
200. See Wittfogel OD, pp. 394-400.
201. Lenin CW 10, p. 177.
202. See MEW 23, p. 533; 25, p. 807. See Wittfogel, "Communist and Non-Communist Agrarian System, with Special Reference to the U.S.S.R. and Communist China," in *Agrarian Policies and Problems in Communist and Non-Communist Countries,* ed. W.A. Douglas Jackson (Seattle and London: 1971), p. 31. Hereafter cited as 1971.
203. Lenin CW 3, pp. 176 and 503.
204. CW 9, p. 48.
205. CW 22, pp. 255 and 258.
206. According to the old Russian calendar this event occurred on October 25. According to the Western calendar, which the Soviet regime adopted early in 1918, it occurred on November 7, 1917.
207. Lenin 26, p. 272.
208. Merle Fainsod, *How Russia is Ruled* (Cambridge: 1955), p. 358.
209. Ibid., pp. 391 and 395.
210. Lenin CW 28, p. 249.
211. Ibid., pp. 423.
212. Ibid.

213. For Lenin the French Revolution ended in 1794 (CW 32, pp. 326). Since he spoke of this revolution as having lasted roughly one year, he evidently contemplated the rule of the Jacobins as the French Revolution in the narrower sense of the term.

214. Lenin CW 28, p. 414.

215. Ibid., p. 420.

216. Ibid., p. 428.

217. Ibid.

218. Lenin CW 32, p. 282.

219. See Franz Borkenau, *World Communism* (Ann Arbor: 1962), p. 114, 118, and 213.

220. Lenin CW 32, p. 152.

221. Ibid., p. 473.

222. Ibid., p. 477.

223. Ibid., p. 215.

224. Ibid., pp. 214 and 233.

225. Lenin CW 20, p. 403.

226. Ibid., 19, pp. 552 and 587.

227. See above.

228. Lenin CW 32, p. 351. Italics added. In the original the word "exchange" is italicized.

229. Ibid., p. 350. As in OD, p. 399, I have corrected the official translation, which obfuscates Lenin's crass formulation behind queer sounding words. For the Russian original, see Lenin *Sochinenia* 32, p. 329.

230. Lenin CW 32, p. 215. CF. Paul Avrich, *Kronstadt* (Princeton: 1970), pp. 196.

231. Lenin CW 32, pp. 478.

232. Ibid., p. 479. Italics added.

233. Lenin CW 33, pp. 498.

234. Lenin CW 32, pp. 347; 33, pp. 467.

235. Lenin CW 33, pp. 473 and 488.

236. Lenin CW 32, pp. 323, 459; and 33, pp. 501.

237. Lenin CW 33, p. 474.

238. Ibid., p. 481.

239. Ibid., pp. 427.

240. Ibid., p. 470.

241. Ibid., p. 487.

242. Ibid., p. 463.

243. Wittfogel OD, p. 394.

244. Lenin CW 33, p. 501.

245. Ibid., p. 474.

246. Ibid., p. 502.

247. Ibid.

248. See Wittfogel OD, pp. 495.
249. Lenin CW 33, p. 477.
250. Weber 1922, p. 205.
251. Max Weber, *Gesammelte Aufsaetze zur Religionssoziologie,* (Tuebingen: 1920), pp. 341 and 348.
252. Ibid. p. 10. For the date, see Weber 1926, p. 687.
253. For the basic form of this concept, see above.
254. Weber 1906, pp. 347.
255. For this concept, see Wittfogel OD, p. 440.
256. MEW 9, p. 396.

Part II

Diplomacy and Strategy

2

The USSR in World Affairs: New Tactics, New Strategy

Joseph Schiebel

Attempts to understand and explain Soviet foreign policy in the early 1970s seem most often to be based on a search for new patterns, goals, and methods. Much commentary assumes that the Soviet leadership is acting under a new realism, a new perception of international relations and the place of the Soviet Union in them, that compels a policy of accommodation, a preservation of the status quo, and a preoccupation with defense, both of the Soviet Union and of the existing international power relationships. A sizable body of opinion holds that the Soviet Union, on the brink of strategic obsolescence because of the risk of losing the momentum of production and technological development, needs, and therefore seeks, a permanent alignment with those domestic and foreign forces that represent the tide of the technological future, and is compelled to pursue a policy of subordinating its traditional political and strategic goals to survival as a going economic production concern.

To be sure, a good deal of this analysis reflects the rhetoric of the political leaderships, East and West, and as such is not necessarily meant to be an accurate reflection of reality, but it has been taken up by serious analysts, amateur as well as professional.

Many of these conclusions regarding innovations and new directions in Soviet strategy assume major changes in objective national and international conditions. Quite apart from the question of whether such change has occurred on a large scale or not, there is no connection between political conditions and strategies designed to deal with them so total or necessary that it alone could sustain the argument.

Beyond that, the various arguments regarding fundamental changes in the strategic power balance or the state of the technological capacity of the Soviet Union seem far from firm. It could be shown without too much difficulty that the maintenance of the international status quo and the reorientation of the power economy to a subsistence (or consumption) economy would have been advantageous for the Soviet Union on many previous occasions in her history or were open as reasonable strategic choices for her leadership. The Soviet economy surely has experienced previous crises of production and backwardness every bit as serious as the current dilemma. Yet, in the past, these circumstances did not in themselves compel the kind of reorientation that they are said to do now.

This chapter examines the possibility that, rather than introducing fundamentally new strategies and tactics, the Soviet Union may be serving up new

71

tactical wine in old strategic bottles for the 1970s, that Soviet international behavior may be simply tactical adjustments to changing problems and opportunities, and designed to serve larger strategic goals and methods not essentially different from those of the past.

The argument has been made that the dramatic changes in strategic perception and foreign policy orientation required to give meaning and substance to detente cannot be made by a Soviet leadership that maintains its power under generally unchanged internal institutional and political conditions. No national leadership can substantially transcend its national ideological, conceptual, political, or institutional base in the conduct of foreign policy, and it seems a reasonable hypothesis that profound changes in the restraints and options inherent in the Soviet political and institutional structure need to occur before its leadership can safely abandon the pursuit of goals and values in international relations that legitimize and rationalize its rule at home. This is not meant to suggest that the survival of the Soviet Union itself is at stake here, only the survival of the present leadership group. There is no doubt that Russia could function adequately in international relations under different kinds of leadership, but there is also little doubt that those now in power are not going to volunteer to step aside to test the proposition.

To make the general hypothesis somewhat more specific, the possibility will be examined that the Soviet leadership is now neither so stability-oriented nor in such great economic trouble that it can be expected to become an unqualified defender of the international status quo or a supporter of the new "structure for peace" aspired to by the grand design of the recent American administration.

Certainly, official Soviet rhetoric maintains that the "revolution" is still on, in the sense that "progressive" developments are expected to continue in the advanced countries as well as in the so-called third world and that these developments will be supported. This "revolution," Soviet leaders do not tire of protesting, is not a sideshow, a set of marginal occurrences they can largely ignore (though it is implied that the West will ignore them and thus permit itself to be victimized by them). And the industrial developmental and production priorities of the Soviet Union suggest that the quest for the military means for an active, dynamic, and ambitious Soviet policy of projecting its power abroad is still a serious undertaking, a preoccupation that in turn suggests that the pursuit of strategic advantage against the West has not been set aside. The thesis that the technological crisis compels a Soviet strategic reorientation and political accommodation with the existing international order prompts this observation: as a general rule, systems of total power have placed security ahead of efficiency. The key operational criterion for success for the Soviet leadership appears to be its political control, rather than the material prosperity of its people or the sophistication of its industrial plant. The Soviet economy, at any rate, is operated as a power, rather than a subsistence, economy; its capacity to produce sufficient means for the exercise of political control at home and the projection of power abroad is the measure of its success insofar as the Soviet leadership is concerned.

It is, of course, entirely possible that in the foreseeable future no nation without an enormous and secure fertilizer-energy-technology base will be in a position to play big-power politics. But it is by no means clear that the Soviet leadership accepts this projection or, if it accepts it, plans to convert its command economy, political despotism, and power-oriented foreign policy into a highly modern, necessarily politically open, nitrogen-oil-industrial complex. The weight of Russian tradition would counsel reliance on continued centralized and confiscatory operation of a relatively backward production plant for a sufficiency of power, supplemented by selective inputs and subsidies from the outside. A survey of the military inventory may also suggest that reliance on the ultimate equalizer, the capacity to threaten to bomb the West back into the Stone Age, may provide a margin of time and relieve the urgency of the problem of backwardness.

Again, there is no absolutely necessary relationship between the production and technology crisis in the USSR and the concomitant need to transfer some of both from the West, and the reorientation of Soviet strategic goals from the pursuit of advantage to the maintenance of the status quo. The transfers obtained in exchange for a rhetoric of detente and some diplomatic summitry and conference games may in fact favor the retention of old goals rather than compel the promulgation of new ones. Presumably, conditions can be attached to the transfer of technology and the exchange of products to encourage new perceptions; and other steps can be taken to discourage or frustrate undesirable Soviet international behavior, but the hoped for results appear elusive at best. The principal concern here, at any rate, is not whether the Soviet Union will be successful in her international venture, but what her principal strategic designs may be.

The Nature of Strategic Designs

What are the major Soviet strategic goals and methods? By that I mean the fundamental expectations all national leaderships always have of their foreign policies, and the absolutely irreducible theoretical and conceptual foundations that give meaning and direction to any foreign policy. While it is scarcely startling that all national foreign policies pursue goals and that this pursuit proceeds from a theoretical base, the identification of each is problematic. Exhaustion of all the intricacies of the relationship between strategy and tactics, primary and instrumental goals, overt and hidden meaning, the short, intermediate, or long range, and reality and illusion is not intended here; the inquiry must be confined to optimal goals and the conceptual bedrock.

Two qualities characterize macrostrategic designs: they are seldom explicitly stated, presumably because their open promulgation would preclude the deception or uncertainty necessary to achieve them; and they must be relatively stable over a substantial period of time to be reliable guides for the inevitably extended period required for their pursuit. This makes them at one and the same time elusive to determine and extremely useful analytical tools once they are accurately identified.

To get beyond two of the most prominent defects evident in existing approaches to Soviet foreign policy—that of mere reliance on official theoretical and practical statements, and that of assuming that to observe activity is to understand its goals, or that tactics is strategy—the following broad approach is suggested. First, established operational patterns of strategy can be seen. Second, historical analogies will permit a separation of that which changes from that which remains the same. Finally, behavior must be analyzed to see with what larger purposes it is consistent.

In briefest outline, Soviet strategic goals have seemed to be: first, the defense of the Soviet Union and, within it, the unlimited power of the ruling elite; second, the acquisition, maintenance, and increase of international political status for the Soviet Union and her dependencies; third, and this is, I concede, a controversial point, the development of the political, economic, and military power of the Soviet Union to yield a preponderance of strength in the international strategic balance; fourth, and this is still a problem of projecting into the future, the exercise of this power to force a change in the processes and relationships of the international political system, and to effect a transformation of as many of the world's social systems as can be forced, encouraged, or helped to conform to the Soviet model of social and political organization.

The strategic methods to be employed in this effort—stated nowhere with greater clarity than by Lenin in his speech to the Moscow cadres in September 1920—appear to be these: As a basic ontological premise, Soviet strategy notes that, for the first period of its national existence, the power commanded by the Soviet Union is weak relative to that of the remainder of the world. This precludes any all-out territorial or political frontal advances, and it dictates that, for this period, the USSR must operate within the existing balance and rules of the international order. Together with the proposition that socialism as propounded by Moscow has an exclusive claim on the future organization of mankind, this implies that the period when the balance of power favors the non-Communist world is intended to be limited and that the primary objective of Soviet policy must be to reverse this balance to one of Soviet superiority.

Since the means of a "policy of strength," or gains achieved through the application of superior force, were, for the time being, absent, an alternative method of cooperation with other forces was determined to be most appropriate. The technical terms for the most important of these indirect means to gain increased power and influence are the exploitation of latent contradictions within the non-Soviet world, concessions, popular and united fronts, diplomatic alliances, and revolutionary alliances. Operationally, this means the creation of variants of dual power situations or the exploitation where they exist independently, of sets of adversary relationships outside the Soviet Union, which permit

the Soviet Union to achieve, in alliance with one party against the other, goals
she would either be unable to achieve with her own means, or which would be
resisted by the intended victims. In this way, too, whatever goals are pursued or
attained are legitimized by the association with an established cause or party.
The guiding model for this approach is no doubt the experience of 1917 in
Russia, with the Bolsheviks' emphasis in power diplomacy; more immediate
ideological goals are neither singularly important nor wholly meaningless. On the
one hand, strategic power is necessary to make possible any seizure of control,
a logical precondition for social revolution. On the other hand, proletarian or
other revolutionary movements, that is, agglomerations of people for whom
ideological aspirations have meaning, are necessary and useful instruments
through which the Soviet leadership exerts political influence in other countries.
Ultimately, of course, no one, except perhaps some Western "pragmatists,"
attempts to wield political power without a hard core of fairly stable and necessarily abstract ideas about the nature of man, state, and society and about his
own aspirations—in other words, an ideology.

Ultimately, also, the ideological and revolutionary base of the Soviet Union
provide the indispensable cohesive force through which a multitude of often
highly disparate elements can identify with what, from the perspective of the
Soviet leadership, is a common political enterprise. And organizational poly-
centrism has made the need for a common world outlook even more urgent.

The complementary relationship of official Soviet foreign policy and the
revolutionarly aspirations of the Communist movement, another operational
dualism, should become more clear when it is considered that Soviet ideology
does not claim to represent only the interests of the international working
class in the industrial nations, but that of all oppressed classes and strata everywhere. This point becomes especially relevant when examining Soviet Asian
strategy.

In the theory and practice of Soviet foreign policy, the most basic of
these adversary relationships have been, and in a sense continue to be, the
following:

Europe offered both the most direct potential challenge to Soviet rule and
the most inviting target for penetration. By the skillful manipulation and
exploitation of political tensions among the European states, Soviet diplomacy
was able to prevent the activation of a united anti-Soviet front and could intensify and influence the destabilizing and disintegrative factors that culminated
in World War II, which, among other things, was an indispensable condition for
the dramatic expansion of Soviet power into Central Europe.

Germany was and is the pivot for Soviet support and use of strategic dualism
in Europe. Real and potential adversary relationships between Germany and
the rest of Europe provide the principal Soviet vehicle for substantial participation in European political affairs, which, in turn, makes Soviet policy highly
influential and explains some of its past successes. The Soviet Asian strategy

reveals the manipulation of both international power relations and of indigenous mass revolutionary movements, and a strategy of seeking a dominant power position for the Soviet Union as well as the seizure of power for the establishment of a Communist state in Asia.

Until mid-1920, the seizure of power somewhere in Western Europe appeared possible to Lenin, and appropriate efforts were made. The collapse of those hopes led to an "agonizing reappraisal," of which Lenin's major foreign policy statements of the time were a part, and by 1923 a major shift was made to an intensification of the struggle for Asia. The pivot of that strategy was, and is, China. The two principal goals were the establishment of, or identification with, a Chinese national movement as a vehicle for gaining control of China, and the subsequent use of China for strategic access to the rest of Asia and the projection of Soviet power there. The two principal methods were, on the one hand, support and manipulation of an internal Chinese political dual-power situation, permitting the Soviet Union the use of one of the power centers to gain control as well as legitimacy for its involvement. On the other hand, support for an intensification of adversary relationships between China and her principal Asian strategic competitor, Japan, was used to bring Soviet power to China in alliance with the major Western powers interested in securing that country against Japanese takeover and thus, again, to legitimize Soviet great power aspirations in Asia within the international system. Where tactical stress was laid in Europe on appeals to the proleteriat and intellectuals, in Asia indigenous support was sought among the radical intelligentsia as well as broad elements aspiring to national independence—or "liberation," in Communist jargon—and among the peasantry, whose response to fraudulent promises of land redistribution, as in Russia, provided mass support.

The third major pivot of Soviet strategy is, and has been, the United States, which has played the dual role of principal ally as well as chief enemy (*glavnii vrag*). This means that, in Soviet strategic perspective, a decisive preponderance of influence in the world cannot be exercised until the United States is reduced to secondary strategic status, and therefore, any Soviet gains, against third parties, no matter how strongly the United States contributed to their achievement, are designed to redound ultimately to the disadvantage of the chief enemy. For the Soviet strategist it means also that, since United States power has been, in the twentieth century, the decisive factor in the international balance, no significant gains can be made except in alliance with, or with the concurrence of, the United States. Hence, the so-called "temporary" alliances with the Western powers, termed "democracies" during such periods of alliances, and hence the propensity of the Soviet Union, so upsetting to officialdom and opinion-leaders in the United States, to seek to convert gains made against third parties with American assistance, as in Eastern Europe and Asia after World War II, into power plays against the "former" ally.

This aspect of the Soviet-American strategic relationship contains, however, an additional complication for Soviet strategists. While the ultimate purpose of temporary alliances with the strong United States against weak enemies is to deprive the latter of territory and power which, in the long run will then also be denied to the United States, the short-run result is often that Soviet gains made as the result of a Soviet-American cooperation also produce gains for the United States. The joint destruction of Japanese power in Asia not only made the Soviet Union a major Asian power, but also permitted the extension of the American empire into Asia; and the liquidation of the British empire opened the former colonies up not only to Soviet penetration, but to American commercial and strategic hegemony as well. The result of Soviet-American strategic cooperation, essential as it was for the attainment of the kind of strategic position the Soviet Union needed to operate as a great power in the post-World War II period, was also the consolidation of the American sphere of influence and the strategic stalemate that, I am about to argue, the Soviet Union now seems prepared to break up.

None of the foregoing, made more explicit below, is meant to imply that Soviet strategy represents a dramatic innovation in human affairs or that its mysteries are doomed to elude us. Indeed, it appears strange that a generation of scholars so preoccupied with imperialism be so reluctant to approach the Soviet Union with this analytical yardstick. The strategy of feeding on the contradictions among other countries in order to conquer or control them separately is encountered in history with such frequency that its very iteration is a cliché, and the principle of allying with the strong against the weak is a well-established Muscovite practice. What the Marxist-Leninist system-builders have done is elaborate a quite systematic and rigid analytical method out of working principles suggested by common sense. While their system may well be the most terrible simplification, their concepts, however remote their relation to objective reality, have proven a remarkably effective guide to action wherever they were not challenged either by superior insights or by an adequate perception of Soviet designs. For practical purposes, objective reality is what it is perceived to be, and, to paraphrase a hoary truism, those who have no conception of reality of their own are doomed to order their actions according to that of someone else's. Even when there has been an adequate conceptual basis for dealing with the Soviet Union, it was replaced or abandoned before it could serve its purpose, and perhaps that is in the nature of not only political, but academic pluralism in the West, where an understanding of politics is too often sought through the same democratic procedures through which we regulate our politics, rather than in the great Western intellectual tradition of the study of man, state, and society from Aristotle to Weber and beyond.

The picture of the Soviet leadership that emerges from a dispassionate and unempathetic analysis of Soviet foreign policy is often objected to as regarding them as single-mindedly power-oriented, ethically coldblooded,

and highly intelligent. Bowing to the objection, one would have them to conclude them to be sentimental and stupid. Their visions, actions, and successes
seem to me clearly inconsistent either with sentimentality or with lack of intelligence. The twentieth century provided an extremely tough arena for world
power politics, and to seize power in a minority coup d'etat, butcher about one-
tenth of its own population, wage the most devasting war in history, and become
the strongest power complex in the world would have been patently impossible
if the struggled had been limited by human sensitivity, analytical flabbiness,
and average intelligence.

What follows here is history. The purpose of recalling it is to identify major
Soviet strategic patterns and goals from the 1920s to the 1960s and to analyze
against this background the principal discernible features of Soviet strategy in
the emerging 1970s. This will permit a judgment of whether recent strategic
designs represent significant departures from established patterns or whether
they conform to them, and will suggest a meaning for Soviet international
activities, which are otherwise obscure.

Germany, Europe, and the World, 1927-45

The latent conflict between the victorious Entente powers and their
strategic and economic designs for dominating defeated, "semicolonial" Germany and the natural revanchist interests of that nation were identified by
Lenin as providing the basis for a policy both for preventing a general European
anti-Communist alliance and for projecting Soviet power into Europe. Stalin
echoed that notion by referring to Germany as the "mine under Europe," the
detonation of which would throw that continent into chaos. Yes, I deliberately
mean to imply that endlessly reiterated Soviet protestation of alarm over German
"revanchism" is rhetoric designed to encourage and identify with anti-German
currents in the West, while German pressures to revise her border and status—
against the West—have always been considered strategically advantageous to the
Soviet Union. The main lines of the Soviet German policy between 1921 and
1934 are reasonably clear. Anti-Versailles revisionism was proclaimed and
supported. Economic and diplomatic ties were cultivated. The secret rearmament of Germany in violation of the Versailles provisions was vigorously carried
out. While a domestic Communist struggle for power was supported after a
fashion, the thrust of the Comintern policy imposed on the German Communist
party from 1927 on was to weaken the Democratic left and the center and
indirectly but substantially strengthen the National-Socialists. A case can and
has been made for the proposition that without this Communist support, the
Hitlerites would not have come to power, but we are here concerned not with
the effect but the intent of Soviet strategy.

The interpretation of this policy line is less clear. The standard "apologist" view is that Stalin sought to help Weimar Germany out of empathy for her political and economic predicament and was tragically mistaken. This view assumes that the Soviet leadership is "sentimental and stupid." The standard textbook explanation is that, for practical reasons, the two outcasts of Europe got together for mutual assistance and comfort, which supposes the Soviet leadership to be traditional and pragmatic power politicians. More perceptive minds (George Kennan and Max Beloff, for example) suggest that there was method in Stalin's madness and that he expected the Hitler regime, once in power, to produce in short order the chaos that would facilitate a Communist revolution. This approach sees the Soviet leadership pursuing ideological-revolutionary aims. Key Soviet theoretical statements, the "curious" lack of any but token subversive or revolutionary Communist activity after Hitler's seizure of power, and subsequent Soviet behavior until 1941, how-ever suggest that Stalin expected first, to encourage anti-Western revisionist politics in Germany and provide it with the means to challenge the West; second, to help the potentially most militant and anti-Western party in Germany into power; third, to incite or enable that government to go to war against the West; and fourth, to benefit strategically from the outcome of that war. This interpretation is consistent with the hypothesis that the Soviet leadership follows a grand strategic design of creating major adversary relation-ships among other powers and benefiting from the resulting conflict.

While this "grand design" is simple, the execution is complicated, if for no other reason than that the Soviet Union could do little more than influence the behavior of the other nations involved, and those nations would act to pursue their own national interests. In what ought to be the classical defini-tion of strategy, the Soviet Union had to find ways of influencing the internal decision-making process of other countries, and in what ought to be the classi-cal definition of diplomacy, she sought to do so by encouraging them to com-mit themselves to policies that conformed to Soviet strategic designs, but that were adopted because they served the nation's own national interests.

The Soviet Union's German policy yielded her by 1934 not only a poten-tially highly volatile conflict situation in Europe, but some risk to her own security as well. What followed from then until 1941 was a policy of capitaliz-ing on this situation by making the Soviet Union an indispensable or desirable partner for both sides, and in this way gaining the big power status that thus far had eluded her. The policy of reinforcing in each of the emerging adversary camps those trends most conducive to an intensification of tensions served both the defensive purpose of preventing the danger of a reasonably stable anti-Soviet Europe and the dynamic end of destabilizing the European political balance to the point of a severe political or military crisis which would create the opportunity for the Soviet Union to achieve either a significant political role in Europe or territorial gains.

Both the risk and the promise of this strategy became real by 1936 as the

German-Italian-Japanese alliance and the anti-Comintern pact took shape. It presented, on the one hand, the strategic nightmare of a two-front war for the Soviet Union and the existence of a power bloc whose main political orientation was anti-Soviet; the risk was compounded by possible indifference to, or collusion with, this trend by the major Western powers. The promise, however, lay in the fact that, whereas the rhetoric of the Axis became anti-Communist, the strategic orientation became anti-British. Soviet strategists were fully aware, certainly by 1940, that the principal preoccupation of joint Axis planning was the liquidation of the British empire, with Japan taking over the Asian possessions, Italy expected to break Britain's supply lines to Asia, and Germany reordering the political map of Europe without British interference.

The Soviet Union secured her interests by intensifying her efforts toward a European collective security system against Germany and Italy, and attempting to build popular fronts aimed at undermining a substantive current of opinion in Western Europe that thought German aspirations reasonable and tolerable and coexistence with Hitler possible. The Spanish Civil War, whatever else the Soviet Union expected of it, certainly served to sharpen the ideological battle lines in the West and to create a close identification among the European and American "left-liberal-progressive" complex with the Soviet Union. The ease with which the Grand Alliance was made operational on June 23, 1941, one day after the German invasion of the Soviet Union, suggests that substantial groundwork for it had been laid. Indeed, the Soviet leadership began to capitalize early on the strategic and political conceptions of the Roosevelt administration toward Germany and Europe, which were anti-German in the extreme and accommodationist, to say the least, toward the Soviet Union, and of that faction in British politics that, in which might well serve as its epitaph, proclaimed that it would ally itself even with the devil against the Nazis, being less than fastidious about any distinction between intolerable Nazi aspirations and legitimate German national interests.

By late 1938, liberal statesmen and the public opinion that supported them in the West had accepted, for reasons of its own, the Soviet view of the matter, namely, that neither the internal nor the external developments and aims of Germany and Italy could be accepted, that they had to be resisted "without compromise," as James Reston and other hawks of yesteryear put it, and that cooperation with the Soviet Union in a bipolar international system was essential to quarantine, contain, roll back, and "whatever" the international power aspirations of Germany and Japan. Yet a point of view, no matter how influential, is not policy, and it seems to me that what the Soviet Union faced was the posibility that Axis goals would be achieved or resisted without the Soviet Union deriving any benefit from either because she did not have "a part of the action." She therefore needed to force the issue to a head.

The German—Soviet Nonaggression Pact of August 1939, together with its various addenda, culminated an intense period of Soviet diplomatic activity which resulted in war in Europe. Once again, I state this deliberately, despite the anticipated protest. Given strategic and tactical facts of life, the likelihood of World War II is characterized as "Sitzkrieg," or phony war, bears it out. It was the pact and its strategic impact that alone made war in 1939 possible. Since the Soviet leadership is neither sentimental nor stupid, and knew what it was doing, I have to assume that it wanted the war, which could be the only result of its diplomacy. This is not meant to take Hitler off the hook, but to put Stalin on there with him.

Leaving aside Hitler's so-called master plan, which, at any rate, has yet to turn up after some thirty years of rummaging around millions of captured documents, let us examine the compelling strategic results of the pact: by removing the threat of two-front war, it made Hitler's invasion plans of Poland strategically feasible. By tying the pact to a secret agreement for the joint partition of Poland, it focused German designs on that country. Because of existing firm British and French guarantees of Poland's independence, a German attack on that country could be expected to lead to a state of war between Germany and the Western powers, the real objective of Soviet diplomacy. At the same time, agreement that the Soviet Union would begin to occupy its share of Poland by mid-September reduced the possibility that Hitler would back off or accept a settlement.

Soviet diplomacy preceding the outbreak of World War II is generally credited with having been either a desperate operation to delay an impending German attack, compounded by Western collusion in Hitler's designs, or a general peace policy designed to enhance European security. How one delays a German attack by eliminating a security buffer and bringing the German forces face to face with one's troops I leave to more resourceful minds to explain. At any rate, to preserve peace in Europe in 1939, all the Soviet Union had to do was not sign the Hitler-Stalin Pact and instead move to activate what became the Big Three Alliance. But that would have left the Soviet leaders without the political influence they wanted in Europe and without the political crisis that held the promise of later strategic gains.

Since the desired result of Soviet diplomacy of the period was war, even though it is believed to have been a peace policy, there appears little choice but to credit it with having succeeded in selling a war diplomacy as a peace offensive.

That such a policy was highly risky must be acknowledged, though that does not necessarily justify the conclusion that these risks must have been too great for Stalin. The Soviet position was precarious at any rate, and to do nothing to upset the political stability of Europe carried risks of its own.

In 1941 the greatest risk faced by Stalin, a German invasion of the Soviet Union, did in fact occur. But that setback also yielded the greatest promise for an eventual expansion of control and influence. The German *Ostpolitik* of 1939-41, having led to a dramatic "normalization" of relations between Germany and the Soviet Union and the political disintegration of Western and

Eastern Europe, now was followed by an *Ostpolitik* of Great Britain and the United States. Eastern Europe was in need of liberation, and the major Western powers committed themselves to a close military and political alliance for this liberation, which, furthermore, they agreed should be carried out by Soviet forces and benefit the Soviet Union.

After World War II reached its strategic turning point in June 1943, the Soviet Union set in motion an offensive that yielded her not only political and military domination in Eastern and Central Europe, but the formal approval and cooperation of the Western powers in this first major Soviet expansion. While the West could comfort itself with the thought that these Soviet gains came at German expense, and that they were concessions to obtain Soviet cooperation in establishing a new world order, the fact is that in the long strategic perspective, these gains were made at Western expense, for the territories transferred from German to Soviet control were also strategically important to the West. As a result, the Soviet Union entered the postwar international arena with greatly expanded geostrategic power. The gamble had paid off, the risks were justified, the European strategy had been a success. The Soviet Union now controlled Central Europe and occupied a position from which significant influence in Western Europe could be claimed.

China, Asia, and the World, 1923-49

The Soviet Union's China policy, in an active sense, begins in 1923. While its strategic elements make it different from the German policy, there is a correlation between the two. One of these correlations is that the doctrinal base holds the two strategies to be intimately related and mutually complementary. The struggle for China was activated when the revolutionary prospects in Germany vanished in the early 1920s. While the principal adversary relationships in Germany were seen as between exploiting bourgeoisie and exploited proletariat and those in Europe as between competing capitalist imperialisms, the class antagonisms in China, Asia, and the rest of the so-called third world were stated to be those between indigenous landed exploiters and the landless revolutionary peasantry on the one hand, and exploiting nations and exploited peoples, including the emerging national bourgeoisie—the pigs of tomorrow—on the other. The class struggle, it was stated, had become internationalized and the revolutionary liberation of the colonial peoples, under Soviet auspices, was expected to undermine the principal capitalist powers and improve the geostrategic position of the Soviet Union. The replacement of Western imperialism by Soviet imperialism was the goal; the national liberation and democratic development of colonial peoples, the rhetorical cover-up.

Another complementary aspect was the expectation that while the political losers in Europe and in Asia would be Germany and China, the big strategic losers would be the United States and her principal Western allies, according to the sound principle that he who controls either Germany or China controls the continents to which they hold the strategic key.

In the 1930s, the German-Japanese alliance compelled Soviet strategists to treat both theaters of operation as closely related. Ostensibly separate Soviet strategies toward Germany and China not only permitted a formulation of tactics designed to deal flexibly with the unique conditions prevailing in each area, but also facilitated a strategy of a mix of peace, cold war, and hot war all at the same time. A probably inadvertent but nevertheless significant factor in this strategy has been the helpful confusion among policy-makers and advisors in the West about what constituted Western vital interests and where the lines were to be drawn, or the phenomenon of "doves" prepared to abandon strategic positions to the Soviet Union in one continent who are "hawks" in their readiness to go to the brink in another.

By 1923, the Soviet Union had identified the two factions in China's dual-power situation and decided to commit herself to the manipulation of both of them. In this conception, the Chinese equivalent of the provisional government was the Peking government, and the Soviet Union entered into a relationship with it designed to maintain it as the principal adversary for the equivalent to the Soviet, the Kuomintang revolutionary movement, which it contracted to help organize, support, and lead to victory through a united front arrangement. The Soviet Union, of course, wanted neither side to prevail in the end. She supported the Peking government because without a strong adversary, the Kuomintang needed no outside help. She favored the Kuomintang, first, because the Chinese Communists themselves could not hope to gain control of the country alone; second, because her penetration of that movement would place the Chinese Communists in a position to seize power once the Kuomintang was on the verge of controlling China; and third, because the sponsorship of Chinese aspirations represented by Sun Yat-sen's movements gained her popular support and legitimized her role.

The attempted seizure of power in 1927 was a failure in the short term, but a success in the long term, because it left the Soviet Union in control from then on of a firmly established Communist revolutionary movement in China. From 1927 to 1935, the Chinese Communist movement gained a territorial and man-power base in China and some international status. Although Mao Tse-tung could not be gotten to see the wisdom of the new policy until early 1937, the Soviet Union, at the Seventh Comintern Congress in 1935, promulgated a new united front for China in which the Chinese Communist movement was to join the Nationalist government, partly in order to regain the political and military status lost after the "Long March," but mainly to support a common national policy in line with the larger Soviet design of activating a big-power adversary relationship in East Asia. Ostensibly, what resulted was a domestic alliance within China and an international alliance composed of the Soviet Union, China,

Great Britain, the United States, and other powers interested in preserving
Chinese national interests against Japanese designs. The outcome by 1945
was the buildup of an enormous Chinese Communist movement and army
that neither the Chinese government nor its Western allies were in a position
to check because of the terms of the political and military cooperation, and
the Soviet Union found herself in a vastly improved position to renew the
civil war—by proxy, of course—for control of China, which she had lost in
the 1927-35 period.

From 1945 to 1949 a dual-power relationship once again proved advantageous to the Soviet Union. Both sides were supported, the Nationalist government formally, the Communists substantively, and the Maoist victory was
expected to provide for the Soviet Union sufficient control over China to permit her to project her strategic power into Asia.

The dualism in China was complemented by a dualism in the American
analytical and political community when one faction proposed that the victory
of the Chinese Communists be welcomed, while another worked actively to prevent it. In a real sense, the Chinese political and military civil war was reflected
in the American political and academic intelligentsia, and the casualty count of
that civil war has yet to be completed—or all the scores settled.

At any rate, for the time being, the China gamble had paid off, the risks
seemed justified, and the Asian strategy had succeeded in making the Soviet
Union a major Asian power.

**The Post-World War II Strategic Plateau and
Its Consequence: The "Cold War" and the
Bipolar Stalemate.**

The end of World War II had given the Soviet Union an entree into the
international balance of power as one of the two superpowers. While Soviet
power was initially weak relative to that of the United States, skillful diplomacy
and the gradual mobilization of domestic resources produced in the ensuing
twenty years an approximate parity, a development that at least some American
administrations, building on the strategic conception of FDR, held desirable.
The thinking appears to have been that, inasmuch as nuclear weapons made the
maintenance of peace vastly more urgent than before, a stable international
order had to be maintained. Since one crucial pillar of that international order
was the Soviet Union, it followed that it had to be in the interest of American
policy to help maintain the stability of the Soviet regime. Hence the American
reluctance to capitalize on Soviet disasters in foreign policy (Hungary, Czechoslovakia) and domestic affairs (crop failures, dissidence) and the tendency to
see problems for the Soviet leadership as opportunities of gaining its cooperation
in common peace-building schemes. That the Soviet leadership would avail itself

of the opportunities offered by this Western policy toward it would seem natural during the period in which its power was being consolidated and enlarged. The question, of course, to be taken up in the remainder of this chapter is whether Soviet thinking envisages this level and kind of participation in international relations as a more or less permanent concern, and is going to settle for her present status, or whether the status and power acquired in recent decades are going to serve as a basis for a new offensive, diplomatic or otherwise, on the international status quo. Has the Soviet Union abandoned the international behavior of a revolutionary power in favor of that of a status quo power, as Secretary Kissinger once suggested? After detente, what?

In Europe, the expansion of Soviet power had removed Eastern Europe as an area from which strategic pressure could be exerted against the Soviet Union. At the same time, that area, and especially its northern tier, was converted into a base from which strategic pressure could be brought to bear against Western Europe. The result was the military confrontation in Europe as we have known it. Another result was a Soviet ability to influence the decision-making and political process in West European countries, although that capacity was gradually lost as the United States, contrary to wartime Soviet expectations, did not withdraw from Europe because of preoccupation with domestic crisis, and as the political and strategic revitalization of Europe proceeded along Atlantic and anti-Communist lines. In the end, the Soviet Union faced in Europe a politically and militarily consolidated Atlantic alliance that, besides providing an attractive alternative model for those nations attempting to work out their own national developments, had the potential for generating some political pressure against the Eastern European Communist states.

Given the fact that Western pressures to make strategic inroads in Eastern Europe generally come in the benign form of credits and trade, and in the nonviolent forms of radio propaganda, and that they derive from the premise that that which promotes the stability of the Soviet Union promotes international stability, which, in turn, leads to favorable conditions for American policy, there should be no undue Soviet anxiety about the external enemy on the European flank, especially since that enemy is willing to be useful. If, then, the predominant Soviet objective were the maintenance of a stable political relationship with Europe, her leaders would have cause to be satisfied with the status quo. If it expected, on the other hand, to obtain further influence in Western Europe and to weaken the United States strategically by driving wedges into the Atlantic alliance, a new strategy was indicated from the early 1960s on.

One interpretation of Soviet diplomacy toward Europe, and it commands the largest number of adherents, is to see it as matching publicly stated U.S. and West European goals of a relaxation of military tensions through a variety of force level and quality arrangements, of a normalization of the various sets of political relations that span the border of the "spheres of influence," and of defusing the German issue by converting that nation from an object of contention to a political and economic bridge. If this settlement comes about, it is expected to yield two politically stable halves of Europe with such substantially reduced military means that they cease to carry strategic weight. The quid pro quo would be a Western abandonment of any political-strategic designs on Eastern Europe, in exchange for which the Soviet Union would, for the foreseeable future, be precluded from being a significant political factor in Western Europe.

Another perspective is yielded by the examination, not of the rhetorical content of Soviet diplomacy, but its expected effect on political stability in Western Europe. To the extent that Soviet designs for Europe tend to encourage progressive or leftist political forces and tendencies, radical as well as moderate, in Western Europe, their effect would have to be destabilizing. In addition, Soviet preference for bilateralism rather than bloc-to-bloc relations may not only reflect the practical reason that state-to-state relations are still the predominant mode of the international order, but can also have the effect of encouraging centrifugal trends in Europe, which in turn would tend to destabilize matters. The European Security Conference, even if it does not yield the Soviet optimum goal of excluding American power, though not American responsibility, from Europe, will still leave the Soviet Union with a vastly increased political role in Western Europe to be used as a basis for influencing politics and policy formation there. The effect of concluding a Mutual Force Reduction Agreement on terms thus far advanced by the Soviet side would be not only the withdrawal from West Germany of stationed Allied forces, but a disbandment of a part of the indigenous German forces. Together with Soviet intransigence on proposals designed to reduce its overwhelming ground force superiority, these positions suggest not so much a desire to produce a mutually acceptable disengagement, but decided strategic and political advantage.

Germany again is the key to the Soviet European policy. Until 1954, the thrust of Soviet diplomacy had been to prevent Germany's political and military integration into Europe, and thus the continent's consolidation, by appealing to German interests and sentiments against becoming "cannon-fodder" for an imperialist anti-Soviet scheme. Key events in that period are fondly referred to by the German left as "missed opportunities." The failure of that policy led to a reversal culminating in the "normalization" of relations between the Federal Republic and Moscow in 1955. The promotion and subsidization of anti-German interests and sentiments was then undertaken in the West with the hope that public and political opinion would adopt the view that Germany's political neutralization was in the interest of the democracies in order to avoid becoming partners to German revanchist designs. The highpoint of that campaign was the Berlin crisis of 1961, and its optimal response was Walter Lippmann's conclusions, after interviewing Khrushchev in the Crimea, that the Soviet position on Berlin was justified and that the German issue was the only obstacle to a general East-West settlement. The clear implication was that a sellout of German interests would usher in an era of peace. The expectable effect, however, would have been the political isolation of Germany, the strategic weakening of Western Europe, and the destabilization of European political relationships.

In the event, policy-makers honored Lippman but ignored his advice. The mobilization of Western public and journalistic opinion and the cultivation of left-of-center politicians had yielded no substantive measurable strategic results. Whether by design or accident, Soviet policy then moved toward offering real political concessions and proposing realistic negotiations in order to bring movement into the East-West relationships in Europe (although in *Pravda* parlance, nothing political ever happens by accident). It is possible, of course, that the Soviet Union's concern with liquidating the conditions of an uneasy and fragile confrontation and of finding a cooperative, stabilizing set of settlements, and it is possible that those demands advanced by the Soviet Union that appear unacceptable to the Western side are merely the opening statements of maximal goals, to be moderated as positive responses are forthcoming. It is also possible, on the other hand, that, in keeping with earlier Soviet tradition, the initial offers of concessions and cooperation will gradually give way to ever more concrete and one-sided demands that lead either to a collapse of the negotiations or Western concessions of some magnitude. It seems likely that the outcome of these negotiations will not consist of the substance of any agreements reached, but of the political and strategic effect of the negotiations themselves. The thrust of Soviet goals, then, can perhaps be seen in the expectable effects of the various arrangements already made or proposed.

The core of these negotiations is *Ostpolitik,* its encouragement by the Soviet Union, its specific formulation by West Germany and her allies, and the Soviet response thereto. To begin with, Soviet response to *Ostpolitik,* ostensibly designed to lead to European stability, has been accompanied by the cultivation of bilateral relationships with Germany's European allies, a diplomacy that can only have a divisive and therefore destabilizing effect in Western Europe. Then, *Ostpolitik* would tend to encourage German independence in Europe, which, at the very least, can lead to her isolation and earn her suspicion and animosity among her present allies. In the hands of the proper political forces in Germany, *Ostpolitik* can be encouraged to lead to German assertiveness, a development sure to undermine the fragile political consensus that keeps the European community together. Thus far, the German architects of *Ostpolitik* seemed explicitly aware of this possibility when they insisted that the emerging relations with the Soviet Union and Eastern Europe could be justified only if the German connection with the Atlantic community in general, and the United States in particular, continued to be unimpaired. Perhaps former Chancellor Brandt's political demise was after all the work of the Soviet leaders, who may have suspected that he saw *Ostpolitik* as a double-edged sword and, thus, found his strategic point of view a block to their expectations. Recalling the episode in the 1920s, in which the Soviet Union intensified the military rearmament of a Germany increasingly isolated politically, it is not inconceivable that the current leadership, noting that political negotiations rendered Germany more independent of her European allies and her political leadership more inclined to assert itself, would reverse its position on the military force reduction negotiations to settle for an undiminished German military establishment, while making the concessions necessary to bring about a withdrawal of allied forces from that country.

The very existence of a heavily armed Germany cut loose from her Atlantic political moorings would make Germany, rather than the Soviet Union, the principal strategic concern of the other European states. The resulting adversary relationship in Europe would have a profoundly destabilizing effect, it would make Germany once again the bone of European political contention, and it would significantly cripple the United States strategically by forcing her to choose sides or to retreat into isolation. For strategic purposes, the general disintegration of the Atlantic political community would be sufficient to make the Soviet Union a vastly more powerful factor in Europe, and a localized European war would not be necessary. (Wars on the flanks and breaks in the flow of Middle Eastern supply of energy would be sufficient to keep pressure on Europe, and such wars would carry the requisite low risk of escalation.) It is suggested here that the expectable results of Soviet diplomacy in Europe, rather than stated goals, hold the key to analyzing Soviet objectives, and these objectives point in the direction of a general political destabilization in Western Europe with the opportunities for Soviet political and strategic gains inherent in it.

Soviet Policy in Asia After 1949: Who Contains Whom?

The Chinese Communist victory in 1949 provided the Soviet Union with obvious strategic gains. Particularist tendencies among her leaders notwithstanding, the Chinese People's Republic certainly was organizationally and philosophically closer to the Soviet Union than to the West, from whose strategic grasp the revolution and civil war had extricated China. The Soviet Union thus could look forward to being the superpower that dominated the Chinese regime, to using China as a strategic base for the projection of her power into Asia, and to enlisting Chinese Communist cooperation in the effort to decolonialize Asia and Africa and to "assist" peoples in their "national liberation," through which the Soviet Union sought, in the postwar period, a changing of the strategic guard in the former colonies, preferably with the cooperation of the United Nations and the intended victims, the former colonial powers and their dependencies.

To maintain her strategically advantageous position in China, however, the Soviet Union, to forestall any possible early rapprochement between the Chinese Communist regime and the West, had to establish and perpetuate a major US-Chinese adversary relationship. The Korean War was a substantial element in this policy, which lasted for twenty years, and generated, from the Soviet point of view, the powerful pressures on the Chinese leadership to remain in the Soviet strategic orbit and denied her policy alternatives. From the American point of view, the relationship led to the containment of China in Asia, which had the positive effect of permitting the economic, social, and political consolidation and growth of the non-Communist states of the Western Pacific, but had the negative effect of securing the Soviet strategic position in Asia. As the American military presence in East and Southeast Asia had precluded any but a pro-Soviet Chinese orientation, however severe the conflict between the two Communist powers became, so it was the withdrawal of this American power in recent years that left the Chinese Communists free to look elsewhere for diplomatic and economic relationships. And as it had been the American containment of China that preserved the Soviet strategic position in Asia, so it was the Sino-American rapprochement that effectively ended major Soviet influence and vastly reduced her access to the Indian and Pacific Ocean area.

The immediate strategic goal for the Soviet Union, therefore, must be the restoration of her controlling role in China and of strategic access to Asia. The accumulation of a large military force on China's northern frontier is a part of that effort, as are Soviet expectations to play a positive role in any forthcoming internal Chinese political upheavals and successions. But current Soviet moves indicate that a larger strategic game is being played, with a variety of options to be pursued as opportunities arise.

One obvious option would be the activation of a new conflict in Southeast or East Asian country, with the intent of once again drawing the United States to the Chinese border with massive military forces. Both the pertinent conceptions of the Nixon Doctrine, and the state of political opinion in the United States on the matter of military intervention in what are thought to be "civil wars" between indigenous forces, make this a questionable enterprise, and no concrete moves in this direction are evident. (On the contrary, it seems more likely that the Soviet Union would move to reactivate the Vietnam War, or a similar conflict, *after* a strategic rapprochement with the Chinese People's Republic.)

Another option is suggested by the historical analogy of the mid-1930s, in which a renewed Chinese-Japanese conflict reopens a Soviet drive for Asian hegemony, either in alliance with Communist China against a Japan supported by the United States, or in an alliance of both Communist powers with the United States against an isolated Japan, with past strategic patterns suggesting that the Soviet Union, not prepared to risk major confrontations with the United States, would prefer American support for, and approval of, any Soviet offensives. A relatively low-key, but consistent policy of attempting to promote tensions between Japan and the United States on the one hand, and between China and Japan on the other, has been maintained for a number of years, with limited success even in the more recent period when substantive rivalries have come to the surface, and any expectation of being able to draw either China or Japan into exerting major pressures on the other power must seem remote to the Soviet leadership. There is no reason to suppose, however, that the Soviet Union is not prepared to capitalize on such opportunities as radical changes in the internal political situation of either or both countries may create.

A third option lies in a move to assemble in East and Southeast Asia a Soviet military presence of sufficient strength to exert the pressure on Chinese policy-makers once provided by the American military presence there. The effect would be an all-Soviet strategic encirclement of China, which as late as 1969 was perceived by the Chinese leadership to be the effective result of Soviet-American strategic collusion against China. One key to that strategy is the question of access. A major Soviet military presence can be supported neither from Vladivostok nor from the Black Sea, and politically secure bases on the Indian Ocean are required, bases reasonably securely linked to the Soviet Union geographically. This enhances, and perhaps explains, greatly increased Soviet activities with respect to India and Pakistan, and particularly the area where Soviet Central Asia borders on both.

The Indian option has three major dimensions. One is the dual-power situation in Indian internal politics, with the Congress party, the Populists and Mensheviks of India, being supported and used against the West, while the Indian Communist party is a Soviet instrument for eventually disposing of the Ghandi-ites. Another is India's continuing role as a link in the Soviet chain of pressure brought to bear against Communist China, made more acute by the acquisition of a nuclear capacity by India and the strategic, if not political, possibility of Soviet nuclear weapons aimed from Indian positions at Chinese targets now elusive for such weapons emplaced in the Soviet Union. The third is the prospect of an India so oriented in its foreign policy toward the Soviet Union that it would permit not only the maintenance of Soviet military facilities on the Indian Ocean, but the use of her communications facilities for supply transit from the Soviet Union. Unfortunately, from the Soviet point of view, geography has made a sizable and tactically secure land connection between India and the Soviet Union problematical. The optimal solution would be a strategic corridor comprised of northeast Afghanistan, northern Pakistan, and portions of Kashmir, assuming that the western section of Sinkiang Province remains inaccessible. That, of course, would entail a major rearrangement of the political map of the area. Soviet activities in the area, however, may suggest just such designs.

An additional option, then, might envisage the dismemberment of what remains of Pakistan. This dismemberment has already been dress-rehearsed in the events leading to the establishment of Bangladesh. In addition to Soviet-Indian collusion, however, Afghanistan would need to be engaged in this scheme to create a land corridor for the Soviet Union to the Indian subcontinent. Such collusion, judging from long-standing and recently sharply accelerated Soviet support for Baluchi and other assorted national liberation movements, could reasonably be expected by compensating Afghanistan for northeastern territory to be yielded with southwest Pakistan, territory "liberated" in the dismemberment of Pakistan a compensation that would not only exceed the size of what was lost, but gain for Afghanistan access to the Indian Ocean. A dividend for the Soviet Union of a Pakistan divided among herself, India, and Afghanistan would not only be access to India, but, by the Indus River Valley, to Pakistan's Indian Ocean ports.

It is, of course, possible, as the general line has it, that Soviet activities in this area are actuated by a sincere desire to stabilize Asian political relations, and Soviet sponsorship of a general Asian Security System is usually cited in support of Moscow's pacific bent. But the collective security arrangement proposed for Asia may be intended to serve purposes similar to those of the Soviet-proposed security systems for Europe in the 1930s and the 1970s: to destabilize political relations, create major adversary relationships, and promote the Soviet Union as the political guardian and guarantor of smaller states. The interpretation proposed above of Soviet activities in South Asia and their connection with an effort to regain strategic access to East Asia may be objected to as farfetched and unreal, but there are reasons for examining it seriously. There are precedents for such political dismemberments as that of Pakistan (suffice it here to recall that the dismemberment and partition of Poland in 1939 led to the outbreak of World War II), and the Soviet Union has in the past rearranged political maps at least as drastically (as in Eastern Europe after World War II) as may be envisaged for her Central Asian neighbors. The Soviet Union is economically, politically, and militarily involved in the area to the extent of accepting considerable risks and of supporting a substantial degree of political and armed violence. The Soviet involvement in the assorted so-called liberation movements, especially in Pakistan and parts of Afghanistan and India, is at least as great as her involvement in such movements at similar early stages in their development in China, Cuba, Greece, and elsewhere.

It must once again be reiterated that the concern here is with probable Soviet optimal strategic designs, not with what is necessarily going to happen. Neither India nor Afghanistan are wholehearted partners in the Soviet effort, nor have countermoves from Pakistan, Iran, the United States, and elsewhere been lacking. From the perspective of mid-1974 it may be that both the perspicacity of United States strategists in an early and accurate identification of Soviet designs and their determination to frustrate them in a timely and, therefore, low-risk manner have reduced the Soviet Union to pursuing the option of a strategic partnership arrangement with India as most feasible under the circumstances.

The United States: Reluctant Ally and Eventual Victim?

The apparent contradiction between Soviet strategic designs and tactical deployments around the world on the one hand, and the single-minded pursuit of detente with the United States is too obvious to be elaborated here. It remains for the Soviet Union a strategic fact of life that she is not in a position to challenge the United States should that power show an inclination to resist Soviet advances, political or otherwise. Thus, the theoretical and practical strategy remains to engage the United States in diplomatic relationships that require her to support or acknowledge those Soviet gains that United States long-term national interests should counsel her to resist. Returning to the argument mentioned at the outset that the Soviet Union is compelled to seek a friendly relationship with the United States to stave off, through transfers of technology, investments, and management systems, a production disaster, there can be a connection between the economic transfusion sought and the need to acquire the production capacity and military means required to follow through on the strategic designs now being initiated. There is a connection between geostrategic access to the Indian Ocean and the ships to place there in the event it is obtained. There is a connection between an increase in Soviet force levels on the Chinese borders to the point where they replace the withdrawn American troops and the manpower deficiencies in Soviet industry, part of which rest on inefficiency. And there is a connection between the multitude of schemes for the political penetration of numerous countries and the ability to deliver in the commercial relationships that are being designed for the purpose. By acquiescing in, or reacting favorably to, Soviet diplomatic or military moves, either because this is deemed essential in the search for a stable world order or because it confers advantages against competitors within the Western alliance, the United States and other major industrial nations are an essential element in any Soviet design to enlarge her strategic position in the international balance. And because of the technology and productivity lag, those same nations play an essential role in any Soviet schemes to acquire the productive power base and military inventory to provide the strategic weight that will permit her to move from being compelled to operate in world politics according to the "rules of the game" derived from the Western tradition, to a setting in which the Soviet version of how states must behave and what peace and security mean in practice hold sway.

I submit that my tentative interpretation of the nature and aims of Soviet strategy in the 1970s is credible, if not conclusive, because, first, there is a theoretical foundation and practical precedent for each of the designs I have identified; second, because practical Soviet initiatives and reactions can be explained, though again not necessarily exclusively, when judged by the criteria I have employed; third, because the thrust of Soviet resource allocation, production priorities, and research and development programs suggest that the concrete means are being acquired for a greatly increased projection of Soviet power in international affairs; and finally, because the intellectual, spiritual, and political malaise in much of the West may encourage the Soviet leadership to continue an otherwise senseless and self-destructive enterprise in the hope that eventually her adversaries will succumb to pressures and temptations that they now understand and resist.

3

The Summit Meeting as a Form of Diplomacy in American-Soviet Relations in the 1970s

Charles E. Timberlake

Before 1972 American and Soviet heads of state had, during the approximately forty years of diplomatic relations between the two governments, met only eight times. Three were formal World War II summit conferences: Teheran in 1943 and Yalta in February 1945 brought together Roosevelt, Stalin, and Churchill, and in July 1945 the Potsdam meeting brought together Truman, Stalin, and Churchill (Atlee replaced Churchill in the second portion of the conference). Two formal meetings occurred during the Eisenhower Administration: the Geneva Summit Conference in 1955 brought Eisenhower together with Bulganin, Khrushchev, and Zhukov of the USSR, and Faure and Anthony Eden from France and Britain, respectively; Khrushchev visited Eisenhower at Camp David in September 1959, but the third formal meeting planned during Eisenhower's Presidency (the Paris Summit Conference of May 1960) did not bring Eisenhower and Khrushchev together as planned, for Khrushchev refused to participate unless Eisenhower apologized for the U-2 incident.[1]

Two other meetings between American and Soviet heads of state were informal: Kennedy met Khrushchev in Austria in 1961, and Johnson met Kosygin at Glassboro on June 25, 1967, while Kosygin was in the United States to address the UN General Assembly on the Middle East War. By 1972 only one American President had visited the USSR (Roosevelt at Yalta) and only one Soviet Premier had visited the United States (Khrushchev in 1959).

By 1972 some twenty-seven years had passed since Roosevelt's Soviet visit, and thirteen years had passed since Eisenhower had accepted the invitation Khrushchev extended to him at the Camp David meeting to visit the Soviet Union. The U-2 incident and the fiasco of the aborted Paris Summit Conference of 1960 prevented Eisenhower from making the visit, scheduled for spring of that year; President Kennedy planned to return the visit in 1964, but he was assassinated in 1963; President Johnson abandoned the Soviet visit he had scheduled for October 1968 when the Soviet Union invaded Czechoslovakia in August of that year. Finally, President Nixon proposed to make the trip in May 1972. Nixon's mining of Haiphong Harbor on the eve of the May meeting bore some resemblances to Eisenhower's sending the U-2 mission over the USSR on the eve of the May 1960 Paris conference, but the Soviets did not withdraw their invitation, and the president arrived in Moscow on May 22 to participate in a week-long summit meeting. Since 1959 Moscow had been only some twelve to fifteen hours flying time from Washington, but the trip had taken thirteen years diplomatically.

As if to make up for missed opportunities, Nixon and General Secretary Leonid Brezhev (not officially head of state, but functioning as a head of state normally would during a summit meeting) have met once per year in 1972, 1973, and 1974, and President Ford and Brezhnev have now agreed to meet in 1975. President Nixon proposed that a summit meeting between himself and Brezhnev become an annual custom. If President Ford should continue the meetings annually until the end of Nixon's elected term in 1976, Nixon and Ford will have had five formal summit meetings with Soviet heads of state in the five-year period of 1972 through 1976. This is equal to the total number of formal meetings held by all previous American presidents with Soviet heads of state.

An official meeting of several days duration between Soviet and American heads of state is a highly complex event, and its place in the over-all diplomacy between two governments is difficult to assess. Such a meeting has both an image and a substance that are very important for future relations, and separating the image from the substance often requires the passage of time. The most successful peacetime summit conference utilizes both the creation of images and the achievement of substance to make its impact upon future relations

This essay argues that the Moscow Summit Conference of 1972 utilized the image and substance well to signal the arrival of a new period in American-Soviet relations, but the Washington Summit Conference of 1973, while significant, was less impressive in form and substance. The inability of the two leaders during the two summit meetings to assemble a cluster of agreements sufficient to convince Congress to alter radically American-Soviet commercial relations was a noticeable failure of the Nixon-Brezhnev scheme of personal diplomacy to build detente. Added to the disappointment of June 1973 were the strains that the Middle East War of October 1973 produced in the form of the most serious confrontation (or at least the appearance of it) between the US and the USSR since the Cuban crisis of 1962.

Against this background the summit meeting in Moscow in 1974 had to be the least successful during the 1970s. The fading image of the summit meeting and the summit meeting's inability to solve the trade problem in 1973—even after substantial success had been made between the two summits to remove diplomatic barriers blocking closer commercial relations—are reflections of the deep-seated fears and antagonisms between the US and the USSR that have developed since 1917 and cannot be overcome dramatically, but must await the passage of time and further patient, continuing negotiations. An occasional summit meeting may speed up this process, but it is a dramatic form that suggests quick solutions, and it is, therefore, not well suited to play the role of the major diplomatic instrument for radically altering American-Soviet relations. This instrument has worked nicely in 1972 and 1973 to supplement traditional diplomacy, but because only a narrow margin of trust exists for negotiated changes in American-Soviet relations, that margin can soon be exhausted and the walls of resistance confronted. To push back those walls and expand the margin for further agreements, those agreements already concluded must be successfully implemented. With declining achievement of substance, the device of the summit meeting becomes less effective the more frequently it is employed. It loses the aura and drama surrounding it; its novelty is gone. It should be held in reserve for those instances when its unique features can be most effective as a supplement to traditional diplomacy.

The Moscow Summit Meeting of 1972

Despite its inauspicious beginning, the Moscow meeting exhibited most of the characteristics of a successful peacetime summit conference. Among its many reasons for success, the most important was that, for the first time since World War II, both sides wanted it to accomplish something tangible to improve American-Soviet relations. The Soviets were especially interested in increasing trade with the U.S., and Nixon, although he referred early in 1970 to an approaching "era of negotiation" in American-Soviet relations, made sufficiently clear the necessity that improved political relations precede improved economic relations.[2] Soviet leaders began emphasizing within a month after Nixon's speech that the Soviet Union did not consider that "increased trade needs to wait for improved political relations."[3] Desiring purchases of American-produced mining and oil-drilling equipment, American designs for steel foundries and, especially, computer systems, the Soviets made substantial purchases in 1971 and 1972 in the US.[4]

The constant barriers the Soviets met in increasing trade with the US were their inability to get long-term credits and the high tariff rates they had to pay because they were not among America's "most favored" trading partners. To obtain long-term credits and to gain most-favored-nation status, the Soviets would have to overcome considerable mistrust in the U.S., some of which dated back to American businessmen's experiences in the Soviet Union in the 1920s, and much of which resided in Congress. Much of that mistrust stemmed from the Soviet political-social-economic system generally, and some particularly emanated from the Soviet Union's refusal to repay the US for equipment assigned to the Soviet government under the lend-lease program of World War II.[5] At the very least, the Soviets would have to settle the lend-lease debt to clear the way for long-term commercial agreements and credits and for obtaining most-favored-nation tariff privileges.

Soviet domestic factors in 1972 forced the government into a situation where, even if favorable loans could not be obtained in the US, Soviet negotiators would have to bargain for the best deal they could get anyway on wheat, for the harvest of 1971 had been poor, and massive spring rains in 1972 had prevented planting and would surely lead to another poor harvest.[6]

By spring of 1972 both the Soviets and Americans saw possible gains from the forthcoming summit meeting. The Soviet side intensely wanted various

American manufactured products and American grain. The Americans strongly hoped that the Communist Party leadership in Moscow would pressure North Vietnam to negotiate a peace settlement that would allow the US to withdraw from Vietnam. Preparations for the meeting were proceeding well: several agreements had been concluded by April, and others were nearing completion. Yet, on the eve of the summit, the North Vietnamese began an offensive that was supported materially and verbally by the Soviets, and to blunt the drive— and, undoubtedly to keep his bargaining position strong at the summit-meeting—President Nixon had mines placed in North Vietnam's main harbors, trapping several Soviet vessel in port and damaging four of them.[7]

The continuation of American-Soviet competition in the Third World areas— even intensification of that competition initially in Vietnam, and later in the Middle East—is the strange backdrop against which the two leading actors perform the play called "detente." As though Haiphong had never happened, Nixon addressed his official Soviet hosts at a formal reception on the evening before the first formal day of negotiations saying: "Summit meetings of the past have been remembered for their 'spirit.' We must strive to make the Moscow summit memorable for its substance."[8] A week earlier he had called the Vienna, Geneva, Glassboro and Camp David summits "cosmetics . . . all froth and very little substance."[9] For a variety of reasons, the desire that both sides shared to create the appearance of a new era in American-Soviet relations proved stronger than the desire to break off the summit.

The Moscow summit did present the appearance of substance in that it produced eight agreements covering areas in which little or no American-Soviet cooperation existed. The creation of the image of a new era was the result not only of substance, but also of a highly successful orchestration of the negotiations that created a talk-sign-talk procedure that began Tuesday with the signing of the less significant agreements, substantively, and culminated on Friday, the last day of the talks, with the signing of the most significant agreements, substantively, before a national television audience. The final act in image building was President Nixon's address to the Soviet people via Soviet television on Sunday. This scenario dramatized the significance and achievements of the summit meeting by suggesting a cause-and-effect relationship between the talks and the signing of agreements when, in fact, no such relationship existed for more than half of the agreements signed.

An analysis of the events during the four-day period of Tuesday, May 23, through Friday, May 26, illustrates the maximum publicity, yet leisure and flexibility, the talk-sign-talk procedure afforded the participants. The scenario that both sides accepted in advance called for signing agreements each day of the main negotiating period: Tuesday, agreements on pollution and health; Wednesday, on space and technology; Thursday, on trade; Friday, on arms limitation.[10] The four agreements to be signed on Tuesday and Wednesday had already been prepared for signature through previous negotiations.[11] Thus, both sides had all day Tuesday and Wednesday free to discuss world problems generally and to work out the details for the more difficult areas of trade and arms limitation scheduled for signing on Thursday and Friday.

On Tuesday, May 23, the first officially scheduled session of the summit meeting began at 11:00 a.m., with Nixon and Brezhnev, each in the middle of a three-man delegation, facing each other across a small table. To Nixon's right (and facing Kosygin, who sat at Brezhnev's left) was Secretary of State William Rogers; on Nixon's left (and facing Podgorny, who was at Brezhnev's right) was Henry Kissinger, special advisor for national affairs. After a two-hour session, the group broke for lunch, and another two-hour session in the afternoon involved only Nixon and Brezhnev and interpreters and occasional aides whom they called into the room. At the end of the afternoon session, both sides left the negotiating room and assembled to sign the agreement on efforts to protect the environment and the agreement on health research.[12]

The agreement on environment protection was a slight revision of an understanding reached by negotiators a month earlier. The agreement called for the exchange of people and data, the holding of bilateral conferences, and the creation of direct contact between scientific institutions for the purposes of cooperating to combat pollution and predict earthquakes. To implement the agreement, a US–USSR Joint Committee on Cooperation in the Field of Environment Protection was to be established and meet once every year in Washington and Moscow, alternately. Each side was to name a coordinator to maintain contact with his counterpart between sessions of the joint committee and to supervise implementation of the cooperative programs and coordinate the activities of organizations participating in the programs. The agreement was to be in force for five years and was to be renewed for successive five-year periods unless one party notified the other at least six months in advance of the expiration date that it was terminating the agreement.[13]

The agreement on cooperation in medical science and public health formalized an understanding reached by HEW and the Soviet Ministry of Health in an exchange of letters on February 11, some three months before the summit meeting. American and Soviet specialists were to "direct their initial joint efforts" toward heart diseases and cancer. Both sides would proceed in the same manner as in the environmental agreement: exchange of persons and information, creation of conference, etc. The agreement would be implemented by an additional joint committee, the US–USSR Joint Committee for Health Cooperation, that would meet "periodically," could establish working subgroups, and would be financed cooperatively by both governments. This agreement was also for a five-year period and would be renewed and/or cancelled in the same manner as the environment protection agreement.[14]

After both sides had signed these two agreements, Nixon and Brezhnev met from 7:15 until 10:00 p.m. for an unscheduled session. At the end of the first day, the president and the general secretary had spent six hours and forty-five minutes in sessions devoted to topics other than those about which they had signed agreements that day. Although the exact content of the discussions are still not known, the American side revealed that at some time during the day Vietnam was discussed "at length."[15] Trade talks were also being conducted by special teams, and Secretary of State Rogers revealed at dinner that evening that those talks were not making significant progress toward an agreement for Thursday.[16]

Wednesday's activities also followed the talk-sign-talk scenario. After a two-hour morning session between Nixon and Brezhnev (the contents of which are unknown) and a two-hour afternoon session devoted to European military and political conditions, the two sides signed agreements on cooperation in space exploration and in the fields of science and technology.[17] Both agreements had been negotiated well in advance of the summit meeting. Negotiators for NASA and USSR Academy of Sciences had reached a preliminary understanding on January 21, 1971 and on April 6, some one and one-half months before the summit, had agreed upon principles for developing compatible space vehicles for docking. In fact, representatives of the Soviet space program were in Houston at the time of the summit in May.[18] The docking, scheduled for 1975, will be more significant as a symbol than for its substance, for both sides have already docked with their own vehicles many times. Furthermore, each country must make modifications in the spacecraft that are to dock. Since these modifications will not be made to other existing spacecraft and will not become standard for new spacecraft, other spacecraft of the two countries will not be able regularly or spontaneously to dock in space after 1975. The agreement on cooperation in space exploration is to be in force for five years with possible extension. Except for promising to work toward creating a system of international law in space, the agreement's provisions all deal with the venture of 1975.[19]

The agreement on cooperation in science and technology created a US-USSR Joint Commission on Scientific and Technical Cooperation to meet "not less than once a year in Washington and Moscow, alternatively . . . to develop and approve measures and programs" to implement the agreement and designate agencies to carry out the activities. Activities to be included are exchange of scientists and scientific information and documents; joint development and implementation of programs and projects; joint research, development and testing, and exchange of results by scientific research institutions; joint courses and conferences, and other such joint activities.[20]

With the signing of the day's scheduled agreements accomplished, Nixon, Kissinger, and at least two other American officials spent from 7:00 to 11:00 p.m. with Brezhnev, Kosygin, and Podgorny on a yacht and at a dacha outside Moscow where they discussed "international matters, among them Vietnam." From 11:00 to midnight the group had dinner.[21]

After Wednesday's extensive evening activities, Nixon spent Thursday morning in his quarters in the Kremlin "conferring with his staff." A session originally scheduled for 11:00 a.m. was postponed until the afternoon.[22] At 2:00 p.m. the American side (composed of his chief trade advisor, Peter Flanigan, William Rogers, and Henry Kissinger) met Soviet negotiators Podgorny, Kosygin, Dobrynin and two others to begin talks on trade, the first topic thus far for which an agreement was scheduled, but about which no preliminary understanding had been reached. At 5:00 p.m., when, according to the scenario, a trade agreement was to be signed, the two sides signed instead an agreement to prevent accidents of military craft at sea, an agreement concluded well before the summit. The two sides had failed to reach an agreement on trade, which, with arms limitation, was one of two major issues, and perhaps the one most important for the Soviets. But the talk-sign-talk scenario was preserved by the agreement (had it purposely been held in reserve?) on preventing incidents on and over the high seas.[23] On this day the world's newspapers carried headlines about success over the naval agreement, and short or no columns about trade failures.

The naval agreement was aimed at eliminating the rather frequent "mock attacks" by Soviet ships during American naval maneuvers and of American "buzzing" of Soviet vessels off the US East Coast. It established a promise that both parties would make significantly greater use than either had in the past of the International Code of Signals to announce their intentions at sea. To be in force for three years, the agreement will be renewed every three years unless one side announces six months in advance of the expiration date its intention not to renew.[24]

Friday morning both sides tried to salvage the trade talks and, after further discussions, signed an agreement to create a Joint Commercial Commission that would continue to work on problems not resolved by the talks. Two major problems blocked a trade agreement. The first was maritime matters, including the higher freight rates the Soviet government would have to pay for grain American vessels would haul to the USSR when final sale of grain was approved. (Both sides had already agreed that any grain purchased would be sent half in American and half in Soviet bottoms.) The second problem was settlement of the lend-lease claims. Although the latter issue was being negotiated through normal diplomatic channels, its resolution was clearly an integral part of the general Soviet-American trade problem. Therefore, it was discussed at the summit, and both sides came closer to an agreement on the dollar amount of the Soviet debt than they were at the beginning of the talks, when the Americans were insisting upon $800 million and the Soviets $300 million. At the end of the talks the only unresolved portion of the lend-lease issue was the question of the length of time the Soviet Union should have to pay the debt.[25]

The Joint Commercial Commission was delegated several specific tasks. It was to negotiate an over-all trade agreement that included reciprocal most-favored-nation status, devise arrangements for each side to provide credit to the other, negotiate provisions for the establishment of business offices in each country by enterprises of the other country, and set up an arbitration mechanism for settling commercial disputes arising from trade. The first meeting of the commission was to be held in Moscow in July of 1972, with further meetings to be in Washington and Moscow, alternately.[26]

Soviet officials sought to present the growth of pessimism because of the temporary failure of the two sides to sign a trade agreement. Mikhail I. Misnik, deputy chairman of the State Planning Committee, held a meeting for the press in his agency's headquarters in Moscow to convey a message to American businessmen. Attempting to whet the appetites of American businessmen, he dangled far-reaching prospects for American investment opportunities for profits in the USSR. Calling upon American businessmen to abandon their concept of "classic" trade, "bartering a sheep for half a camel," he proposed advancing to "large-scale arrangements in which the United States would provide plant and equipment and we would pay with raw materials and the end products of such plants."

Misnik also suggested: the USSR might possibly build a large passenger-car plant that the United States would supply with capital equipment, and the Soviets would pay for that equipment with finished cars the Americans could market wherever they wished, perhaps in Western Europe. He also suggested Soviet delivery of the YAK-40, a highly successful Soviet short-haul jet, for adaptation to American requirements. Two other proposals were for shipping Siberian liquefied gas in tankers from Murmansk to the American East Coast and from the Yakut region to the American West Coast.

To transform these possibilities, and many others, into realities, he said, the United States must first extend most-favored-nation treatment for Soviet imports, then grant credits for purchases in the US, and third, remove maritime and shipping restrictions on Soviet vessels in American ports.[27]

After the morning negotiations that resulted in creation of the trade commission, Nixon and Brezhnev, assisted by the chief SALT negotiators, Gerard Smith and Vladimir Semenov, met for two hours to prepare final details of two agreements on arms limitation. Those agreements were signed before a television audience after a formal dinner that Nixon gave at Spasso House in honor of his Soviet hosts.[28]

The two agreements were the Treaty on the Limitation of Anti-Ballistic Missile Systems that dealt with "defensive weapons," and the Interim Agreement on Certain Measures with Respect to the Limitation of Strategic Offensive Arms. The latter was an executive agreement and did not require congressional approval, but the first, being a treaty, required approval by the US Senate. Both sides committed themselves to begin abiding by both agreements immediately, however.

The treaty on defensive weapons limited the total number of antiballistic missile (ABM) launchers and missiles to two hundred of each per country. Each country was allowed two areas of specified size with no more than one-hundred launchers and one-hundred missiles per area. One "ABM deployment area" was to protect the capital city and was defined in area as having a 150-kilometer radius from the capital. Within that area, in addition to the launchers and missiles, each side was allowed "ABM radars within no more than six ABM radar complexes, the area of each complex being circular and having a diameter of no more than three kilometers." The second site was to be 150 kilometers in radius from the center of an ICBM silo area. In addition to the one-hundred ABM launchers and one-hundred missiles permitted, each side could maintain two "large phased-array ABM radars" of specified quality and no more than eighteen ABM radars of a specified quality.

The treaty provided for a maximum of fifteen ABM launchers at present test ranges, but both sides promised not to develop, test, or deploy ABM systems that were, sea-, air-, or mobile-land-based. Each also promised not to develop launchers, or modify existing ones, to launch more than one missile or to reload missiles rapidly. Such launchers would have provided one party a qualitative advantage within the quantitative limitation of two-hundred launchers provided for in the treaty. With only that exception, the treaty allowed for "modernization and replacement" of the systems and their components. Both parties also promised not to give ABM systems or components to other nations and not to deploy their own systems outside their national boundaries, and both promised not to "assume any international obligations which would conflict with this treaty."[29]

Verification of compliance with the treaty, long a major obstacle for any American-Soviet arms limitation agreement, had become less of a problem by 1972, for both sides had begun using reconnaissance satellites early in the 1960s to ascertain, for other purposes, the same type of data that would be needed for verification of compliance with the treaty. Without openly admitting the past, current, or future utilization of reconnaissance satellites, both sides agreed, nonetheless, to continue to use them and to permit the other side to use them for treaty verification. The phraseology in the treaty that rendered that provision acceptable was: in a manner "consistent with generally recognized principles of international law," each party would use "national technical means of verification at its disposal" and would "not interfere with national technical means of verification of the other party." Each also promised not to "use deliberate concealment measures" to prevent the other from checking on treaty compliance. To deal with problems that might arise during verification and to implement other provisions of the treaty, the parties created a standing consultative commission.[30]

The treaty was for unlimited duration and would be reviewed every five years. The treaty allows either party to withdraw from the agreement six months after having given the other party a statement of the "extraordinary events related to the subject matter of this treaty [that] have jeopardized its supreme interests."

The interim agreement on limiting offensive weapons was intended to regulate developments in that area during the interim between the Moscow summit meeting and the Washington summit meeting the following year, at which time both parties hoped to sign a final agreement prepared for them by their negotiators during the second phase of the Strategic Arms Limitation Talks (SALT II).[31] The agreement committed both parties to construct no additional fixed land-based intercontinental ballistic missile (ICBM) launchers after July 1, 1972, to refrain from converting into launchers for heavy ICBMs any other type of ICBM launcher, and to limit submarine-launched ballistic missile launchers and modern ballistic missile submarines to the number in existence and under construction at the date of ratification of the agreement.

Verification procedures were the same as those written into the treaty on ABMs, and the standing consultative commission created in the ABM treaty performed the same tasks for the interim agreement.[32]

With the conclusion of the signing of the two agreements on arms limitation on Friday evening, May 26, the substantive portion of the Moscow summit meeting of 1972 was completed. If one counts the arms limitation agreements as two separate agreements (as opposed to a two-part agreement, as some have done) and if one counts creation of the joint trade commission as an agreement, then the total number of agreements signed in Moscow was eight. Five of those agreements were already completed in detail before Nixon arrived in Moscow, and the final details of the arms limitation agreements were apparently very close to completion. Thus, what did the talks add to the substance of American-Soviet relations that had not been produced through regular diplomatic channels? The only two issues where differences apparently remained were trade and arms limitation. No substantive agreement on trade emerged. Creation of a commission to solve problems merely transferred to the members of the trade commission those problems that American and Soviet heads of state had been unable to solve themselves.

Ascertaining whether the details of the arms limitation agreements were the results of American-Soviet negotiators at SALT or the result of compromises made by Nixon and Brezhnev in Moscow is very difficult. At different points during the week one side or the other would report that the agreement was already a reality, then a later report would cite "certain last-minute technical problems." Until further information is released, we will wonder whether the threat of not signing an agreement was an effort one side or the other was using as pressure to win support for some point in the trade negotiations or some other issue during the private portion of the Moscow talks that was unrelated to the topics about which agreements were signed. If the talks added substance to any agreement signed during the week of the summit, that substance was limited to those details that had not been completed by the SALT negotiations before May 23 but that appeared in the two arms limitation agreements.[33]

The image of success that the 1972 Moscow summit meeting has acquired resulted more from the form of the meeting than from the substance of the agreements. Utilization of the talk-sign-talk scenario to suggest results, and the novelty of the event of the first American president visiting the Soviet capital city (Roosevelt had merely moved a few paces into the war-ravaged city of Yalta in 1945) gave the meeting an aura, a drama, and a newsworthiness.

Collectively, these psychological aspects of the situation constructed an image of success, and in international relations images are important, even when they are not congruent with reality.

Between Summits

The 1972 meeting's very success in image-building and in signing substantive agreements made comparable success at the 1973 Washington summit meeting all the less likely. The second meeting was less newsworthy, for relatively frequent summit conferences are, of course, less exotic than ones separated by thirteen years, just as the second walk on the moon was less exotic than the first, and the third less exotic than the second. Further, the two most delicate substantive issues of the 1972 meeting, trade and limitation of offensive arms, were unfinished items at the end of the Moscow talks. Because both parties had committed themselves to success in both areas, those two issues had to be negotiated closer to a solution if the 1973 conference was to be comparable in substance with the 1972 meeting, and substance for the 1973 meeting had to be achieved in one year, rather than thirteen.

To begin preparation of agreements for 1973, the Joint Commercial Commission, under the chairmanship of Secretary of Commerce Peter Peterson, met in Moscow from July 20 to August 1, 1972. Both governments had decided at the end of the summit meeting to treat collectively the many factors affecting expanded trade, for many of the issues were interrelated. For examples, the president was unwilling to extend Export-Import Bank credit to the Soviet Union until the lend-lease problem was satisfactorily resolved, and the Soviet Union, in turn, did not wish to pay its lend-lease debt until the question of most-favored-nation status was satisfactorily resolved.[34]

The Joint Commercial Commission approached the related points through separate working groups. Working groups were created during the first ten days for each of the following problems: (1) reciprocal credit, (2) lend-lease, (3) licenses, patents, copyright, and taxes, (4) the maritime agreement, and (5) the trade agreement (which had two subgroups, one on the most-favored-nation problem and one on business facilities). The fifth group also devoted its attention to the question of arbitration of conflicts arising from trade. Peterson, with others, devoted attention to joint projects between the two countries. At the end of the meeting of the joint commission on August 1, Peterson and Soviet Minister of Foreign Trade Nikolai S. Patolichev signed the terms of reference and procedures of the commission, and the two agreed to meet again in 1972, the exact date to be mutually determined depending upon the progress made by the individual working groups that would continue to negotiate. The group on maritime matters had already made "substantial progress" by August 1.[35]

By September the working groups and other negotiating teams had made sufficient progress to warrant discussions at a higher level. At Brezhnev's invitation, Nixon sent Kissinger to Moscow, where from September 11 to 14, Kissinger spent some twenty-one hours with Brezhnev and about three hours with Gromyko, discussing trade, European security, and mutual balanced force reductions, the latter in connection with resumption of SALT. As a result of that meeting, the Soviet Union sent three negotiating teams to Washington near the end of September, one each to discuss with American officials lend-lease, MFN, and a maritime agreement.[36]

During the American-Soviet negotiations in Washington, both sides concluded a set of three agreements, signed on October 14 and 18, that encompassed all the key issues related to American-Soviet trade. The first agreement, signed October 14, was an agreement on details related to maritime matters that would, or might, arise when American and Soviet vessels began transporting cargo between the two countries. The agreement covered rates to be charged by American carriers, navigation procedures to be used by American carriers entering Soviet ports, a list of forty ports in each country that would be "open to calls upon notice," and specific details related to carrying raw and processed agricultural products. All the provisions were to be retroactively operative from July 1, 1972. Thus, all shipment of American grain to the USSR as a consequence of the grains agreement of July 8 would be covered by this agreement, for shipment was to begin August 1, according to the grains agreement.[37]

The two agreements signed on October 18 were a trade agreement and the Agreement Regarding Settlement of Lend-Lease, Reciprocal Aid and Claims. The trade agreement included a clause where each country accorded "to products originating in or exported to the other country treatment no less favorable than that accorded to like products originating in or exported to any third country."[38] Thus, the Soviet Union had its most-favored-nation clause, although final approval rested with Congress. The lend-lease settlement established the Soviet debt at $722 million, a figure much closer to the American claim of $800 million than to the Soviet figure of $300 million at the beginning of the Moscow summit. But the manner in which the debt was to be paid tied final payment to congressional approval of the most-favored-nation clause of the trade agreement. The Soviet Union agreed in advance to pay $48 million of the debt, as follows: $12 million on October 18, 1972, the day the agreement was signed; $24 million on July 1, 1973; and $12 million on July 1, 1975. The date that payment would begin for the remaining $674 million would be determined by the date on which "a note from the Government of the United States of America is delivered to the Government of the Union of Soviet Socialist Republics stating that the Government of the United States of America has made available most-favored-nation status for the Union of Soviet Socialist Republics." After that date, the balance was to be paid in equal installments through the year 2001, with the Soviet side allowed to defer payments on no more than four occasions during that period, and with 3 percent interest due on the deferred payments in 2001. The deferred amounts would still be due by July 1, 2001.[39] The White House hoped Congress would approve most-favored-nation status no later than 1974, and it calculated the annual Soviet payment due from July 1, 1974, through July 1, 2001, as $24,071,429.[40] The lend-lease agreement made no provisions regarding payment in the event that most-favored-nation status was not granted. Because the president had a Soviet commitment regarding lend-lease payment, he authorized the Export-Import Bank of the United States to begin extending credit to the USSR on October 18, 1972.[41]

On the basis of the commercial agreements, the president prepared a broad trade bill, the Trade Reform Act of 1973, that he submitted to Congress in April 1973. If Congress approved it before Brezhnev arrived in Washington in June, the Washington summit meeting would have an aura of triumphal celebration for the two chief players, in addition to congratulations for any new substantive agreements the meeting might produce. The matter of further arms limitation was still an area designated for agreement, and success in the area of trade could help offset any disappointment that might arise from inability to reach agreement on further arms limitation. Without favorable action on MFN and without an agreement on arms limitation, what could the two actors then make of the summit meeting?

Three important events that occurred between the summits threatened much of the American-Soviet constructive diplomacy that resulted in the agreements of October 1972. First was the $750 million grains deal of July 8, 1972, which, although it aided many Americans, came to be popularly regarded in the US as the major culprit that had sent food prices soaring between July 1972 and May 1973.[42] The second event was the Soviet Union's imposition, in August 1972, of the special "education tax" on Jews wishing to emigrate. The third event was the scandal related to the American presidential election of 1972 that seemed, by June of 1973, the time set for the Washington summit meeting, likely to result in removal of President Nixon from office.

Of the three events, the first to become a problem for American and Soviet diplomats was the "education tax." The details of the new tax began to filter to Americans in mid-August. The *New York Times* reported August 16, for instance, that the "general fee" of $1000 for Soviet emigrants was being replaced by a fee ranging from $5000 to $26,000.[43] The following day, presidential candidate Senator George McGovern referred to the USSR's action as holding Jews "hostages of the state."[44] The Soviets had become aware of American hostility toward the policy and discussed the issue with Kissinger during his visit of September 11 and 14.[45]

Congressional hostility escalated throughout September. On September 21, McGovern called the fee a "slave tax" in a speech to the Conference of Presidents of Major American Jewish Organizations.[46] The following day the *New York Times* reported that the existing fee was higher than originally assumed: the range was $15,000 to $37,440 rather than $5000 to $26,000 as previously reported,[47] and on that day the House of Representatives adopted an amendment prohibiting the Export-Import Bank to grant loans to any country charging more than $50 for an emigration fee.[48] Finally, on October 4, Senator Henry Jackson and seventy-one other US senators introduced an amendment to key portions of the trade bill that would remain in effect until the exit fee was abolished. The amendment would bar credits, credit guarantees, and MFN status. The action was, Jackson said, a direct result of the August "diploma tax."[49]

The Soviet government began attempting to remove congressional hostility, once the agreements of October were signed. On October 18, the day on which the trade agreement and lend-lease settlements were signed, the Soviet government suddenly permitted nineteen Moscow Jewish families to emigrate to Israel without paying an exit fee. Six of the families had been told forty-eight hours earlier that they would have to pay a total of $195,000 in fees.[50] By October 20, the Soviet government had extended the same offer to 139 Jewish families, and by October 25, to 190 families.[51] On October 23, the well-known Soviet Jewish activists R. Rutnam (who reported being imprisoned with other scientists outside Moscow for ten days during Nixon's visit to Moscow in May 1972),[52] M. Klyachkin, and G. Shapiro (who had an American wife) were given permission to emigrate.[53] The Soviet periodical *Za rubezhom* (Abroad) attacked McGovern for linking increased American-Soviet trade and the emigration fees.[54]

By April of 1973, when the Nixon administration submitted its trade bill to Congress, the administration had already added defense of the Soviet Union's emigration policy to the defense it had to make of itself for inflation from the grains agreement and for the scandals of the 1972 election. The major clause of the Trade Reform Act of 1973 that related to the Soviet Union, the president explained to Congress, provided that the president have authority to extend most-favored-nation treatment "to any country when he deemed it in the national interest to do so. . . . Any such extension to countries not now receiving most-favored-nation treatment could be vetoed by a majority vote of either the House or the Senate within a three-month period." He said the "new authority would enable us to carry out the trade agreement we have negotiated with the Soviet Union and thereby ensure that country's repayment of the lend-lease debt." Noting the "deep concern" that "many in the Congress have expressed over the tax levied on Soviet citizens wishing to emigrate," he asserted that denying MFN status was not "a proper or even an effective way of dealing with this problem."[55]

Other spokesmen for the administration's Soviet policy went further in defending Soviet actions. One example will suffice to present the general argument administration officials developed repeatedly in April and May of 1973. Addressing the Subcommittee of the House Committee on Foreign Affairs, Walter J. Stoessel, Jr., assistant secretary for European affairs, noted a substantial change in Soviet policy toward Jewish emigration since 1969. Before that year the annual average emigration of Jews from the Soviet Union had been "not more than a few hundred." The number "jumped" to 3000 in 1969; "fell" to 1000 in 1970; "went much higher—to 14,000" in 1971; "rose further" to 31,000 in 1972 ("an average monthly rate in excess of 2500 was attained"); and for 1973 "that level is holding . . . We are gratified by these developments." A "concurrence" existed, he said, between the Soviet government's having permitted "some 60,000 Jews to leave over the last four years" and "significantly improved" American-Soviet relations, "including trade," during that same four-year period. To encourage liberal emigration policies, he argued, the US should "continue in a positive vein [rather] than a punitive vein. An essential step," he added, was for Congress to approve the portion of the Trade Reform Act of 1973 to expand the president's authority to grant most-favored-nation status.[56]

Because of the scandal of the 1972 presidential election, because of the "education tax" levied on Soviet Jews, and because of the popular belief in the US that the Soviets had outsmarted US negotiators during the grain deal so that the American public was paying for its government's ineptness in dealing with the Soviets, Nixon and Brezhnev were tainted characters in American eyes on the eve of the Washington summit meeting. A meeting between the two was much less welcomed than it had been one year earlier. Furthermore, each of the two men had been forced, because of domestic events in the other's country, to give support to his counterpart for policies that were quite probably personally repugnant: Nixon's Watergate, Brezhnev's Jewish policy. But because the image of detente had its credence in close personal ties as much as in the substance of documents generated over the past two years, each of the two men had to preserve the public appearance of friendship and sympathy for the other's misfortunes in order to nurture the image.

The Washington Summit of 1973

Brezhnev arrived Saturday, June 16, at Andrews Air Force Base and went to Camp David, where he spent the remainder of the day and all of Sunday preparing with aides for the first formal day of the summit meeting (Monday, June 19). President Nixon spent Saturday and Sunday at Key Biscayne, Florida, conferring with his aides, especially Kissinger, in preparation for the meeting. Sunday afternoon Kissinger called on Brezhnev at Camp David to establish the agenda for the meeting.[57]

US officials related that the agenda would include discussion of: a joint statement containing guidelines for further negotiations to limit offensive nuclear weapons; the European Security Conference meeting scheduled for autumn 1973, to seek a formula to reduce military forces in Europe; Nixon's endorsement of some large business deals reached between US companies and Soviet agencies, as well as a full discussion of prospects for future trade and the granting of most-favored-nation status to the USSR; a review of international

conditions, especially the Middle East and Indochina; and conclusion of a series
of agreements already worked out or in their final stages of preparation.[58]

The 1973 conference was arranged to maximize contact between the two
chief participants and emphasized far less the actual signing of agreements than
the talk-sign-talk format did at the 1972 Moscow conference. During the first
day of the formal talks, Nixon and Brezhnev spent three hours and forty-five
minutes in private conference and concluded their talks with a gala dinner at
the White House that lasted all evening and past midnight. Early in the evening,
the two announced that they had authorized their ministers and secretaries to
sign three agreements, previously completed by experts, the following morning
(Tuesday) at 10:30. These were agreements on cooperation in oceanographic
research, cooperation in transportion, and cultural exchanges. A fourth agreement—on cooperation in agriculture—might also be ready for signature by
morning. At the end of the dinner, near midnight, press secretary Ronald
Ziegler announced that the agricultural agreement was ready for signature the
next day. Nixon postponed the following day's session by one hour so the
participants could recover from the night's activities.[59]

Tuesday morning at 10:30 the four agreements were signed at the State
Department. Nixon and Brezhnev were on hand to toast the occasion. The
agreement on oceanographic research was an effort to implement two of the
agreements reached, in principle, during the Moscow summit of 1972: the
Agreement on Cooperation in the Fields of Science and Technology (May 24,
1972), and the Agreement on Cooperation in the Field of Environmental
Protection (May 23, 1972). The agreement also further expanded the Agreement on Exchanges and Cooperation in Scientific, Technical, Educational
Cultural and Other Fields of April 11, 1972. It established a number of specific
research areas that would be the initial focus of joint American-Soviet attention: studies of large-scale ocean-atmosphere interaction; ocean currents of
planetary scale; geochemistry and marine chemistry; geological and geophysical
investigation; biological productivity; and intercalibration and standardization
of oceanographic instrumentation and methods. The agreement included a
listing of the usual forms of cooperation: joint planning, exchanges of personnel and information, joint conferences, etc. To implement the agreement, a
US-USSR Joint Committee on Cooperation in World Ocean Studies was
created, to meet once a year, alternately in the US and the USSR. It was to be
in force for five years, but its termination would not necessarily terminate
joint projects.[60]

The agreement on transportation, also for five years, provided for cooperation in researching problems related to construction of bridges and tunnels,
especially in cold climates; railway transportation and construction, especially
in cold climates; civil aviation; maritime transport; and automobile transportation. Possible forms of cooperation were the same as those for implementing
the oceanographic agreement.[61]

The agreement on cultural relations listed all the agreements of 1972 and 1973, including those signed that day (June 19), and reaffirmed both parties' commitment to implement them in practical form. It reiterated the details of the current agreement for exchange of students and scholars, and added to the general list of cultural items that might be exchanged documentary films on science, textbooks, course syllabi, radio and TV programs, and traveling exhibitions.[62]

The Agreement on Cooperation in Agriculture was also an expansion of the 1972 agreements on environmental protection, science and technology, and exchanges. Areas for specific immediate cooperation in agriculture were exchanges of information on such topics as: estimates on production, consumption, demand, and trade of major agricultural commodities; methods of forecasting production, especially the use of econometric methods; plant science; livestock and poultry science; soil science; mechanization of agriculture; use of mineral fertilizers; processing, storage, and preservation of agricultural commodities; land reclamation and reclamation engineering, and uses of equipment, designs and material for that purpose; and the use of mathematical methods and electronic computers in agriculture, including mathematical modeling of large-scale agricultural enterprises. Implementation called for the usual exchange of personnel and information and specifically added exchanges of plant germ plasm, seeds, living material, animals, chemicals; models of new machines, equipment, and scientific instruments; and exchange of agricultural exhibitions. A Joint Committee on Agricultural Cooperation would be created and would meet annually, alternately in US and USSR, to serve as the implementing agency. Subsections of the joint committee were to be a Joint Working Group on Agricultural Economic Research and Information and a Joint Working Group on Agricultural Research and Technological Developments. Each of these two groups was to meet twice per year alternately in the two countries. The joint committee was free to set up other working groups. No project undertaken already on the basis of the agreement of March 21, 1973 (US-USSR Joint Commission on Scientific and Technological Cooperation) was to be interrupted, but administration of projects in progress would be added to the responsibility of the new joint committee when the latter became operative.[63]

Once the ceremony surrounding signing of the agreements was concluded, Brezhnev left the State Department building to attend a four-hour luncheon with the Senate Foreign Relations Committee in Blair House, Brezhnev's residence during the summit meeting. There, while lobbying for congressional approval of most-favored-nation status for the USSR, Brezhnev confronted, for the first time in his political career, the problems a government executive has dealing with the legislative branch in a republican form of government. He delivered a two-hour address, then answered questions about the Jewish policy of the Soviet government. In response to a question from Senator Hubert Humphrey, he cited the same figures Nixon and State Department spokesmen

had been using in April and May, to assure Humphrey that 60,000 applications
had been approved within the past four years for Jews wishing to emigrate from
the USSR.[64] In the end, he proved no more successful than other executives
as promoters of self-interested legislation.

Abandoning the less comfortable world of lobbying with the legislative
branch, Brezhnev moved from the Blair House luncheon to the White House for
a two-hour conference with Nixon (who was joined by Treasury Secretary
Shultz, Secretary of State Rogers, and John Connally). Brezhnev was assisted
by Patolichev and Gromyko. After the session Nixon took Brezhnev for a
cruise aboard the presidential yacht on the Potomac River, and the two flew to
Camp David for the night.[65]

Wednesday, June 20, Nixon and Brezhnev conferred privately for fifteen
minutes at approximately one o'clock and, accompanied by aides, talked until
3:15 p.m. about strategic arms limitation. During those talks the two reached
agreement on a declaration of principles that would spur final agreement on a
permanent limitation of nuclear offensive weapons. The formal signing of the
final draft of the accord would transpire on the following day, Thursday,
June 21.[66] While Nixon and Brezhnev talked, Treasury Secretary George Shultz
and Foreign Trade Minister Nikolai S. Patolichev signed the Convention on
Matters of Taxation, which aimed at preventing double taxation for firms and
citizens of one country operating on the territory of the other. This accord
was another in the long string of ground-clearing acts preparing for an orderly
state of extensive commerce between the two countries. Following the signing
of the agreement on taxation, Shultz and Patolichev continued what they
called "intensive discussions on economic and trade issues."[67]

On Thursday, June 21, Nixon and Brezhnev met at Camp David from 11:30
to 12:30, took a break, and resumed the talks from 1:20 until approximately
3:20, when they returned to Washington, where in the East Room of the White
House at 3:30 they signed two agreements: Basic Principles of Negotiations on
the Further Limitation of Strategic Offensive Arms, and the Agreement on
Scientific Cooperation in Peaceful Uses of Atomic Energy. The agreement on
principles for further limitation of strategic offensive arms was to serve as a
set of guidelines for continuation of the recessed SALT II negotiations in
Geneva. (The second round of SALT had begun in November 1972, with
Ambassador U. Alexis Johnson as the US representative at the talks.) Whereas
round one of SALT had produced an agreement limiting defensive weapons,
round two had as its objective a permanent agreement limiting strategic offensive weapons that would replace the interim agreement signed in May 1972
during the Moscow summit and that went into effect in October 1972, to run
for five years.[68]

The "essence" of the interim agreement was, as Kissinger explained at a
news conference before the 3:30 signing, that both sides "froze their offensive
weapons at the levels they had achieved last May" and at the levels that were

predictable over the five-year period the interim agreement was to cover. The major problem in negotiating a permanent agreement was dealing not only with the quantity of arms, but also the quality of arms, for which no mathematical formula could be used, and in addition, the reduction of arms was to be as much an integral part of the permanent agreement as limiting arms. By April 1973, SALT II was still so far from producing a permanent agreement that both sides realized that more time would be needed than remained before the June summit meeting. Therefore, Nixon and Brezhnev decided to try, through correspondence, to establish some general principles upon which agreement might be possible and to enter into full discussions of those principles during the Washington summit. Agreement on those principles during the summit might then facilitate completing the permanent agreement before the end of 1974. The agreement on principles was achieved, then, during the Washington discussions.[69]

The agreement affirms both sides' determination to continue negotiations over the next year, with the objective of signing the permanent agreement in 1974. The second principle is that both sides promise not to attempt to achieve unilateral advantages through the permanent agreement. The third principle is that a permanent agreement will attempt to place limitations not only on the quantitative aspects, but also on the qualitative improvement of strategic offensive weapons.

The fourth principle is that monitoring by national technical means must be included, and the fifth is that modernization and replacement of strategic offensive arms will be permitted under conditions that will be formulated in the final agreement. The problem for the permanent agreement is how to modernize and replace weapons within the guidelines of limiting qualitative changes of weapons systems.

The sixth principle is that both sides are prepared to reach agreements on separate measures to supplement the existing interim agreement of May 26, 1972, assuming completion of a permanent agreement. That is, Kissinger explained, both sides are willing to conclude separate supplementary agreements shorter in duration than the interim agreement and that would regulate the situation until 1974, when the permanent agreement will be signed, and these separate agreements will be included in the permanent settlement.

The seventh principle is that both sides will continue to take "organizational and technical measures" for preventing accidental war. Kissinger summed up the statement of principles as formally committing the two countries to the urgency of completing a permanent agreement and setting a deadline of 1974 for completing that agreement; it included reduction and not simply limitation of arms as an objective; and "limitation" referred not merely to numbers of weapons, but also sought to limit their qualitative improvement, a dimension not a part of the SALT negotiations.[70]

The Agreement on Scientific Cooperation in Peaceful Uses of Atomic

Energy, the second agreement signed at 3:30 in the White House, defined three areas in which the two countries would engage in joint cooperative research: controlled thermonuclear fusion, fast-breeder reactors, and research on the fundamental properties of matter. To manage these ventures, the two sides proposed establishing working groups of scientists and engineers to design and execute the joint projects; joint development and construction of experiments, pilot installations and equipment; exchanges of personnel, data, and equipment; and joint seminars, panels, conferences. A Joint Committee on Cooperation in the Peaceful Uses of Atomic Energy was to be created, to meet once per year in the two countries, alternately. It was to be in effect for ten years.[71]

At the Soviet Embassy on this evening of June 21, Brezhnev, (assuring his audience, "The Soviet Union's line at improving relations with the United States is not some temporary phenomenon. It is a firm and consistent line reflecting the permanent principles of Soviet foreign policy formulated by the great founder of the Soviet state, V.I. Lenin") invited Nixon to visit the Soviet Union in 1974. Nixon accepted the invitation.[72]

On Friday, June 22, Nixon and Brezhnev signed the Agreement on Prevention of Nuclear War, and Secretary of the Treasury Shultz and Soviet Minister of Foreign Trade N.S. Patolichev signed the Protocol on US-USSR. Chamber of Commerce and the Protocol on Commercial Facilities. The accord on preventing nuclear war was, in effect, a treaty of nonaggression, each side promising to "refrain from the threat or use of force against the other," and against "the allies" of the other, and even against "other countries, in circumstances which may endanger international peace and security." At any time when a "risk of nuclear war" between the two countries seems to exist, the two "shall immediately enter into urgent consultations with each other and make every effort to avert this risk." The agreement was for a period of "unlimited duration."[73]

The Protocol on the Chamber of Commerce had as its objective creating "in the United States private sector" and in the USSR a Soviet-American chamber of commerce. If sufficient desire were found to exist, the US-USSR Joint Commercial Commission would be notified and, apparently, take steps to create the chamber of commerce.[74] The Protocol on Commercial Facilities included the promise that each side would open a separate office on the territory of the other no later than October 31, 1973, to promote trade. It also noted steps taken by both sides to provide separate, enlarged quarters for the commercial officer of the respective embassies, and the Soviets listed ten US companies that the Soviets had accredited to establish representatives in Moscow.[75]

Saturday, June 23, US and Soviet aides signed a Protocol on Expansion of Air Services that allowed the American "designated airline" (currently PanAmerican) to add to its New York-to-Moscow service flights from New York to Leningrad, and for the Soviet designated airline to add to its

Moscow-to-New York service flights from Moscow to Washington. The agreement also allowed for more frequent flights between New York and Moscow. On June 23, Brezhnev taped his radio and television address at San Clemente, and it was played the following day.[76]

Sunday, June 24, Brezhnev and Nixon signed a joint communiqué that was released simultaneously the following day in Moscow, Washington, and San Clemente.

The joint communiqué contained little new information and merely summed up what had already been written into agreements. It did shed light on the two leaders' concept of the scope of future trade. It listed the objective of "2-3 billion dollars of trade over the next three years."[77] Kissinger explained in a news conference at San Clemente on June 25 that the figure referred to the total amount of trade that would occur between 1973 and 1975, excluding agricultural commodities. The US-USSR trade in 1973 was about $1.3 billion, including agricultural commodities, and approximately $600 million without agricultural commodities. Thus, the $2-3 billion figure would represent an increase of some 50 percent.[78]

The Washington summit meeting, while it produced a larger number of agreements than the 1972 Moscow meeting, achieved less substantively. All the agreements but three promised to exchange larger numbers of personnel, materials and data, and several were merely slight revisions of existing agreements, e.g., air flights and cultural exchanges. The two heads of state could not move trade relations any farther, except by lobbying with congressmen, for granting MFN rested with Congress, and settlement of lend-lease awaited the outcome of the MFN question in Congress. They also could not achieve the permanent agreement on limiting strategic offensive weapons they had anticipated at the end of the Moscow summit, and they had to settle for an agreement on principles. Only the agreement to prevent nuclear war was a substantive issue beyond scientific and cultural exchanges. The promise that both sides made to help reduce the risk of nuclear war was severely compromised by the Middle East War of October 1973.

The very success of the 1972 Moscow summit made equal success at the Washington summit less likely. The easier areas for agreement had been used up, and one year between the two meetings was inadequate to erode away the walls of suspicion sufficiently to create room for a new agreement.

The Washington summit was also less successful in form. No orchestration resembling the talk-sign-talk progression of Moscow existed. A very large portion of the contact between Nixon and Brezhnev occurred in the seclusion of Camp David rather than in front of the media in Washington. During the Moscow talks only the Wednesday evening session aboard a yacht and in a dacha outside Moscow resembled the seclusion of the Camp David portion of the Washington summit.

In both summit meetings Nixon and Brezhnev used every public opportunity

to create and groom an image of personal detente. They then sought to use
that personal detente to increase detente between the two nations they represented. Personal detente has progressed much more rapidly than national
detente, however, and served as a substitute for it in October 1973 during the
Middle East War. As long as the American and Soviet heads of state can communicate personally by letter or electronic means, and as long as the annual
meeting occurs with all its ceremonies, personal detente will exist. Between
such annual meetings, both sides can battle vicariously through their allies in
the Middle East, the Soviets can punish dissident intellectuals and Jews, and
the US can deny the USSR most-favored-nation status.

Certainly personal contact is better than none at all among heads of important, powerful countries, unless the contact creates an image of detente that
obscures hostilities that remain unchanged. The image of detente might possibly
create a broader margin of trust between the walls of hostility and thereby the
image might help produce substance, but we should never allow ourselves to
consider the image and the object to be totally identical. Detente is a status
in the relationship between governments that can be documented in agreements
and treaties and in the practices employed by both sides throughout the year;
it is more than an annual, week-long exercise in good manners between two
persons, regardless of their positions in the nations they represent.

Notes

1. For a summary of the summit conferences through 1960, see Keith Eubank,
   The Summit Conferences, 1919-1960 (Norman, Oklahoma: University of
   Oklahoma Press, 1966). Elmer Plischke, *Summit Diplomacy: The Personal
   Diplomacy of the President of the United States* (College Park, Md.: Univer-
   sity of Maryland Press, 1958) analyzes the advantages and disadvantages of
   utilizing the summit meeting as a form of diplomacy. See David Wise and
   Thomas B. Ross, *The U-2 Affair* (New York: Random House, 1962) for a
   record of events surrounding the Paris Summit Meeting of 1960. See also
   New York Times, 19 June 1973, p. 14.

2. President Nixon referred to American-Soviet relations in his State of the
   Union Message, January 22, 1970, as follows: "I would not underestimate
   our differences, but we are moving with precision and purpose from an era
   of confrontation to an era of negotiation" (Department of State *Bulletin*,
   February 9, 1970, p. 146). On February 18, however, he made clear the
   necessity that political issues would have to be resolved before trade could
   improve when he wrote, in his message to Congress on foreign relations,
   "We look forward to the time when our relations with the Communist
   countries will have improved to the point where trade relations can increase
   between us" (Ibid., March 9, 1970, p. 312).

3. A representative of the Institute of the U.S.A. of the Moscow Academy of Sciences made this point to an assembly of businessmen in St. Louis in March. Representatives made the same point on April 30 at the National Convocation on the Challenge of Building Peace, a public discussion between American and Soviet public figures sponsored by the Fund for Peace in New York City. New York *Times,* April 30, 1970, p. 37. And, of course the Soviet government offered Henry Ford the deal to build a plant for producing trucks in the USSR at the end of April 1970.

4. Several periodicals recorded these deals. See, for example, *U.S. News and World Report,* January 10, 1972, p. 70.

5. See Antony Sutton, *Western Technology and Soviet Economic Development, 1917 to 1930* (Stanford: Hoover Institution Publications, 1968) for an analysis of the failures of several American firms working Soviet concessions in the 1920s.

6. Severe winter weather in 1971-72 killed a significant part of the winter wheat crop, and an unusually hot dry summer in 1972 took a heavy toll on the spring wheat crop (*New York Times,* 23 April, 1972, p. 3; 7 September, 1972, p. 13). As early as September 1972, the Soviet government was revising priorities and devoted some $1.5 to 2 billion for grain purchases and distribution (Ibid., 7 September, 1972, p. 13 and 21 October, 1972, p. 13).

7. The president assumed after Haiphong that the summit meeting had no better than "a 50-50 chance" of being held, despite the presummit accomplishments (*Newsweek,* 29 May 1972, p. 35).

8. Department of State *Bulletin,* 26 June 1972, p. 865.

9. Ibid., 12 June 1972, p. 803.

10. UPI report from Moscow, Columbia *Missourian,* 24 May 1972, p. 1.

11. *New York Times,* 25 May 1972, p. 1. Hedrick Smith was one of the rare journalists covering the summit meeting to appreciate the significance of the talk-sign-talk orchestration of the talks. See his article, "The Split Level at the Summit Conference," in ibid., p. 4.

12. *New York Times*, 24 May, 1972, has a photograph of the representatives in this session. An informal two-hour session was held between Brezhnev and Nixon Monday afternoon shortly after Nixon settled into his Kremlin quarters. (Ibid., 23 May, 1972).

13. The text of the agreement is in the Department of State *Bulletin,* 26 June, 1972, pp. 921-22.

14. Ibid., pp. 923-24.

15. *New York Times,* 25 May, 1972, p. 1.

16. Ibid.

17. Ibid.

18. Ibid.

19. Text of the agreement is in the Department of State *Bulletin,* 26 June, 1972,

pp. 924-25. See also *Space World,* Vol. I, No. 11 (November), 1972, pp. 4-15, for data on the venture, and especially pp. 11-12 for a chronology of events and agreements from October 1969 to July 1972 between the U.S. and USSR regarding cooperation in space exploration.

20. Ibid., pp. 925-26.
21. See Kissinger's comments at the Kiev news conference, May 29 (ibid., p. 892).
22. *New York Times,* 26 May, 1972, p. 1.
23. Kissinger maintained at a news conference in Moscow on May 29 and later in Kiev on the same day that no agreement on matters of substance related to trade was expected. He said the negativism in the press about a deadlock in the trade negotiations was unjustified. The objective of the trade talks was to create a commercial commission, he said (Department of State *Bulletin,* 26 June, 1972, pp. 884 and 890). Yet the scenario called for "an agreement" related to trade to be signed Thursday, and President Nixon had said on May 19, before departure from Washington, "I met with congressional leaders discussing such matters as most favored nation and others, the matter of credits. I would say that the chances for some positive results are good—not certain, but certainly good. You will be wanting to follow that very closely during the course of our visit there" (ibid., p. 804).
24. Ibid., pp. 926-27.
25. *New York Times,* 29 May, 1972, p. 1.
26. Ibid. Text in Department of State *Bulletin,* 26 June, 1972, p. 898.
27. *New York Times,* 29 May, 1972, p. 1.
28. Ibid.
29. The text of the agreement is in Department of State *Bulletin,* 26 June, 1972, pp. 918-20.
30. Ibid., (Article XII), p. 919.
31. The five-year period for which the treaty was to be in force was qualified by the expression "unless replaced earlier by an agreement on more complete measures." Both sides pledged themselves to concluding "such an agreement as soon as possible" (p. 921). Their objective was to have the permanent agreement ready for signature by the June 1973 summit set for Washington. Kissinger indicated this objective in his news conference June 21, 1973 (Department of State *Bulletin*, 23 July, 1973, p. 135).
32. Text of the interim agreement is in Department of State *Bulletin*, 26 June, 1972, pp. 920-21.
33. Coverage of the meeting during the week by the *New York Times* is illustrative of the alternating optimism and pessimism that appeared in the press.

    According to one researcher, major problems remained unsolved when Nixon arrived in Moscow. Nixon and Brezhnev discussed SALT for approximately five hours Tuesday afternoon and evening (May 23), and the final treaty was worked out by Soviet and American negotiating teams in Moscow and Helsinki during the week. The details and wording were completed only minutes before the scheduled signing of 11 p.m. in Moscow. But the document, still under revision on the plane from Helsinki to Moscow, contained so many errors that it was retyped Saturday morning, and Brezhnev and Nixon held a second and private signing that morning of the corrected documents. For a highly interesting, but undocumented, account of the activities related to SALT from May 23 to May 26, 1972, see John Newhouse, *Cold Dawn: the Story of SALT* (Holt, Rinehart and Winston, New York, 1973), pp. 249-260.

34. See Peterson's press conference of August 1 in Moscow. Department of State *Bulletin* 11 September, 1972, p. 288.

35. Ibid., p. 286.

36. See Kissinger's news conference of September 16, 1972, in Department of State *Bulletin,* 9 October, 1972, pp. 389-91.

37. The text of the grains agreement of July 8, 1972 is in *United States Treaties and Other International Agreements,* vol. 23, document #7423. (Hereinafter *U.S. Treaties*). The text of the maritime agreement is in ibid., document #7513.

38. The text of the trade agreement is in Department of State *Bulletin,* 20 November, 1972, pp. 595-99.

39. Ibid., pp. 603-4. (The $722 million included $45 million unpaid portion of the "pipeline account" for goods shipped to the USSR immediately after World War II (White House Fact Sheet, p. 594 of ibid).

40. Ibid., p. 594.

41. Ibid., p. 604.

42. An AP story, datelined Washington and carried in the Columbia (Mo.) *Daily Tribune,* October 8, 1973, p. 10, illustrates the problem. Entitled "Russian grain sale helped inflate food prices," the article compares prices of selected consumer items in May of 1972 and May of 1973; it discusses the shortages of railroad cars the shipment of grain from the Midwest to port cities caused; and it blames the shortage of railroad cars for creating higher freight rates and for producing a shortage of fertilizer when it was needed for spring use.

43. *New York Times,* 16 August, 1972, p. 1.

44. Ibid., 17 August, p. 8.

45. Department of State *Bulletin,* 9 October, 1972, pp. 395, 397-98.

46. *New York Times,* 22 September, 1972, p. 1.

47. Ibid., 22 September, 1972, p. 3.

48. Ibid., p. 17. The Senate Appropriations Committee later deleted the amendment, for, among other reasons, Israel charged an exit fee of more than $50 (Ibid., 28 September, 1972, p. 50).

49. Ibid., 5 October, 1972, p. 1.

50. Ibid., 19 October, 1972, p. 1.

51. Ibid., 22 October, 1972, p. 11; October 25, 1972, p. 3.

52. Ibid., 19 October, 1972, p. 1.

53. Ibid., 24 October 1972, p. 13.

54. Ibid.

55. Department of State *Bulletin,* 30 April, 1973, pp. 518-19.

56. Ibid., 11 June, 1973, pp. 861-62. Secretary of State Rogers's statements to the House Committee on Ways and Means on May 9, 1973, which included the same figures and made the same argument, is in ibid. pp. 837-38.

57. *New York Times,* 18 June, 1973, p. 1. Several thousand demonstrators gathered at the Capital steps to oppose Soviet policies on Jewish emigration. Senator Jackson addressed the group and called upon Nixon to press Brezhnev for a more liberal emigration policy. The group marched to Ellipse Park, near the White House. The entire block on which the Soviet Embassy is located was cordoned off.

58. Ibid.

59. *New York Times,* 19 June, 1973, p. 1. Early Monday morning the Senate Watergate Committee announced suspension of its hearings for the week in order not to detract from the summit negotiations.

60. Text of the agreement is in *U.S. Treaties,* vol. 24, document #7651.

61. Ibid., document #7652.

62. Ibid., document #7649.

63. Ibid., document #7650.

64. *New York Times,* 20 June, 1973, p. 1.

65. Ibid.

66. *New York Times,* 21 June, 1973, p. 7.

67. Ibid.

68. Department of State *Bulletin,* 23 July, 1973, pp. 134-35.

69. Ibid., p. 135. The Moscow summit meeting in 1974 also failed to produce the permanent agreement. It issued, instead, another set of "principles."

70. Ibid. Text is also in *U.S. Treaties,* vol. 24, document #7653.

71. *U.S. Treaties,* vol. 24, document #7655.

72. Department of State *Bulletin,* 23 July, 1973. pp. 118, 120.

73. *U.S. Treaties,* vol. 24, document #7654.

74. Ibid., document #7656.

75. Department of State *Bulletin,* 23 July, 1973. pp. 173-74.

76. Ibid., pp. 174-75. Also in *U.S. Treaties,* vol. 24, document #7658.

77. Department of State *Bulletin,* 23 July, 1973, p. 132.

78. Ibid., p. 151.

Part III

Some Elements of Philosophy, Ideology, and Theology

4

The Papal-Communist Detente, 1963-73:
Its Evolution and Causes
Dennis Dunn

The Past

Over the past ten years, the Catholic church and the Communist states have been steadily ameliorating their relations. Such a reformation comes as a shock to many observers, since the church and the world's various Communist governments, with the exception of Castro's Cuba, have been the bitterest of foes.

In the past, the Catholic church has been one of the bulwarks of anticommunism. It was generally, although not implacably, opposed to the Soviet government, which assumed power in 1917. The church's hostility followed from the Communists' atheistic philosophy and the fear that malevolence would follow their coup. The church, however, could have accepted the Bolsheviks if they had practiced religious toleration. Lenin's government, however, was of no mind to endure the "sycophants of religion" and, following the civil war, it launched a brutal policy of persecution that decimated the organizational structure of the Roman Catholic church in the Soviet Union. Stalin continued to pillory Catholicism, leaving, by the time of the Nazi attack, a few scattered churches and an apostolic administrator in Moscow who was tolerated because he was serving, simultaneously, as chaplain to the American Embassy.[1]

Soviet persecution of Catholicism swelled the Vatican's opposition to communism. In 1937, Pope Pius XI issued a resounding condemnation of Marxism-Leninism in his famous encyclical, *Divini Redemptoris*.[2] The papacy also felt compelled to support, although indirectly and with reluctance, anti-Communist forces, including fascism.[3]

Once the Soviet Union was invaded by Germany, Stalin's antireligious stance underwent a change. The transformation, like the original policy of persecution, was yoked to power politics. Before World War II, Communist Russia had battered religion because it believed, out of Marxist convictions, that the extirpation of religion would enhance its rather tenuous hold on the State. The Nazi invasion, however, like an electric shock, jolted Stalin into the reality that many an earlier politician had learned; organized religion could be a buttress of power. Stalin, accordingly, quickly revived Orthodoxy and, for the remainder of the war, tendered feint conciliations to the Vatican, although these gestures were compromised by a number of factors, chief of which was that the wedding with Orthodoxy kept the Soviet government on an anti-Catholic course because of Orthodoxy's animosity toward Catholicism and its desire to assimilate the Ukrainian Catholic Uniate church.[4]

121

As could be anticipated, given Stalin's dissimulation, the Vatican did not warm to the Soviet government. Instead, the papcy, throughout the course of the war, adopted an anti-Soviet stand and became increasingly apprehensive as it became obvious that the Axis powers were going to be defeated and that the Western powers, particularly the United States, were oblivious to the danger of Communist expansion into Catholic East Europe.[5]

In the immediate postwar period, Stalin, in the hope of obtaining Catholic backing to facilitate Soviet hegemony in East Europe, sponsored a general, nonpersecutory policy toward the Catholic Church.[6] His action, however, was rendered barren, as far as the papacy was concerned, by his predilection for totalitarianism, by isolated attacks upon the church, notably in Slovakia, by Tito's truculence against religion, and, most aggravating, by Orthodoxy's coercive absorption in 1946 of the Ukrainian Uniate church.[7] Naturally, the Vatican did not respond positively to Stalin's position in Eastern Europe but, on the contrary, rallied behind and strengthened the West's burgeoning anti-communism. The papacy also denounced the suppression of the Uniate church and worked diligently to defeat the Italian Communist party in the national election of 1948.[8]

By the spring of 1948, Stalin, moved by his fears of an American scheme, as reflected in the Marshall Plan, to "roll back" Soviet domination of Eastern Europe, by the Vatican's unresponsiveness, indeed, by its explicit anticommunism, and by his apprehension of Titoism spreading to the other satellites, implemented a ruthless policy to integrate the Eastern European countries into his totalitarian system.[9] His program included a violent, systematic campaign to end the independence of the Catholic church in Eastern Europe, to subordinate the church to the surrogate governments, and, finally, to sever all ties between the papacy and Catholics in Soviet-controlled territories.[10] The Vatican reacted to the onslaught by, first, maintaining its anti-Communist positions, including support for the evolution of NATO, and, second, by issuing, in July 1949, a decree, *Responsa ad dubia de Communismo,* which prohibited Catholics from belonging to and backing Communist parties.[11] That document froze Catholic-Communist relations into a state of mutual hostility. When Communist China emerged at the end of 1949, it also fell into the already polarized pattern.

The early 1950s witnessed the high-water mark of the Communist world's onslaught against the Catholic Church. With Stalinism climaxing in 1953 and 1954, the church was buffeted with the arrest of clergy and the organization of regime-backed splinter churches. In 1956, as the policies of de-Stalinization and peaceful coexistence took root, some placation took place. Cardinal Stefan Wyszynski, for example, the primate of Poland, who had been imprisoned in 1953, was freed. However, the improvement, as far as organized religion in general was concerned, was only transient, and by the end of the 1950s, Khrushchev, fearing that peaceful coexistence might undermine the party's internal control, launched a campaign to keep the ideological fires of

Marxism-Leninism burning. An essential element in that foray was a renewed attack upon religion.[12] The Soviet government was well aware of what Stalin had learned, that religion could be a boon to those in power, but that reality had to be balanced with the ideological exegencies of a government based upon atheism. The revived antireligious plan, however, did not stretch to include, except in propaganda, the Roman Catholic church in the satellites. Such a strategy indicated that Khrushchev, like Stalin, probably, would have been amenable to some understanding with the Vatican, particularly in an atmosphere where the Soviet Union was interested in preventing nuclear war and in garnering public support for its puppet regimes in Eastern Europe.

Pius XII was not moved, but in late 1958 he died and was replaced by Pope John XXIII. Pope John initiated, with the Vatican Council and his encyclical *Pacem in Terris,* a dramatic change in the Catholic church's attitude toward the Communist world. In 1962, spurred by Khrushchev's continuing policy of peaceful coexistence, by the Russian leader's "show of statesmanship" in the Cuban missile crisis, and, conceivably, by the Soviet bloc's intermittent, as opposed to consistent, intolerance of the Catholic Church, Pope John made the first offer to thaw Communist-Catholic relations. Late in the year, using Norman Cousins, the former editor of *The Saturday Review* as an intermediary, the pope asked Khrushchev if he would like to reach a reconciliation and, if so, if he would, as a sign of his intentions, release from prison Archbishop Joseph Slipyi, the head of the Ukrainian Uniate church.[13] The Vatican knew that the key to a general accord with the Communist world was an assuagement of relations with the Kremlin. In early 1963, Khrushchev vouchsafed Pope John's request and thereby launched a slow but steady detente in Communist-Catholic relations. In March 1963, Khrushchev sent his daughter and son-in-law, Aleksei I. Adzhubei, then editor of *Izvestia,* to meet Pope John and extend the dialogue.[14]

The death of Pope John in June 1963 did not alter the new course. In fact, his successor, Pope Paul VI, became an ardent advocate of *Ostpolitik* and, especially since 1970, the Vatican and the Eastern European Communist countries have established a precarious modus vivendi. Within the past few years, China also, because of the Sino-Soviet conflict, has involved itself in a peripheral way with the Vatican. It must be pointed out, of course, that the adjustment met with considerable internal opposition both within the church and the Communist bloc. The new pope met his resistance head on by initiating a major shakeup of the Vatican's chief administrative body, the Curia. Khrushchev, and later Brezhnev, found it more convenient and desirable to ignore criticism from such opponents as Albania and to stymie domestic objections by allowing a genuine mollification toward the Catholic church in the satellites but not in the USSR itself.[15] What follows is a brief country-by-country survey of the papal-Communist accommodation, from 1963 to 1973, and then an explanation of the causes of this dentente.

Detente, 1963-74

The estrangement between the Catholic church and the Communist world involved a variety of issues, but the most basic problem was the staunch unwillingness of the Communist regimes to tolerate in their midst an independent, foreign-controlled religious institution. Another important cause of alienation, was the lack of dialogue between the church and the various governments. Other general problems were such governmental machinations as blocking or hindering interminably the construction of new churches (especially in the new housing complexes); unreasonably taxing church property and personnel; limiting religious services and celebrations; restricting vocations and seminaries; prohibiting, in most cases, the organization of a hierarchy; organizing fifth columns; precluding religious publications; supporting measures in favor of atheistic education and against religious education; disallowing church organizations; discriminating against believers in jobs and schooling; and, finally, interfering in internal church matters, including personnel selections and papal communications.[16]

The indictment seems to be onesided—and indeed it is. The church, to be sure, adopted anti-Communist postures, but its position was, *a posteriori,* the result of the Communists' attitude.

USSR

The interaction between Pope John XXIII and Khrushchev did not result in any significant mollification of the Soviet government's attitude toward Ukrainian or Baltic Catholics. The Uniate church remains suppressed, and some 3.2 million Roman Catholics, living mainly in Lithuania, are languishing.[17] There is no chance whatsoever that the Soviet Union will again legitimize the Ukrainian Uniate church, and the Vatican seems to have reconciled itself to that noisome reality.[18] The inspiration of the papacy, in driving towards concord with the USSR, is that it will be able someday to administer freely to the Baltic Catholics. In that regard, the church, as will be shortly seen, has some slight cause for optimism.

The real and immediate significance of the contact between the pope and Khrushchev was that it established a dialogue between the Vatican and the Soviet Union, and most important, it opened the door for the regularization of relations between the church and the Eastern European Communist states. The interlocution continued in 1965 when Pope Paul met Soviet Foreign Minister Andrei Gromyko at the United Nations and in April 1966, welcomed him at the Vatican. In January 1967, the colloquy advanced as the pope received Nicholai Podgorny, the Russian head of state. *Pravda* reported the visit on the front page.[19]

Until 1970 further public associations were eschewed, although the *New York Times* intimated that confidential discussions were proceeding.[20] In 1970 two visitors, Vasken I, the Supreme Catholicos of the Soviet Armenian Church, and Andrei Gromyko called at the Vatican. In 1971 the traffic began to flow in the other direction, as Archbishop Agostino Casaroli, the secretary of the Council for Public Relations of the Church, Father Pedro Arrupe, the general of the Jesuit Order, and a high-level Vatican delegation, sent to attend the election of Metropolitan Pimen as patriarch of the Russian Orthodox Church, arrived separately in Moscow. The years 1972 and 1973 witnessed a growing communication. In February 1972 a delegation of Russian Orthodox church officials visited Rome, and in May 1973 a group of Vatican ecumenists returned the courtesy and, while in Moscow, signed a joint statement with their Orthodox counterparts acknowledging that "there is a strong tendency toward some sort of socialism in many parts of the world."[21]

In general, the on going dialogue revolved around the status of Roman Catholics in the USSR, the strengthening of ties between the Russian Orthodox church and the Vatican (especially in the realm of library and theological student exchanges), and, finally, means by which the papacy and the Soviet government could cooperate on mutual international goals, primarily the maintenance of peace and world security.[22] The fruit of the discussions, up to this point, has indeed been meager, but it includes the Vatican's agreement to the Soviet-American-sponsored nuclear test ban treaty, the papacy's participation in the Soviet-sponsored European Security Conference, a diminution in the USSR's anti-Vatican propaganda, unilateral declarations for peace (especially in Vietnam and the Middle East), and the consecration, in November 1972, of one bishop, the Most Reverend Valerian Zoudaks, who is serving in Latvia.[23] The last-mentioned development has been the only concession the Soviets have made to the church in the USSR, although since the self-immolation of a young student in May 1972, in protest against Russian suffocation of Lithuanian nationalism, the onslaught against Baltic Catholicism has slowed.[24]

Poland

In Poland, where the Catholic church represents more than 90 percent of the population and where the cardinal primate has been called "the second most powerful man," the process of adjustment over the past decade has gone by fits and starts. In addition to the general problems associated with church-state relations in a Communist country, disharmony in Poland stemmed from the unwillingness of the Vatican to name permanent Polish bishops to the northern and western territories, which Poland annexed from Germany following World War II, and from the overwhelming influence of the church. Nonetheless, with the Russians' actions and Vatican Council II providing openings, the process of detente crept along. In April 1963, Franz Cardinal Koenig, who heads the Vatican's Secretariat for Non-Believers and is one of the church's experts on Communist affairs, arrived in Warsaw and initiated negotiations. His visit precipitated a meeting, the first in two years, between Cardinal Wyszynski and the

Communist party head, Wladyslaw Gomulka. The potential inherent in these events remained, in 1964, untapped and then, in December 1965, gave way to renewed tensions in the aftermath of the Polish episcopate's conciliatory letter to the German bishops. The Polish epistle extended and begged "forgiveness" for mutual past transgressions between the German and Polish peoples, and although it became an important factor in the evolvement of Willy Brandt's *Ostpolitik,* the letter's pacificatory language and incursion into the sensitive Oder-Neisse question enraged the Polish government.[25] In retaliation, the regime downplayed the 1966 Christian millenium celebration, balked at giving the pope a visa to attend the festivities, and prohibited Cardinal Wyszynski from traveling outside the country for two years.[26] Bitter recriminations colored church-state relations for the remainder of Gomulka's reign.[27]

The freeze thawed dramatically again in December 1970, in the wake of the Baltic Coast workers' riots. Edward Gierek, like Gomulka before him, appealed to the church for support, but, unlike Gomulka, made some significant concessions.[28] In January, the government announced that it was setting in motion the machinery to grant the Catholic church full title to the church lands in the territory won from Germany.[29] The church in Poland and the Vatican responded by calling for civil concord in the still seething Baltic region.[30] In March, Premier Piotr Jaroszewicz and Cardinal Wyszynski discussed their outstanding antagonisms. In April, Cardinal Koenig visited Poland, and in May the Vatican and the Polish government jointly reported the commencement of negotiations. On June 23 the regime fulfilled its January pledge and turned over to the church full title to nearly seven thousand former German church buildings and two thousand acres of land in the Oder-Neisse region. Discussions on an accord reached a high level in November, when Archbishop Casaroli arrived in Warsaw.

On February 28, 1972, the government, in another concession, ruled that the church would no longer be required to submit reports on its income and expenditures or maintain records of its assets.[31] The regime also abetted a nationwide celebration of the anniversary of the beatified martyr priest Maximilian Kolbe and permitted increased travel to Rome for the Polish episcopate.[32] The papacy, for its part, fulfilled the longstanding Polish demand and named, on June 28, permanent bishops (that is, raised the canonical status of the Polish apostolic administrators) for the Oder-Neisse lands.[33] In November 1973, with the Polish foreign minister, Stefan Olszowski, calling at the Vatican, the government and the church verged on establishing diplomatic ties. Numerous problems remain to be solved, but there is light in Poland.

Czechoslovakia

In Czechoslovakia, where the church counts close to 78 percent of the population among its adherents, church-state collaboration over the past ten years has experienced more valleys than peaks. Complicating the standard picture of Communist-church ties has been the Czechoslovak government's reluctance to liberate imprisoned or restricted bishops and priests, its aversion to allowing the Vatican to fill vacant episcopal posts, and finally, the "Czech Spring" and Russian invasion of 1968. Nonetheless, in the wake of the Khrushchevian initiative and Vatican Council II, rapprochement began.

In July 1963, Cardinal Koenig arrived in Prague to lay the foundation for some congruity. Evidently his action resulted in the government's decision to free, in July, three imprisoned bishops and, then, in October, five more, including the primate of Czechoslovakia, Archbishop Josef Beran, who had been under house arrest for twelve years.[34] For the next four years, pessimism displaced the excitement of those initial events as the Novotny regime sent the primate into exile at Rome and, in an attempt to split the faithful, persisted in backing the "peace priest" movement.

The picture changed spectacularly in January 1968, when Alexander Dubcek replaced Antonin Novotny. The new rulers reopened discussions with the church through the person of Bishop Frantisek Tomasek, the apostolic administrator of Prague, and in general relaxed all antireligious measures.[35] The religious "Prague Spring," however, gave way to the Novotny status quo, with Gustav Husak replacing Dubcek in the aftermath of the Soviet invasion of Czechoslovakia on August 20. For the next four years, although oscillating discussions took place, relations remained acrimonious.[36]

Finally, the Czechoslovak government, regaining its equilibrium, allowed, on February 27, 1973, the Vatican to fill four vacant episcopal posts, although the pope qualified the appointment of Josef Vrana because of his past work with the regime-backed "peace priests". This concession gave an episcopal presence to six of the nation's thirteen dioceses.[37] The Czechoslovak-Catholic nexus, however, is far from symmetrical, although serious dialogue proceeded throughout 1973.

Hungary

Hungary, with a 68 percent Catholic population, had most of the characteristics of the Communist-Catholic axis. Furthermore, constructive negotiations were stymied by the Cardinal Josef Mindszenty problem. The cardinal, incarcerated for alleged treason in 1948 and released to find asylum in the US Embassy in Budapest during the 1956 revolution, was an insurmountable obstacle to Vatican-Hungarian accord.

Despite the Mindszenty question, church-state relations in 1963, as elsewhere in the Soviet bloc, fumbled forward. In the spring, Cardinal Koenig and Archbishop Casaroli both descended on Budapest to try to solve the Mindszenty enigma and to discuss episcopal appointments. In September 1964, the Vatican and the government reached an accord whereby the papacy, with governmental approval, could fill empty episcopal posts and communicate freely with its new Hungarian hierarchy.[38]

The next six years saw little progress as the Vatican tried to persuade Cardinal Mindszenty to leave Hungary.[39] Discussion, however, persisted, and in September 1971 the church and the government jointly announced that Cardinal Mindszenty was leaving Budapest.[40] A compromise was reached whereby it was agreed that the cardinal would not interfere in Hungarian affairs and the regime admitted, *de facto* if not *de jure,* that he had not been guilty of treason. That development moved church-state relations into high gear, and in March 1972 the Vatican was permitted to name four more bishops. In an atmosphere of relaxed give-and-take, negotiations for a concordat through 1973 took on a note of seriousness.

Yugoslavia

Yugoslavia, with a 35 percent Catholic population centered in Slovenia and Croatia, has been, over the past decade, the leader in papal-Communist intercourse. The church in Yugoslavia today has a full episcopal complement and controls forty-six ecclesiastical secondary and high schools, seminaries, hospitals, nursing homes, and numerous freewheeling publications. The former archbishop of Zagreb, Cardinal Franjo Seper, is presently head of the Vatican's Congregation on Doctrine and Faith, the first East European bishop to hold a high papal post.

The church's extensive influence and role in Yugoslavia has been coming under criticism by Communists who fear the religious freedom might be suicidal to an officially atheistic regime and might become a center nationalism among the Croatians and Slovenians.[41] Tito seems to believe, however, that the church, rather than being a fissiparous force, is a buttress to Yugoslavia's heterogeneous polity. At any rate, the detente goes on and is flourishing, and the Vatican holds up its concord with Tito for the rest of the Communist world's emulation.[42]

This harmony began in 1964 with a series of negotiations that eventually, in 1966, led to a restoration of diplomatic ties, broken in 1952, below the ambassadorial level.[43] In January 1967, Premier Mika Spiljak advanced associations with a call at the Vatican. In August 1970, the Vatican and Yugoslavia, with contacts growing quite warm, raised their diplomatic association to the full ambassadorial level.[44] In March 1971 rapport was capped with Tito's reception by the pope in Rome.

The Other Communist States

Ties with Romania, where the Catholic church holds a 10 percent representation, moved forward at a snail's pace. Sporadic exchanges, from 1967 to 1973,

have been pressing the detente ahead. In November 1967, Cardinal Koenig
visited Bucharest and revealed some progress by reporting that the Ceausescu
regime had freed the imprisoned bishop of Alba-Iulia, Aaron Marton.[45] Julius
Cardinal Doepfner, the archbishop of Munich, journeyed to Romania in November
of 1971. In March 1972, a delegation of Romanian Orthodox churchmen made an
unprecedented stop at the Vatican. Finally, in May 1973, President Nicholae
Ceausescu and Pope Paul met in Rome. These dialogues have won the church toleration and a base of communication with the dominant Orthodox faith.[46]

In East Germany, where there are only 1.3 million Roman Catholics,
normalization has crept along. The past few years, however, have witnessed an
acceleration, and presently there are rumors that the government of Erich
Honecker and the Vatican will establish diplomatic relations. There have been
increasing contacts between Cardinal Alfred Bengsch, the archbishop of Berlin,
who resides in East Berlin, and the GDR. The principal hitch has been the
reluctance of the papacy to isolate the East German Catholics from West Germany by creating new dioceses in large East German areas, including Erfurt,
Scherin, Magdeburg, and Meiningen, which are still technically a part of the
West German dioceses of Fulda, Paderborn, Osnabrück, Hildesheim, and Würz-
burg, respectively. In July 1973, however, in a major move for reconciliation, the
Vatican named East German apostolic administrators to the disputed territories.[47]

The one great mystery for the church has been China, where the estimated
3.2 million Catholics have been totally cut off from the Vatican. Pope Paul
has made it a major goal of his pontificate to renew relations with China, but
in general the response has been disappointing. In January 1967, the pope,
in a dramatic appeal, offered friendship and dialogue to the Chinese, but
before the year was out, he found himself berating the antireligious extremities
of the cultural revolution.[48] In July 1970, however, the Chinese government
freed Bishop James E. Walsh, an American Maryknoll cleric who had been in
prison since 1958.[49] In November 1970, in a whirlwind tour of the Far East,
Pope Paul attempted to stoke the flickering flame, and by the end of the year,
some peripheral contact between church representatives and the Chinese Embassy
in Belgrade was initiated.[50] In 1971-72, exchanges apparently continued, and in
April 1973, the Vatican lauded the Christian ideals in the philosophy of Maoism.[51]

The countries where detente has not evidently taken root include Bulgaria,
North Vietnam, North Korea, and Albania, all of which have an insignificant
Catholic population and the last which remains, of all the Communist states,
quite hostile to the Vatican. In Cuba, of course, relations are excellent and
have been from the beginning.

Papal Motives

The most obvious motive for the Vatican in mollifying the Communist world
is that a modus vivendi is the best means available for protecting and improving

the status of Catholicism in the Communist sphere. Over 90 percent of the people in Poland and Cuba, 80 percent of the people in Lithuania, 78 percent of the people in Czechoslovakia, 68 percent of the people in Hungary, 35 percent of the people in Yugoslavia, 25 percent of the people in Latvia, and 10 percent of the people in Romania are Catholic. In addition, the Church has interests in East Germany, Bulgaria, North Vietnam, North Korea, Albania, Estonia, Urkaine, Belorussia, and, most important, China. The general condition of the church, with the glaring exception of the Soviet Union and a few other countries, as the survey clearly reveals, has indeed been ameliorating, and that success alone would seem to justify the papal *Ostpolitik.*

Second, the Vatican has perceived that the "winds of change," to borrow a phrase from Neville Chamberlain, are clearly blowing in Africa, Asia, and Latin American and that these gales are howling, despite the setback in Chile, in a leftist direction. The Roman Catholic Church is an overwhelming force in Latin America and a respectable presence in Asia and Africa. The papacy recognizes that if it wants to maintain its position and, more important, given the priorities of a church that believes itself to be the true faith, expand its influence, it must address itself to the have-nots of the third world. Increasingly, Catholic clerics, who are close to the suffering masses, are working with and leading socialist movements. After the Latin American Bishops' Council in Medellin, Columbia in 1968, the Catholic Church as a whole in Latin America moved toward a progressive position and soon such groups as the Chilean Christians for Socialism, the Argentinian Third World Priests movement, and the Columbian Golconda Group emerged to lead the struggle. The Communist media has noted these development with plea-sure.[52] At the same time, where the church has been slow to respond to social injustice, it has been attacked.[53] Certainly the Vatican realizes that if it tarries, time will pass it by. It is, therefore, moving to embrace socialism, which it senses as the wave of the future in the third world. The strong socialist currents in some developed countries, particularly Italy, serve to reinforce this trend. Historically the church has been able to adjust to the pangs of change and, granted its past record of durability, its present shift in policy is an object lesson.

Third, the Vatican grasped, probably in the wake of the Soviet suppression of the Hungarian revolution in 1956, that Soviet control of Eastern Europe was a long-term reality. Through the course of the 1960s and the 1970s, further-more, it became obvious that Soviet military strength, despite the fissiparous tendencies in the Communist world, was growing and, perhaps, surpassing that of the United States. In addition, Soviet leverage in the third world, especially in the Arab countries, could be manipulated, within bounds, to serve Soviet goals. Under these circumstances, the ability of Western Europe to conduct an unfettered foreign policy, one without recourse to Soviet interests, appeared by the 1970s to be in jeopardy. The Soviet Union was becoming the dominant European power, and its status, whether in Eastern Europe or Western Europe, was not about to fade, but, if anything, be enhanced. For the Vatican to remain antagonistic toward this state bordered on naiveté.

Throughout the centuries of its existence, the Catholic church has always been quite amorphous in adjusting to man's sundry political systems. As long as the state would permit the church to perform its spiritual mission of stalking souls, the church could and has accepted polities that vary from democracies to dictatorships. Indeed, the church has shown a marked preference for the authoritarian society and, possibly sickened by the loose morality of the "free world," it feels the Communist prefecture, given a modification of its atheism, would be a more suitable environment for its mission. At any rate, in the 1960s, when the Soviet Union indicated a willingness to reach an accommodation, the Vatican moved quickly to develop the opening.

Fourth, the Vatican, especially in the nuclear age, is interested in preventing war. Its motives are both humanitarian and utilitarian: its acquaintance with the ravages of war moves it to spare mankind such a catastrophe; and the church functions best in an atmosphere of peace and security. The papacy's search for tranquillity forced it to court Russia and, simultaneously, to bring China out of isolation. These policies spoke to the two contingencies that could hurl the world into a nuclear holocaust: war between the West and the Soviet Bloc, and war between the Soviet Union and China.

There were, of course, other trouble spots in the world, such as the Arab-Israeli war, the Indochina war, and the Ulster conflagration, and the papacy addressed itself to these also, but not to the point of condemning Communist inflamation or involvement in these threats to peace. Possibly, however, the Vatican determined that such contained conflicts could be solved if its rapprochement succeeded and led to a genuine understanding and a workable balance between the United States, Soviet Russia, and China. On the other hand, the papacy might have accepted, however reluctantly, such controlled crises as part of the price for a symphony with the Communist world and, in particular, with the USSR. The Soviets have been inflaming, since 1917, the "weak links" of capitalism, and conceivably the Vatican has reconciled its quest for peace with the reality of Soviet foreign policy by accepting Lenin's conviction that lasting tranquillity will only come when the "social injustices" of the capitalist system have been eradicated.

One other possibility exists: the Vatican may believe that the Soviet Union, through fruitful association with the church, will someday abandon its policy of exploiting tension in the world. Be that as it may, the Vatican is sincere in its efforts to secure peace for the world and, in pursuit of that goal, it deems it both prudent and wise to bridge the Iron Curtain.

A possible fifth reason for papal advances to the Communist states is linked to the possible by-product of close cooperation: character assimilation. The church, at the very least, is banking upon, and receiving to a degree, toleration, but it certainly is hoping for much more, including conversion. The process of redemption is a graduated one, and in the case of the Communist world, the initial foundation would be the apostasy of atheism. On that score the church does have some grounds for optimism. Throughout the Soviet bloc, there is growing indifference for antireligious and atheistic work. This is indirectly reflected in the efforts of diehard atheists to resuscitate the atheistic drive and directly mirrored in the telling criticism directed at the Soviet Union and its satellites by their former ideological brethren, principally the Albanians, who now refer to Moscow as the headquarters for religious opium.[54] This indifference might be attributable to the already pervasive secularism of Soviet society, as Bohdan Bociurkiw argues, but it also might be attributable to human nature and, in addition, to the government's ambivalence toward religion: how can it both associate with, and cater to, organized religion and, at the same time, demand that it be extinguished?[55] Michael Bourdeaux, in fact, reports that there is an upsurge of religious belief among the young in the Soviet Union.[56] But no matter what the reason for atheistic apathy, the Vatican certainly expects eventually to eradicate atheism and thus prepare the way for what undoubtedly will be a long, arduous task: the conversion of the Communist camp.

The papacy's final motive for seeking a concordat with the socialist world is connected to its apparently growing ideological conviction that socialism is closer to the ideals of Christianity than is capitalism.[57] Some cynics might claim that the church's ideological metamorphosis followed its recognition of socialism as the wave of the future, but this would be an injustice to the church. As early as *Rerum Novarum,* it had found many desirable qualities in socialism, but it could not, naturally, tolerate or support a movement that portrayed religion as a parasitical tapeworm and planned its funeral. Recently, however, with the disparity between the rich and the poor escalating, particularly in the third world, the church evidently is turning toward socialism, which, in theory, promises an end of exploitation and a more equitable distribution of the world's goods. The essence of Christianity is love of God and man, and even though communism has, in practice, dwarfed and suppressed the human spirit and completely rejected God, its goals are attuned to the substance of Christianity.

The church, of course, certainly realizes that before it can fully embrace socialism, it must turn Marxism on its head (much as Marx turned Hegel on his) and place idealism before materialism and, thus, provide permanent spiritual motives, based upon man's value as a creature of God, for reorganizing world society into an economically classless system. Otherwise, Marxism-Leninism simply deteriorates into a philosophy of power, where the leaders of a given socialist society become more interested in maintaining themselves in power, since materialism offers no higher good, than in advancing the cause of creating a *truly* classless society. The church, in other words, is hoping, through detente, to transform materialistic socialism into Christian socialism.

Communist Motives

As Catholic-Communist relations have heretofore evolved, it has been primarily a relationship involving the Soviet Union, its satellites, Yugoslavia, and

Romania rather than the Communist world as a whole. Albania remains antagonistic, in part because the church in inconsequential in the country, but mostly
because the policy strengthens Soviet revisionism, which propounds not only
peaceful coexistence but, possibly, support for Tito's long-held ambition to
annex Albania. Bulgaria, North Korea, and North Vietnam, although answer-
able to the Soviet Union, have remained uninterested, undoubtedly because the
church is so minute in their countries and because an accord would offer them
no immediate substantive benefits.

China has many good reasons for seeking out the Vatican, especially because
the church is strong in some parts of the third world, which the Chinese consider
their bailiwick, and because the Vatican could provide an excellent means for
bringing China out of its dangerous isolation vis-à-vis the Soviet Union. Representation at the papacy, with its strong links to the West and the third world,
could bring the Chinese the same benefits that memberhip in the United Nations
provided. However, China, while quite recently showing oblique signs of a
desire for a modus vivendi, has, by and large, remained aloof. Its reluctance in
all likelihood is tied to three factors. First, an unwillingness to compromise its
anti-Soviet propaganda by itself becoming a "revisionist," although undoubtedly
its overtures to the United States and the Common Market countries have already
gone far to undermine that prohibition. Second, the Chinese are determined not
to tolerate on their soil a foreign-controlled church, which would certainly revive
unpleasant memories of China's former colonial position. Finally, a decided
resistance to improve relations while the Vatican perseveres in its diplomatic
alliance with Taiwan.

Of the countries that have searched for an exchange with the Catholic church,
the motives have varied. Yugoslavia's desire for a concordat is intimately tied
to two realities. The Catholic church is a significant force in the multinational
state of Yugoslavia, with a preponderance among the Croatians and Slovenians.
Tito's miracle has been his ability to hold together the splintered nationalities
of the Balkans, and he apparently has decided, with a conviction growing in
proportion to his age, that continued religious persecution would serve as a
centripetal agent and possibly, upon his death, contribute to the disintegration
of Yugoslavia. Conversely, he anticipates that supineness will help bridge the
provincial cleavages and reinforce unity. Tito's expectation has been borne out,
for the church is fast becoming one of the pillars of Yugoslavian society and, in
turn, assuming a vested interest in the perpetuation of a compact Yugoslavia.
Second, Tito, as one of communism's mavericks, needs friends to give him
freedom from isolation and provide him with credibility in the West. The Vatican,
as a major Western institution, can, to a degree, provide Yugoslavia with diplomatic support as Tito continues to pursue a course independent of the Soviet
Union, Red China, and the United States.

Romania's desire for contacts with the Vatican are somewhat similar to
Tito's. The church can furnish Romania with a touchstone in the West, where

it seeks trade and diplomatic corroboration of its emancipation from the Soviet line and to where it traces its heritage.

The willingness of the Soviet Union and its satellites to make the church a bedfellow has many motives. First, the Soviet Union hopes to gain what it attempted to win immediately after World War II: the leverage of the church to facilitate its control of Eastern Europe. As the dominant religion in Poland, Hungary, and Czechoslovkia, the church can go far to fortify the status quo in Eastern Europe and make the satellite governments more palatable and popular with the masses.

Second, the church, as a principal religion in West Germany, France, Italy, Spain, Belgium, Ireland, and Luxemburg, can help deliver Western European acceptance of Soviet security goals. This factor has been aptly demonstrated in the Vatican's subvention of the Soviet-sponsored European Security Conference.[58] The church might also prove useful in preparing Europe for eventual assimilation into a Soviet sphere of influence.

Third, the Catholic church is a powerful presence in the third world, espeically in Latin America; the Vatican maintains diplomatic relations with seventy-six countries, most of them from the third world. Thus, the church can be quite efficacious to the Soviet Union by endowing the Russians with a stamp of endorsement among the Vatican's third world friends and by cooperating with Soviet-backed schemes in the third world. For example, the Vatican's rapport with the Communist world has certainly reinforced the disposition of those third world Catholics who are already, as mentioned earlier, working with socialist movements. In addition, the papacy's tendency to support the Arab position in the Arab-Israeli feud has, to a degree, brought the Vatican's moral authority behind the Arab cause, which the Soviets also side with. The Vatican maintains diplomatic relations with Egypt, Tunisia, Algeria, Libya, Iraq, Sudan, and Kuwait—but has steadfastly refused to recognize Israel. Needless to say, it makes no difference that the church's stands have not been assumed to please the Soviets. Nonetheless, the Communists do accrue the benefits.

Fourth, the Vatican can collaborate in maintaining order in the USSR. The Ukrainian Uniates, although their church has been suppressed, are still a force of disruption in the Soviet Union. There is ample evidence that the Uniate church continues to operate as an underground movement and such sub rosa activities, in the totalitarian society, are anathema.[59] In addition, hundreds of Uniate émigrés constantly point up the shortcomings of the Soviet system and have recently demanded that the Vatican establish a patriarchate for the Ukrainian Catholics and name Cardinal Joseph Slipyi, the head of the Ukrainian Uniates-in-exile, the patriarch.[60] Such an irredentist development would send shudders up and down the spines of the Soviets, and to appreciate their potential paroxysm, one only has to point to Stalin's incredible fears, in 1939, that Hitler would use the gnatlike Carpatho-Ukraine to annex the elephantine

Soviet Ukraine.[61]   Naturally the Soviet Union expects, as part of the Vatican's price for compatibility, that the church would not afford succor or encouragement to the Ukrainian Uniates. In fact, the church has not, although it persists in sympathizing with the Ukrainians' plight, as Pope Paul recently indicated in an address to a group of twelve exiled Uniate bishops: "We have a continuing interest both for Ukrainian living abroad—the generous witness to the name Christian in both the new and the old world—and for your fellow countrymen who have remained in the Ukraine, to whom our fatherly, vigilant and shared concern goes out.[62]

Besides the Uniate Catholics, there are also Lithuanian, Latvian, and Polish Catholics in the Soviet Union. The Lithuanian Catholics, particularly, are a numerous group, and the Soviet government, while it slowly dilutes the Catholic concentrations in the Baltic states through Russian migration, anticipates that the Vatican will, again as part of the quid pro quo, vouchsafe moral sustenance for the continuation of Soviet domination in its western borderlands and, possibly, terminate its diplomatic relations with the Lithuanian government-in-exile.

At the same time, however, the Soviet government, as its share in the concert, must provide evidence to the Vatican that Catholics are being tolerated, permitted freedom of religion, and accepted as legitimate national minorities. The two policies are obviously at variance, one of many areas where interests clash, but one could hazard a guess that the church will probably win the battle, since Catholicism is endemic to the national identity of the Lithuanians and since the Russians will find it easier to accept a Catholic church to bolster them than to create a martyrology that could lead to internal disorders and compromise their confederation with the Vatican.[63]

Fifth, the Soviets wish unanimity because the papacy can be utilized, as Russian Orthodoxy has been used,[64] to garner world opinion behind the two major thrusts in Soviet foreign policy: disruption of the capitalist world order through the support and exploitation of tension and prevention of war, that is, not allowing the first theme to go so far as to involve the USSR in a nuclear holocaust. In regard to the first policy, Catholicism, as a force for change in Latin America and, to a degree, in Spain and Italy, and as the major religion of the revolutionary IRA in Northern Ireland, can be an accomplice in protracting the chaos that weakens the capitalist states and their diplomatic, military, and economic arrangements.[65]   Ulster, for example, has been a constant drain on Britain, and the Communists, in their propaganda, have made hay out of the British disconfiture and castigated the English for persecuting a minority religious group.[66]   The Vatican, as a major religious and moral force for peace, can also prove quite an effective buttress to Soviet pursuance of peaceful coexistence. The church, for example, has influence in the United States, and it can use its weight to help keep the Americans committed to peaceful coexistence. It must be pointed out, however, that the Catholic church's desire for peace and for social justice in the world is not predicated upon fulfilling Soviet wishes, any more than was the Arab oil embargo against the West. It simply happens to be another case where methods but not intentions coincide.

Sixth, fellowship with the Vatican gives the USSR a positive image among religiously conscious people in the world, especially in the West, and, simultaneously, belies the charge that the Soviet Union suppresses dissent and minority groups. The latter development, particularly if the Vatican would use its influence in Washington in Russia's favor, might prove in the future to be quite useful to the Soviet government in its attempts to gain most-favored-nation status from the United States Congress.

Finally, concurrence with the papacy reinforces the Soviet Union's recent policy of detente with the United States. Even though the present American government only maintains a subambassadorial envoy at the Vatican, the Catholic church is a powerful influence in the United States. In a world where war may erupt between China and Russia, a neutral United States is imperative to the Russians, who feel they can defeat China on a one-to-one basis. Obviously any program that tends to commit the United States to friendship with the Soviet Union is desirable, and undoubtedly the Kremlin feels that coaction with the Vatican is such a policy.

The Communist-papal rapprochement has produced and can create advantages to both sides, but as is often the case with former enemies working out a modus vivendi, one's triumphs are the other's setbacks. Despite the mutual drawbacks, the reciprocal advantages seem to indicate a strengthening and flowering of the detente.

Notes

1. Dennis J. Dunn, "Pre-World War II Relations Between Stalin and the Catholic Church," *Journal of Church and State* 15 (1973): 193-204.
2. Pius XI, *Divini Redemptoris, Acta Apostolicae Sedis* 29 (1937), 65-106.
3. See Guenter Lewy, *Catholic Church & Nazi Germany* (New York, 1964) and Saul Friedlander, *Pius XII and the Third Reich: A Documentation* (New York, 1966).
4. Dennis J. Dunn, "Stalinism and the Catholic Church During the Era of World War Two," *The Catholic Historical Review* 49 (October 1973), 404-28. For some excellent studies on the suppression of the Uniates, see: Bohdan R. Bociurkiw, "The Uniate Church in the Soviet Ukraine: A Case Study in Soviet Church Policy," *Canadian Slavonic Papers* 7 (1965), 89-113; Denis Dirscherl, S.J., "The Soviet Destruction of the Greek Catholic Church," *Journal of Church and State* 12 (1970), 421-39; Roman Reynarowych, "The Catholic Church in the West Ukraine After World War II," *Diakonia,* no. 4 (1970), pp. 372-87; Ivan Hrynioch, "The Destruction of the

Ukraninian Catholic Church in the Soviet Union," *Prologue,* vol. 4, no. 1-2 (1960); Dennis J. Dunn, "The Disappearance of the Ukrainian Uniate Church: How and Why?" *The Ukrainian Historian,* 1-2 (33-34) 1972), 57-65.

5. Pierre Blet et al. (eds.), *Actes et documents du Saint Siège relatifs à la seconde guerre mondiale,* 7 vols. to date, vol. V: *Le Saint Siège et la guerre mondiale (juillet 1941-octobre 1942),* nos. 480, 484, 486.

6. *Ibid.,* vol. 3: *Le Saint Siège et la situation religieuse en Pologne et dans les Pay Baltes* (1939-1945), part 2, no. 598; also see Dunn, "Stalinism and the Catholic Church During the Era of World War Two," pp. 426-27.

7. *Diiannia Soboru Hreko-Katolyts' koi Tserkvy, 8-10 bereznia 1946, u L'vovi* [Proceedings of the Council of the Greek-Catholic Church in Lvov, 8-10 March 1946] (Lvov, 1946); Bociurkiw provides an excellent analysis in his "The Uniate Church in the Soviet Ukraine," pp. 104-7; also see: *First Victims of Communism: White Book on Religious Persecution in the Ukraine* (Rome, 1953); for examples of the isolated attacks, see: Ludwig Nemec, *Church and State in Czechoslovakia* (New York, 1955), pp. 202-18; T. Zubek, *The Church of Silence in Slovakia* (Whiting, Indiana, 1956), pp. 29-30.

8. Dennis J. Dunn, "Stalinism and the Vatican" (doctoral dissertation, Kent State University, 1970), pp. 116-40.

9. For an excellent survey of Soviet foreign policy, see: Adam Ulam, *Expansion and Coexistence: A History of Soviet Foreign Policy, 1917-1967* (New York, 1968).

10. For good, general accounts of the postwar, religious conditions, see: Albert Galter, *The Red Book of the Persecuted Church* (Westminster, 1957); Walter Kolarz, *Religion in the Soviet Union* (New York, 1962); Robert Conquest (ed.), *Religion in the USSR* (New York, 1968); Gary MacEoin, *The Communist War on Religion* (New York, 1951); G.W. Schuster, *Religion Behind the Iron Curtain* (New York, 1954); Robert Tobias, *Communist-Christian Encounter in East Europe* (Indianapolis, Ind., 1956); Paul Mailleux, S.J., "Catholics in the Soviet Union," and V. Stanely Vardys, "Catholicism in Lithuania," *Aspects of Religion in the Soviet Union 1917-1967,* Richard H. Marshall, Jr. (ed.) (Chicago, 1971), pp. 357-78 and 379-403 respectively.

11. Acta SS. Congregationum, *Decretum: Responsa ad dubia de communismo, Acta Apostolicae Sedis* 41 (1949): 334.

12. Michael Bourdeaux (ed.), *Religious Minorities in the Soviet Union (1960-1970),* (London, 1970), pp. 3-6; Donald A. Lowrie and William C. Fletcher, "Khrushchev's Religious Policy 1959-1964," *Aspects of Religion in the Soviet Union,* pp. 131-55.

13. Norman Cousins, "The Improbable Triumvirate: Khrushchev, Kennedy, and Pope John," *The Saturday Review* 54 (October 1971): 27, 34.

14. *New York Times,* 7 and 8 March 1963.
15. *L'Osservatore Romano,* 14 March 1963; *New York Times,* 12 November 1963; 17 September 1964; 4 June 1967; 14 January 1968; 16 January 1968; 1 May 1969, 16 November 1970; 24 November 1970; 3 May 1972; 11 March 1973; 5 July 1973.
16. For an interesting summary of the church-state problems in East Europe, see: Bohdan Bociurkiw, "Religion in Eastern Europe," *Religion in Communist Lands* 1 (July-Oct., 1973): 9-14; also see: Joshua Rothenberg, "The Legal Status of Religion in the Soviet Union," *Aspects of Religion in the Soviet Union,* pp. 61-102.
17. Vardys, op. cit.; V. Stanley Vardys, "Geography and Nationalities in the USSR: A Commentary," *Slavic Review* (September 1972), pp. 564-70; Kathleen Matchett, "Recent Events in the Lithuanian Catholic Church," *Religion in Communist Lands* 1 (January-February 1973): 9-11; Janice Broun, "Lithuania in the Valley of the Shadow," *America* (December 22, 1973), pp. 482-84.
18. Ukrainian émigrés are very much aghast at the papacy's attitude. See: *New York Times,* 2 January 1971; 17 March 2971; 24 December 1971; 20 February 1972; 20 June 1973; 18 November 1973.
19. *Pravda,* 31 January 1967; *Izvestia,* 31 January 1967; Radio Vatican, 31 January 1967; *L'Osservatore Romano,* 30 January 1967.
20. *New York Times,* 5 July 1973.
21. Ibid.; *Izvestia,* 6 June 1971; Radio Moscow, 7 July 1971.
22. *New York Times,* 28 April 1966; 13 November 1970; 24 February 1971; 25 February 1971; 26 February 1971; 1 March 1971; 4 March 1971; 5 July 1973.
23. Radio Moscow, 8 February 1972; *New York Times,* 2 April 1972; 13 November 1972; 5 July 1973.
24. *Nauka i religia,* no. 5 (May 1972) pp. 26-28; *Sovetskaya Litva,* 21 May, 1972, p. 4; Tass, 4 April 1972; 25 May 1972; Radio Moscow, 24 May 1972; Radio Vilnius, 27 May 1972; also see the references in note 17, above.
25. Radio Warsaw, 12 December 1965; *New York Times,* 5 December 1965; 11 December 1965. For a good explanation of the problems of church-state relations in Poland, see: Lucian Blit, "The Insoluble Problem: Church and State in Poland," *Religion in Communist Lands* 1 (May-June 1973): 8-11.
26. Radio Warsaw, 3 June 1966; 6 June 1966; 8 June 1966; *New York Times,* 16 January 1966; 31 January 1966; 11 February 1966; 6 March 1966; 16 May 1966; 1 June 1966; 21 June 1966; 25 June 1966; 15 December 1966; 19 December 1966; 5 November 1968.
27. *New York Times,* 6 March 1967; 26 May 1967; 9 April 1967; 24 September 1967; 30 September 1967; 1 October 1967; 30 October 1967; 18 December 1967; 26 December 1967; *L'Osservatore Romano,* 8 February 1968.

28. Radio Warsaw, 30 January 1971; *New York Times,* 24 December 1970.

29. Radio Warsaw, 20 January 1971; 30 January 1971. The lands had been leased to the church since 1945.

30. Radio Vatican, 1 February 1971; 12 February 1971; Radio Warsaw, 11 February 1971.

31. Polish Press Agency, 4 March 1972 (hereinafter PAP).

32. Ibid., 9 November 1972.

33. Radio Warsaw, 28 June 1972; Radio Vatican, 29 June 1972.

34. *L'Osservatore Romano,* 3 October 1963; 4 October 1963; *New York Times,* 21 July 1963; 4 October 1963.

35. *New York Times,* 20 April 1968.

36. Ibid., 30 August 1970; 12 February 1971; 6 March 1971; Radio Prague, 30 July 1971; 24 November 1971.

37. Radio Vatican, 28 February 1973; Czechoslovak Press Agency, 3 March 1973.

38. *L'Osservatore Romano,* 16 September 1964; Radio Budapest, 18 September 1964; *New York Times,* 16 September 1964.

39. *New York Times,* 13 June 1965; 7 March 1966; 19 October 1967; 26 March 1968; 5 February 1969.

40. Radio Budapest, 28 September 1971; Radio Vatican, 28 September 1971; *New York Times,* 30 September 1971.

41. For examples, see: Yugoslav Telegraph Service, 11 January 1972; 6 October 1973 (Hereinafter cited as Tanyug); Radio Zagreb, 31 October 1972. For a pessimistic assessment of recent developments associated with nationalism, see: Christopher Civic, "Recent Developments in Church-State Relations in Yugoslavia," *Religion in Communist Lands* 1 (March-April, 1973): pp. 6-8.

42. *New York Times,* 26 August 1967.

43. Radio Belgrade, 25 June 1966; Radio Vatican, 25 June 1966.

44. Radio Belgrade, 14 August 1970; Radio Vatican, 16 November 1970.

45. *New York Times,* 25 November 1967.

46. Radio Bucharest, 11 November 1971; *New York Times,* 27 May 1973.

47. East German News Agency, 11 October 1973; *New York Times,* 24 July 1973.

48. *L'Osservatore Romano,* 7 February 1967; *New York Times,* 7 January 1967.

49. Radio Peking, 10 July 1970.

50. *New York Times,* 3 November 1970; 5 November 1970; 5 December 1970; 5 July 1973.

51. *New York Times,* 19 April 1973.

52. PAP, 4 January 1973.

53. *New York Times,* 15 September 1968; 19 September 1968; 12 February 1971; 12 January 1973; 17 June 1973.

54. *Pravda,* 10 August 1971; 18 August 1971; 15 September 1972; 20 February 1973; 16 June 1973; *Izvestia,* 15 September 1971; *Nauka i religia,* no. 4 (April 1972), pp. 46–47; no. 5 (May, 1972); Radio Moscow, 23 November

1971; 21 December 1971; 2 June 1972; Radio Minsk, 24 August 1972; Radio Vinnitsa, 4 February 1972; Radio Tirana, 27 January 1971; 10 February 1971; 25 February 1972; 27 February 1972; 9 March 1972; 2 July 1973; Albanian Telegraph Agency (ATA), 29 August 1971; 6 September 1971; 29 December 1971; 9 February 1972; 15 February 1972; 3 September 1973; 20 September 1973.

55. Bohdan Bociurkiw, "Religion and Atheism in Soviet Society," *Aspects of Religion in the Soviet Union,* pp. 45-60.

56. Bourdeaux, p. 6.

57. This development is reflected not only in Pope Paul's encyclical *Populorum Progressio,* but also by an array of recent literature and events. See: *New York Times:* 14 November 1965; 17 November 1965; 29 March 1967; 6 January 1971; 15 May 1971; 19 April 1973.

58. Ibid., 23 June 1973; 5 July 1973.

59. Bourdeaux, pp. 19-20; *The Chronicle of Current Events,* no. 7 (April 30, 1969) and no. 8 (June 30, 1969), found in Peter Reddaway (ed. and trans.), *Uncensored Russia* (New York, 1972), pp. 331-33; Also see: Radio Kiev, 7 April 1972; *Nauka i religia,* no. 5 (May 1972), pp. 26-28; *New York Times,* 12 November 1963.

60. *New York Times,* 2 January 1971; 17 March 1971; 26 September 1971; 24 October 1971; 20 February 1972; 20 May 1973; 18 November 1973.

61. I.V. Stalin, *Sochineniya,* ed. Robert H. McNeal (Stanford, 1967) I (XIV), 340; Ulam, *Expansion and Coexistence,* p. 264.

62. *The Texas Catholic Herald,* 4 January 1974.

63. V. Stanley Vardys is inclined to be optimistic. See his "Catholicism in Lithuania," pp. 402-3.

64. See the excellent book by William C. Fletcher for the relationship between Soviet foreign policy and the Russian Orthodox Church: *Religion and Soviet Foreign Policy 1945-1970* (London, 1973).

65. *Pravda,* 9 February 1971; 7 March 1971; Radio Moscow, 18 December 1971; 23 April 1972; Radio Warsaw, 4 January 1973.

66. To cite but a few of the many references in Communist media: *Pravda,* 4 February 1971; 10 August 1972; *Izvestia,* 5 February 1972; Moscow Radio, 11 March 1971; 15 January 1972; 16 March 1972; 30 July 1972; 18 September 1972.

5 Soviet Scholarship and Existential Theologians
William C. Fletcher

Until the middle 1960s, contemporary theology was a terra incognita to Soviet scholarship on religion. The influence of atheism, the position officially sanctioned by both party and state in the USSR, was so pervasive as to exclude almost entirely any serious consideration of alternate positions. Theological doctrines of contemporary churches abroad were treated in the vocabulary of polemic ("obscurantism," "superstition," "exploitation," etc.); the leading proponents of the various theological schools were mentioned sparingly and only insofar as they came into direct contact with the Soviet religious milieu, and their theological predecessors were noticed not at all. The result was that serious Soviet treatment of religious thought seldom progressed much further than Leibnitz, and were Soviet scholarship to be the guide, Feuerbach (a very minor light indeed in the non-Soviet constellation of noted thinkers) would have appeared the most important theologian of recent times.

In 1954, Nikita Khrushchev inaugurated a serious, long-term effort at building up Soviet antireligious scholarship.[1] There was ample room for improvement. A Soviet scholar, writing a dozen years later, himself derided a 1954 article in *Voprosy Filosofii* (Problems of Philosophy), the most prominent Soviet journal of philosophical scholarship), which had treated Kierkegaard "as a freak [yurod]" and presented his philosophy "as a mere curiosity."[2] Indeed, when the vigorous antireligious campaign of the 1960s was well underway,[3] an eminently out-of-date compendium on contradictions in the Bible by Emel'ian Iaroslavskii from prewar days still was being touted as the most effective work of scholarly atheism availabile.[4] Clearly, Soviet antireligious scholarship was poorly equipped to meet the challenge of the increasingly sophisticated religious environment in the USSR.

In the middle 1960s, however, serious efforts to overcome this weakness began to appear. Existential theologians were mentioned increasingly in Soviet scholarship, and their systems of thought began to receive serious attention. For the first time Western theologians, both the leaders and even many of the lesser known figures, became subjects of Soviet writings, infrequently, to be sure, but often enough to indicate serious and continued consideration.

This article attempts to illustrate some of the dimensions of this new departure, in order to evaluate in part how successful Soviet scholarship has been in its study of contemporary theology. To keep the study within manageable proportions, a "case study" approach inspects a sampling of Soviet philosophical and religious studies insofar as they concern four of the major influences

141

in contemporary Western theology: Kierkegaard, Tillich, Barth, and Bultmann. It should not be inferred that Soviet scholarship has limited its purview to such stalwarts, for a large number of contemporary theologians have been examined. Nevertheless, inspection of Soviet treatment of these four figures will give some indices of the level of development of the larger field of contemporary theology in Soviet scholarship.

Soren Kierkegaard

With the possible exception of Nikolai Berdiaev, probably no theologian has received more frequent mention in recent Soviet scholarship than the Dane Soren Kierkegaard (1813-55). Has influence is felt not only in theology, but in philosophy as well, and hence Soviet scholars in both fields have occasion to study him.

> Already in the forties of the last century the philosophical mutiny in Kierkegaard, with the religious-mystical position of Protestantism against the rationalistic, dialectical-logical conception of the world of Hegel, laid the bases of the irrationalistic tradition of the most recent existentialism.[5]

Kierkegaard's influence in the contemporary world has been so immense that Soviet scholarship can scarcely avoid noticing him, not only in attempting to comprehend contemporary existential theology, but secular or even atheistic existential philosophy as well. The leaders of existential thought make no secret of Kierkegaard's influence on their thoughts.[6]

A second reason for the amount of attention devoted to Kierkegaard is his proximity to Hegel. Because of the special affinity between Marxism and Hegelianism, and because Karl Marx himself arrived at his philosophical discoveries through studying the Hegelian tradition, Hegel occupies a special place in Soviet philosophical scholarship. The fact that "Kierkegaard in his time fought against the panlogism of Hegel"[7] would in itself tend to attract the attention of Soviet researchers.

Finally, there are good grounds for study of Kierkegaard because of his influence on theology.[8] To a man, contemporary existential theologians are the children of Kierkegaard (nearly always admittedly so) and hence his influence is ubiquitous throughout the field. If such theological luminaries as Tillich, Barth, and Bultmann are worthy of study, Kierkegaard is much more deserving of attention, for his impact is felt throughout the broad circles of followers of each of these theologians as well as numerous others besides them. Furthermore, Kierkegaard's anticipation of Berdiaev on so many theological issues would tend to make him especially prominent in Soviet eyes, for the burgeoning popularity of Berdiaev, particularly among the intelligentsia, presents an ever more critically important problem even to those Soviet philosophers whose interests are confined to what is pragmatically relevant in contemporary Soviet society.[9]

It would be difficult for the Soviet reader to derive any clear or comprehensive picture of Kierkegaard's thought from references to him (or even, indeed, articles devoted solely to him) in Soviet scholarship. In part, this is doubtless due to the opacity of Kierkegaard's own writings. The inconstancy of attitudes and subjects, the convoluted patterns of thought, the love of the dramatic and the tendency towards overstatement, the reliance on indirecton and illustration rather than rigorous definition, and the exceedingly personal involvement of the author with his work, all combine to render the task of understanding Kierkegaard's writings remarkably difficult. To penetrate through the initial obscurity of much of his work, demands a rather extraordinary degree of insight and sympathy. Furthermore, the relatively large number of works that he produced, ranging from brief essays to immense treatises, demands a considerable devotion of time and energy to the subject if any degree of competence is to be achieved. Certainly there is danger that a cursory, or even intense but relatively brief, immersion in his writings will result in distortions and misunderstandings. It hardly needs emphasizing that if Kierkegaard is approached *en passant*, there is very little chance that his system of thought (if system there be) will be grasped at all. Despite these difficulties, however, certain aspects of his thought, sometimes in distorted form, can be derived from contemporary Soviet writings on Kierkegaard.

Naturally, Kierkegaard's basic denial of the objective approach in favor of the subjective is noted, for this emphasis on the existential, as contrasted with the essential, is widespread in contemporary philosophy. "Kierkegaard, as a subjective idealist, denies the objective character of the historical process, considering that it is not history which is the key to 'I', but 'I' is the key to history."[10]   One can say nothing at all about other people or things outside; one only knows himself and what he perceives and experiences. Morality, for example, is exclusively individual and cannot be applied generally.[11] However, while Soviet scholarship does take note of this individualistic tenor of Kierkegaard's thoughts, at times it seems questionable whether this theme is presented forcefully enough or with sufficient emphasis in Soviet writings to communicate its intensity in Kierkegaard's own works, for this approach permeates nearly every other concept with which he deals.

This deficiency is particularly evident in attempts by Soviet scholars to elucidate Kierkegaardian anthropology. Indeed, in many respects, to use the term *anthropology* at all with respect to Kierkegaard may betray a certain lack of understanding, for its connotations of generality, abstractness, and objectivity might seem very foreign indeed to Kierkegaard's intensely personal approach. It is questionable at best, for example, that "Kierkegaard in his philosophy operates with the concept of abstract man, but he paints him with a cloud; his prototype is the biblical Adam, and by no means a real, earthly man."[12] Kierkegaard's connection of alienation with Adam's discovery of *Angst* is quite rightly noted, [13] but to interpret the use of the doctrine of the Fall as a general thesis about abstract man may be to give it more weight than was intended in the original usage. When Kierkegaard talks of man, one always suspects that he has only one individual (himself) or perhaps two (himself and the individual reader) in mind. And when, especially in a very brief article summarizing Kierkegaard's philosophy, Soviet scholarship concludes that for him morality is categorically inapplicable to women because of their subordination to the man,[14] one wonders whether this is at all what Kierkegaard intended.

Kierkegaard's depiction of the human situation is explained by Soviet commentators as a twofold, paradoxical situation. The individual is isolated, his isolation consisting both of alienation from the world and unification with it; it is this peculiar isolation which places before him the unavoidable act of choosing.[15] Ideally, the individual should be sovereign, free, the molder of his own life in concrete actions, and without subordination of the self to external circumstances.[16]

Soviet scholarship places special emphasis on the Kierkegaardian construct concerning levels of human existence (as developed, for example, in his *Stages on Life's Way*). It does not appear that Soviet commentators have been especially successful in elucidating this ambiguous subject. For example, the aesthetic and the ethical stages are equated with the Either-Or decision that faces man.[17] The crucial distinction within the religious stage between "Religiousness A" and "Religiousness B" seems to be missing from the Soviet analysis. This leads to a very curious interpretation: "The entire life of the person in the given [religious] stage presents itself as an uninterrupted ascent to god, an approach to complete union with him in the afterlife."[18] That such an interpretation is directly opposed to Kierkegaard's doctrine that progress does not come gradually but rather by a radical leap, rightly noted by the author earlier in the same article,[19] seems to have escaped his attention.

> There is no hope or progress, and therefore the person performs an unmotivated leap and enters into the next stage of his development. This strange conclusion has for him great convincing power: first, the ways of the lord are inscrutable, and second, the atonement for the primeval sin by the martyr's death of Christ gives the person hope for communion with god, in which, properly, according to Kierkegaard, is his development. Thus, the problem of the development of the person receives for Kierkegaard a theological interpretation in the spirit of the anthropological principles of Protestantism.[20]

Indeed, Kierkegaard's anthropology, according to Soviet scholarship, is not so much an anthropology as a theology. In discussing his approach to ethics, for example, the following conclusion is reached:

> All of these arguments are based on complete ignorance of the social motivations of moral actions and moral norms. If one departs from the social determinism of morality, then one proceeds with logical inevitability to derive morality either from the depths of the psyche, which for Kierkegaard, who considers man sinful, is ruled out, or from divine commandments, reaching man by one means or another. Thus, the moral doctrine of Kierkegaard is theocentric. Theocentrism colors all his philosophical anthropology. This is evident from those explanations which he gives to the ethical stage of the life of the person.[21]

In the last analysis, Soviet scholars see in this theocentric approach a denial of the subjective methodology with which Kierkegaard began: Kierkegaard's subjectivism really leads him to posit the objectivity of God in place of the real, bourgeois world that he denies.[22]

If Soviet treatment of Kierkegaard seems somewhat inchoate, this is not primarily due to lack of available sources. While there is no evidence that Soviet scholars are working in the original sources, nor that direct translations from the Danish to Russian are available, Soviet scholars do have access to the German translation of his complete collected works.[23] A fair sampling of his individual works appears in direct citations: *Either-Or,*[24] *Final Unscientific Postscript,*[25] *On the Concept of Irony,*[26] *Fear and Trembling,* and *On the Difference Between the Genius and the Apostle.*[27] Due note is taken of the 1962 bibliography by Y. Himmelstrup, *Soren Kierkegaard,* with its 6995 entries.[28] However, there is perhaps an unhealthy tendency to rely on secondary works about Kierkegaard, rather than on his own writings themselves.[29]

In summing up Kierkegaard's importance as an influence on contemporary philosophy and theology, Soviet scholarship seems to be far from unanimous. A well-researched article, for example, was devoted to a denial of *Slavic Review's* (June 1966) comparison of Kierkegaard and Hertzen.[30] Even within Protestantism, his system cannot be universally acceptable:

> Calvinism, it is true, accepts the Lutheran justification by faith and also is a religious expression of bourgeois mercantilism and the spirit of individualism. However, Calvin's doctrine of predestination decisively condemns Kierkegaard by contradicting the unmotivated free will of the individual and excluding a person's free decision and choice of his actions.[31]

One Soviet author evaluates him as "a reactionary Danish philosopher-mystic of the 19th Century"[32] which, at first glance, may seem a bit unusual, but which can be supported on the basis of the social doctrines of Marxism. Even on the question of whether Kierkegaard can properly be called an existentialist there is some controversy:

> In this connection the question arises that allegedly existentialism existed earlier, beginning with Kierkegaard. We do not have momentous bases to agree with this position of bourgeois philosophical historiography. It is known that Kierkegaard as an "existentialist" was born only after the appearance of contemporary existentialism. That the religious thinking of Kierkegaard belongs to existentialism seems debatable to us. The very term *existentialism* in general did not exist at all before the thirties of our century. From our point of view, so-called "religious" existentialism is simply a part of Christian theology, inasmuch as it arose as a reaction to those numerous "existential" human and social problems which first were raised and answered by existentialism. It seems to us quite difficult to prove that theology may be existentialist, and existentialism theological, if we, in sum, are to be consistent in the interpretation of the concept of existence.[33]

Others, however, disagree, explicitly ascribing the beginnings of existentialism to Kierkegaard.[34]

Soviet scholarship's summary interpretation of Kierkegaard is expressed in terms of the received tradition of Marxism. His rejection of the Church as mediator between God and man in favor of an individual relationship with God was nothing other than a reflection of the bourgeois fear of the masses and the bourgeoisie's misanthropism in view of its awareness that the collapse of capitalism was imminent.[35]

Paul Tillich

The appearance of Paul Tillich (1886-1965) on the horizon of Soviet scholarship was a relatively late phenomenon. In part, this may be due to the fact that Tillich's influence in the major denominations is perhaps less visible than that of other theologians, and despite the highly philosophical tenor of his writings, he stands somewhat to one side of the mainstream of existential theology. For whatever reason, Tillich comes into view infrequently in contemporary Soviet scholarship.

When Tillich is mentioned in Soviet writings, considerable confusion prevails almost always. In this regard, Soviet commentators are one with a vast number of Western writers who have similarly failed in the attempt to present Tillich's thought in condensed form. This is largely due to the complexity that is interwoven into Tillich's system of theology. Tillich is one of the few truly systematic theologians of the twentieth century, whose thought is an organic whole, indivisible, with each concept presupposing a grasp of the entire system for its understanding. Furthermore, his theology is so dependent—indirectly, perhaps, but nonetheless heavily—on the works of predecessors in a number of fields (German idealistic philosophy, nineteenth-century theology, psychoanalytic psychology, modern art and aesthetics, etc.) that it becomes very difficult indeed to gain an accurate assessment of his thought without considerable study of these background disciplines.

Of recent articles on Tillich, perhaps the least susceptible to detectable error was one by a United States author which was translated in *Voprosy Filosofii* in 1968; it should be noted, however, that this article dealt almost entirely with Tillich's predecessors and his impact, and made no excursions whatsoever into the dangerous region of the content of his theology.[36] Other Soviet endeavors are rather less fortunate. One Soviet author, for example, seems to connect Tillich with the *Honest to God* approach of J.A.T. Robinson by enlisting the aid of a single quotation taken out of context from Tillich:

> This depth is what we mean by the word *god*. And if this word has no great meaning for you, translate it and speak of the depth of your life, the spring of your existence, your most important interest, and what you take unreservedly seriously. Perhaps in this case you will have to forget everything traditional that you have been taught about god, perhaps even the very word *god*.[37]

In another case, a Soviet author spends more than 60 percent of a five-and-a-half-page article on background matters and then attempts, with rather remarkable lack of success, to present Tillich's theology in two pages.[38]

A fairly high proportion of Soviet attention to Tillich is devoted to his Method of Correlation, treating it primarily in terms of a means of joining philosophy with theology rather than as a means of bridging the gap between the individual and the problems raised by the world around him.[39] This other function of the Method of Correlation is not entirely absent, however:

> "Both in philosophy and theology," reasons Tillich, "the ontological question inevitably arises—the question of being, but this question of philosophy and theology is raised from different positions: for philosophy interest is placed in 'being in itself,' for theology 'the meaning of being for us.' "[40]

Other doctrines of Tillich very often are in imminent danger of being inundated by confusion. Whether the chaos that threatens is due to insufficient understanding on the part of the Soviet author in question, or whether it is due to an overly bold attempt to simplify and condense, must remain an open question.

> *Kairos* signifies an historical process, its pattern and connection with the advent of Christ (the second *kairos,* etc.) and the motive power of this process. Theonomy, autonomy, and heteronomy are various periods of development. "Autonomy is the dynamic process in history. Theonomy is the substance and meaning of history." Autonomy prepares the way for theonomy. "Theonomy is the answer to the question contained in autonomy." Heteronomy is the demonic beginning of history, the attempt to suppress autonomy, to limit the creation and to subordinate human life to a law which is foreign to inner consciousness. The principle of autonomy is connected with the destruction of freedom. Tillich limits its activity. "All thoughts about autonomy are accompanied by consciousness of sin, and this was the basic experience of my life."[41]

Oddly enough, the ontological basis of Tillich's theology, which may represent the system's most subtle aspect, seems to fare rather better at the hands of Soviet scholarship. "The being of a human, according to Tillich, is always confronted with nonbeing, for man is mortal."[42] Except for the rather minor error of attributing an inspriational function to what may actually serve Tillich as an illustrative vehicle, Tillich's attribution of ontological meaning to the biblical doctrine of the Fall is clearly understood: "He proceeds from the Old Testament history of the fall of Adam, which he views as a symbolic expression of 'alienation,' as the move from 'essence' to 'existence,' in which man is condemned to abide."[43] Alienation and *Angst* follow from this ontological realization.

> The threat of nonbeing, which possesses man, gives birth to dread. Dread Tillich describes as "the existential discovery of nonbeing," as the finality which is experienced "as my personal finality."
> ... Dread is not a temporal but a permanent, "existential" condition of man, evoked by "nonbeing", i.e., by that which cannot be understood. Dread cannot be eliminated; for Tillich, it characterizes the very existence of man.[44]

Perhaps understandably, because Tillich is very seldom clear and precise when treating the subject, the concept of God he derives from his ontological analysis of existence ("ground of being," etc.) receives somewhat less successful elucidation in Soviet scholarship. "Attempts are made to show the failure of human reason when faced with revelation, which descends on man in a moment of ecstasy, giving the possibility of penetrating to some sort of 'depth of reason,' 'chaos,' 'absolute,' 'ultimate concern,' etc. (as a rule, Tillich, when speaking of god, uses symbolic designations, metaphors)."[45] Perhaps wisely, Soviet scholarship seldom endeavors to isolate more precisely what Tillich means by the word *God* (although it should be noted that such summary treatments as this may run considerable risk of misrepresentation—to understand Tillich's "ultimate concern" as a direct metaphor for God is possible only by tropical extension).

Tillich's approach to ethics has also come under scrutiny in Soviet scholarship. Here the ground seems somewhat firmer, perhaps due in part to the ability of Soviet specialists to draw upon the not entirely dissimilar emphases of Berdiaev.

> The basic method for supplying a foundation for the absoluteness of the "moral demands of god" in contemporary Evangelical ethics is the division of the sphere of morality into two parts, one of which is presented as absolute. Paul Tillich, for example, introduces the concepts of "moralism" and "morality" to this end. "Moralism," according to Tillich, presents itself as the content of the moral imperative and is concerned with such circumstantial and changing values as traditional, consentual, political and religious authorities, and therefore "moralism" (the concrete rules of conduct) is also variable and circumstantial. "Morality" serves for Tillich as "the pure form of the essential self-assertion of man." It is unconditional and absolute, because in it, according to Tillich, we are not related to any external, changing powers.[46]

Tillich's insistence that no laws stemming from an outside agency, explicitly including the state, can be considered anything more than conditional is noted without comment.[47]

In summary, it would not seem that Soviet commentators have succeeded well in the attempt to understand and portray Tillich's theology. For example, one Soviet writer concludes, "In a word, the doctrine of Christ, as also the doctrine of god, for Tillich are products of revelation, and they are portrayed as theological, not philosophical products."[48] Such a statement, while superficially documentable, would seem to run a perilous risk of ignoring the entire ontological basis that unites philosophy and theology in Tillich's mind, as Soviet scholarship illustrates elsewhere in treating the Method of Correlation. Nor can the following summary of Tillich's doctrine of the New Being inspire great confidence in the Soviet author's accuracy of understanding Tillich:

> The overcoming of all conflicts and contradictions of the consciousness of the individual is connected, according to Tillich, with the

individual's conversion to "Being," "the Transcendent," i.e., to
god. Thus, in the last analysis he arrives at "absolute faith" as
the panacea for all problems and contradictions of actuality.[49]

Finally, to place too much emphasis on Tillich's recognition of the value of certain essentialist (as opposed to existentialist) positions[50] may not accurately
convey the depth of Tillich's commitment to existentialism.

In large measure, deficiencies in Soviet studies on Tillich are due to insufficient immersion in (or unavailability of) his works. It would appear that the
first two volumes of his *Systematic Theology* are available to Soviet scholars[51]
but, in one illustrative example, the author of a Soviet article on Tillich cites
pages 3-4 and 18 of volume I and includes one general reference to volume II;
otherwise, he relies almost entirely on M. Horton's *Tillich's Role in Contemporary Theology*.[52] In view of the difficulty in elucidating Tillich's complex
and interconnected system, reliance upon secondary sources is an especially
tenuous means of approaching his theology. It is only slightly less misleading
to rely on his more popular works, such as *The Protestant Era, Interpretation
of History*,[53] *The Courage to Be, The New Being*,[54] or a German translation,
Auf der Grenze.[55] These works, although written by Tillich and designed for
a less technically oriented readership, all seem to presuppose a knowledge of
his system. To use them as an approach to, much less a substitute for, his
Systematic Theology can result in serious misunderstandings.

One possible advantage that Soviet scholarship may possess in approaching
Tillich is that his works were written in English and would not seem to be
available in Russian translation. English for these scholars is a second language
just as it was for Tillich, and hence Tillich's peculiar use of certain English
words, in which he gives them their exact definition rather than admitting
their more common connotations (e.g., "essential") is less subject to misconceptions. At times, Tillich quite openly reinterprets a word for his own use
and ignores its customary content, and Soviet scholarship quite properly
takes note:

> At its basis lies a not very clever etymological manipulation of the
> word *protestantism*, with the aid of which it is given a meaning
> which has nothing in common with its historical content. According
> to Tillich, "Protestantism is a protest against form." And, as such, it
> is also a protest against itself. "Any era is subject to protestant pro-
> test," he writes. "This relates to the era of the Reformation."[56]

At other times, however, Tillich's reinterpretation of English words is more
deft, and in this regard Soviet scholars may be less likely to draw incorrect
conclusions than would a native American.

Ultimately, it would not appear that Soviet scholarship is able comfortably to classify Tillich neatly and fit him into a general overview of contemporary theology. One author concludes his study very strangely indeed: "In his final conclusions Tillich remains a pastor, in principle having in no way broken with the soil of traditional Lutheranism."[57] More to the point, there seems to be some doubt as to whether Tillich is to be dismissed categorically as representing a reactionary trend as contrasted with progressive Marxism:

> It is interesting to note that Tillich paid respect to Marxist philosophy. "No one can understand the character of contemporary revolution in the world," he asserted, "if he has not been prepared for this by the Marxist analysis of bourgeois society, of the contradictions of this society and its basic tendencies." In another place Tillich gives the materialistic explanation of history its due: "Man—even that man who is occupied with social production—this is he who is the material of all history." Tillich, doubtless, belongs to the number of contemporary thinkers who are trying to preserve peace in the whole world.[58]

Karl Barth

Of the three modern theologians under review, by far the most influential in Western Protestantism is Karl Barth (1886-1968). The Barthian theology, more commonly designated neoorthodoxy, swept through the churches of Europe in the interwar period and was a dominant force in Western Christianity in the decades following World War II. His influence has been enormous. It was primarily through Barth that the power of existentialism, with its immediacy and uncompromising individualism and with its incisive demand for decision, entered into traditional Christianity in the Protestant West. Whereas study of other contemporary theologians may be helpful, an understanding of Barth is essential for a proper comprehension of the postwar evolution of Western Protestantism.

In view of his enormous influence, it seems odd that Barth's name appears relatively infrequently in contemporary Soviet scholarship. In part, this may be due to the fact that when Barth broke with the earlier liberalism in 1920 he consciously elected to return to the language of the Church rather than, as had been increasingly the norm, utilizing the terms and concepts of the secular disciplines (philosophy, history, etc.). The result has been that Barth's influence has been confined almost exclusively within the Church. He has not had any considerable, measurable impact on secular existentialism. In larger measure, however, his receipt of infrequent coverage in Soviet scholarship is due to a semantic or, perhaps, methodological difficulty that has not yet been overcome in Soviet scholarship. There is pronounced tendency to treat the movement in which he has been a dominant figure collectively rather than in terms of individual theologians. "The dialectical theology" is often alluded to and analyzed, but as an aggregate force in which distinctions are seldom drawn between the contributions and positions of Barth and those of more or less closely related theologians (Brunner, Niebuhr, Gogarten, et al.). Indeed, it is often the case that all existential theologians, including Tillich and Bultmann, are lumped together indiscriminately under the rubric "dialectical theology."[59] This is an increasingly questionable approach after the early 1920s, when there was a considerable degree of confluence among such theologians. Particularly if there is danger of extending the usage to include Catholic existential thinkers such as Maritain or even non-Christians such as Buber, this approach becomes very tenuous indeed.

Because of this problem in categorization, an attempt to discern the treatment of Barth in Soviet scholarship will perforce embrace a degree of imprecision. At times, to be sure, Barth is treated specifically and examined from his own works; at other times, however, when dialectical theology is the subject, the treatment will be drawn primarily from Barth, but without indication of what accretions may have come from other thinkers.

Barth's ideational background receives somewhat better coverage than is the norm in contemporary Soviet scholarship on existential theologians. Due note is taken of his Kierkegaardian emphases,[60] and his earlier background in the liberal theology is also noted, with Ritschl, Harnack, and Troeltsch receiving mention as his theological predecessors.[61] Significantly, Schleiermacher also appears in the lists of Barth's forbears.[62] This is fairly atypical, for Schleiermacher's influence generally goes unnoticed in Soviet scholarship (see below), and may be due in part to his appearing in a United States author's treatment translated into Russian: 'Karl Barth became famous as a sharp opponent of the 'psychologization' or religious belief, which had been introduced to Protestant theology thanks to Friedrich Schleiermacher, who brought Kantian categories into Protestant theology."[63]

Generally speaking, because of Barth's proximity to the normative doctrinal patterns of historic Christianity, his theology does not seem to present Soviet scholarship with quite so many quandaries as other forms of the existential approach. His basic attitudes are noted in the Soviet literature, and the frequency of fairly accurate portrayal (as opposed to transmogrification) is relatively high. A case in point would be the crucial doctrine of the role of Scriptures in Barth's theology. One Soviet author in his summary treatment of Barth notes that according to Barth, God's Word cannot be received directly, but only through His Prophets and Apostles, or in other words, through the Bible. Its authenticity is attested to by the first Church, and the Holy Spirit, through subsequent history, also testifies to it. Hence, he notes that Barth, even though he commences by basing all things on the Word, ultimately has recourse to the same philosophical and literary-critical approaches of the older liberalism.[64] Another Soviet author, however, in dealing with Barth's approach to ethics concludes simply, and without limiting qualifications, that according to Barth the believer must obey the laws in the Bible.[65] This conclusion, of course, runs perilously close to overlooking Barth's distinction between the Word and the words, his doctrine that the Bible is the vehicle, not the source, of guidance in the Christian life.

At least in its intention, Barth's system is explicitly and exclusively theocentric, working deductively from God's revelation of himself to derived conclusions concerning man rather than, as had often been the practice in the earlier liberalism, working inductively from man's experience as the starting point. Barth's doctrine of God receives fairly competent treatment in Soviet scholarship. The disjunctive relationship between man and God (God as "wholly other") is noted, as is the dictum that the only knowledge of God possible is that contained in His revelation of Himself.[66] Indeed, man can never learn anything at all about God except that "God is absolutely necessary."[67] Barth's emphasis on the existential dimension in the concept of God is also noted: "God is in heaven, but you are on earth,' he writes. 'The relationship of *this* god to *this* man and *this* man to *this* god is for me the theme of the Bible and the sum of philosophy in one word.'"[68] Study of God is *sui generis*; unlike human contradictions, such as that between capitalism and communism, which operate within a single system (the world), the problems concerning knowledge of God are dissimilar to human contradictions and are hence properly called paradoxes.[69]

As a result of this concept of God, man, for Barth, exists "in a 'field of tension' between two worlds, the earthly and the heavenly."[70]

> At the center of the theological constructions of the representatives of "neo-orthodoxy" stands man, torn by the tragic contradictions of his existence. Fear of death and the condemnation of primeval sin oppress man, looming as the basic characteristics of his being. The theologians of this movement emphasize the impossibility of man overcoming these tragic contradictions by his own powers. Man can overcome them only when he has come into communion with god, only when he has wholly surrendered himself to him. The way of "man's coming into communion with god," in their opinion, is based not on intelligence, but on irrational processes, on blind faith.[71]

With regard to Barth's doctrine of ethics, the existential basis is properly indicated,[72] whereby general rules of conduct are supplanted by the individualized, inner experience of the concrete situation. "Situational ethics," however, is treated rather summarily: " 'Situation ethics' is reduced to 'the ethics of the moment,' to the ethics of absolute relativism and subjectivism, which is the equivalent to a denial of ethics."[73] Its approach has a theocentric rationale behind it: "The will of god is *absolutely free,* and therefore it cannot be placed

in the Procrustean bed of specific rules of conduct."[74]   Soviet treatment of this
subject, however, may be somewhat deficient, for the immense impact of
situational ethics in Western Christendom is neither indicated nor really
explained. An East German article translated into Russian sums up Barth's
approach to Christian conduct in terms that seem to emphasize the traditional
Christian element in his thought rather more than the existential, situational
dimension: "To live in the spirit of Jesus Christ, to follow his laws, to be led
by his word—such is the ultimate conclusion of this understanding of the
divinity."[75]

From the Marxist point of view, Barth's apparent denial of social action in
favor of individualism is considered a serious defect. His doctrine of God as
"wholly other" raises such an immense chasm between God and man "that *in
practice* god has no meaning for man and *in practice* man should seek support
in himself alone and himself bear responsibility for his own life ('god is in
heaven, but you are on earth.')."[76]   Nor is Barth's doctrine that all social,
governmental, moral, and other crises stem from the crisis of the individual
and can be ameliorated only by changing the individual[77] especially compatible
with the Marxist preference for a collective approach to such problems. "In its
social role, contemporary Evangelical ethics is not different in principle from
either traditional Protestantism, Catholicism or Orthodoxy."[78]

Generally, however, Soviet scholarship seems fairly capable in attempting
to summarize Barth's position, covering a sufficient proportion of his important
doctrines to give a fairly reliable picture.[79]   The chief deficiency in Soviet
scholarship on Barth is due to a problem endemic to all serious study of his
work. Barth simply wrote too much. The volume of his theological work has
probably not been equalled since the Reformation and the High Middle Ages,
and as a result, to attempt to cover his theology comprehensively is a challenge
of intimidating magnitude. There is little evidence that Soviet scholarship has
managed to cover even his formidable magnum opus, *Church Dogmatics,*
comprehensively, although occasional reference is made to volumes II, III, IV,
and VII, parts 3 and 4.[80]   Perhaps because much of Barth's writing is extraordinarily difficult without a deep immersion in, and familiarity with, the
theological writings of the Church, and particularly of the Calvinistic tradition,
Soviet scholarship has a considerable tendency to rely on secondary sources.
One illustrative article on Barth cites an article he contributed to a 1960
Festschrift for H. Barth once, *The Epistle to the Romans* six times, and then
relies on secondary sources for the reamining thirty-two footnotes.[81]

Soviet scholarship seems fairly ambiguous in evaluating Barth. A degree
of expedience is detected in the failure to maintain rigorous existentialism
in order to preserve the theology's influence in the parish.[82]   Nevertheless, a
degree of sympathy and, at times, an unusual desire to present his theology
fairly (if, inadvertently, quite inaccurately) is occasionally evident.[83]   Perhaps
in large measure this is due to Barth's rejection of an anti-Communist position,

which for Soviet authors provides grounds for "giving respect to the famous Swiss religious figure for his active participation in the struggle for peace, for averting a new world war."[84] Soviet scholarship takes some pride in Barth's evolution over a half century from an initial hostility to bolshevism to a neutral position, while simultaneously expressing some pique that although Barth condemns capitalism, he also rejects socialism.[85] At one point his answer to Reinhold Neibuhr's attack on him for being neutral on the Hungarian question is approvingly quoted: "And I ask why Neibuhr is silent on American prisons. When he talks about that, I will talk about Hungary."[86]

Rudolph Bultmann

Rudolph Bultmann (1884-   ) is probably the most thoroughgoing existentialist of any of the major theologians of the Twentieth century. Rigorous and uncompromising in his devotion to philosophical existentialism, he has had only minimal impact in the churches. His influence is enormous, however, in religious scholarship, not so much because of his theological position (which has found few disciples), but because of his eminence as a scholar of the New Testament. His command of this field is towering and, to the degree that New Testament scholarship is a sine qua non of contemporary Protestant study, he is a familiar and influential figure throughout the West.

The consistency of Bultmann's existential approach might make him more accessible for Soviet scholars than some of the more traditional theologians. Soviet philosophy has awakened to the necessity of dealing with existentialism, and a great many of the insights derived from secular existentialists would seem applicable to Bultmann. Philosophically, at least, he represents somewhat of a known category to contemporary Soviet philosophical scholarship. "The irrationalistic approach to man lies at the basis of his 'existential' interpretation of Christian mythology."[87]

The key to Bultmann's approach to theology is "demythologizing" the Scriptures, a methodological device intended to translate the concepts of the Scriptures from the myths of the supernatural world view reflected therein into terms understandable to the scientific, naturalistic world view of the twentieth century.

The Christian faith, states Bultmann, is presented in the Bible, and in particular in the New Testament, in mythological form. Bultmann shows, in particular, the mythical character of the Biblical picture of the world. "The world is considered as divided into three stories. In the middle is the earth, above it heaven, below it the underworld. Heaven is the habitation of god and the heavenly creation, angels; the underworld is hades, the place of torment. But even the earth is

not only the place where natural and everyday events occur; it is also
the area of action of the supernatural powers, god and his angels, satan
and his demons. In natural events and in the thought, will and actions
of people the supernatural powers intervene; miracles are not infrequent.
Man does not possess himself; he may be possessed by demons; satan may
reward his evil designs; but god also can lead him by thoughts and will,
can give him the possibility to recognize the heavenly images.[88]

From the scientific point of view, by contrast, the natural order cannot be dis-
rupted by supernatural powers.[89] For this reason "Bultmann tries to represent
the biblical myths not as stories about real events, but only as a *mode* of trans-
mitting to man another, deeper content (the *kerygma*), which is hidden by the
shallowness of the gospel narrative."[90]

For Bultmann, the *kerygma* consists not of a message but rather of a
demand, a demand for an existential decision on the part of the individual to
whom it is presented.

"The Christian life," writes Bultmann, "is always a life from the hereafter as the future, not in the sense of the realization of an idea, but
always only in the given moment, in decision. And real decisions never
accept the form of the matter; they never are objectified in the affair,
which may have been called Christian; this characteristic of it has
already disappeared together with the moment. Not the extratemporal
eternity of an idea determines the moment, but the requirement now
approaching me, the meeting." Only in the decision of the moment
may we come to the help of our neighbor. Only here does Christian
love exist. Only "noncasuistical thought" does not give us stagnation
in inactive complacence, it simply keeps our conscience on the alert,
a feeling of responsibility in a condition of full readiness.[91]

According to Soviet scholarship, Bultmann's theology is anthropologically
oriented, as witness his statement "Theology sees the world and man always
in relation to god. Each thesis about god is simultaneously also a thesis about
man, and conversely. Therefore in this sense . . . theology is simultaneously
anthropology."[92] Some ambiguity exists, however, for the same author also
takes note of Bultmann's condemnation of liberal theology for speaking not
of God but of man.[93]

Various degrees of confusion seem to be evident in Soviet analysis of
Bultmann's thought.

The term *kerygma* designates the "true" positions of the New Testament. Together with them in the New Testament there are also
"myths." The New Testament *kerygma* speaks of god's plan of

salvation, equally inviting all generations. The mythical part, though, sets forth the divine actions in accordance with the notions of the first century of our era. However, reminds Bultmann, actions are always "eschatological events," which enter into history as possibilities for construction of a meaningful life.[94]

Certainly there seems room for questioning whether the author has clearly understood Bultmann's position in the above passage. A more basic error is evident in the following:

> He rejects the purely philosophical interpretation of Christian mytho-
> logy. Bultmann tries to combine together the "existential" interpre-
> tation of the gospel myths with an acceptance of the reality of the
> "earthly history" of Christ, his suffering and death on the cross.
>   Bultmann tries to cleanse the New Testament of "miracles," of
> the immediate intervention of supernatural powers in earthly life.
> Therefore from the gospel history of Christ Bultmann accepts as real
> only those facts that relate to earthly events of the life of Christ (in
> this point he is close to the liberal theology). . . . Thus, despite all the
> "radical" designs of "demythologizing" the New Testament, Bultmann
> appeals to it as the sole source of the Christian faith.[95]

This is a rather astonishing summary in view of Bultmann's position, derived from his rigorous application of the disciplines of New Testament scholarship, that we have almost no reliable knowledge about Jesus and, indeed, know very little about the theology of the earliest Church. Nor is it consistent with Bultmann's approach to historiography, in which history is considered not as events, but as the interpretation of events.[96] Finally, on theological grounds it is impermissable, in view of the Bultmannian dictum that "natural data in no case may be used as a foundation for faith."[97]

It would seem that the chief problem in Soviet study of Bultmann is insufficient attention to his writings. On relatively rare occasion his *Glauben und Verstehen*[98] and an article contributed by him to the anthology *Kerygma and Mythos*[99] will be cited. Usually, however, there is fairly obvious reliance on secondary works and reactions to Bultmann by other thinkers (e.g., Thielecke), a questionable procedure at best.[100] The chief reason for this inattention to his own writings would doubtless be that the chief source of his theological position is to be found in his *Theology of the New Testament*. Although this work has been quoted on at least one occasion,[101] in itself it presumes such a high degree of familiarity with the technical procedures of New Testament criticism that it would probably remain totally opaque to nearly all Soviet observers who have not had the training necessary to fol-low such intricacies. "For us, these attempts to translate the Bible into contemporary 'existential' language offer no special interest. We are interested in the general thought, the philosophical and social direction of the ideas of Bultmann."[102] The difficulty, of course, is that ultimately the two are inseparable.

Conclusions

Despite the greater degree of attention devoted to contemporary theology by recent Soviet scholarship, as contrasted with the almost total absence of the subject in earlier endeavors, it seems clear that this field is far from fully developed in Soviet philosophy and study of religion. On relatively infrequent occasions a minimal degree of understanding is evident, but there is certainly no indication as yet of any towering competence in studying existential theology. Soviet treatment of this field of knowledge is still sufficiently under-developed that one turns to their writings on contemporary theology more as an index of the development of Soviet philosophical scholarship than as a possible source of added insight into the works of the theologians.

On certain points, however, it may be conceded that the particular traditions of Marxist-Leninist philosophy in which Soviet scholarship is steeped give rise to insights and interpretations that may merit inspection. In particular, the attempt to analyze the social role of the existentialist theologians has occupied much of the attention of Soviet scholarship. Existential theologians are described as hostile to socialism because of their emphasis on the individual, following Kierkegaard.[103] More concretely, such theologians reflect the general crisis of capitalism of the current era.[104]

> Every philosophy is the daughter of its time; more than that, it is
> nothing else than the era itself, intelligible from the position of
> whatever class or social group. The philosophy of Kierkegaard was
> the vulgar romantic reaction to the bourgeois ideology and the idea
> of socialism in the 1840s; but this was its social role in the past. In
> the present time this philosophy is bourgeois, contradicting demo-
> cratic ideology and Marxist socialism. One of the most important
> reasons for its spread in bourgeois countries of the West is the crisis
> of the person in bourgeois society in the epoch of imperialism; the
> danger of thermonuclear catastrophe and destruction of all man-
> kind have only strengthened the process of rendering the person
> worthless; the control of monopoly and the bourgeois state apparatus
> over the conduct and form of the thoughts of the citizens suppress
> the person and lead, on the one hand, to conformism and the deper-
> sonification of the person, and on the other, evokes an answering
> individual reaction in the bourgeois, petit-bourgeois, and especially

intelligentsia ranks. And all this takes place in the conditions of the contemporary second industrial revolution, which reinforces the influence of mechanization and automation of production to the degradation of the person of the worker, enhancing the role and significance of the technical intelligentsia in production and in the life of society and thereby broadening the social base of petit-bourgeois illusions and individualistic hopes.[105]

The cultural nihilism and moral relativism Soviet scholarship detects in existential theology is ascribed to the crisis of capitalism.[106]

Finally, it is necessary to bear in mind that bourgeois consciousness is a reaction to the major feature of our era—the transformation of the world of socialism in the decisive power of the development of the conditions of our era. The bourgeois consciousness is forced to react both to the growth of the power and capability of world socialism, and also to the growing popularity of the ideas of social-ism and communism. In the arsenal of bourgeois ideology anti-communism is strengthened, and one of its means comes forth as individualistic philosophical anthropology, in which the pastors of capitalism wish to find a weapon against the attractive power of socialistic collectivism.[107]

It is by no means a novelty to ascribe the popularity of existentialism to the crises of the twentieth century (indeed, the term *crisis theology* itself suggests such an explanation). Nor is there lack of precedent for considering existen-tialism symptomatic of a collective loss of nerve in the face of the horrors of the twentieth century, as contrasted with the tranquil optimism of the previous generation. To suggest, however, that the chief threat occasioning the rise of existentialism is the growth of communism may seem a novel insight to Western students of contemporary theology.

One of the most marked deficiencies in Soviet study of contemporary theology is a striking lack of understanding of the historical backgrounds of the existential theologians. As has been noted, the development of the existentialist influences in contemporary theology has been examined some-what, but treatment of the historical development of modern theology seems totally lacking. Thus, for example, while Adolph von Harnack and Ernst Troeltsch are occasionally mentioned in connection with theological liberal-ism,[108] there is no mention of the evolution of Christian historiography towards the view, currently widespread, that history is a most unreliable science, repre-senting not facts themselves but current opinions about what happened in the past. The approach of Bultmann, as has been indicated, is inexplicable without the historiographic key.

More important, the towering influence of Friederich Schleiermacher (1768-1834) is almost totally lacking. He is mentioned only on rarest of occasion in summaries of the backgrounds of contemporary theologians,[109] but there is no hint of the immense influence of "the father of modern theology" on contemporary theologians. Schleiermacher reversed the tradition of centuries by working inductively from the individual's experience in constructing his theology, rather than deductively from a body of received scriptures or dogma. In so doing, he initiated the approach that all subsequent liberal and post-liberal theology has followed. Not even Barth, who consciously attempted to center his theology on God's revelation of Himself, entirely departed from the tradition of Schleiermacher (compare his approach to the Word and the Scriptures). Even in specifics, in many respects, contemporary theologians are engaged in elucidation of themes originally posited by Schleiermacher in his *The Christian Faith*. Tillich, for example, in his highly metaphysical, ontological analysis of "the ground of being," would seem to be expressing in different terms almost precisely Schleiermacher's concept in "the feeling of absolute dependence." Bultmann, following Schleiermacher's methodological approach, defines God and, hence, theology according to a specific form of individual experience, the response to the *kerygma*. The failure of Soviet scholarship to divine the influence of Schleiermacher in contemporary theology represents a serious weakness.

To some degree, Soviet understanding of contemporary theology is impeded by Marxism-Leninism, acceptance of which seems to make it extraordinarily difficult to achieve a profound understanding of existentialism. For example, the impact of the individualistic approach of existentialism seems foreign to the Marxist experience:

> Only Marxism-Leninism gives a genuine presentation of man, his existence, the place of man in society. In the works of the classics of Marxism is given a complete doctrine of man as a social and active being, of his interrelationships with other people, of all possible social relationships, which indeed constitute the genuine human existence. "Man's being," writes K. Marx, "is not abstract, an inherently separate individual. In its activities it is an aggregate of all social relationships." A man is not an abstract individual possessing an immutable and simple essence. To approach an evaluation of the being of man concretely is impossible without analysis of his membership in one or another class, his place in the class struggle, and the like. We find nothing like that in the works of K. Barth, for he speaks of man in general, unrelated to time, place, class membership, etc.[110]

Surely, such a contradistinction between man in the abstract and the concrete is not entirely coterminous with the existential distinction between man as an abstraction and as an individual.

The most serious deficiency that threatens to vitiate Soviet studies of contemporary theology is ultimately a methodological problem. Soviet researchers are exclusively and outspokenly utilitarian in these studies, approaching the subject not in order to understand these systems in and for themselves, nor out of a general thirst for knowledge, but in order to provide equipment for more specific, nonscholarly endeavors. A parallel may be seen in the field of psychology of religion: "Soviet psychology of religion from its first steps took shape as a scientific discipline called to life by the needs of atheist education," notes one author, and he proceeds to explain that this is the reason why it is so much more proficient than bourgeois efforts.[111]

Among the concrete reasons motivating Soviet scholarship to inspect contemporary theology is the large influence these theologians have in the Western world. For example, the World Council of Churches has devoted much attention to the theological ideas of Tillich, Barth, and Bultmann.[112] More generally,

> disagreements at the theological summit inevitably are expressed by changes in the tactics of the church and in its daily intercourse with believers. And it is important for us Marxists to study these disagreements and changes, which are closely connected with different variants of the religious trading on the theme of mankind.[113]

In addition, there are domestic reasons for examining contemporary Western theologians. One is their affinity with Nikolai Berdiaev.[114] The growing popularity of Berdiaev among the Soviet intelligentsia has elicited a considerable renaissance in Berdiaev studies among Soviet academicians, a response which is beyond the scope of this paper, but which is deserving of considerable study in itself. That the Western theologians are participants in the tradition exemplified by Berdiaev necessitates their study.

Probably the dominant reason for Soviet study of existential theologians is the hope of discovering additional weapons to be added to the arsenal of the antireligious campaign within the USSR.

> Analysis of contemporary evangelical ethics has great significance for the practice of atheistic education in our country. Believers cannot but be strongly impressed with the fact that the ideology of contemporary Protestantism, which is second in number of believers in Christianity, in fact no longer insists on the doctrine of the divine creation or the eternality and immutability of the basic rules of morality. In addition, this proves the incorrectness of a number of general formulae relating to the basic peculiarities of all of contemporary Christian ethics. In no circumstances is it correct to ascribe

to all of Christianity those views which representatives of one of the three of its basic branches have long since renounced. Genuine scientific atheism should study all of the substantival changes that have taken place in contemporary religious ideology.[115]

According to this line of reasoning, should the discoveries of Soviet scholarship on existential theologians result in products that can be applied in the endeavor to reduce the confidence of Russian believers in the Church, then the effort will have been eminently successful.

Obviously, such utilitarian motivations suggest that maximum proficiency of Soviet in this field of knowledge will be a long process. As yet, there is little evidence of the development of a core of Soviet scholars specializing intensively in contemporary theology who might, regardless of their own positions, succeed in gaining a truly profound understanding of any or all of these systems of thought, and who then might be able to give them a sympathetic and competent treatment in their own writings. That such theologians are being studied at all is a significant change from the earlier pattern; it seems apparent, however, that existential theology is still an infant discipline in Soviet scholarship.

Notes

1. *Pravda,* 11 November 1954.
2. V.A. Karpushin, "Seren k'erkegor—predshestvennik ekzistentsialistskoi antropologii" [Soren Kierkegaard—fore-runner of existential anthro-pology], *Voprosy filosofii* [Problems of Philosophy], no. 12 (December 1967), p. 103.
3. See Donald A. Lowrie and William C. Fletcher, "Khrushchev's Religious Policy, 1959-1964," in Richard H. Marshall, Jr., ed., *Aspects of Religion in the USSR, 1917-1967* (Chicago: Chicago University Press, 1971), pp. 131-55.
4. *Literaturnaia gazeta* [Literary Gazette], 10 April 1962.
5. G.E. Smirnova, "Sovremennaia burzhuaznaia filosofiia istorii i neotomizm" [Contemporary Bourgeois Philosophy of History and Neo-Thomism], *Voprosy filosofii,* no. 2 (February 1967), p. 131.
6. E. Iu. Solov'ev, "Ekzistentsializm" [Existentialism], *Voprosy filosofii,* no. 12 (December 1966), p. 85, note 1.
7. N.S. Narskii, "Problema otchuzhdeniia v ekzistentsializme i religiia" [The Problem of Alienation in Existentialism and Religion], *Filosofskie nauki* [Philosophical Sciences], no. 1 (1966), p. 67.
8. Karpushin, p. 109.
9. Cf. I.F. Balakina, "Religioznaia filosofiia N.A. Berdiaeva i ee sotsial'naia napravlennost' " [The Religious Philosophy of N.A. Berdiaev and its

Social Direction], in Academy of Sciences of the USSR (hereafter cited as AN SSSR), *Voprosy nauchnogo ateizma* [Problems of Scientific Atheism], (Moscow: Mysl', semiannually, 1966--) I, 142.

10. T.T. Gaidukova, "Printsip ironii v filosofii K'erkegora" [The Principle of Irony in the Philosophy of Kierkegaard], *Voprosy filosofii*, no. 9 (September, 1970), p. 112.

11. Karpushin, p. 107.

12. Ibid., p. 112.

13. Narskii, p. 66.

14. Karpushin, p. 108.

15. Gaidukova, p. 118.

16. Ibid., p. 116.

17. Ibid., pp. 119-20.

18. Karpushin, p. 108. When quoting Soviet publications, this study will make no attempt to correct the Soviet practice of "orthographic atheism," whereby the dignity of capitalization is denied to the divinity. See Aleksandr Solzhenitsyn's comments on this convention in his "Epilogue" to *August, 1914* (Paris: YMCA Press, 1971, quoted in *New York Times*, 16 June, 1971).

19. Karpushin, p. 105.

20. Ibid., p. 106.

21. Ibid.

22. Gaidukova, p. 120.

23. Tadeush M. Iaroshevskii, "Kontseptsiia 'podlinnoi zhizni' Martina Khaideggera" [The Conception of "Genuine Life" of Martin Heidegger], *Filosofskie nauki*, no. 5 (1970), p. 119; Karpushin, pp. 105, 107.

24. Ibid.; Gaidukova, pp. 109-20.

25. Karpushin, pp. 105, 107.

26. Gaidukova, pp. 109-20.

27. Narskii, pp. 66, 69.

28. Karpushin, p. 103.

29. Ibid., pp. 109-20.

30. Z.V. Smirnova, "Ob odnoi lozhnoi istoricheskoi paralleli" [One False Historical Parallel], *Voprosy filosofii*, no. 10 (October 1968), pp. 114-124.

31. Karpushin, p. 108.

32. Zh. G. Golotvin, "Problema cheloveka v 'dialekticheskoi teologii' K. Barta" [The Problem of Man in the "Dialectical Theology" of K. Barth], in AN SSSR, III, 300.

33. L.P. Mikhailova, "Interpretatsii ekzistentsializma v sovremennoi zapadnoi filosofii" [Interpretations of Existentialism in Contemporary Western Philosophy], *Voprosy filosofii*, no. 12 (December 1967), p. 165.

34. Iaroshevskii, p. 119.

35. Narskii, pp. 69-70.

36. Pol' Krosser [Paul Crossier?], " 'Teologiia krizisa' Paulia Tillikha" [The

"Theology of Crisis" of Paul Tillich], *Voprosy fillosofii,* no. 10 (October 1968), 78-83.

37. I. Kryvelev, "Contemporary Attempts to Modernize Religious Mythology," *Politicheskoe samoobrazovanie* [Political Self-Education], no. 4 (April 1967), pp. 71-78, translated in *Research Materials* (Geneva, Switzerland), I, 5 (July 1967), p. 2.

38. O.T. Vilnite, "Paul' Tillikh–'teolog krizisa' " [Paul Tillich–"Theologian of Crisis"], *Filosofskie nauki,* no. 2 (1968), pp. 64-69.

39. Iu. V. Krianev, "Prakticheskaia i teologicheskaia podgotovka khristianskogo ekumenizma" [Practical and Theological Preparation for Christian Ecumenicity], in AN SSSR, 8: 298-301.

40. Vilnite, p. 64.

41. Krianev, p. 301.

42. D. M. Ugrinovich, "Popytki 'ekzistentsial'noi' interpretatsii Khristianstva" [Attempts at an "Existential" Interpretation of Christianity], *Voprosy filosofii,* no. 8 (August, 1966), p. 97.

43. Vilnite, p. 68.

44. Ugrinovich, p. 97.

45. Vilnite, pp. 67-68.

46. V.M. Boriskin, "Krizis evangelicheskoi etiki" [The Crisis of Evangelical Ethics], in AN SSSR 1: 98.

47. Ibid.

48. Vilnite, p. 69.

49. Ugrinovich, p. 98.

50. V.V. Lazarev, "Ekzistentsialistskaia kontseptsiia cheloveka v SShA" [The Existentialist Concept of Man in the USA], *Voprosy filosofii,* no. 3 (March 1967), p. 162.

51. Krianev, pp. 299-301.

52. Vilnite, pp. 64-69.

53. Krianev, pp. 299-301.

54. Ugrinovich, pp. 97, 100.

55. Boriskin, pp. 88-118.

56. Ibid., p. 94.

57. Vilnite, p. 69.

58. Krosser, p. 83.

59. E.g., Boriskin, p. 89, note 2.

60. Krianev, p. 304; Goltvin, p. 300.

61. Ibid., p. 303; Krianev, p. 304.

62. Ibid.

63. Krosser, p. 82.

64. Krianev, pp. 305-6.

65. Golotvin, p. 314.

66. Ibid., p. 305.

67. Ibid., p. 311.
68. Ibid., p. 307.
69. Ibid., p. 308.
70. Boriskin, p. 90.
71. Ugrinovich, p. 96.
72. Boriskin, p. 105.
73. Ibid., pp. 110-11.
74. Ibid., p. 109 (unless otherwise specified, all italics are in the original of the text quoted); cf. p. 103.
75. Olof Klor, "Krizis evangelicheskoi teologii" [The Crises of Evangelical Theology], *Voprosy filosofii,* no. 11 (November 1968), p. 100.
76. Ibid., p. 97.
77. Golotvin, pp. 317-18.
78. Boriskin, p. 105.
79. Cf. Krianev, pp. 304-7.
80. Ibid., pp. 304, 305, 307; Boriskin, pp. 88-118.
81. Golotvin, pp. 299-320.
82. M.M. Skibitskii, "Krizis khristianskoi apologetiki" [The Crisis of the Christian Apologetics], *Voprosy filosofii,* no. 4 (April 1968), p. 161 (reviewing G.A. Gabinskii, *Kritika Khristianskoi apologetiki* [A Critique of Christian Apologetics] [Moscow: "Mysl'," 1967]).
83. Golotvin, pp. 299-320.
84. Ibid., p. 301.
85. Ibid., pp. 319, 320.
86. Krianev, pp. 307-8, quoting *Christianity Today* 6: 7.
87. Ugrinovich, p. 101.
88. Ibid., pp. 100-101.
89. Klor, p. 97.
90. Ugrinovich, p. 101.
91. Boriskin, p. 111.
92. Quoted by Golotvin, p. 310.
93. Ibid., p. 304.
94. Krianev, p. 303.
95. Ugrinovich, p. 103.
96. Krianev, p. 302.
97. Klor, p. 98.
98. Boriskin, pp. 88-118.
99. Ugrinovich, p. 100.
100. Krianev, pp. 301-3.
101. Golotvin, p. 310.
102. Ugrinovich, p. 102.
103. Karpushin, p. 110
104. Krosser, p. 79.

105. Karpushin, p. 110.
106. Ibid., p. 111.
107. Ibid.
108. Ugrinovich, p. 96.
109. Vilnite, pp. 66-67; Karpushin, p. 104.
110. Golotvin, pp. 311-12.
111. R.A. Lopatkin and M.A. Popova, "Problemy psikhologii religii" [Problems of Psychology of Religion], *Voprosy filosofii*, no. 7 (July 1969), p. 151.
112. Krianev, pp. 291-92.
113. Vilnite, p. 69.
114. Boriskin, p. 121.
115. Ibid., p. 99, note 1.

Part IV

Soviet Agriculture: Some Analysis and Interpretation

6

The Continuing Perplexities of Soviet Agriculture: The Performance of Northern Kazakhstan

W.A. Douglas Jackson and *Richard Towber*

Despite persistent and large annual variations in gross output, it is evident that since 1965 there has been a general improvement in Soviet agricultural performance. The agricultural sector seems clearly to have gained a flexibility that has allowed more immediate response to changes in the weather. A very substantial increase in inputs has, of course, contributed to this situation (table 6-1), but equally important, such inputs have led to larger yields per acre in certain key commodities (table 6-2). Although gross agricultural output, and especially the production of grain, has fallen short of expectations in some years, still, blessed with good growing conditions, the farm economy has achieved a number of record harvests that, if sustained, could point to a better future for industrial and agricultural worker alike. Even so, as Alec Nove pointed out in 1970, Soviet agriculture, compared to the West, remains "the least efficient sector of the Soviet economy. The production gains of recent years have been achieved at high cost."[1] That assessment remains no less true in 1974.

The current, or ninth, five-year plan (1971-75) has called for significant increases in agricultural output volumes over previous years. Much of this increase, the plan stated, is to be gained by higher yields per unit area.[2] Indeed, for every hectare of state and collective farm agricultural land, production is to be raised by one-third. Not only if the gross harvest to exceed annually that of the preceding plan, but the production of grain is to reach new levels, averaging 195 million metric tons per year. Particular concern, moreover, is directed toward the expansion of the feed base and, accordingly, targets for meat and dairy products as well as for eggs are high.

Khrushchev had projected an increase in agricultural output of 70 percent for the seventh plan, but he realized only 15 percent. In the eighth plan, Brezhnev called for a growth of 25 percent but achieved only 21 percent, despite the fact that on the whole the weather was kind to the cultivator.[3] The ninth plan, apart from the setback of the crop year of 1972, seems destined to surpass the increases of the preceding plan, but judging by performance to date, it most likely will be less than anticipated.

Any attempt to project future Soviet achievements in agriculture is confronted by many difficulties. Because of some very basic geographic factors, the weather over the Soviet farm belt will always cause concern. Soil conditions can be modified through various types of reclamation schemes, but throughout much of the cropped area only a balanced program of soil feeding and rotation

Table 6-1
Inputs to Agriculture—USSR

	1960	1965	1970	1970 as a Percent of 1960
Sown area, m. hectares	203.0	209.1	206.7	102
Labor, m. persons	29.4	28.0	26.8	91
Capital investments, b. rubles	36.3	55.8	81.5	225
Motor power, m. horsepower	155.9	236.6	336.4	215
Fertilizer, st. units. th. tons	11404	27066	45649	400
Gross Agricultural Product b. rubles, 1965 prices	63.0	70.9	87.0	138

Source: *Selskoe khoziaistvo SSSR. Statisticheskii sbornik* (Moscow, 1971), pp. 25, 108-10, 137, 357, 373, 446.

Table 6-2
Grain Crop Yields—USSR (centners/hectare)

	1959-65 Average	1966-70 Average	1966-70 as a % of 1959-65
All grains	10.3	13.7	133
Winter wheat	15.3	19.6	128
Spring wheat	8.1	11.1	137
Winter rye	9.5	11.3	119
Spring barley	10.9	14.8	136

Sources: *Selskoe khoziaistvo SSSR. Statisticheskii sbornik,* (Moscow, 1971), pp. 150-51. *Selskoe khoziaistvo SSSR. Statisticheskii sbornik,* (Moscow, 1960), pp. 208-9.

will bring about more immediate positive results. Plant research has achieved some notable gains in the past and will continue to do so in future. The availability and more efficient use of machinery can wrench a crop from the soil when undue delay may spell lower yields if not outright disaster. Still, as Professors Johnson and Kahan pointed out in 1965, "Anyone who attempts long-term projections of agricultural output in the USSR—in any country for that matter—could be called foolhardy and perhaps should be."[4]

The purpose of this paper, then, is not so much to attempt the foolhardy as to raise some troublesome questions concerning agricultural performance in the past that may have a bearing on the present and future. In particular, the focus here is on the role played by Northern Kazakhstan in Soviet grain production and the continuing uncertainties associated with it.

Not only does the Soviet Union possess the reputation of being the world's largest producer of grain, but over the past decade, because of an inability to supply its own diverse requirements, it has become one of the world's principal importers.

Since 1953 the eastern regions of the country—the territories stretching from the middle Volga eastward to the Altai Mountains—have made on the whole substantially larger contributions to the Soviet grain supply. Indeed, over the past two decades, the eastern regions have contained almost half the total grain area, have produced over a third of all grain, and have often delivered more than half of the nation's annual grain (table 6-3). The western, or European, part of the country has yielded the bulk of the winter grain as well as much of the feed grain. It is a characteristic of weather patterns over the USSR that poor crop conditions in the west are frequently offset by good conditions in Siberia and Kazakhstan, or vice versa. Winter kill, for example, can cause severe damage in the west, although the losses in 1970 and 1971 were nowhere as severe as those experienced in 1969, when 14 million hectares were damaged.[5] Still, the rather extensive winter kill of 1972, together with the subsequent summer drought, not only was partially offset by more favorable crop conditions in the spring grain regions but led some Soviet and Western commentators to hail the reliability of the virgin lands of Kazakhstan.[6] A closer look at grain production in that republic, and especially in the northern oblasts, however, raises questions that on balance do not warrant such unqualified enthusiasm.

First of all, it should be understood that this reassessment of Kazakh grain production is not an attempt to argue the success or failure of the virgin lands. No one need quarrel with the statement that since the 1950s the republic has become a major grain-producing region of the country, although subject to incredible fluctuations in output.

In a 1970 review of W.H. Parker's *An Historical Geography of Russia,* Professor James Gibson of York University implied that Parker had developed an erroneous estimate of the virgin land scheme; that he had in effect assumed what was termed the "Jacksonian myth of the failure of the Virgin and Idle Land Scheme." Gibson, on the other hand, had come to the conclusion that the venture had "greatly increased the quality and reliability of the Soviet grain crop and considerably improved the livestock sector."[7] It would be useful, we think, to see what Professor Parker actually wrote and to weigh both his and Gibson's comments against the evidence of the time.

"Rapid population growth outran grain production," wrote Parker, and Khrushchev launched the "Virgin and Idle Lands Scheme" on the steppes of Kazakhstan to remedy this; he also promoted the

Table 6-3
The Importance of the Eastern Regions[a] for Soviet Grain Production

Year	Sown Area	Eastern Regions as a Percent of USSR Gross Harvest	and Deliveries
1940	31.5	23.7	32.4
1950	31.1	31.7	35.0
1960	51.6	46.5	61.9
1965	49.3	28.2	30.0
1966	48.6	43.9	55.1
1967	49.1	35.9	50.2
1968	49.6	43.7	57.1
1969	50.5	35.2	44.7
1970	49.5	39.3	51.4

[a]Includes principally the oblasts between the Volga and the Altai Mountains, and including Northern Kazakhstan.

Sources: *Narodnoe Khoziaistvo SSSR v 1961g. Statisticheskii sbornik* (Hereafter Narkhoz-) (Moscow: 1962), p. 374; *Narkhoz-1962*, pp. 246-47, 256-57, 268, 292; *Narkhoz-1963*, p. 294; *Narkhoz-1964*, pp. 279, 296, 325; *Narkhoz-1965*, p. 341; *Narkhoz-1969*, pp. 308-9, 324, 345; *Narkhoz-1970*, pp. 294-95, 309; *Selskoe khoziaistvo SSR. Statisticheskii sbornik* (hereafter Selkhoz-) (Moscow: 1960), pp. 132-33, 147, 226-29; *Selkhoz-1971*, pp. 108-9, 115, 148-49, 154-55; *Posevnie ploshchadi SSSR. Statisticheskii sbornik* (Moscow: 1957), pp. 6-7, 60-61, 206-11, 218-21; *Narodnoe khoziaistvo RSFSR v 1958 g. Statisticheskii sbornik* (hereafter Narkhoz RSFSR-) (Moscow, 1959), p. 232; *Narkhoz RSFSR-1959*, pp. 227, 252; *Narkhoz RSFSR-1960*, pp. 207-8, 236-37; *Narkhoz RSFSR-1962*, pp. 188-91, 228-29; *Narkhoz RSFSR-1964*, pp. 183, 220; *Narkhoz RSFSR-1967*, pp. 184, 229-30, 254; *Narkhoz RSFSR-1968*, pp. 205, 223, 232; *Narkhoz RSFSR-1969*, pp. 159, 187, 200; *Narkhoz RSFSR-1970*, pp. 175, 209, 223; *Narodnoe khoziaistvo Kazakhskoi SSR, Statisticheskii sbornik* (Almo-Ata, 1957), pp. 72-73, 80-81, 112-13, 116-17, 120-21, 124-25; *Narodnoe khoziaistvo Kazakhskoi SSR v 1960 i 1961 gg. Statisticheskii sbornik* (Almo-Ata, 1963), pp. 84-85, 118-19, 152-53; *Narodnoe khoziaistvo Kazakhstana v 1968 g. Statisticheskii sbornik* (Almo-Ata; 1970), pp. 37, 102, 116, 132.

cultivation of maize. Both campaigns were ill conceived and worse executed. They failed to take account of climatic and soil conditions and they diverted men and equipment from established areas and crops, but losses incurred in this way were not made good by corresponding gains from the innovations. The Virgin Lands Scheme was at first very successful. Grain production rose remarkably from 82 million tons in 1953 to 140 million tons in 1958, but by 1963 had fallen back to 107 million tons. An investment of 30 billion rubles, which could have achieved much in drainage in the west or irrigation in the southeast, had been largely dissipated. Furthermore, in 1963 nearly 2-1/2 million tons of wheat had to be imported from Canada alone at a cost of 14.3 million rubles.[8]

One need not support entirely Parker's assessment, but there was little evidence to assert, as did Gibson, that the virgin lands "had greatly increased the quality and reliability of the Soviet grain crop and considerably improved the livestock sector." Certainly it would seem that Professor Gibson was not fully aware of the difficulties that had developed in grain farming in Northern Kazakhstan. These difficulties have been documented since 1965 but were apparent even at a much earlier date.

Jackson wrote, in a March 1962 reappraisal of Soviet progress from 1953 on;

> In the eastern steppe regions of the Soviet Union, dry farming is at all times a calculated risk. A short growing season, accompanied by early autumn frosts and snow, along with the regular danger of drought, are factors that confront the steppe farmer. They are factors that allow little margin for miscalculation and error. Prior to 1953, grain yields in the steppe regions had been low and, from the point of view of the Soviet regime, unsatisfactory. . . . In order to remedy the situation, the regime decided that by ploughing the extensive tracts of virgin or long-fallow land, scattered through the steppe farms or lying along the southern margin of crop cultivation, large increases in wheat production could be achieved. Indeed, with a yield of only ten centners per hectare, the Soviet regime hoped to obtain no less than 32.8 million tons annually. The dimensions of the program, therefore, were enormous, and the expectations of the regime were great; but the results have not been an unqualified success and, judging from the official reaction, in fact have been quite unsatisfactory.[9]

Elsewhere, Jackson, in discussing the nature of Soviet land reserves, had concluded that greater use of steppe lands had always been possible "but only to the extent that proper methods and techniques are employed in cultivation and measures are taken to maintain soil fertility in those lands already under crops."[10] He noted, too, that the use of virgin and idle lands could bring "a temporary halt to the decline in durum wheat acreage and production since durum, because of its greater tolerance than common wheat of conditions in the steppe, is in a position to guarantee some success to Soviet efforts."[11] Success there, it should be noted, would have indeed contributed significantly to the quality of the wheat and especially to its protein content.

During the Khrushchev era, only the crop years of 1956 and 1958 actually met Soviet expectations, and both were years of very favorable weather conditions. Even so, due to the inability to get all of the crop out of the fields at harvest time when bad weather set in, there were significant losses. In the remaining years, especially after 1960, a failure to heed sound agronomic advice and general mismanagement compounded the failures induced by weather. The results were so disappointing as to compel major changes in party leadership in Kazakhstan. The crop failure of 1963 most certainly contributed to the downfall of Khrushchev himself.[12]

With the removal of Khrushchev, criticisms of the management of the grain lands in Kazakhstan came to the surface, and these tended to support Jackson's earlier contention. Writing in *Literaturnaia Gazeta* in 1965, Leonid Ivanov remarked, "Stereotyped instructions, identical for all regions of our vast country, prevented judicious farm management and in no way promoted the productive use of our principal wealth—the land."[13] The stereotyped instructions to which Ivanov referred applied not only to the question of fallowing but also to methods of tilling the soil, the unwise curtailment or use of which had caused immeasurable damage and losses.

Ivanov noted that in order to avoid the instructions, many farm managers had to resort to clandestine or "underground" fallowing, "as we call it in Siberia, to commit a fraud. But if this was a lie, it was a white one." Although the farms were given the right to plan sown areas

> It was necessary to keep an eye on the established plan for the sale
> of the grain to the state, and for many grain regions of the country,
> particularly Siberia and Virgin Land Territory, the plan was, as the
> saying goes, a very tight fit: It was necessary in a number of cases
> to sow more than 70 percent of the arable land to grain crops. To
> all intents and purposes no land remained for other crops. Under
> such conditions, the right to independent planning was in fact
> nullified.

Faulty tilling, associated with the widespread use of the moldboard plough, which cut deeply into the fragile, lighter soils of the Kazakh Steppe, led to dessication and serious problems of erosion. The plough had simply been transferred from European Russia with its heavier soils to the droughtier lands of the east with little official regard to the consequences. "The virgin land," as one Soviet commentator noted in 1970, "soon began to avenge itself for these stereotyped attitudes with bad harvests, dust storms and grain that remained unharvested until the snows came."[14] Hence, the agronomists from European Russia who were responsible for the system of farming introduced into the eastern steppe "were transferred elsewhere or penalized, as though it were possible to compensate for the absence of a scientific approach in farming by an administrative reshuffling."

More telling evidence of malpractice in the virgin lands may be found in a very revealing work by F.T. Morgun, published in Moscow in 1969.[15] Taking to task those Soviet critics who claimed that the virgin lands project was a mistake from the very beginning, Morgun argued that prior to 1959 virgin land farming had by and large been highly profitable.

This success could have been reinforced only under the condition of allocating a rational amount of weedy lands to clean fallow, but, since this was not done, the economic indications of the new farms took a marked turn for the worse. In 1959-1962, the cost of grain on the kolkhozes and sovkhozes of Northern Kazakhstan was higher than in the remaining grain-raising regions of the nation.[16]

Since this region harvested more spring wheat in 1964 than did the entire nation in 1940, the virgin lands, according to Morgun, "could have produced significantly more even in the poor, precipitation-shy years" (table 6-3).

Declining yields, of course, led directly, as Morgun noted, to rising production costs. The average yield of grain on the new sovkhozes in the five oblasts that constituted the Virgin Krai was reported initially at 11 centners per hectare, costing only 2.88 rubles to produce.[17] In 1957-58, on those farms where yields did not exceed 4.5 centners, costs rose to 5.67 rubles, with such farms producing 23.4 percent of the total harvest.[18] Where yields ranged from 4.5 to 6.8 centners, the cost was less (4.36 rubles), but only 14 percent of the harvest was produced at that figure. The rest of the farms, attaining yields of 11 centners or more, produced 32 percent of the harvest at only 2.58 rubles. The average cost in 1957-58 was 4.2 rubles, with average yields well below 9 centners per hectare. In 1960-61, when yields fell from 8.6 to 6.3 centners, the cost rose from 4.5 to 5.4 rubles. These trends are confirmed in tables 6-4 and 6-5. For the seven-year period 1958-64, it cost 5.52 rubles per centner to produce grain averaging 6.9 centners per hectare. In 1965 the average cost had risen to 6.5 rubles per hectare.[19]

Soviet harvests in the past have been notoriously poor in quality. Grain harvests in particular are known to have contained grain of various stages of ripeness, a relatively high proportion of weeds, trash, and moisture—what is described in the United States as "bunker weight."[20] Through the years the regime has attempted to improve the situation, in part by disseminating improved seed adapted to the local region. Along with this there has been an effort to expand the planting of hard and durum wheats. According to Koval, from 1957 to 1962, within the USSR as a whole, the area sown to hard spring wheat increased by four times and totalled in the latter year more than 19 million hectares. During the same period durum sowings declined from 4 to about 2.5 million hectares.[21] In 1959 in Kazakhstan durum and hard wheats occupied only 13.3 percent of the spring wheat area. However, by 1965, the ratio had risen to 38.4 percent, an increase that included a quadrupling of the area in durum.[22] Still, substantial fluctuations in plantings were the rule. In any case, the yields of spring wheat in Northern Kazakhstan averaged 8.8 centners per hectare in 1959 but fell to a disastrous low of 3.1 in 1965.[23]

The 1965 March Plenum, as is well known, brought a number of reforms

Table 6-4
Cost of Production of Grain on the State Farms of Kazakhstan,
(By Natural-Economic Zones, in Rubles)

Years	Average Republic	Steppe	Droughty Steppe	SemiArid Steppe	Arid Steppe	Tian-Shan	Altai Region
1956-60	3.98	4.16	3.75	4.69	6.49	3.53	4.07
1961-65	5.84	5.99	5.78	6.04	9.16	4.64	5.26

Source: R. Iu. Kuvatov, *Sebestoimost selsko-khoziaistvennoi produktsii* (Alma-Ata, 1969), p. 141.

Table 6-5
Cost of Production of Grain on the State Farms of Kazakhstan,
(By Oblast, in Rubles)

Years	Kustanai	Tselinograd	Kokchetav	Pavlodar	North Kazakhstan	Ave.
1954-58	4.12	3.47	3.67	4.31	3.76	3.80
1959-63	5.93	4.91	5.48	5.92	4.24	5.32
1964-66	5.64	5.96	5.96	10.1	5.37	6.06

Source: A.E. Karminskii et al., *Ekonomika zernovo khoziaistva* (Moscow, 1970), p. 401.

to Soviet agriculture.[24]   Among the recommendations were requirements for an expansion of clean fallowing, a short fallow-grain crop rotation, the abandonment of the repeated tilling of the soil by moldboard ploughs, and the exclusive use of horizontal moldboardless implements.[25]

Following upon the disastrous year of 1965, when to the new regime's embarrassment gross grain production in Kazakhstan dropped to 7.6 million (cf. 23.g in 1964 and 10.6 in 1963) and in the virgin lands to 4.3 (cf. 10.1 in 1962 and 3.1 in 1955), a bumper harvest was recorded in 1966.[26]   The weather conditions were almost perfect, especially at harvest time, losses were abnormally low, and the moisture content of the grain was less than average. Since the area in grain was the lowest it had been since 1961, higher yields were realized (equal to those in 1956). The greater availability of machinery and the increased use of fertilizer may have been among the principal factors.

Poor crop weather again descended on Northern Kazakhstan in 1967. Seed was planted under unsatisfactory conditions, and although the rains that fell in May and June were timely, the ensuing drought brought poor plant development and lower yields. Indeed, the output of wheat in Kazakhstan and Siberia fell below the average achieved during the 1956-63 period inclusively.[27] 1968 was a better year, permitting Morgun to note, "One can already feel the measures undertaken by the party: the restoration of clean fallow and the rejection of routine recommendations."[28]

These improvements notwithstanding, Soviet agriculture faced another setback in 1969. Unfavorable weather prevailed at both the beginning and the end of the crop season. A late spring delayed planting by about two weeks; dry weather in early July retarded growth. The ensuing rains provided some relief, but at harvest time there were further delays. While the gross harvest of grain in 1969 exceeded that of 1968 and 1969, the moisture content, ranging from 25 to 28 percent, was higher than usual.[29] Still, the Soviets stated that with the application of new techniques of cultivation, the yields of grain in several of the oblasts of Northern Kazakhstan increased. Thus, compared with 1962-65 yields in the 1966-69 period in Kustanay jumped from 5.9 to 9 centners per hectare, in Kokchetav from 5.5 to 9.1, and in Northern Kazakhstan from 7.2 to 13.4.[30]

1970, the year of the eighth plan, proved to be something of a bumper crop year, although the gross grain output of the 186.8 million tons fell short of target. Kazakhstan performed well,[31] surpassing by 200,000 tons in its official gross estimates the 22 million produced in 1958, but remaining under its totals for 1966, 1964, and 1956. Yields were good. Kustansy oblast achieved 13.1 centners per hectare, Kokchetav 10.6 and North Kazakhstan 14.3. Pavlodar and Tselinograd were less successful, reaching only 4.3 and 7.4 respectively. The new Turgay oblast, carved out of surrounding territory, reported 6.2 centners. Equally good, if not better yields were reported from peripheral oblasts: East Kazakhstan, 15.0; Uralsk, 11.6; Aktyubinsk, 10.9; and Sempalatinsk, 7.0. Karaganda, however, did substantially less well, with only 3.2 centners.[32] In 1970, moreover, durum and hard wheats occupied 91.6 percent of the sowings of spring wheat, although in actuality less than 600,000 hectares were sown to durum, only half the amount planted in 1965.[33]

If one compares the average performance of the virgin lands oblasts during 1965-70 with that of the preceding years back to the bountiful harvest of 1956, the results are somewhat less encouraging, raising questions as to the real state of farming during the first Brezhnev plan period (tables 6-2 and 6-3).

During the latter, total sowings were up, but the grain area was down, as was that of wheat. The cultivation of other crops, together with an expansion of clean fallowing, account for the changes. While the gross output of grain in the USSR rose substantially, there was only a slight increase in that of Kazakhstan, but the output from the virgin land oblasts was down. On average, Kazakhstan produced as much wheat in 1965-70 as in 1956-64, but the virgin lands harvest was off by a million tons. Not only that, state grain and wheat purchases from the virgin lands were down, although the republic as a whole fared better.

To some extent reductions in sowings in the virgin lands were offset by increased plantings in the normally droughtier peripheral oblasts. Even so, output and deliveries to the state from these secondary grain areas were below those of the earlier period.

Finally, if the average yields of grain produced in the virgin lands during the eighth plan are compared with those of preceding years, a downward tread is detectable. This was equally true of the peripheral oblasts, although the decline throughout Northern Kazakhstan as a whole was overshadowed by an improvement in the southern oblasts, thus registering a gain for the republic as a whole. In the case of wheat, the drop in average virgin land yields was even more dramatic, contributing to the republic's over-all lower wheat yields.

In the first year of the ninth plan, grain and wheat production in Kazakhstan fell, but in 1972, to offset the losses in winter grains in the western part of the country, the eastern regions responded with increased spring plantings.[34] Because of this and the relatively good weather, the republic was able to produce 29 million tons, or 17 percent of the gross grain crop of 168 million, a production not matched since the banner year of 1956.[35]

The grain area in 1973 remained above previous years' averages, and the resultant harvest exceeded all expectations. Even when allowances are made for the somewhat greater than normal amounts of foreign matter and of moisture in the gross output, because of heavy precipitation during harvesting over large areas of the Soviet Union, the 1973 crop will nevertheless remain the largest ever produced in the USSR.

In short, while the Soviet Union has succeeded in boosting its total output of grain, the role of the virgin lands continues to raise some questions that, at this date of writing, remain unanswered. Prior to 1971, the record was uneven, despite a sharp increase in investments, particularly after 1965. With the improved harvests—at least measured in gross terms—of the past three or four years, it is possible that a turning point may have been reached. But verification of this change can only be demonstrated with the passage of time.

Notes

1. Alex Nove, "Soviet Agriculture Under Brezhnev," *Slavic Review* 29 (Sept. 1970): 410.

2. N.K. Baybakov, *State Five-Year Plan for the Development of the USSR National Economy for the Period 1971-1975* (Moscow, 1972), part I. pp. 169-70 (JPRS 56970-1).

3. Keith Bush, "Soviet Agriculture in the 1970's," *Studies on the Soviet Union, New Series* 11:3 (1971), p. 37.

4. D. Gale Johnson and Arcadius Kahan, *The Soviet Agricultural Program: An Evaluation of the 1965 Goals,* RM-2848-PR (Santa Monica, Calif.: The RAND Corporation, May 1962), p. 110.

5. *Foreign Agriculture,* 12 May 1969; 12 January 1970; 26 October 1970; 20 March 1972.
6. Theodore Shabad, "Asian Russian Grain Crops Set Record," carried in the *Seattle Post Intelligencer,* 15 October 1972.
7. *The Canadian Geographer* 14 (Winter 1970): 387.
8. W.H. Parker, *An Historical Geography of Russia,* (Chicago: Aldine Publishing Company, 1969), p. 348.
9. W.A. Douglas Jackson, "The Virgin and Idle Lands Program Reappraised," *Annals* Assoc. of Amer. Geogr. 52 (March, 1962): 79.
10. W.A. Douglas Jackson, "The Soviet Approach to the Good Earth: Myth and Reality," *Soviet Agricultural and Peasant Affairs,* Ray Laird (ed.) (Lawrence, University of Kansas Press, 1963), pp. 177–78.
11. W.A. Douglas Jackson, "Durum Wheat and the Expansion of Dry Farming in the Soviet Union," Reproduced by permission from the *Annals* of the Association of American Geographers, Vol. 52, 1962, p. 410.
12. Werner G. Hahn, *The Politics of Soviet Agriculture, 1960-1970* (Baltimore and London, The Johns Hopkins University Press, 1972), p. 111 ff.
13. Leonid Ivanov in *Literaturnaia gazeta,* 6 April 1965, translated in *The Current Digest of the Soviet Press (CDSP)* 17:16 (1965), p. 11. Translation copyright 1965 by The Current Digest of the Soviet Press, published weekly at The Ohio State University by the American Association for the Advancement of Slavic Studies; reprinted by permission.
14. *Izvestia,* 1 July 1970, translated in *CDSP* 22:26 (1970), p. 5. Translation copyright 1970 by the Current Digest of the Soviet Press, published weekly at The Ohio State University by The American Association for the Advancement of Slavic Studies; reprinted by permission.
15. F.T. Morgun, *Analysis of Virgin-Land Grain Raising,* pp. 1–39. Translated from *Dumy o tseline,* 2nd rev. ed. (Moscow, 1969), chapt. 5, pp. 110–15 (JPRS 57636).
16. Morgun, p. 3.

> During the first years of developing virgin lands, the new lands were clean of weeds, and the farms obtained good grain harvests even without a sufficiently high level of farming. Everywhere the simplest system was used: plow—plant—harvest, and again plow—plant, and so forth. Wheat was sown in one field for 6-7 and more years running. After 4-5 years, and in a number of instances a larger number of years of using the designated system, the basic areas of recently virgin lands have been significantly overgrown with weeds.

See Jackson's commentary on this practice in "Virgin and Idle Lands Program Reappraised," p. 76. See also V.A. Adamchuk, S.B. Baishev and others, *Razvitie i razmeshchnie proizvoditelnykh sil Kazakhskoi SSR* (Moscow,

1967), pp. 145-6, for a discussion of problems associated with farming methods in Northern Kazakhstan.

17. *Voprosy ekonomiki selskogo khoziaistva na sovremennom etape* (Moscow, 1963), p. 12.

18. *Ekonomika zernovogo khoziaistva* (Moscow, 1970), p. 401.

19. Ibid., p. 401.

20. *Literaturnaia gazeta,* 18 December 1968, p. 11; see also Harry E. Walters, "New Soviet Plan Implies Farm Policy Switch," *Foreign Agriculture,* 21 March 1966, p. 4; also *Foreign Agriculture,* 22 March 1965.

21. T.A. Kovel, *Zernovoe Khoziaistvo SSSR* (Moscow, 1965), p. 149.

22. Iu. M. Burlakov, *Zernovoe khoziaistvo Kazakhstans* (Alma-Ata, 1972). p. 140.

23. *Narodnoe khoziaistvo Kazakhstana v 1968 g. Statisticheskii sbornik* (Alma-Ata, 1970), p. 122.

24. Nove, pp. 386 ff.

25. *CDSP* 22:26, p. 5. See Hahn, pp. 111-14.

26. Selskoe Khoziaistvo SSSR. Statisticheskii sbornik (Moscow: 1960), pp. 226-27; *Selskoe khoziaistvo SSSR. Statisticheskii sbornik* (Moscow: 1971), pp. 148-49; *Narodnoe khoziaistvo Kazakhskoi SSR v 1960 i 1961 gg. Statisticheskii sbornik* (Alma-Ata, 1963), pp. 84-85; *Narodnoe khoziaislvo kazakhstand v 1968 g. Statisticheskii sbornik* (Alma-Ata, 1970), pp. 116.

27. *Narodnoe khoziaistvo SSSR v 1962 g. Statisticheskii sbornik* (Moscow, 1963), p. 169; *Narodnoe khoziaistvo SSSR v 1970 g. Statisticheskii sbornik* (Moscow, 1971), p. 309; *Selskoe khoziaistvo* (1960), pp. 202-203; *Selskoe khoziaistvo* (1971), pp. 148-49.

28. Morgun, p. 7.

29. *Foreign Agriculture,* 12 January 1970.

30. *CDSP* 22:26, p. 5.

31. *Selskoe khoziaistvo* (1971), pp. 154-55.

32. Burlakov, p. 34.

33. Ibid., p. 140.

34. *Izvestiia,* May 23 (*CDSP* 24:21, 21 June 1972, p. 18; *Foreign Agriculture,* 18 September 1972, p. 9.

35. *Kazakhstanskaia Pravda,* 2 February 1973.

7

Soviet Agriculture in 1973 and Beyond in Light of United States Performance

Roy D. Laird

Problems of Comparison

Some might argue that any comparison of Soviet and United States agricultural achievement is unfair. We would agree to the extent that differing circumstances and experiences do render the two rural scenes incomparable in many ways. Two major differences, for example:

1. The weather is less favorable for Soviet farmers than it is for their United States counterparts. Only relatively small areas (e.g., the Kuban) are comparable to the enormously productive United States cornbelt that stretches from the Western slopes of the Appalachian mountains into the eastern counties of Nebraska and Kansas. As the former minister of agriculture V.V. Matskevich reported in 1971, whereas some 60 percent of the US sown area receives an annual rainfall of over 700 mm., only 1 percent of the USSR sown area receives that much precipitation.[1]

2. Not since the Civil War has rural America been devastated by battle, while war has twice visited much of rural Russia and the Soviet Union during this century. Beyond bringing about the direct destruction of the farms and the farmers, these wars left the nation economically crippled with less available for investment in agriculture.

For these important reasons, any across-the-board comparison of US-USSR agriculture would be unfair. Thus, our own past guess (largely based on Canadian experience) has been that primarily for weather reasons Soviet small grain yields per hectare must be expected to be some 10 percent less than United States yields. However, whatever allowances are made in the name of equity, surely such discounts do not explain the fact that Soviet grain yields remain roughly only one-third those of the United States. Even in the bumper, best year ever, 1973, the implied yield claim of 16.8 centners/hectare,[2] is only half the US 1966-70 average of 32.5 centners/hectare.[3]

The comparative method is one of the most valuable of the social science tools of understanding. If properly qualified, US-USSR comparison can help advance our understanding by providing, among other things: a measuring stick for both recent Soviet production accomplishments and possible future potential; additional insights into the system costs of Soviet agriculture, costs that go beyond the usual economic measures, and a better means of appraising the efficacy of policy innovations.

The United States Extensive Model

Although the United States' agricultural system is rightfully praised for its
successes, it is hardly the perfect Platonic paradigm of farming. For example,
the more intensive Western European systems often outproduce the United
States in terms of yields/hectare. Indeed, our own prediction is that mounting
world demands for food will cause the American farmer to turn more to
European practices of intensive cultivation. Still, given the achievements of
the US extensive system, the model does provide production targets (sometimes cited by Soviet officials) for Soviet farmers to emulate, at least as long
as the Soviet leadership insists upon employing what is, by most measures, the
most extensive system in the world. The imposition of the extensive model on
the rural USSR is at the heart of the Soviet food problem.

Some clarification of terms is called for at this juncture. Although the
world offers a variety of agricultural system combinations, two basic patterns
stand out, the extensive and the intensive methods of cultivation.

Extensive agricultural practice, particularly associated with the United
States, rests first and foremost on a setting wherein a nation is land-rich and
labor-poor, where there is more than enough fertile land to support the population's food needs, while labor for farm work is relatively expensive. A second,
important factor is a relative abundance of machinery and chemical aids for
the farmers. A third key factor, although not ultimately essential, is a market
system wherein profit is the prime measure of success. Given such an amalgam,
those engaged in food production discover that within optimum limits of
scale, profits are maximized by holding relatively high labor costs to a minimum
while increasing the size of the farm that can be managed through purchase of
labor-extending machinery. As illustrated in table 7-1, the United States rural
scene has changed dramatically, largely since 1930, in pursuit of the extensive
model. Production per farm worker has expanded significantly (4.9 times, in
terms of the number of persons fed by one farm worker), while the size of the
average farm has more than doubled (2.5 times), and yet the number of workers
employed in agriculture has been reduced to nearly one-third (-2.8 times) what
it was in 1930. These are remarkable achievements, but there have been prices
to pay, including having to accept lower yields per acre in some instances where
more intensive farming methods would have produced more food per unit of
land.

Intensive agricultural practice exists primarily in those nations in which
land is comparatively short and there is a relative abundance of labor for
cultivating the soil and husbanding the animals. Machinery and chemical aids
tend to be much more dear than in nations predominantly following extensive
practices. While profit may be important to the farmers, subsistence cultivation tends to be more prevalent. Most important, since land is relatively scarce,
both the nation and the farmers cultivating the soil find that they must strive

Table 7-1
United States Agriculture, 1930 vs. 1971

	1930	1971	x difference
1. Number of farms	6,288,698	2,876,110	−2.2
2. Land in farms (acres)	986,771,000	1,117,401,000	+1.1
3. Acres/farm[a]	157	389	+2.5
4. Total farm employment	12,497,000	4,445,900	−2.8
5. Acres/farm worker[b]	79	251	+3.2
6. Persons/farm worker	9.8	48.2	+4.9

[a]Source: *Agricultural Statistics 1972*, United States Department of Agriculture, (Washington, D.C.: United States Government Printing Office 1973), pp. 504, 509, 523, and 542.

[b]No. 2 ÷ No. 1.

[c]No. 2 ÷ No. 4

to maximize yields from every available piece of arable land, primarily by the employment of hand labor to do meticulous tasks that the American farmer could not afford without cutting deeply into profits. The careful rotation of crops, hand weeding, planting, transplanting and harvesting, the application of all available natural fertilizers, and elaborate ditch irrigation are among the types of labor-costly farming practices employed in these nations. Adoption of the American extensive, mechanized methods (even if the people could afford them) could cost dearly in terms of total production. No machine can weed or harvest an acre as thoroughly as can human hands determined to reap the last possible grain from the soil. Tractors may plow deeper than oxen-pulled plows, (usually an advantage), but tractors do not produce the vital natural fertilizer created by draft animals. Even where farmers can afford tractors and where farms are of a size that mechanization can be advantageous, as is most of Western Europe, there is much less specialization. Most such farms plant a wider variety of crops, allowing for carefully planned rotations. To this plains-reared American, one of the most impressive memories of Europe in the spring is that of witnessing its farmers emptying the winter's accumulation from the barns into long steaming rows across the fields. Here alone is a major reason for substantially higher wheat yields in Western Europe than in the United States.

If soaring prices paid for his crops are causing the American farmer to rediscover the manure spreader, increasing Soviet food demands may prove their extensive cultivation model increasingly untenable.

Brezhnev, Grain, and Meat

Stalin employed terror as a key means of keeping the population under control, holding the growth of consumer output to a minimum while maximizing the expansion of industry. Khrushchev presided over the abandonment of mass terror and tried to deliver more consumer items (especially food), largely by introducing relatively inexpensive schemes such as planting corn almost everywhere and plowing up vast tracts of once virgin semiarid soils. The 1963 drought underscored the failure of Khrushchev's agricultural schemes.

Brezhnev has shown a combined sense of quiet urgency and economic realism about farming that was not true of his predecessors. Quite different from earlier times, there is now much more material substance behind Brezhnev's 1972 observation that the "three main components of the party's present policy in agriculture are: comprehensive mechanization, chemicalization, and large-scale land improvement. For these purposes we have allocated more funds than have ever been appropriated for agriculture."[4] Almost from the beginning of his leadership in 1964, "intensification" (underlined by statements that virtually all future output increases must come from increased yields/hectare) has been a central theme of Soviet agricultural policy. Unfortunately, as underlined here, some of the practices that continue, especially regarding the size of the farms (table 7-8), work against the achievement of higher yields per hectare. Nevertheless, during the eighth five-year plan period (1966-70), investments in agriculture reportedly increased by 21 percent.[5] The current ninth five-year plan (1971-75) calls for a further investment increase of 21 percent.[6]

Although official retail prices have not changed for more than a decade, prices paid to the farmers for their produce have risen substantially. Peasant incomes have advanced nearly to the level of the average urban worker's wages. Fertilizer production has significantly increased. Land amelioration projects have gone forward.

Grain production is the major key to Soviet agricultural advance, and output rose by 29 percent from the 1960-65 to the 1966-70 planning period.[7] For decades, Soviet agriculture was required to subsidize urban industrial growth. In a complete turnaround, by 1970, according to the estimate of one colleague, government subsidies of the agricultural sector probably exceeded 11 billion rubles annually.[8] Much of what was needed on the strictly economic front is being provided, and both the words and the deeds of the Soviet leadership reflect a firm resolve to continue along the same lines. Thus, in addition to increased investments, the response to the 1972 crop failure was the expenditure of huge sums on foreign grain imports.

That grain is the key Soviet crop is underlined by US-USSR comparisons. Thus, as shown in table 7-2, whereas during 1966-70 only 45 percent of the US sown land was planted to grains, 75 percent of the Soviet cropland was in what they classify as grain: primarily wheat, oats, barley, rye, corn sorghums,

Table 7-2

US-USSR Sown Land, 1966-70[a]

	US	USSR	x difference
Sown area, million hectares[b]	135.9	170.6	+1.3
Grain area, million hectares	61.7	126.0	+2.0
Wheat area, million hectares	20.0	67.2	+3.4
Percent of Sown area in grain	45	74	+1.6
Percent of sown area in wheat	15	39	+2.6
Percent of grain area in wheat	32	59	+1.8

Sources: Data in this and the comparative tables that follow were drawn from the 1966 through 1962 annual US and USSR statistical volumes, *Agricultural Statistics*—(United States Department of Agriculture, Government Printing Office) and the *Narodnoe khoziaistvo SSR*—statistika, Moskva

[a]+1 hectare = 2.471 acres.

[b]1969 only, latest US census year for such purposes.

rice, field beans, and peas. Even more important than the production of more bread for an expanding population, the Soviet plan to increase the annual grain output from the 167 million metric ton level during 1966-70 to 195 million tons during 1971-75[9] is to produce the feed necessary for more livestock products, especially meat.

Perhaps the most serious of all the leadership's long-run promises to increase consumer satisfaction is the one to achieve Western standards of meat consumption or, at least, the annual human consumption norm developed by the Institute of Nutrition, USSR Academy of Medical Sciences, which is stated to be 82 kilograms.[10] As shown in table 7-3 (which includes other comparisons), when measured in terms of production of meat per capita, the US output was over twice that of the Soviet Union. Here again we must allow for climate differences, which influence the availability of feed grains.

While some one-third of the US grain land is in high-yielding corn, the USSR has relatively little land that has the combination of warmth and moisture to produce that major source of US animal feed. In part, the USSR has less grain, and thus less grain for conversion into livestock products. Further, because of climate, much more of the US wheat is sown to higher-yielding winter varieties, while some two-thirds of Soviet wheat land is in lower-yielding spring varieties. Therefore, comparing US and USSR grain yields directly is hardly fair. However, when US wheat yields are adjusted to allow for climate differences, and Soviet yield claims are adjusted to allow for excess moisture and foreign matter, US wheat yields remain nearly two-thirds greater than USSR yields.

Table 7-3
US-USSR Livestock Production 1966-70[a]

	US	USSR	x difference
Meat, million metric tons[b]	20.1	11.6	−1.7
Kgs. per capita	100.4	48.8	−2.1
Kgs. per capita, academy norm	–	82.0	–
Milk			
Million metric tons	13.2	41.1	+3.1
Kgs./cow	4,068	2,185	−1.9
Kgs. per capita	267	339	+1.3
Eggs			
Millions	68,979	35,840	−1.9
/hen	219	151	−1.5
per capita	344	151	−2.3

Sources: See table 7-2

[a]1 metric ton = 2204.6 pounds, 1 kilogram = 2.2046 pounds

[b]Including fish

Virtually all of Canada's wheat is of spring varieties, and their yields have averaged some 10 percent less than those of the United States. Thus, reducing US yields downward by 10 percent, we have a comparable adjusted yield of 18 centners/hectare. However, Western specialists agree that official Soviet grain figures are inflated (we estimate by 15 percent during 1966-70), so that the adjusted comparable 1966-70 Soviet yield would be 11.3 centners per hectare (note table 7-4).

1973, Fence Row to Fence Row and Beyond

When grain prices are high, American farmers expand their plantings (as they are doing in 1974), even sometimes planting in the ditches beyond the fences. Part of the credit for the best-ever grain crop in the USSR in 1973 must go to increased investments and part to what may have been the most favorable weather conditions of this century, but a large part must go also to sowings that overextended the normally available grain area. Recent sowing patterns, plus a statement by Brezhnev, imply that the response to the 1972 disaster was to gamble on planting 9.9 million more hectares in grain than planned for 1973. This is equal to 24.5 million acres, slightly more than half the total area sown to wheat in the US in 1971.[11]

In 1968, Brezhnev said that in order to achieve the 1971-75 plan goal, which is an average annual production of 195 million metric tons, yields per hectare would have to equal 17-18 centners/hectare.[12] This projection implies

Table 7-4

US-USSR Yields, 1966-70 (Centners/hectare)[a]

	US	USSR	x difference
All grain	32.5	13.3	−2.4
Wheat	20.1	13.4	−1.5
Wheat adjusted (US−10 percent, USSR−15% percent)	18.0	11.3	−1.6
Vegetables and melons	137	132	−
Potatoes	243	116	−2.1
Sugar beets	401	228	−1.8

Sources: see table 7-2

[a]1 centner = 220.46 pounds, 1 centner/hectare wheat and potatoes = 1.487 bushels/acre

a planned sown grain area of 118 million hectares on the average, which (as shown in table 7-5) precisely fits the actual cropping practices in recent years, that is, until 1973.

Soviet and Western authorities alike have agreed that the area sown to grain in the recent past, which reached its peak in 1964, was overextended, especially in the moisture-deficient areas of the once virgin lands. While it is hoped that higher yields per hectare would make up the difference in production needs, more land would be left to fallow and more planted to other needed fodder crops. Clearly, therefore, the successful 1973 gamble was paid for largely by a reduction of land slated for fallow and for the other fodder crops. However, the extraordinary weather of 1973 cannot be expected to reoccur in the near future, and the extensive grain sowings of 1973 could be repeated only at great peril.

Although the USSR is more than twice the size of the US, its cropland is only slightly larger. Indeed, as shown in table 7-6, when all of the land in farms is compared, the US figure is substantially higher.

In 1969 the US had more than 50 million hectares of cropland idle or in pasture (table 7-6), most of which could be sown to grain if needed. Sown to wheat yielding the average 20 centners per hectare, this land could produce an additional 100 million metric tons. Implied Soviet plans, the recent sowing record, and other evidence indicates that even in 1969 more Soviet land was sown to grain than would be expected for a normal balance of crops. However, in the desperate search for more livestock output, the herds were increased beyond the land's carrying capacity, and so 1973 witnessed huge grain imports followed by a repeat of Khrushchev's earlier gamble on overextending the sown area.

Table 7-5
USSR Land Sown to Grain, 1964–73, and Implied 1971–75 Plan[a]
(million hectares)

	1964	1965	1966	1967	1968	1969	1970	1971	1972	1973	1974	1975
Actual	133.3	128.0	124.8	122.2	121.5	122.7	119.3	117.9	120.1	127.9	–	–
Implied Plan								118	118	118	118	118
1973 over plan											9.9	

Sources: *Narodnoe khoziaistvo SSSR* volumes 1965 through 1972; Brezhnev's 1968 report; and USSR Statistical Administration Report.

[a] 1 hectare = 2.471 acres

Table 7-6
US-USSR Farmland as of 1969[a]
(millions of hectares)

	US	USSR	x difference
Sown to crops	135.9	170.6	+1.3
Clean fallow	20.6[b]	8.1	-2.5
Sown to grasses	35.6[c]	38.0	+1.1
Cropland total	192.2	216.7	+1.1
All land in farms	428.9	244.1	-1.75

Sources: See table 7-2

[a]1 hectare = 2.471 acres

[b]US, idle or in cover crops

[c]US, cropland in pasture

The 1971-72 shortfalls were followed in 1973 by a disruption of the cropping plan beyond just the 9.9 million extra grain hectares. The USSR Statistical Administration also reported that expanded sowings were made to "sugarbeets, cotton plants, sunflowers, potatoes, and vegetables and some other crops," or a total expansion of plantings 3.8 million hectares greater than 1972.[13] In the moisture deficient new lands regions of Kazhakstan alone, the expansion over 1972 amounted to an additional 1.4 million hectares sown to spring grains.[14]

Beyond the Point of Diminishing Returns

As of 1973 the US remains land-rich and labor-poor, so that its extensive agricultural practices remain economically rational. The USSR, however, probably never should have opted for an extensive system, which on several counts goes far beyond US measures. Surely the recent record implies that they have gone beyond the point of diminishing returns for their present system. Indeed, the Soviet leaders own insistence that virtually all future production advances must come from yield increases supports such a contention. Moreover, their own planners, while stating a planned 21 percent increase in agricultural investment for 1971-75 (the same as that claimed for 1966-70) anticipated only a 16 percent increase in grain production in contrast with the 29 percent increase claimed during 1966-70.[15]

Perhaps the most important of all the indicators for the future of Soviet food output is revealed in the 1967 calculations made by two of the leading Soviet authorities on their land resources. As shown in table 7-7, the specialists

Table 7-7
USSR Land per Capita, 1967 vs. 1980 Projections
(million hectares)[a]

	1967	1980
Arable land	224.3	235-230
Amelioration plan		+17
Loss to cities		– 4
Gain		+13
Arable land per capita	0.95	.86
Sown area	206.9	219.4

Sources: See note 16 and *Narodnoe khoziaistvo SSSR 1968*
[a]1 hectare = 2.471 acres

projected (allowing for additional new lands from costly amelioration projects, minus land lost to urban growth) a possible arable area of 235-236 million hectares in 1980. The sown area in 1967 was 206.9 million hectares. Thus, allowing the same amount of fallow, which actually should be expanded, if the amelioration plan is fulfilled (and it has lagged), and if all the added land were sown to crops, the sown area would reach 219.4 million hectares. These same authorities further calculated that the area of arable land per capita in 1967 was .95 hectares, and that if the added 12-13 million hectares were available by 1980 (given projected population advances) there would be only 0.86 hectares per capita in 1980, a "drop . . . by 9.5 percent."[16]

Without repeating the involved explanation here, we would note that in a 1971 article, in which we employed North American comparisons along with past Soviet experience, we calculated that before adjustment (for moisture and foreign matter) the average grain output during 1971-75 should be some 185 million metric tons (161.5 when adjusted downward by 15 percent).[17] Three of the five years of the current plan period are past, and the claimed 1971-73 achievement (including grain from the unanticipated oversowing in 1973 of 9.9 million hectares) is 185 million metric tons (table 7-8).

Based on that analysis, extra grain for feed (plus other additional sources of fodder) implied a meat achievement during 1971-75 of some 13.6 million metric tons and 14 million tons during 1976-80, if only domestic sources of feed were depended upon. Utilizing a population projection series that has been on the mark to date[18] and our estimates of possible increases in animal feed, we project that the per capita output can be expected to increase significantly from 1966-70 to 1971-75 (48.9 kgs/capita to 54.6). However, such an increase would be short of the promise implied in the plan (to 57.8

Table 7-8

USSR Average Annual Grain Production and Projection, 1961-80 (million metric tons)

	Production			Plan	Author's Projection	
	1961-65	1966-70	1971-73	1971-75	1971-75	1976-80
Official claim	130.5	167.5	185.0	195.0		
Unadjusted					185.0	208.0
Adjusted	111.0	142.0			161.5	181.0

Sources: See note 17

kgs./capita), and during 1976-80 an actual decline (to 52.8 kgs./capita) is projected. However, the Soviet reentry into the world grain market in 1972 demonstrated the leadership's resolve not to let such a decline occur.

In sum, Soviet consumption of meat per capita is roughly half that of US. Part of the problem is a Soviet perference for potatoes (a point made by former minister of agriculture V.V. Matskevich at a Minsk agriculture conference in 1970); part is a problem of less favorable growing conditions; part is a need for even further investments in agriculture (especially reflected in the lack of availability of mineral fertilizer). Our own past research has documented that an important additional source of Soviet food production shortfalls stems from system inefficiencies, which may account for some 15 percent losses in grain production alone.[19] Some of the system inefficiencies are illuminated by the additional US-USSR comparisons presented in table 7-10. Surely, whatever the exact mix of causes, the USSR cannot, without continued massive feed grain imports, produce the stated norm of 82 kgs. of meat per capita (much less the 100 kgs. per capita produced in the US) at any foreseeable date.

Notes

1. *Ekonomicheskaia gazeta,* no. 11 (1971), p. 5.
2. The claimed output for 1973 is "more than 215 million metric tons (*Sel'skaia zhizn,* 12 November 1973, p. 1), and the area sown to grains was 127.9 million hectares (*Sel'skaia zhizn,* 26 July 1973, p. 1).
3. Compiled and calculated from volumes of *Agricultural Statistics* 1966 through 1972, United States Department of Agriculture (United States Government Printing Office).

Table 7-9
USSR Population, Milk, Meat, and Meat Per Capita, 1956-70, and Projections to 1980

	Past Claims			Plan	Author's Projection	
	1956-60	*1961-65*	*1966-70*	*1971-75*	*1971-75*	*1976-1980*
Population (millions)[a]	205	222	237	249	249+	265[b]
Milk (million tons)++	51.7	64.7	80.5	92.3	89.9	89.9
Meat (million tons)[c]	7.9	9.3	11.6	14.3	13.6	14.0
Meat per capita (kgs.)[c]	38.5	41.9	48.9	57.4	54.6[d]	52.8[d]

Sources: See notes 17 and 18

[a]Mid year of the five-year periods

[b]Revised downward slightly from our 1971 article.

[c]Average annual production

[d]Excluding production based on imported feedstuffs

Table 7-10
US-USSR Farm Size and Labor Comparisons, 1966-70

	US	USSR	x different
1968 population (millions)	200	237	+ 2.0
Number of farms	2,580,000	48,000[a]	−54.0
Hectares/farm	166	5,150	+31.0
Total labor force (millions)	75.9	122.5	+ 1.6
Farm Workers (millions)	4.8	40.0[b]	+ 8.3
Farm Workers as percent of population	2.4	16.9	+ 7.0
Farm Workers as percent of labor force	6.3	32.6	+ 5.2
Workers/farm	1.9	833.0	+43.8
Hectares of cropland/farm worker	41.1	5.4	− 7.6
All grain tons/farm worker	59.1	4.2	−14.1
Wheat tons/farm worker	11.9	2.3	− 5.2

Sources: See table 7-2

[a]Kolkhozy + sovkhozy, excluding private plots

[b]Including an estimate of some 10 million engaged primarily in private plot production

4. Brezhnev, "Report on the Fiftieth Anniversary of the Union of Soviet Socialist Republics" (*Sel'skia zhizn,* 22 December 1972), pp. 2-6.
5. Brezhnev, "Report to the 24th Congress" (*Pravda,* 31 March 1971), pp. 1-4.
6. A.N. Kosygin, "Report on the 1971-75 Plan Directives at the 24th Congress" (*Pravda,* 7 April 1971), pp. 1-3.
7. Brezhnev, Report to 24th Congress, pp. 1-4.
8. A personal conversation with Professor Alec Nove during 1970.
9. Kosygin, Report . . . Plan Directives, pp. 1-3.
10. Which includes pork fat. See S. Duden, *Ekonomika sel skogo khoziaistva,* no. 2 (1971), pp. 9-14.
11. *Agricultural Statistics 1972* (Op.Cit.)
12. Brezhnev, "Report to the 1968 Plenum of the CPSU" (*Pravda,* 31 October 1968), p. 1.
13. *Sel'skaia zhizn,* 26 July 1973, p. 1.
14. Ibid., 14 June 1973, p. 1.
15. Brezhnev and Kosygin Congress Reports.
16. Academician S. Udachin and Director of State. Institute for Land Resources V. Sotnikov, *Ekonomika sel'skovo khoziaistva,* no. 4 (1969), pp. 17-25.
17. Roy D. Laird, "Prospects for Soviet Agriculture," *Problems of Communism,* September -October 1971, pp. 31-40.
18. See Series A, p. 17, "Estimates and Projection of the Population of the U.S.S.R. by Age and Sex, 1950-2000, *International Population Reports,* Series P-91, no. 23 (March, 1973), pp. 1-29.
19. R.D. Laird, B.A. Laird, Sung-Il Choi, "The Impact of Farm Size and Management upon Production Efficiency in Soviet and Eastern European Agriculture," *Agricultural Typology and Land Utilization* (Verona, Italy: Center of Agricultural Geography, pp. 23-39 and Roy D. Laird and Betty A. Laird, *Soviet Communism and Agrarian Revolution* (Harmondsworth, Middlesex, England: Penguin Books, 1970).

Part V

Changes and Perspectives in
Soviet Culture

8

Soviet Art in the 1970s
John E. Bowlt

Investigation of the formation and development of modern Soviet art, specifically painting and sculpture, must bear in mind many distinctive and peculiar circumstances—simply because the history of the Soviet visual arts follows a pattern of political and cultural interaction quite different from that of the Western world. In order, therefore, to understand the predicament of Soviet art in the 1970s, it is essential also to understand the political and historical background against which it has developed and against which it will continue to develop. In this sense, any attempt to chart the vagaries of modern Soviet art or to forecast its imminent course from a purely aesthetic standpoint would be a hazardous venture indeed, the more so since the last twenty years have witnessed a series of ideological reversals and modifications of direct relevance to the evolution of Soviet culture.

At first glance, therefore, it would seem that the dependence of Soviet art on political vicissitude would create an artificial climate for its growth and prosperity, at least to a Western observer. The sporadic cultural liberalization that began with Khrushchev's accession in 1953 and has continued until the present has therefore been welcomed on both sides of the Iron Curtain, even though this process may prove to be as pernicious to artistic development as the rigid strictures of the Stalin era. In any case, this process of mitigation may, or may not, be maintained for long. For example, at the time of writing, the editorials and lead articles appearing in the official art magazines *Iskusstvo, Tvorchestvo,* and *Khudozhnik* differ little in their ardency of purpose and ideological conviction than the first Stalinist decrees on art issued over forty years ago.

What has to be considered in any examination of the contemporary Soviet art scene is whether traditional artistic criteria are still being maintained at all official levels, whether the original values of socialist realism are still supported by the party and by the Union of Artists of the USSR; or whether they have been altered—whether, in fact, as one union member said, "Contemporary life is rapidly overtaking artistic tradition."[1] Indeed, it might appear a curious anachronism that those socialist realist principles, elucidated at the First Congress of Soviet Writers in 1934 and at other concurrent events, should still hold sway in 1973-74, in a society that, materially and culturally, has changed a good deal since the first years of the Soviet régime. On a more specific level, it would seem strange that after the condemnation of Stalin and the criticism addressed to Zhdanov over the last few years, the Congress of 1934—over which their shadows loomed so large—should still be regarded as the official platform on which the future program of Soviet art was decided.

But the paradox certainly remains that the many formal declarations continually being made by the Soviet administration echo those very ideas proclaimed by Bukharin, Gor'ky, Radek, Zhdanov et al. at that Congress and shared by Igor Grabar' (then representing the visual arts workers of the Soviet Union) as well as many of the former literary and artistic avant-garde (Inber, Pasternak, Shklovsky, Sergei Tretyakov, etc.); the meaning and phraseology of dicta such as "reality in its revolutionary development," "truth and historical concreteness of the artistic depiction . . . . combined with the task of ideological transformation and education of the working people in the spirit of socialism," "labor as the central hero"[2] have changed little during the last forty years. But the fact that these principles, together with the qualities of optimism and topicality so closely identifiable with Soviet socialist realism, achieved immediate popularity and that they have survived until the present would testify, surely, to rather more than the effectiveness of a political imposition and might indicate that they were not, perhaps, so very alien to the nation's cultural consciousness. Of course, the personal artistic tastes of Stalin and his *confrères* and the rigid policies of the political machine conspired to force a single and definite direction on the development of Soviet art throughout the 1930s, 1940s, and early 1950s, but it might be argued that Soviet art would have developed in more or less the same way and would have reached similar conclusions today even without the excessive ideological pressure.

For the Western art historian to attempt to evaluate modern Soviet painting and sculpture and to divine its potential course of development is a very difficult task, unless he has an adequate knowledge of the brief but dynamic history of Russian art of both the nineteenth and twentieth centuries. It is, perhaps, a neglect of the foremost traditions of nineteenth-century Russian art which has caused the modernist movement, especially its contribution to the nonobjective world, to assume such an extraordinary stature in the eyes of Western observers, and yet to experience such neglect at the hands of their Soviet counterparts. The importance of the Russian avant-garde to universal twentieth century art must not, of course, be underestimated, and the nonobjective achievements of Kandinsky, Malevich, Popova, Tatlin, and others cannot be disputed; but what was equally as profound and innovative as their totally abstract work was their representational or applied work—in other words, the weight of the Russian avant-garde lay not necessarily in its nonobjective creation, but in its figurative, or at least "relevant," work; the cubo-futurist and aerial suprematist phases of Malevich, the functional designs of Tatlin, the emotional landscapes of Kandinsky, even the rayonist painting of Larionov, which, according to the theory, was still a representational art form.[3]

The very presence, then, of a representational tradition, whether on a narrative, philosophical, or metaphysical level, within the very center of the Russian avant-grade can be accommodated comfortably within the general spectrum of nineteenth-century realism and twentieth-century socialist realism. The basis for this argument might be extended to include the tradition of the *lubok* and the icon, so patently representational and so broadly intelligible.

The general inference can thus be made that the Russian people and even the intelligentsia during the nineteenth and twentieth centuries felt, perhaps more than any other nation, that art was a cultural activity, not intrinsic, but extrinsic; not "useless," but "useful." It is not the task of this essay to explain the reasons for the peculiarly tactile aesthetic of the Russian visual arts, although the "era of the object, its affirmation and its cult,"[4] the static and controlled way of life experienced by so many in nineteenth- and early twentieth-century Russia served as a fitting background to that very material interpretation of reality favored by such diverse artists as Perov and Repin, Larionov and Tatlin, Boris Ioganson and Vladimir Serov: art was, therefore, regarded as a part of the physical universe and was not a clinical deduction or a self-sufficient unit that the rational, abstract mind of a Western artist would have formulated. It was into this artistic ambience that the Russian realists entered in the 1860s and 1870s, achieving such wide popularity with their social and political episodes immediately comprehensible both to the masses and to the intellectuals. And as the first distinctive *movement* in modern Russian art they attracted an enthusiastic and disproportionate attention, and still do—disproportionate, that is, to a Western taste nurtured on the ideals of technical finesse and formal innovation.

The dominance of realism and the materialist interpretation of art by apologists such as Belinsky, Chernyshevsky, Dobrolyubov, and Stasov during the nineteenth century helps to explain why the emergence of nonobjective art just before and after the Revolution was so unexpected, so radical and also so short-lived. For example, within the space of a few years Malevich had returned from the purity of the initial phase of suprematism to representational painting and Tatlin had advanced from his aesthetic assemblages of materials to functional objects and then back to representational painting; many of the nonobjective artists, in fact, experienced this shift of values especially with the rise of industrial design after 1920. Moreover, many younger artists, often recent graduates from the new Soviet art schools in the early 1920s, reacted consciously and sincerely against the "utter rootlessness of further analytical and scholastic aberrations. . . . We want to create realistic works of art."[5]

It was within this framework that such well-known artists and subsequent supporters of realism as Deineka, Goncharov, and Pimenov came to the fore. Yet before they embraced the realist ideal, many of these new figurative artists experimented with symbolism (Goncharov), expressionism (Deineka), and surrealism (Tyshler, Barto), artistic methods that were constituent parts of modernist Russian painting (we think of the symbolist *Blue Rose* group, the expressionist currents in the *Union of Youth,* and the surreal elements in Chiurlienis, Masyutin, et al.). This "neoromanticism" provided a viable and often exciting alternative to the rigid canons of nineteenth-century realism exemplified by artists such as Arkhipov, Kasatkin and, later, Brodsky and Katsman.

Immediately, therefore, we can detect two different interpretations of representational art during the mid- and late 1920s: a rather photographic, although sufficiently didactic one, favored by the members of AKhRR and called heroic realism,[6] and a more lyrical, more subjective rendition identifiable in particular with members of OST, such as Goncharov, Shterenberg, Tyshler, and Vil'yams.[7] This divergence within the confines of Soviet representational art is particularly manifest today and serves to erode the ostensible solidarity of the orthodox cultural establishment.

Paradoxically, the principles of socialist realism, as formulated in the early 1930s, make allowances for both attitudes toward reality. The general conception of socialist realism as advocated at the 1934 Congress was that it entailed the imposition of a sociopolitical ideal on a depiction of concrete reality, and this combination of the real and the unreal could prompt Zhdanov to maintain "Romanticism cannot be alien to our literature . . . but it must be a romanticism of a new kind, a revolutionary romanticism. . . revolutionary romanticism must enter literary creativity as an integral part."[8] The resultant tension, therefore, between image and idea allowed the more whimsical artist some degree of elasticity, even when the cult of personality became especially evident from the late 1930s onwards: the abundant scenes from collective farm life bathed in sunshine, the smiling faces of construction workers, the tranquil professor seated at his desk, the depictions of Stalin clothed in the white raiments of a Chirst,[9] such paintings were as romantic and as removed from the truth of Soviet reality as the idealized peasant scenes of Venetsianov or the subjective visions of Borisov-Musatov had been many years before.

It is at this juncture, in fact, that the term surrealism comes to mind, for the industrial and agricultural utopias depicted by artists such as Kotov, Laktionov, and Plastov, particularly during the 1930s and 1940s, were founded on that same interaction of dream and the waking state as were the contemporaneous works of Dali and Tanguy. In this sense, it can be argued that the fantastic art early socialist realism produced continued that philosophical and mystical tradition that was clearly identifiable with Russian ecclesiastical art and with the creativity of the *Blue Rose* artists and with Kandinsky, Malevich, et al.

Moreover, on these grounds, it becomes comprehensible why the most widespread (but, unfortunately, not the finest) art trends supported by the modern Soviet avant-garde are variants of surrealism and expressionism and not, for want of a better word, neoplasticism. Again, we find that it is the "poetry" of reality which attracts the younger generation of official realists, so that even at the grand Moscow exhibitions such as "The USSR is Our Mother-land" (1973), the over-all mood is a reflective, lyrical one and lacks that vigor and unanimity of purpose which, for example, the old AKhRR exhibitions invariably generated. Indeed, many of the early socialist works, however rhapsodical and hyperbolic, still treated of dynamic themes in a very forceful and direct way: pictures were big and obvious, subjects were innovative (e.g., the industrial and transport landscape), their determined heroes were "everyman" and could inspire collective confidence.

The endeavors of the young Soviet realists today, however, follow a different pattern: pictures tend to be much smaller, scenes are often highly personal (a development symbolized, perhaps, by the noticeable move from outdoors to indoors, from panoramic vista to intimate genre), "heroes" are no longer types, but diverse individuals, compositions are more complex and less immediate, often because of a superficial and eclectic application of cubist, primitivist, and decorative principles. In this respect, the neoromantic work of today, as exemplified by artists such as Obrosov, Tordiya, and Zhilinsky, reminds us of the similar development in the late 1880s and 1890s when the vivid realism of the first generation of *Wanderers* gave way to a much more sentimental and nostalgic art form. And in both cases we find that the move was parallelled by a new attention to lyrical poetry; in the Soviet context of the 1950s, of course, the sudden advent of a personal, introspective literature (Voznesensky, Evtushenko, et al.) after the hack-work of the Stalin era played a vital role in the formation of new artistic and critical attitudes. Although the "poetic" tendency in art is criticized for its lack of "significance" as is the tendency towards excessive ornamentation,[10] the fashion continues, so forming a link, however tenuous, with the contemporary pop culture of America and Western Europe, with its preference for effete sentimentality.

The two approaches to representational painting identifiable with the 1920s and early 1930s and, on a somewhat different level, with the present day attracted particular attention in the late 1950s and early 1960s. Opinions were polarized in 1957 with the establishment of the Union of Artists of the USSR, an organization that had been contemplated since 1932. The union, with its direct party support, its material reserves and, of course, its unfailing patronage of socialist realism, immediately took on a role as guardian of traditional Soviet art, endeavoring to counterbalance the increasing trend towards antirealism. Throughout the 1960s and early 1970s the union has continued to act as the practical extension of party policy vis-à-vis the visual arts: it now numbers over 12,000 members; between 1969 and 1972 it placed commissions for over 15 million rubles; and every year it organizes about four thousand art exhibitions. Obviously, for material reasons alone, it is extremely advantageous for a Soviet artist to be a member of the union; but although a voluntary body, its procedure of enrollment is a difficult one, consisting of a series of interviewing committees, rigorous examination of works according to realist criteria, and testimonials from union members.

An open conflict between the orthodox artists of the union and the unorthodox artists outside its perimeter took place in December 1962 at the now famous exhibition "Thirty Years of Moscow Art" held at the Manège.[11] One very significant aspect of the Manège affair was that the "romantic" interpreters of reality, represented by Drevin, Fal'k, Goncharov, Neizvestnyi, Shterenberg, et al. enraged Khrushchev just as much as, if not more than, the nonobjective artists, represented by Belyutin and his abstract expressionist group. It has been suggested[12] that Vladimir Serov, then president of the Academy of Fine Arts, was responsible for the inclusion of deviationists in the exhibition, since he knew full well that Khrushchev would respond with the bitter words "We are going to maintain a strict policy of art. . . . Gentlemen, we are declaring war on you!"[13] This statement echoed Hitler's declaration voiced in similar circumstances in 1937: "From now on we are going to wage a relentless cleaning-up campaign against the last subversive elements in our culture."[14] On many occasions Serov also expressed his antipathy to the works of the "troubadours of formalist searches"[15] and upheld what he considered to be the fundamental tenets of socialist realism until his death in 1969. It was during the early 1960s, in fact, i.e. during Serov's hegemony, that the division between the official and unofficial factions within Soviet art was recognized as a serious and corrosive process, prompting Khrushchev and other leaders to emphasize that the "strength of Soviet literature and art—the method of socialist realism—is in the truthful depiction of the chief and decisive elements in reality."[16]

But despite official disfavor, the underground continued to flourish, both as a protest medium and as an aesthetic experiment, thereby forming an organic link with the delicate and clandestine avant-garde of the Stalin era: the drip canvases of Rodchenko, the surrealist easel and decorative work of Tyshler, the abstract painting of Kakabadze. Just as public poetry readings were held, so private art exhibitions were organized, both bypassing the censor; just as manuscripts began to circulate with astonishing rapidity, so a new network of private collectors began to acquire the old and new Russian avant-gardes; just as Evtushenko became the hero of the new Soviet writers, so Neizvestnyi became the accepted leader of the new generation of artists; and despite his recantation in *Pravda* in March 1963,[17] Neizvestnyi went on to become the subject of international discussion, of publications, and of the attention of such august institutions as the Museum of Modern Art in New York.[18] Now, like Evtushenko and Voznesensky, Neizvestnyi is remembered for past glories, while his work, more original and lasting than Evtushenko's, has lost much of its contemporary relevance. Of course, Evtushenko and Neizvestnyi were symbolic figures whose gestures gave direction and encouragement to a new wave of writers, artists, and artistic events. Other unofficial artists appeared in the wake of Neizvestnyi, such as Krasnopevtsev, Plavinsky and Zver'ev, each attracting his own Soviet and Western clientele; important exhibitions opened, such as the Fal'k retrospective in 1966, the Filonov in Novosibirsk in 1967, and the Rodchenko in

1968; private collections such as Yakov Rubinshtein's went on tour; above all, society and its tastes were changing: all factors conspired to threaten the edifice of socialist realism.

One very urgent demand for change in the principles of socialist realism, at least in the context of the visual arts, came from architecture and industry, as Alain Besançon pointed out as early as 1963.[19] With the higher output of consumer goods, it became more desirable to streamline design, to implement a more economical style of basic geometrical units for furniture and building, and to reject the costly munificence of the Stalin neo-Palladian *"ampir vo vremya chumy."* The new architecture of elemental forms, of stark contrasts in glass and concrete had become manifest as early as 1960 (see the Kremlin Palace of Congresses), and now, of course, it has already neutralized much of the distinctive architectural character once possessed by Moscow.

The application of the international style, which finds its roots in the 1920s, has meant, in turn, that the constructivist architecture of that period, until recently regarded as "formalist," has become quite acceptable. Logically, therefore, one would expect at least a partial recognition of the main stimuli to Russian constructivism, i.e., Malevich's suprematism and Tatlin's reliefs; and while such art and artists are still not celebrated publicly, it is significant that detailed references to them do appear now especially in the context of design, architecture, the decorative arts, and aesthetics. On a very practical level, modern Soviet architects have stressed the need for a new concept of decorative or monumental art since, quite obviously, the kind of grand panneaux executed in the Stalin buildings such as the Hotel Moskva (painted by Evgenii Lancéray in 1937/38) or Deineka's sports scenes on the subway station Mayakovskaya (1939) would be inapplicable to the austerity and linearity of such buildings as the New Arbat complex or the SEV skyscraper.

Unfortunately, the abstract or highly schematic decorative panneaux the new buildings require have not been created, and instead, large areas on external and internal walls have been devoted to Rivera-type scenes of society at work or to simplistic images of technological and cultural progress. Of course, the tradition of monumental art in Russia is a very long and important one, and we can see an ideological parallel between the ancient church fresco and the Communist mural, but just as Soviet painting and sculpture have been unable to shake off the yoke of representationalism, so monumental art has remained conventionally figurative. As one critic put it: "We've grown tired of a good deal over the last few years. We're tired of triptychs. . . . We're tired of "strong" heroes with their huge muscles and thick skins, with their faces knowing no doubts and scorning introspection. We're tired of figures utterly motionless in their poses."[20]

The striking contrast between the new minimal architecture and the old elaborate depictions of happy episodes from working life or of past triumphs has forced many to view socialist realist painting as stagnant and anachronistic; and this realization, particularly on the part of the architectural and design

communities, has been strengthened by many segments of a society that has
changed considerably over the last few years and that must surely question even
Lenin's attitudes to art. When, for example, Lenin declared in 1920 that a socialist government must fight against "bourgeois inclinations . . . pornography . . .
anything which divulges state or military secrets" in art,[21] he was talking in a
different age and to a different audience, one whose concept of pornography,
for example, would not be shared by the younger generation of Soviet citizens
today, just as the description "bourgeois art," once applied to impressionsim,
Art Nouveau and constructivism, but now applied rather to surrealism, expressionism and nonobjective art, has proved to be an indecisive and elusive term.

Moreover, many of Lenin's pronouncements on art lack specific information, necessitating commentary and elucidation; but it was natural that as a
spectator and not as an art specialist Lenin could deftly formulate the business
of art in such platitudes as "[Art] must be intelligible to the masses and must
be loved by them . . . it must unite the feelings, thoughts and will of these
masses . . . . it must arouse artists in them and nurture them."[22] It is surprising
that a civilized society that could produce such sophisticated musicians, writers
and painters as Richter, Solzhenitsyn, and Tyshler could still attempt to compose
artistic policy in accordance with such generalizations.

The advances in technological and scientific achievement, the changing taste
of Soviet society, the intellectual's wish for an art form more delicate and
abstruse, the general move away from the collective to the individual—such
factors must surely dictate a shift of emphasis within the spectrum of official
art. But, paradoxically, when we come to examine the statements on art and
aesthetics by members of the party or of the Union of Artists during the late
1960s and early 1970s, we find that the tone is the same as forty years ago.
Zimenko, for example, secretary to the board of the Union of Artists and chief
editor of the journal *Iskusstvo,* could assert in 1971 that the entire system of art
within a developed socialist society could be planned in advance,[23] and idea that
recalled Zhdanov's demand of Soviet literature that it "catch a glimpse of our
tomorrow. This will not be a utopia, because our tomorrow is being prepared
today by our systematic and conscious work."[24] However, the suggestion that
the creative process could be calculated and formulated was vigorously criticized
by other members of the union: "The Union of Artists is a creative organization.
Artists do not fulfill production plans, they create."[25] The discussion of nationalism and internationalism in art is also a perennial issue, reaching conclusions as
rhetorical and as exaggerated as those of Gorky's speeches at the 1934 Congress.
The call to artists to frequent factories, shipyards, Red Army units, etc. is voiced
just as urgently as it was in the 1920s and 1930s. The third and fourth congresses
of Soviet artists (1969 and 1973) used the same vocabulary, despite the important cultural events that had occurred between them, concurring in their desire
to "educate the artist in the spirit of intransigence to any manifestations of
bourgeois ideology, to any of the various modernist, formalist and naturalist
directions and tendencies in art."[26]

An issue that has taken on particular significance during the last two or three years and that has never been examined satisfactorily is the function of Soviet art criticism. This question has worried the party considerably over recent months, culminating in the publication of the decree "On Literary-Artistic Criticism" in 1972[27] and prompting Brezhnev to affirm at the Twenty-Fourth Party Congress, "The progress of Soviet literature and art would be even more significant and their defects eliminated more quickly, if our literary and artistic criticism would implement the party line more actively, if it would perform with more *printsipial'nost'* "[28]

Following the advocation of socialist realism in the early 1930s, Soviet art criticism, like literary criticism, adopted an exclusively sociological, extrinsic approach to the work of art, resulting in numerous "life and work" studies of national and foreign artists. By its very nature, of course, such a system of art appreciation has been unable to evaluate the work of art independently, as a self-sufficient unit; it has not been concerned with formal structure of a given painting or sculpture. In literature recent developments have overcome the resulting stagnation of the sociological method, and the structuralist studies of Lotman and his colleagues have provided new criteria and new insights after the pedantic and predictable work of critics such as Metchenko and Vengrov.

In the visual arts, this exciting development has been parallelled only by the isolated endeavors of the late Lev Zhegin, Sarab'yanov and a few others,[29] and the school of ciriticism that relates the artisti's life and the story of his work still dominates art publications; so that while opening up new fields of research, particularly within the eighteenth century and the end of the nineteenth/beginning of the twentieth, scholars such as D'yakonitsyn, Kogan, and Podobedova have presented factographies as devoid of formal analysis as the Stalinist academic works of Aleksei Milkhailov and Neiman.

The first major and open confrontation between the traditional and innovative camps of Soviet art criticism appeared with two very interesting and contradictory essays in *Iskusstvo* in 1972, each illustrating the polarization of critical attitudes evident amongst Soviet art historians: Sarab'yanov's "Iskusstvoznanie i literaturovedenie" and D'yakonitsyn's "Problemy russkogo iskusstva kontsa XIX nachala XX veka"[30]: Sarab'yanov expressed concern over the reluctance to apply new methods in Soviet art criticism and the consequent lack of progress being made in the discipline; D'yakonitsyn warned against any rash attempt to alter traditional critieria and to neglect the "scientific Communist principle of *partiinost'*."[31]

Sarab'yanov's call to "examine the violation of structure as an artistic convention . . . . the exposure of a syntagmatic, i.e., inner, immanent . . . . level of expressivity in the work"[32] has not attracted many followers so far, although it undoubtedly will; but it is most significant that a more formal, more constructive approach to art has already been favored by some practicing artists. This evolution of art towards a more scientific, more exact pattern constitutes, in fact, a very exciting development on the contemporary front of the Soviet visual arts and surpasses in vision and originality the countless essays in eroticism and surrealism now associated with the Moscow avant-garde.

The new trend towards construction, or "artistic technology," owes much to Lev Nusberg, a self-taught Moscow artist, who, during the late 1950s, had rapidly assimilated the devices of Kandinsky, Klee, Malevich, and Miró, finally arriving at the kinetic method in 1961 for which he is now known. Together with Franciso Infante, Krivchikov, and others, Nusberg founded the Dvizhenie group in 1962,[33] and the following year some of their constructions were shown at the Moscow House of Art Workers under the title "Exhibition of Ornamentalists," a description that connected the group automatically with the decorative arts and hence obviated the direct demand for overt political content.

Thereafter kinetic constructions were shown at various institutions in Moscow and Leningrad, and associates of the group took part in conferences devoted to such themes as "Light and Music" (Kazan, 1969) and created the layout of several scientific and cultural exhibitions, such as "Fifty Years of the Soviet Circus" (Moscow, 1969). In 1965 Dvizhenie issued a program entitled "What is Kinetism?" which presented the principle tenets of Nusberg and his colleagues (at that time):

> We demand the utilization of all potentials and all media, all technological and aesthetic, physical and chemical phenomena, all forms of art, all processes and forms of perception as well as the interrelationship of physical reactions and the action of various human mental impressions as a means of artistic expression.[34]

Because of personal and ideological frictions, the collective is continually changing, although Nusberg remains the leader, and onetime colleagues, who include technicians, painters, actors and musicians, branch out on their own. The political position of the present collective and of kinetists outside its confines, such as Koleichuk and now Infante, is an ambiguous one: on the one hand, their work is recognized by certain governmental organs such as the Ministry of Building and the Ministry of Radiotechnology Industry, yet on the other, it is disregarded by the Ministry of Culture and the Union of Artists. It is because of this curious divergence of views that the kinetists were allowed to formulate various exhibitions and even to contribute to the Leningrad decorations in honor of the fiftieth anniversary of October,[35] but that Nusberg was refused permission to join the Union of Artists; Infante and his colleagues, now forming a rival group called ARGO (*Avtorskaya rabochaya gruppa*), created an "artificial kinetic environment with the active use of chromomusic, plastic organization of space, and various forms of movement"[36] for the international chemistry exhibition in Moscow in 1970, yet Infante has never had a public one-man show. Perhaps the saddest consequence of this twilight existence is that beyond official

commissions, materials are very hard to come by, so that many projects remain
at the graphic and design stage: among many such embryonic schemes are
Nusberg's designs for a total pleasure garden environment and for a pioneer
camp center (partly implemented at a Black Sea resort in 1968).

Indebted to Nusberg's initial kinetic ideas and also, on a different level, to
Johannes Itten and Adolf Fleischmann, but already a long way beyond them, is
Infante, one of the Soviet Union's most talented artist-constructors. Convinced
of man's ultimate inhabitation of space, Infante has designed a series of forms
that, while floating and revolving, would create artificial environments in the
cosmos or would act simply as abstract constructions—units in which color,
sound, and light would play roles as important as the structural axes themselves.
He describes his new conception in one of his manifestoes:

> All the beautiful monuments of man's spirit which have copied
> nature one way or another belong to the classics. Our age is
> remarkable for a new quality—it has begun to create systems and
> models which, *in their effect,* can reproduce processes and phenom-
> ena analogous to natural ones. This is no longer the reflection of
> nature, but the creation of *artificial* systems, "living" according to
> the laws of nature and developing by analogy with nature. . . . Apart
> from their creative, heuristic and psychological values, the issues of
> scientific and technological development designate for us . . . media
> and instruments for the possible realization of our conceptions.[37]

It is precisely in the work of Infante and ARGO, of Nusberg and Dvizhenie,
and of Koleichuk (working independently) that we can perceive the support and
evolution of the great Russian constructivist tradition of the 1920s, especially as
it affected the whole notion of architecture and urban planning. Not only do
the actual constructions of the Moscow kinetists have total architectural meaning in that they are destined to serve as microenvironments, but also even the
small-scale ornamental graphic designs, especially the pieces of Bitt, Bystrova,
Grigor'ev, Infante and Nusberg, maintain that linear fluidity and spatial balance
that we identify with Rodchenko's drawings of 1915-19 or with Miturich's
spatial graphics of 1920-21; the prototype constructions of Infante and Koleichuk also remind us of the wood and metal constructions of Medunetsky,
Rodchenko, and the Obmokhu group (1920). On a different level their concern
with a synthetic presentation of form and movement, with a spatial definition
by light, color and sound, recalls the optical and perspectival experiments of
Klyun, Matyushin, and the Enders during the mid- and late 1920s.

It is this audacious, experimental approach to three-dimensional reality,
together with a full acceptance of technological advance, which links the Moscow kinetists to such pioneers as Gabo, Lissitzky and Tatlin (however different
their respective aesthetic systems). But, of course, the kinetists are interested

in a mobile art form, something scarcely investigated by the old avant-garde, although Gabo certainly used light as a constructive and dynamic element in his work as early as 1923, and the fantastic architect Georgii Krutikov transferred constructive principles to mobile architectural complexes floating in space.[38] Tatlin and Miturich, too, were close to the kinetic method in their projects for flying machines.

However, it is not only their concentration on movement, whether actual as in constructed mobiles, or illusory as in *trompe-l'oeil* graphics, which distinguishes the kinetists from their precursors, but also their application of the illogical to their basic constructive schemas, expressing that same combination of intuition and calculation we find in a Kandinsky or a Malevich. It is in this direction that the work of Nusberg seems to be developing, as his Alice in Wonderland Pioneer Camp or his layout for a Museum of the Soul would indicate. Infante remains a little more rational, applying his designs to environments that still appear feasible, even though his incredible "Necklace" project intended to encircle the earth, testifies to his profound imagination and sensibility. Koleichuk remains at a more abstract, nonutilitarian stage than either Nusberg or Infante and brings to mind Yaacov Agam, Nobert Kricke, and Franz Küsters. In the case of Nusberg and Infante, it is precisely their masterful combination of the logical and the fantastic that distinguishes them from parallel trends in other European countries: in Poland, for example, Jan Chwaczyk has created light constructions; in Czechoslovakia, Dalibor Chatrný, Karel Malich, and many others work in a constructive idiom; but the essential idea of a *kinetic artificial environment* predestined for a cosmonautical epoch is missing from their work and it remains as aesthetic as the happenings of Western Europe and America. Contrary to this, the kinetic art of Dvizhenie and ARGO has, ultimately, a utilitarian and social function, however visionary and unfeasible this may seem; and it is precisely this external value of the Moscow kinetic art that links it directly to the central traditions of Russian and Soviet art.

There is no doubt that for a resurgence of Russian art we must look to the Moscow kinetists, even though they themselves avoid the term "artist," perhaps agreeing with Gan's declaration of 1922: "Art is finished! . . . Labor, technology, organization!. . . that is the ideology of our time."[39] It is the clarity of vision, the prospect of an "on-going" art and its supreme modernity that separate the Moscow kinetists from the other representatives of the contemporary Soviet avant-garde, from those painters and sculptors who remain loyal to traditional media and who tend to support a surrealist or expressionist rendition of existence. With few exceptions, the work of these artists, like that of so many of their East European colleagues, does not create the impression of innovation or of potential; and even though their search for a more mystical, subjective interpretation of reality does, in itself, constitute an ideological and social protest, it remains so often a quaint confusion of vulgar eroticism and religious nostalgia: Vladimir Yankilevsky's distorted adoration of the female anatomy produces little of novelty to a Western market saturated with such art; Ilya Kabakov and Erik Bulatov, very competent technicians, possess a precision and a clarity welcome after the coarseness of Yankilevsky, but both, all too obviously, owe their thematic derivation to Magritte;[40] Michel Chemiakin, now living in Paris, shares a grace and discipline identifiable with the *World of Art* and with the Russian book illustrators and caricaturists of the nineteenth century, but his art is static, it is "finite";[41] the work of Oskar Rabin is already well-known in the West, perhaps because of its specifically Moscow subject matter: churches, Stalin buildings, wooden houses, and the remarkable intensity of his textures provide his work with a force and intensity not present in his often shallow imagery; Evgenii Rukhin is perhaps the most exciting of all the contemporary underground painters, for his work manifests a fertility and sense of purpose lacking in so many of the pieces by his colleagues: his textural contrasts, achieved by appliqué of various materials—cloth, wood, glass—to the surface, testify to the artist's unflinching search for new spatial definitions while still within the basic confines of the canvas. It is perhaps indicative of Western bourgeois taste that artists such as Yankilevsky, Rabin, and Krasnopevtsev find a ready market amongst both the diplomatic circles of Moscow and the dealers of Paris, London, and New York. The kinetists, however, are patronized by comparatively few collectors either at home or in the West, although they have achieved a positive reputation through their contributions to Western exhibitions, particularly to the recent show at the Gmurzynska Gallery in Cologne.[42]

The fluctuations in the cultural policy of the Soviet Union over the last two decades make any prognosis of artistic development a difficult and perhaps fruitless task. Yet there are certain signals that might indicate a dramatic change in the very near future. One of these is the fact that so many members of the old Russian avant-garde, who only a few years ago were scarcely mentioned, are now regarded as positive contributors to Russia's artistic heritage: Al'tman, Chagall, Fal'k, Filonov, Goncharova, Larionov, Rodchenko are now recognized, even though, for obvious reasons, certain aspects of their work receive disproportionate attention; for instance the neoprimitivist phase of Larionov is emphasized, but his rayonism is ignored; Rodchenko's design work is praised, but not his nonobjective painting.

Western acknowledgement of the avant-garde also focuses attention on such names, and the network of private collectors in the Soviet Union, such as Costakis, Rubinshtein and Chudnovsky, does much to familiarize artists and scholars with the creative achievements of the pre- and post-Revolutionary periods. The fact that Costakis was allowed to lecture about his collection in the US and England in the fall of 1973 and that negotiations with the Ministry of Culture to show his collection in the US are already underway also points to a political and artistic readjustment. Moreover, a few Soviet art historians express the hope that some of the works in the *zapasniki* will be displayed in the new Tretyakov Gallery when it is opened in 1974/1975.

On the other hand, such optimism is countered by the fact that Mme Furtseva could gladly exchange a Malevich suprematist piece for a Goya in 1973 and that pieces by Klyun, Malevich, and others from the Soviet Union regularly turn up for auction in London, in most cases with the Ministry of Culture's knowledge and with its blessing. Nevertheless, the climate has certainly altered over the last few years and the circumstances referred to above are playing a vital role in propagating the avant-garde and in introducing "formalist" trends to the public at large—even though they may not necessarily change the dictatorial attitude of the Ministry of Culture and the Union of Artists. For that we must rely on internal changes and pressures: many of the Stalinist diehards, such as Aleksandr Gerasimov, Katsman and Serov, are dead or nearly so; the "lyrical" (and very pernicious) alternative to strict realism now dominates official exhibitions and art salons: and such work *is* pernicious, because in a very sentimental and bourgeois manner Orosov's *Little Girl with Swallows* (see cover to *Iskusstvo,* 1973, no. 4), Mylnikov's *Morning,* a nude asleep in an idyllic landscape—justified by one critic as a "conception of the higher harmony between man and nature, of the noble morality of reality,"[43] or Narimanbekov's *Still-life* (see cover to *Iskusstvo,* 1973, no. 6) erode the majestic principles of "practical work . . . . supreme heroism and grand prospects"[44] which, surely, ought to be identifiable with socialist realism.

Undoubtedly, there is anxiety within the Union of Artists regarding this more flexible interpretation of socialist realism, and many members are dissatisfied with the tendency to depict the "poetry" of reality rather than its concrete phenomena. Added to this is the fact that many of the "lyrical" pictures are inspired by Western artists past and present: Mikita's *For Our Nephew's Happiness* (see *Tvorchestvo,* 1973, no. 3) obviously derives from Bosch; Raksha's *Contemporaries* (see *Iskusstvo,* 1972, no. 12) bears a curious resemblance to Norman Rockwell's *Freedom from Want* of 1943. It is hard to imagine that critical comments alone, as naive as "Why is it necessary to stick newspaper cuttings on to an oil painting?"[45] could halt the progress of this tendency; in any case, party and union declarations concerning art can be so verbose and nebulous that they give little idea as to what specifically is wanted of the artist. It is at this juncture, in fact, that a coercive return to a more precise, more rigid artistic policy might be seen to be the most sensible solution.

On the other hand, if a cultural mollification does occur in the near future, then both the official and the unofficial artists will suffer. The situation might even develop whereby the Stalinist works of Brodsky, Katsman, Serov, etc. would become more desirable as collector's items than those of the underground, because in so many cases the latter are acquired principally for their symbolic value, for their function as protest art. Deprived of that extra-aesthetic quality, they would become less meaningful and less sought after. And in many cases the loss would not be great.

Unfortunately, the "lyrical" realists would retain their popularity simply because "mood art" always has a wide appeal. By the same token, the position of the kinetists would not change much, although with materials more accessible they would be able to implement many more of their constructions and to test them as microenvironments on a much broader scale. But even if these thoughts prove mere speculation and a reversal in artistic policy is imminent, it would certainly seem that socialist realism has lost that vigor, that grandeur, that sense of mission it possessed in its original condition. As they wander through the dark labyrinth of the Tret'yakov Gallery, halting often in the deserted halls of Soviet painting, the ghosts of Stalin and his entourage must surely echo the words Diaghilev pronounced on the occasion of his Russian portrait exhibition in 1905; "Do you not think that the long gallery of portraits of people great and small. . . . is but a grand and convincing reckoning of a brilliant, but, alas, mortified period of our history?"[46]

Notes

1. G. Korzhev at the Fourth Congress of Artists of the USSR, 1973. Quoted from: "Vmeste c partiei, vmeste s narodom," *Iskusstvo*, no. 7 (1973), p. 3.
2. First two statements from A. Zhdanov's speech at the First All-Union Congress of Soviet Writers. Quoted from: I. Luppol et al. (eds.): *Pervyi Vsesoyuznyi s'ezd sovetskikh pisatelei. Stenograficheskii otchet*, M., 1934, p. 4. Third statement from Gorky's speech (Ibid., p. 13.)
3. M. Larionov: *Luchizm*, M., 1913. A variant of this appeared a few months later as "Luchistskaya zhivopis'," *Oslinyi khvost i mishen'*, M., 1913, pp. 83-124.
4. N. Punin: *Noveishie techeniya v russkom iskusstve*, pt. 2, L., 1928, p. 5.
5. Preface to the catalogue of the first exhibition of NOZh (New Society of Painters), Moscow, 1922.
6. For details on AKhRR (Association of Artists of Revolutionary Russia) and AKhR (Association of Artists of the Revolution) see: I. Gronsky and V. Perel'man (compilers): *AKhRR*, M., 1973. This contains the manifestoes of AKhRR.
7. There is no monograph on OST (Society of Easel Artists). For some details, see R. Zherdeva: "Tema truda v proizvedeniyakh khudozhnikov OSTa," *Iskusstvo*, no. 8 (1973), pp. 29-38.
8. A. Zhdanov, p. 4.
9. This curious resemblance is evident, for example, in I. Toidze's picture "I.V. Stalin at the Ryon Hydro-Electric Power Station" (1935) in the Marx-Engels-Lenin Institute, Tbilisi.
10. See G. Konyakhin: "Esteticheskie illyuzii i khudozhestvennaya real'nost'," *Iskusstvo*, no. 11 (1969), p. 5; M. Anikushin: "Sovremmenost' eto soderzhanie," *Tvorchestvo*, no. 2 (1973), p. 3.
11. For accounts of the exhibition see R. Etiemble: "Pictures from an Exhibition," *Survey*, no. 48 (1963), pp. 5-18; P. Sjeklocha and I. Mead: *Unofficial*

Art in the Soviet Union (Berkeley and Los Angeles: University of California Press, 1967), pp. 91 *et seq.*; T. Whitney: *The New Writing in Russia* (Ann Arbor: University of Michigan Press, 1964), pp. 27 *et seq.*

12. R. Etiemble.

13. "Khrushchev on Modern Art," stenographic report in *Encounter,* no. 115, (1963) pp. 102-3.

14. Quoted from J. Willett: *Expressionism* (New York/Toronto: McGraw-Hill, 1970), p. 205.

15. I. Popov: "Novatorstvo istinnoe i lozhnoe," *Iskusstvo,* no. 11 (1968), p. 2. For Serov's statements, see: *V Bor'be za sotsialisticheskii realizm. Sbornik statei i rechel VI. A. Serova,* M., 1963.

16. Quoted from Whitney, p. 19.

17. Neizvestnyi's recantation appeared in *Pravda* for 15 March 1963.

18. See J. Berger: *Art and Revolution. Ernst Neizvestny and the Role of the Artist in the USSR* (Harmondsworth: Penguin, 1969). The Museum of Modern Art, New York, purchased some of Neizvestnyi's sculptures and drawings.

19. A. Besançon: "Soviet Painting: Tradition and Experiment," *Survey,* 1963, no. 46, pp. 83-93. Significantly, in the same year appeared V. Khazanova's *Iz istorii sovetskoi arkhitektury 1917-1925,* M., a pioneer work which helped to lift the anathema from constructivism.

20. D. Sarab'yanov, "Pod znakom iskanii. Zhivopis' Sovetskogo Zakavkazya," *Iskusstvo,* no. 2 (1972), p. 14.

21. Quoted from G. Kunitsyn: "Leninskie kriterii v otsenke iskusstva," *Iskusstvo,* no. 4 (1969), p. 2.

22. Ibid., p. 3.

23. V. Zimenko: "Struktura izobrazitel'nogo iskusstva v razvitom sotsialisticheskom obshchestve," *Iskusstvo,* no. 9 (1971), p. 3.

24. A. Zhdanov, p. 5.

25. I. Bogdesko: "Nado nastupat'!" *Tvorchestvo,* no. 2 (1973), p. 4.

26 "Postanovlenie III s'ezda khudozhnikov SSSR," *Iskusstvo,* no. 2 (1969), p. 3.

27. In *Pravda,* 25 January 1972.

28. *XXIV S'ezd Kommunisticheskoi partii Sovetskogo Soyuza. Stenografi- cheskii otchet,* M., 1971, vol. 1, p. 113.

29. See L. Zhegin, *Yazyk zhivopisnogo proizvedeniya,* M., 1970; D. Sarab'yanov: *Russkaya zhivopis' kontsa 1900-kh - nachala 1910-kh godov,* M., 1971.

30. Sarab'yanov's piece appeared in *Iskusstvo,* no. 5 (1972), pp. 38-43; D'yakonitsyn's appeared in *Iskusstvo,* no. 10 (1972), pp. 69-71.

31. L. D'yakonitsyn: "Problemy russkogo iskusstva. . . ," p. 71.

32. D. Sarab'yanov: "Iskusstvoznanie. . ," p. 43.

33. Over the last few years there have been many scattered references to Nusberg and Dvizhenie in Western publications. Of particular use are

Chroniques de l'art vivant, no. 23 (1971), pp. 17-19 (apart from commentary by Michel Ragon, this issue contains a chronicle of Soviet kinetic events 1961-70); Catalogue to *Progressive russische Kunst/Lev Nusberg und die moskauer Gruppe "Bewegung,"* Galerie Gmurzynska, Cologne, 1973 (this contains a translation of the Ragon article and an anonymous essay "Lev Nusberg und die Gruppe 'Bewegung' ").

34. "Lev Nusberg und die Gruppe "Bewegung' " (unpaginated).

35. For commentary see V. Petrov: "Prazdnichnoe ubranstvo Leningrada," *Stroitel'stvo i arkhitektura Leningrada,* no. 1 (1968), pp. 2-10; O. Nemiro: "Oformlenie Leningrada v dni 50-letiya Oktyabrya," *Iskusstvo,* 1969, no. 2, pp. 37-41.

36. F. Infante: "O kineticheskoi srede i metode sozdaniya kineticheskikh proizvedenii primenitel'no k praktike kineticheskikh sred-vystavok i nekotorykh proektov," p. 4. Unpublished manuscript.

37. F. Infante: " 'Arkhitektura' iskusstvennykh sistem v kosmicheskom prostranstve," p. 1. Unpublished manuscript.

38. On Krutikov see S. Khan-Magomedov: "Proekt 'letayushchego goroda'," *Dekorativnoe iskusstvo,* no. 1 (1973), pp. 30-36. It is of interest to compare Krutikov's theories with those of Koleichuk; see V. Koleichuk: *Mobil'naya arkhitektura,* Moscow, 1973.

39. A. Gan: *Konstruktivizm,* Tver', 1922, p. 48.

40. Some details and illustrations concerning Yankilevsky, Kabakov and Bulatov will be found in *Chroniques de l'art vivant,* pp. 11-13; also see Catalogue to *Avant Garde Russe. Moscou 73,* Galerie Dina Vierny, Paris, 1973.

41. On Chemiakin, see Catalogue to *Michel Chemiakin. Saint-Petersbourg 71. Avant-garde Russe,* Galerie Dina Vierny, Paris, 1971.

42. See note 33.

43. V. Sysoev: "Khudozhniki Rossiiskoi Federatsii," *Iskusstvo,* no. 3 (1973), p. 13.

44. A. Zhdanov, p. 4.

45. G. Konyakhin, p. 5.

46. S. Diaghilev: "V chas itogov," *Vesy,* no. 4 (1905), p. 45.

9 Some Sociological Aspects of Soviet Cinematography

Victor Rashkovsky

In February of 1922, the founder of the Soviet State, Vladimir Lenin, declared in a conversation with the minister of education, Anatoly Lunacharsky: "Of all the kinds of art, the most important one for us is the cinema." These words, repeated thereafter a million times in books, articles, and reports, stamped on the walls and decorating as slogans every cinema of the Soviet Union, reflect the constant and close attention of the Soviet regime to the art of the cinema.

The nature of this phenomenon is not hard to explain. First of all, for Russia, a country then almost completely illiterate, the cinema was, indeed, the only kind of art available for the masses. Besides, in the very nature of the cinema there is authenticity, a convincing connection with reality, and that's why it has the greatest emotional and propaganda impact. Finally, the cinema is capable of appealing to the greatest audience. In 1972, the daily cinema audience in the Soviet Union was about five million persons. All of this explains why Soviet authorities regard the cinema as the most important art form. And that is why the Soviet authorities try to use the cinema as one of the strongest instruments of social pressure, as a part of their comprehensive propaganda machinery.

Relations between the Soviet regime and the cinema operate in two dimensions. On the one hand, officially the cinema exists as a form of an art. There are professional critics, studying the problems of image structure, of means of expression, genre and special stylistic features, and providing aesthetic evaluation of all the details of cinematographic activity. A number of special books and journals dealing with the art of cinema are published. Official articles and speeches extoll in glowing phrases the creation of the rich and wonderful spiritual world of the Communist society by the genuine means of art and particularly of the art of cinema.

But these are mere words, nothing but an official cover. In fact, Soviet authorities are completely uninterested in art; indeed, they are afraid of it, as they are afraid of anything that encourages the independent thought. The whole state propaganda machinery operates for brain washing, and any creation of art that does not fit the constraints of propaganda poses a danger to the state.

One of the best known examples is the movie *Andrei Rublev*, directed by Andrey Tarkorsky. Many people in the West know that the showing of this movie was forbidden in the USSR for five years, and it was only shown last year, in spite of the fact that this movie had been sold abroad and even awarded the International Association of Cinema Critics prize at the Cannes Film Festival. What was it that frightened Soviet officials in this extraordinary movie about

215

a great Russian icon painter of the fifteenth century? First of all, it was cruel realism in the description of a bloody and severe period of Russian history, the bitter truth about betrayals and barbarism of the Russian people themselves, which helped maintain the Tartar yoke in Russia. Moreover, the authorities regarded as dangerous the philosophical ideas, inherent in this movie, about the relations between an artist of genius and the society, between the artist and the people, and the problem of interpretation of reality in an artistic creation.

It would be wrong to think that the Soviet leaders want or, in view of their cultural level, are even capable of understanding every phenomenon of cinematic art. Nothing of the sort! But there is the complicated, cumbersome, and multi-stage system of state control over the cinematography—determining the fate of a movie during every stage, from the proposal of a scenario to the eventual showing in the cinema theatres. This system acts as an ideological censorship, augmenting official censorship itself. Every script, before shooting, must pass (in different stages) through three editorial boards and must be approved by a manager of the cinema studio and by the State Committee of the Cinema (that is to say, the ministry). After tryouts for any movie, all actors for main parts must be approved also by the editorial board and by the manager of the studio, and in some cases, by the state committee. In other words, the movie director has no right to choose his actors independently.

It is important to emphasize that the authorities are guided exclusively by ideological rather than artistic considerations. Some years ago there was the hidden instruction of the chairman of the State Committee prohibiting the casting of film actors Rolan Bykov and Inna Churikov as main characters in historical and revolutionary movies. Both of them are very talented and popular, but they have somewhat unprepossessing appearances. It was explained in this instruction that the characters of the heroes of the Revolution and of the civil war must be performed only by actors whose appearance is perfect, because the appearance of actors must be in harmony with the perfection of the revolutionary ideals of the characters they are to portray.

Once the movie is completed, its fate may be considered at several stages and determined by most unexpected factors. The movie *The Sordid Tale,* directed by Alexander Alov and Vladimir Naumov, was forbidden as a slander of Russian national character, although the directors only followed accurately the spirit of the Dostoevsky story on which the script was based. In 1968, director Gennady Polloka filmed the movie *Intervention.* It was based upon the classic Soviet play, which told about the intervention of the Allied armies in Odessa in 1919. The movie was forbidden, and it was explained unofficially to the director that the word *intervention,* can evoke undesirable associations; a few months before the Soviet Army had occupied Czechoslovakia.

Any movie may be forbidden, or only a small number of prints may be made, with the explanations: "It's very gloomy," or "It distorts the image of a Party member", or "It's incomprehensible." This latter explanation is usually invoked in connection with the charge of "formalism", that is, the subjugation of content to the form. This happened, in particular, with two superlative films: *The Color of Pomegranates,* directed by Sergei Paradjanov, and *Prayer,* directed by Abuladze. These represented attempts at poetic biographies of two great national poets, the Armenian, Sayat Nova and the Georgian, Vazha Pshavela.

In the high official circles, the greatest fear is not of overt anti-Soviet attacks, which, in any case, are impossible under the described multistage system of controls, but the dread of innuendoes, analogies, and allusions. The authorities are afraid not only of the text but also of the "subtext." Many Soviet films, if not forbidden outright, were corrected or modified, because the bureaucracy perceived in them "an unmanageable subtext." This expression is often utilized in official evaluations, when they do not want to accuse the film authors of intentionally creating an undesirable "second plan," but the officials are afraid that "enemies" or "unconscionable elements" may "misinterpret" the entire film or a particular episode in it.

At times, humorous situations arise when film authors insist that the officials explain to them exactly what constitutes the "unmanageable subtext." For example, last year director Zhelakyavichus filmed *This Sweet Word—Freedom,* a description of the escape of a group of Communists from a South American jail. It seemed that all of the ideology was correct. But the film had excessive discussion of the necessity of freedom for every human being, and in general the concept of freedom was discussed on the screen in excessively broad terms. The director experienced several tough months of fighting to save his film from absolute prohibition.

Several years ago an even more interesting episode occurred in Soviet cinematography. The famous director of the older generation, Michail Romm, produced a two-part serial documentary, *Ordinary Fascism.* In this truly outstanding film, created with brilliantly expressed individuality and splendid commentaries by the director himself, the topic was the genesis and development of fascism in Germany, how it was possible to brutalize and completely bamboozle a great people possessed of a rich cultural and historic past. Romm, a great master and a man of seasoned wisdom had lived a long and hard life, survived the loss of many friends and relatives during the Stalin era, and abhorred fascism of any shade—brown, red, or yellow. The film had an easily perceived "second plan." The allusions were rather transparent, and the suggestions embodied in some of the episodes would be understood by anyone except the youngest children. For example, the visit to an art exhibit by Hitler immediately called forth an association with a similar visit to an art exhibit by Khrushchev, which was followed by a virtual pogrom of artistic intelligentsia. Moreover, one of the portraits included in the exhibit—a portrait of Hitler—reproduced in absolute detail of composition and pose the portrait of Stalin well-known to every citizen of USSR and declared a classic by the official bureaucracy.

After the film was completed, a series of incomprehensible events took place. At no single stage was the film rejected or forbidden. To approve the film would have meant the acceptance of a very heavy responsibility, for the "second plan" was apparent to anyone. To reject or forbid the film would have meant to express in so many words, out loud, the heretical thought: "It is stated not only for Germany but also about us, the Soviet Union!" In this manner, it would have been necessary to acknowledge openly the existence of certain analogies. Naturally, no one wanted to do it. Ultimately, the task was passed upward to the summit of the hierarchical pyramid. The film was viewed by the members of the Politburo of the Central Committee of the Communist Party of the Soviet Union. It is hard to say what was said or what was thought by the Soviet dictators, but they reached a judgment of Solomon. The film was approved for showing in cinema theaters, the press was ordered to praise it, and moreover, it was awarded a state premium. Yet, simultaneously, it was forbidden to be shown on television and for units of the Soviet Army. The state TV network was forbidden to use even fragments of the film on any telecasts.

I will note, in passing, that the film engendered extraordinary interest on the part of Soviet viewers. It was seen by more than 30 million persons, an unheard of audience for such a film. This was a record for documentaries; it persists to the present time and, I believe, will stand for many more years. And Michail Romm remained true to himself; he died two years ago before completing the film *Great Tragedy,* a film about "the cultural revolution" in China, yet another variety of fascism.

I want to emphasize once again that the entire system of control exists only for the purpose of ideological screening, but it does not prevent the production and showing of low-quality, antiartistic films. Perhaps this is the reason why many of the top cinematographic posts are filled with persons of low cultural and professional level. For example, for some ten years the manager of a major Soviet cinema studio, Mosfilm, was a former trumpet player of a jazz orchestra, and currently the studio is managed by a former police officer and author of cheap detective novels. But such officials are not, in fact, the most frightening and dangerous; these conscientious and intellectually limited hacks are capable of letting through some films they do not understand, but are fearful of displaying their incompetence. Others are more frightening—persons with university diplomas, erudite, and fond, on occasion, of citing the executed writer Isaak Babel or the great poet Osip Mandelshtamm, who lost his mind and perished in Stalin's concentration camp. They are sufficiently intelligent to know the value of Soviet regime and to comprehend clearly the nature of the contemporary world. And they are sufficiently cynical, while understanding all of it, to make a career of serving as faithful Cerbers, guardians of the ideological sterility of Soviet art. True, there are not many in cinematography, perhaps a few dozen. But they are running the shows. They hold instructional positions in the

Institute of Cinematography; they sit on art councils; they serve as principal editors of professional journals; and they attend international symposia. Western intellectuals are often charmed by their brilliant minds, great erudition, and lovely manners.

In the meantime, it is precisely this kind of person who carries the greatest responsibility for the system of ideologic deception in the Soviet Union. It is precisely these people who determined, in particular, the nature of the peculiar societal phenomenon—Soviet movie criticism.

It is generally accepted that a critic is one capable of analyzing professionally a creation of art and communicating his judgment to a wide audience. In the Soviet Union this is hardly the case. Creation of art is evaluated by high-ranking officials. For example, the editor-in-chief of the journal *The Art of Cinema*, Eugenii Surkov, before commissioning a critical essay of a film, would first inquire from the State Cinema Committee whether to praise the film or to damn it. If he is unable to find out the official attitude, then he attempts to second guess. After the the editorial board of the journal would attempt to find that critic who would agree to produce the essay in the recommended channel. In other words, the critic in this case is the person capable of expressing professionally the viewpoint of official leadership, rather than his own.

Here is how the same Eugenii Surkov, the purest incarnation of the official hack, defines the principal task of Soviet cinema criticism: "The task of a critic is to assist all the viewers to develop the sole perception of a given work of art." Quite outspoken, is it not? In a totalitarian society there may not be differing points of view on any questions. It follows that artistic creations must be evaluated also by everybody in the same manner, in accordance with party leadership.

The centralized production system existing in the USSR plays a very important part in the utilization of cinema as an instrument of social pressure. In the Soviet Union, annually, some 120-125 feature films are produced. Approximately the same number of films are annually purchased or received in exchange from abroad. The major portion of foreign cinema productions are films from the socialist countries. Western films usually selected are entertaining comedies and melodramas. But of the serious films only those are selected that contain sharp criticism of some aspects of society. However, in all films, episodes are cut out which in some respect fail to accommodate Soviet censors. For example, scenes out of Stanley Kramer's *Bless the Children and the Beasts*, were deleted including an event taking place in a synagogue. The same principle apparently guided the deletion of parts of the film "Funny Girl"; in the episode deleted, the heroine of the film says that she is Jewish, and the screen shows Jewish storefronts with names written using Hebrew letters.

The production of Soviet films is planned one to two years in advance.

The films are grouped according to themes and genre. True, these plans, much as others in the planned economy of the USSR, are hardly ever fulfilled.

In order to attract major writers to the task of fulfilling the "social objectives," i.e., the creation of scenarios on themes required by the government, a system of limited competitions has been inaugurated. The participants in these competitions are invited individually and they are guaranteed higher than usual honoraria. The system of competitions is yet another example of how generously the Soviet government rewards the fulfillment of state commissions. No one country in the world, no one producer, could, for example, finance the production of such a super giant as *War and Peace* by Sergei Bondarchuk. The total expenditure on this film was never made public, and perhaps it could not even be computed. For example, in filming of such episodes as the battles of Borodino and Austerlitz, up to 100,000 soldiers of the Soviet army took part, without any fee of course. During the five years required for its production some forty-three factories were working full time supplying the needs of the film: costumes, military ammunition of the period, and other authentic items. With special permission of the government, gold articles and treasures were made available by the state depositories and principal museums.

We will not discuss whether a country with its economy in ruins can permit itself the luxury of such expenditures. For us, at present, a more important consideration is that the principal motivation for the creation of that super giant was the vain attempt to "do in the eye" the American version of *War and Peace.* Similarly, the production of the five-part colossus *Liberation,* directed by Yurii Ozerov, was dictated by purely ideological motives. This film was called forth to create a specially falsified version of World War II and the "liberation" of Eastern European countries by the Soviet army.

Both of these films, of course, resulted in financial losses to the government. But the films fulfilled their ideological propaganda tasks. Much as in the space race the Soviet Union, lagging behind the United States by more than one decade, managed to create for a limited time the appearance of its primacy by the dint of improbable expenditures to the detriment of other parts of the economy, so also the production of these super-gigantic films served to demonstrate to the whole world the blossoming of Soviet culture, and to shake the imagination by the scope of the financial effort, which only the richest and the mightiest country could afford.

There seem to be two categories of persons whose interests touch the relationship between the Soviet government and the cinema. The first group is relatively small, a few thousand persons who make the films. The second groups, comprised of tens of millions persons, are the film viewers. It is impossible to evaluate correctly Soviet cinematography without taking into consideration the inner situations of each of these groups.

Let us start with the creative workers of the cinema. Or, more precisely, we will speak in this case about the directors, because they are the ones who have the greatest influence within the world of cinema, and it is precisely upon them that the authorities concentrate their attention. Soviet professional directors are trained by the State Institute of Cinematography. The entrance examinations for this institute serve as the first selection stage. The principal criterion is not the creative talent of the future director but his ideological devotion to the regime. A tremendous part in the selection of candidates is played by responses in the application form: party membership, the occupation and communal behavior of parents, the absence of any relatives in Western countries and, undoubtedly, the nationality of the applicant. The widely heralded ideological fiction of equality of all Soviet citizens is preserved by the operation of a Special Mandate Commission, which, after completion of the examinations, reviews the application data and renders the final decision, which is not subject to appeal and does not require the disclosure of reasons for rejection.

Upon graduation from the institute, the potential director faces a choice. To start with, he finds himself a member of a highly privileged social group; upon dutiful behavior and appropriate direction of effort, he is guaranteed a very high (by Soviet standards) standard of living. Moreover, he may receive many other privileges: an assignment to special homes for creative artists, trips abroad, rights for better housing, etc. But all of this must be paid for by rejection of one's creative individuality and obedient fulfillment of all official directions.

To tell the truth, the screening system just described operates quite dependably, and therefore the majority of Soviet directors do not torture themselves with doubts for long, since they do not possess genuine talent, and their attitude to the regime is cynically utilitarian. It is precisely this type of person who is responsible for filming 110 to 115 out of the 120 movies produced annually in the Soviet Union.

The fate of the few exceptional persons is substantially harder, and even tragic. I have in mind those truly talented persons who are prevented—if not by conscience, then at least by taste—from filming primitive situational movies or utter garbage.

The fate of any talented person in the Soviet Union, to put it mildly, is not to be envied. A writer, however, can write for himself or submit his writings to an underground publisher. A painter can decorate the walls of his own apartment with his creations. A director, on the other hand, is denied an opportunity of creative activity unless he becomes a cog in the state machinery. This is why the foundation of the cinematographic career of *every* director must necessarily involve a film deal, in one way or another attesting to the willingness and capability of the director to cooperate with the regime. Woe to one who does not manifest such a desire. His name is entered on a "black list"; under the best conditions he may be given a second chance in a few years to demonstrate his willingness to capitulate. It is understood, of course, that the level of compromises differs, as well as further relations between the artists and the regime.

Persons with stronger principles and minimal willingness to compromise spend many years of their lives and cripple their nervous systems in "going through the channels" and in endless arguments with officials. If they are fortunate, they may receive permission to produce a film. This is why one of the most talented Soviet directors, Andrei Tarkovsky, has made only three films in fourteen years. Of course, the behavior of Soviet authorities has its own simple logic. The authorities finance the films in order to obtain the results they want.

The paradox in the situation is that the authorities are also compelled to make certain concessions. They are not able to simply force out all of the talented directors from the industry. The Soviet Union is very sensitive about its prestige in the international arena, including the prestige of its art. Nothing so enhances the value of a director as the recognition he receives in international film festivals. This is why permission was granted to produce films such as *Andrei Rublev* and *The Color of Pomegranates*." But even those few films, the exceptions, released annually in the USSR and having the right to be counted among works of art, would have been completely different had their authors been afforded creative freedom.

The noted Russian philosopher Nikolai Berdiaev, wrote, "Russia is a country inhabited by an oriental people and a western intelligentsia." This is true even today, with the only difference being that the layer of intellegentsia, tradition-ally thin in Russia, is even thinner now. This polarization between the people and the intelligentsia must be kept in mind in any evaluation of the attitude of audiences towards the cinema.

Until recent times, consideration of all questions related to the audiences had in the USSR a purely speculative character. It was known that there exists an elitist part of the public, several tens of thousands of persons, living mostly in Moscow, Leningrad, and other major cities. It is precisely these people who would spend a night standing in line for tickets during the Moscow inter-national film festivals. It is they who read books and magazines on cinema. They organize film clubs, discussions, and meetings with film workers. For this part of the movie-going public both the social impact of the film and its aesthetic perfection are of equal importance.

In parallel with them there exists a multimillion mass of so-called ordinary viewers. It is in the name of this amorphous and silent mass that Soviet official-dom state with authority, "The people like this" or "The people do not need this."

The first concrete sociological research related to the mass cinema using audiences in the USSR was begun only a few years ago. In the course of this research, several facts were established relevant to the present study. It was shown, for example, that Soviet movie making does not satisfy completely either group. For the elite, it is unacceptable on account of its aesthetic poverty and propagandistic falsity. And for the mass of film-goers, Soviet films are, on the one hand, inadequately entertaining and, on the other hand, far removed from the real and serious problems of the Soviet population.

The lack of satisfaction of viewers with domestic movies has for the government not only moral consequences but a sharply felt material effect: 52 percent of all Soviet movies do not realize the cost of their production.

Another curious phenomenon surfaced: a record number of viewers have been attending for the last few years rather primitive Arab and Indian melodramas. Apparently, the first consideration is the so-called "compensatory" function of art, the spectator attempts with the help of cinema to separate himself completely from real, everyday life and to transport himself into the exotic atmosphere of lurid ethnography and hypertrophic emotions. Let us note in passing that the films of so-called historical-revolutionary genre, which are accorded by Soviet leadership primary significance, occupy one of the last positions in the list of viewers' preferences.

The reaction of the general mass of Soviet moviegoers to the critical appreciation of films in the press is also of interest. If the film is panned in the press, particularly for ideological errors, then it must be seen!

The fundamental conclusion that can be made on the basis of completed sociological investigations seems to be that the Soviet propaganda machine currently does not possess unlimited influence on wide layers of the population. This conclusion probably could have been validated with far greater definition if the methodology of sociological investigations did not necessitate the use of questionnaires. The problem is that any questionnaires suggest to a Soviet respondent an irresistible association with KGB, the secret police. Therefore, each interviewee, with very few exceptions, tries to stay within the constraints of his social role and attempts to guess the answers that would earn for him the most favorable impression.

A few more words in conclusion. The harsh system of government control of cinematography operates to reduce considerably the fruitfulness of research of all aspects of history, theory, and contemporary problems of Soviet film making from a purely aesthetic point of view; it is necessary to take into account the social factors as well. Of course, these factors are considered in the study of *any* form of art, in *any* country, in *any* historical period. But in the present case, without an adequate weighing of all the accompanying circumstances of social character, the picture will not only be incomplete, but absolutely wrong.

It seems to me that the formulation of a social History of Soviet Cinema must be conducted in the common area of three disciplines: history of cinema, general history and sociology, to the extent that all the aesthetic processes and phenomena must be analyzed with continuous reference to the history of development of Soviet society. Such a study must not only tell the creative and personal fates of several famous masters about their destruction or gradual degradation, but must also treat the many talented artists whose paths came to a tragic end after only one or two films. This book must serve as a memorial to those who have perished and as a warning for those living and working today.

Of much interest to me is the investigation of the means and methods that reflect in films the Soviet reality and its social processes. This theme can be developed from materials of Soviet cinema with a maximum effect, since Soviet cinema makes possible the study of both direct and indirect methods. I will explain, using an example. In the early fifties in the Soviet Union a film, *Kuban Cossacks,* was produced, and directed by Ivan Pir'ev. The film was approved by Stalin himself and received all possible official awards. The film described the rich and merry life of collective farmers on the Kuban. The heroes of the film had no serious problems in life; they lived in completely carefree surroundings and luxurious abundance. And at the same time, while well-fed and handsome cinema actors sang and danced on the screen, real collective farmers in the entire country existed in a half-starved condition, and when horses were lacking for the spring plowing, they either used cows or placed themselves between the shafts. In this manner the film *Kuban Cossacks* can give rich information not of direct nature, about the happy and rich life of Soviet collective farmers, but about social processes that engendered such films in the period of hunger and suffering.

Within the framework of the same theme is the investigation of "Aesop's language," which many film masters use to communicate to those who want to see and hear considerably more than is permitted by the Soviet censorship.

Let me state, finally, that I would be glad to cooperate with any person or institution interested in further study of these and other subjects, related to and inherent in Soviet cultural history and reality.

Part VI

Education, Literature, and Censorship

10

Soviet Literature in Soviet High Schools (and Here)

Wladislaw G. Krasnow

There is no need to prove interdependence between the structure of a given society and the ways it perpetuates itself through education of the young. Two different types of society—two different types of education. Thus, both Soviet society and the Soviet educational system are as rigid and uniform as those of America are not. It is not my intention, however, to make any value judgment, and the characterization of the Soviet system as "rigid and uniform" is to be understood as merely descriptive.

With this in mind I shall survey the teaching of Soviet literature in Soviet high schools during the last twenty years. By doing so I intend to focus upon the consequences of such teaching for both the Russian language and the American students of it. Some suggestions as to the teaching of Soviet Literature in American colleges also will be made.

If someone had asked me right after my graduation from a Soviet high school in 1954 to name the ten foremost Soviet authors, he most likely would have received the following list: Gorky, A. Tolstoy, N. Ostrovsky, Sholokhov, Fadeev, Mayakovsky, Demyan Bedny, Isakovsky, K. Simonov, and N. Tikhonov,

This list of prose writers and poets (five of each for the sake of parity) could have safely been lengthened to include such names as Furmanov, Serafimovich, Makarenko, Lebedev-Kumach, Tvardovsky, Surkov and the like. And I would have named all those authors not because I personally liked them, but simply because they were *the names*. Actually, any high-school graduate of the time would have come up with virtually the same list.

An American student majoring in Russian literature would, I imagine, have given a rather different "top ten" list on Soviet literature. With the possible exception of Gorky and Mayakovsky, there would be altogether new names: Zamyatin, Pilnyak, Babel, Olesha, Zoshchenko, Blok, Pasternak, Akhmatova, Mandelshtam, and Tsvetaeva. The list could have been expanded with such names as Ilf and Petrov, Paustovsky, Esenin, Gumilyov, Klyuev, not to mention, for the sake of synchrony, the authors who became prominent after Stalin's death.

Comparing the two lists, one cannot help wondering whether we are speaking of the same subject matter at all, that is, of Russian literature of the Soviet period—so great is the disparity.

Such disparity existed in the beginning of the fifties, when the cult of Stalin was at its height. One is certainly justified in expecting a considerably different situation in the sixties when, in the wake of the anti-Stalin campaign, many Soviet authors were rehabilitated, some of them posthumously.

227

To observe the situation in the sixties, let us take a closer look at a Soviet program on literature, translated and introduced by John Fizer in the Winter 1968 issue of SEEJ.[1]

For the Soviet period, the program singles out only five authors and their works. They are Mayakovsky, Sholokhov, Fadeev, N. Ostrovsky, and, of course, Gorky. As to the more modern authors, the program only mentions "two or three other works from contemporary Soviet literature."

Comparing this Soviet program with what we in the early fifties had been studying in high school, I fail to see any significance difference excepting perhaps just one: the name of A. Tolstoy is conspicuous by its absence (evidently because of his novella *Bread* (*Khleb*), where Stalin was eulogized.

Although this program is preceded by elaborate guidelines for both student and examiner(s), in which the role of literature as a tool of the party is strongly stressed, one gains very little insight into the actual educational practices of Soviet high schools. Therefore, I would like to offer some recollections from my own tenth, graduating, year in a high school when Soviet literature was systematically studied the whole year. It was Kirov high school no. 21 in the city of Perm, and as one of the better in the region, the school is representative of the urban Russia.

The textbook on the subject was *Russkaya Sovetskaya literatura* by L.I. Tomofeev,[2] a well-known scholar and a corresponding member of the Soviet Academy of Sciences. The same textbook had been used virtually by all high-school students who graduated from the forties on. Texts, edited and often abridged, were taken from anthologies like *Sovremennaya literatura: Khrestomatiya dlya 10-go klassa.*[3] Some works, however, were assigned to be read from separate publications.

The class work centered around the textbook. Classes were held three hours a week throughout the year. The main form of instruction was a rather extensive presentation by the teacher of biographies and works of the authors within the sociopolitical context of their time, with the leading role of the party always stressed. Understandably, the teacher's presentation was in complete accordance with the textbook. The rest of the hour was spent on questioning the comprehension of the pages assigned. Once a month or so students were asked to write either a classroom composition or a homework paper, the so-called *sochinenie.* One could choose from two to four topics on a given author and work. Thus, after having covered the novel *The Young Guards* (*Molodaya Gvardiya*) by Fadeev, the class might have been given a choice of the following topics: (1) the role of the party in Fadeev's *The Young Guards*; (2) The Komsomol as a faithful helper to the party; or (3) Oleg Koshevy as a typical representative of the heroic Soviet youth during the Great Patriotic War. Here is a sample of other topics: The patriotism of the Soviet people in Azhaev's novel *Far from Moscow* (*Daleko ot Moskvy*); features of socialist realism in Furmanov's Novel *Chapaev*; the image of Lenin in the poem

Lenin by Mayakovsky. The last type of topic was especially popular with both students and teachers because of its predictability: whenever a portrait of Lenin, Stalin, or Voroshilov appeared in a text, one could expect a question about him.[4] Only once was such expectation thwarted: those students who had done homework for "The Image of Stalin in the novella *Bread* by A. Tolstoy" had to reorient themselves quickly and switch instead to Lenin or Voroshilov when the teacher announced at the last moment that the topic on Stalin had been eliminated.

As to the content, every student was smart enough to know the best way to fill the paper. Writing a paper on Mayakovsky, for instance, he would never fail to take as an epigraph Stalin's "the best, most talented poet of our Soviet Age"; then he would proceed to describe the heroic period of the civil war (or the reconstruction period); in the main part of the paper, he would establish both the identity of Lenin with the party, and of the party with the people, all of this supported by a dozen quotations memorized. Eventually he would come to the conclusion that the poet very well indeed fulfilled the "social requirement" with the help of his famous "pen-bayonet."[5] When, in a final sentence, the smart student pointed out the aptness of the epigraph of the paper, a full circle was accomplished. Now he need worry about nothing but misspellings and commas. Since all students were smart enough not to commit political or ideological blunders, errors in grammar and in punctuation became virtually the sole criteria for the evaluation of such papers. This phenomenon, which might be called the "terror of the comma," is a negative side effect of the Soviet educational system, and it concerns Soviet young people in a very practical sense. I have yet to meet an American student who would accept the idea that a few commas could pull his grade down, possibly deciding whether he is to go to college at all.

Quotations, whether from poetry or prose, were expected to be memorized, and there were a lot of them. The real task of the student was to incorporate them as smoothly as possible into the body of the paper. The definition of a thought as the "shortest distance between two quotations" was in wide circulation among students. Moreover, since every single graduate from high school was processed through the same program, one can assume that all those quotations became, for better or worse, part of the national language. It would be hardly an exaggeration to say that a familiarity with those deposits of Soviet literary "wisdom" is as important for understanding of the Soviet ethos as a familiarity with the Bible is important for the comprehension of Judaeo-Christian culture. Any Soviet intellectual awakened in the middle of the night and given the name of, say, Gorky, will immediately, as if reacting to the Pavlovian conditioned reflex, start producing a web of quotations like, "Man, oh, how proudly this sounds," "Pity degrades Man," "If the enemy does not surrender, he should be annihilated," "Recklessness of the brave—in this is the wisdom of life," and so on and so forth.[6] Some of the quotations could be found in such reference books as *Krylatye Slova,* which is neither extensive nor devoted exclusively to the Soviet period.[7]

In almost every issue of the Soviet press, a native Russian easily recognizes those quotations either in headlines or in slogans. If a Soviet citizen sees, for instance, in *Pravda* or on the wall a slogan like "Kommunizm–éto molodost' mira" ("Communism is the youth of the world") he would hardly fail to recognize in it the pen of Mayakovsky and would even be able to complete the sentence "*. . . i ego vozvodit' molodym.*" (". . . and it shall be built by the young.") The same could be said about "Partiya i Lenin–bliznetsy bratya" ("The Party and Lenin are twin brothers") and a dozen similar slogans. In fact, judging by the range of dissemination through the mass media, a comparison of the Soviet literary clichés with American commercials rather than with the Bible appears to be more to the point.

Gorky and Mayakovsky comprised roughly half of the whole Soviet literature course. The rest of the year was devoted to Tolstoy's novella *Bread* (*Khleb,* 1937) appended to his trilogy *Road to Calvary* (*Khozhdenie po mukam*) with the specific purpose of eulogizing Stalin's role in the civil war; Furmanov's short novel *Chapaev* (1923) about a hero of the civil war; Nikolay Ostrovsky's autobiographical novel *How the Steel Was Tempered (Kak zakalyalas' stal',* 1932-34);[8] Sholokhov's *The Virgin Soil* (*Podnyataya tselina,* 1932) about collectivization of peasants in the Don region; Fadeev's early novel *Rout (Razgrom,* 1927) about the civil war in the Far East and his documentary novel *The Young Guards* (*Molodaya gvardiya,* 1946), which had to be later rewritten since the first edition failed to emphasize the fole of the party in an underground youth movement against German occupation; Boris Polevoy's *Tale About a True Man (Povest' o nastoyashchem cheloveke,* 1946) about a pilot who became an air ace in spite of the fact that both his legs had been amputated; and Vasiliy Azhaev's *Far from Moscow* (*Daleko ot Moskvy,* 1948)[9] a tribute to the "heroic rear" during the war. Somewhat less attention was paid to such works as Serafimovich's *Zhelezny potok* (1924) Makarenko's *Pedagogicheskaya poema,* about a Soviet orphange in the twenties; S. Babaevsky's *Kavaler Zolotoy Zvezdy* (1947 about a postwar reconstruction of *kolkhozes,* and Vsevolod Kochetov's *Zhurbiny* (1952), a tribute to the Soviet working class. Among the poets none came close to the stature of Mayakovsky. To be sure, poets like Demyan Bedny, Isakovsky, N. Tikhonov, A. Surkov, K. Simonov, S. Shchipachev, A. Tvardovsky (for his war poem *Zoya* about Zoya Kosmodemyanskaya, a guerilla heroine) enjoyed a stature much higher than either Esenin or Blok, though the two were granted a few pages in the textbook.

Among the authors not studied at all and not even mentioned were such prose writers as Zamyatin, Babel', Pilnyak, Ilf, Petrov, and Olesha to name a few, and such poets as Mandelshtam, Tsvetaeva, Gumilyov, and Pasternak. Only Zoshchenko and Akhmatova had the dubious advantage of having been named: we learned about them in the 1946 decisions of the Central Committee that the former was a slanderer of Russia and the latter was something between a "half-nun" and "half-prostitute."

Such was the situation in Soviet high schools toward the middle of the fifties. As we have seen, there has been no substantial changes by the middle of the sixties. What kind of changes can we expect now, at the start of the seventies, when the Soviet School system, because of the failure of Khrushchevian reforms, is back on its ten-year schedule?[10]

When in the fall of 1970 Soviet students started the tenth grade, they had to buy again a textbook with the title *Russkaya Sovetskaya literatura*.[11] This time, however, the textbook is not by Timofeev, but by A. Dementyev, E. Naumov, and L. Plotkin. Why the preference has been given to the three authors instead of Timofeev is not for us to surmise. It is known, however, that both Dementyev and Naumov had earlier criticized Timofeev for his failure to present Soviet literature as "a completely new phase in the development of Russian and world literature"[12] and accused him of indulging in tracing influences on Soviet authors of the Russian classical tradition. Besides this change of approach—not a change for the better—the new textbook bears very few signs of receptiveness to the fresh ideas that have marked Soviet intellectual life since Stalin's death.

Nevertheless, some of the changes have to be pointed out.

1. Blok and Esenin are finally elevated from subchapters into separate chapters.

2. So is Tvardovsky. Besides *Vasiliy Tyorkin*, his new work *Za dal'yu dal'* is discussed extensively. However, *Tyorkin na tom svete* (*Tyorkin in the Other World*) is not even mentioned.

3. *Bread* by A. Tolstoy is deleted, but not its author: he retains a separate chapter, which means he is still in the "top ten."

4. Rehabilitation of Babel', Pilnyak, Tsvetaeva, and Olesha did not mean their recognition: they are not even mentioned.

5. Pasternak and Akhmatova are noted, but reluctantly, and only for their patriotic poems during the war.

6. Ehrenburg is praised as a patriotic publicist during the war period, but his *Ottepel'* (*Thaw*) is not mentioned.

In short, one notices very few signs of a thaw as far as the "Literature of the Thaw" is concerned. Dudintsev's *Ne xlebom edinym* (*Not by Bread Alone*) is not mentioned, and neither is Kazakov, nor Aksenov. Paustovsky, Soloukhin, V. Panova, V. Ovechkin, and O. Berggolts are barely mentioned. Absence of Solzhenitsyn's name in the textbook is also conspicuous, though not surprising. Nominated in 1964 for the Lenin Prize, the author of *One Day in the Life of Ivan Denisovich* was bound to be banished from the official Soviet literature after such events as the ouster of Khrushchev, who personally authorized his first publication in the USSR, his own letter to the Fourth Congress of the Writer's Union demanding an abolition of censorship, and after publication abroad of *Cancer Ward* and *The First Circle*. The textbook's authors did not even have the audacity to mention the fact of his expulsion from the writers' union.

On the other hand, Leonov's *Russky les,* Auézov's *Abay,* and Aytmanov's stories are given special attention, since all three have been awarded the Lenin Prize. As for modern poets: Evtushenko, Rozhdestvensky, and Voznesensky are given three pages in all. Evtushenko's *Bratskaya GES*, is briefly discussed, but *Heirs of Stalin* (*Nasledniki Stalina*) and *Baby Yar* are omitted. Among the playwrights, the Lenin Prize winner Pogodin is singled out, and his play *Kremlevskie kuranty* (*The Kremlin Chimes,* about Lenin) is discussed in detail.

Literature of non-Russian nationalities no longer retains a separate division in the book as it had in Timofeev's. Instead, a Tartar poet, Musa Dzhalil', executed by the Nazis in Berlin but not recognized as a hero until after Stalin's death, and the Ukrainian novelist Oles' Gonchar are treated side by side with Russian authors. Finally, in the discussion of the *Mirovoe znachenie sovetskoy literatury* (*World Significance of Soviet Literature*) no references to Red China, Howard Fast, Louis Aragon, or any other living Communist are to be found. Instead, only the dead—and therefore evidently presumed infalible—Dreiser, Bernard Shaw, Fučik, and even Nehru are allowed to praise Soviet literature.

Quite obviously the field of Soviet education has not responded significantly to the change of intellectual climate that took place after Stalin's death. The rostrum of ten foremost Soviet authors with which this article started remains essentially the same in spite of more than fifteen years of intellectual ferment. A possible substitution of the names of Blok and Esenin for those of Bedny and Tikhonov does little to bridge the gap between the Soviet and American lists. Perhaps this gap has become even wider in the wake of Pasternak, Sinyavsky, Daniel', Solzhenitsyn, and of the works of *Samizdat.* Even the award of the Nobel Prize to the "official" Soviet writer Sholokhov did little, if anything, to heighten the status of "orthodox" Soviet literature abroad. Besides, it was more than counterbalanced by the award of the same prize to the "unofficial" Solzhenitsyn. And even if a few authors appear occasionally on both lists, they are more often than not appreciated for different reasons and for different works.

Why such a divergence? Perhaps some would blame it on the cold war. On the other hand, one could argue that the last fifteen years have witnessed an unprecedented increase in the flow of American tourists to the USSR and the flow of Soviet books to the USA. Were those years in vain?

The rationale behind the Soviet list is that peaceful coexistence is not meant to extend to the realm of ideology. Since literature is believed to belong to that realm, it is to be guided instead by the principle of the "ideological struggle against any bourgeois tendencies." In practice it simply means an exclusion of, and intolerance toward, any author or any work that does not conform to the current Central Committee version of Marxism-Lenin-ism in general, and of socialist realism in particular. Hence, there will be no publication of such novels as *Doktor Zhivago,* the underlying philosophy of which is anything but Marxist-Leninist, or of any formalist experiment that might conceal some "alien" ideas. There is even less hope for high-school instruction about such works. The authors of the textbooks simply do well to follow the latest party directives. One can add that this rationale is a rather consistent one, excepting perhaps the curious way of "struggle" by avoidance. But the Soviets can always say that they define their own terms.

As to the rationale behind the American list, one can say that the authors on it are mainly selected on artistic grounds—because we like them, because they give us either new insights into life or deepen our appreciation of the artistic forms. Nevertheless, one question should be asked: Should the top ten necessarily be the taught ten? There is a tendency at American colleges to answer "yes." As a result, the awareness of American students of the official Soviet literature is bound to be insufficient.

But why should one bother about the official literature? One reason is that this literature enjoys the widest attention in the USSR. For better or worse, it permeates both the language and the awareness of all Soviet citizens. Not to know who the *Geroi Krasnodona* (Heroes of Krasnodon) are in modern Russia is roughly the same as not to know who Joe Namath or Marilyn Monroe are in American English. And to ascribe a quotation like *"Umri, no ne davay poceluya bez lyubvi"* ("Die rather than allow a kiss with-out love") to a Pushkin is the same as to attribute a line like "Ultra-bright gives your mouth sex appeal" to a Hawthorne. It is in the official Soviet liter-ature that we find the origin of many *Pravda* clichés and also of the phrases used to drill American exchange students in Leningrad and Moscow. In short, I think that the study of the Russian language and of Soviet literature could be brought closer to each other to the benefit of both, and the descriptive method of linguistics could be, to a certain extent, applied in the teaching of literature.

Another reason for a wider study of the official Soviet authors is more complex. Imagine a conversation on Soviet literature between an American tourist majoring in Russian and a young Soviet intellectual. First, the conver-sation will be inhibited by the awareness of the "anti-Soviet propaganda" law. The American will be reluctant to talk to his Russian friend about *Doktor Zhivago* or *Rakovy korpus (Cancer Ward)*, which he has most likely studied in his college. Wishing to keep up the conversation without getting involved with controversial names, his Russian colleague would mention that even such notorieties as Ostrovsky or Fadeev had troubles with their novels, you know? At this point he is likely to discover that our American friend has never heard even the names of the authors. At worst, the Soviet friend might draw the conclusion that there is truth in the allegations of Soviet propaganda about "anti-Soviet indoctrination" in American colleges. In short, the American educational system, by an unintentional exclusion of the official Soviet literature from its purview, is needlessly made vulnerable to accusations of partiality.

Whether we accept the Soviet challenge to "ideological struggle" or, instead, challenge them ourselves to extend peaceful coexistence into the field of litera-ture, we should try to encompass in our presentation of Soviet literature both "official" and "unofficial" authors, unless we want to commit the Soviet fallacy of avoidance in reverse.

If what I am saying about the present situation is true—not being familiar with the whole scene, I have spoken only of certain tendencies—I would suggest some remedies.

One of them could be a comparative study of Soviet literature, when an official author is studied side by side with an unofficial one, preferably of the same period, genre or themes. For example: Mayakovsky/Pasternak, Tsvetaeva; Isakovsky/Klyuev, Akhmatova, Esenin; Gorky/Zamyatin; Sholokhov/Bulgakov, Babel'; Ostrovsky/Olesha; Kochetov/Zoshchenko, Solzhenitsyn; and so forth. By this I do not mean to suggest a fifty-fifty approach, for an inclusion of even just one "official Soviet" author may help to achieve the effect desired.

Another solution could be found in the type of "handbooks" for which Edgar Lehrman argued in the fall 1969 issue of *SEEJ*.[13] He focused upon the need for background information for readers of Russian classics. In my opinion, no lesser need exists as regards Soviet literature.

Finally, even such an easy step as an inclusion of the Soviet high-school anthologies and textbooks in both undergraduate and graduate reading lists may prove to be helpful.

It is my hope that the suggested alterations will both enhance the relevance of literature courses and create better conditions for an increased intercourse between the countries. By the same token, they will detract nothing from the authors we cherish most. Given the necessary background information and having read a typical Soviet "social requirement" novel in a comparative course, a student will be even more appreciative of the purely artistic qualities of the heterodox authors. His confidence in American education will increase. His Soviet colleague will think more of him, and, hopefully, argue for similar changes in the USSR.

As to the prospects for the seventies and beyond, one can only hope that what Solzhenitsyn said about his recent book, *Arkhipelag Gulag,* will come true in respect to all now unpublishable books: "I am certain that the time will soon come when this book will be read widely and even freely in our country."

Notes

1. John Fizer, "The Soviet Program for the Entrance Examination into vuzy in Russian Language and Literature," *Slavic and East European Journal,* vol. 12, no. 4. (Winter 1968).

2. L.I. Timofeev, *Russkaya Sovetskaya literatura,* 7th ed. (Moscow, 1952).

3. *Sovremennaya literatura: Khrestomatiya dlya 10-go klassa,* 11th ed. (Moscow, 1950).

4. The other *obrazy* were popular too, like Ostrovsky's Pavel Korchagin or Gorky's Pelageya Nilovna. They were, in fact, called *obrazá* (icons) in student slang.

5. From his line: *Ya khochu, chtob k shtyku priravnyali pero. . . .*

6. See, for instance, how ironically Solzhenitsyn uses Gorky's "Pity degrades Man" in his *The First Circle.*

7. *Krylatye slova,* sost. N. Ashukin, M. Ashukina, 3rd ed. (Moscow, 1966).

8. The title itself belongs to the "winged words" of Soviet Russian. One chapter of Solzhenitsyn's *The First Circle* bears a title that implies an antithesis to Ostrovsky's adage "One has but one life."

9. Prisoners in Solzhenitsyn's *The First Circle* succinctly refer to it as *Far from us.*

10. See Abraham Kruesler, "The New Reform of Soviet Education," *SEEJ,* vol. 13, no. 4 (Winter, 1969).

11. A Dementyev, E. Naumov, and L. Plotkin: *Russkaya Sovetskaya literatura* (Moscow, 1970).

12. See Gleb Struve, *Soviet Russian Literature 1917-1950,* University of Oklahoma Press, 1951), p. 354.

13. See Edgar H. Lehrman, "Needed: American 'Handbooks' for Masterpieces in Russian," *SEEJ,* vol. 13, no. 3 (Fall, 1969).

11

Copyright, Censorship, and Dissidents in the Soviet Union

John H. Langley

International Law

It is very difficult to discuss United States-Soviet copyright problems without first looking at some aspects of international copyright law. Three basic conventions or treaties control copyright in the Western world.

The first is the so-called Berne Convention, ratified in Berne, Switzerland, in 1887. The Berne Convention for the Protection of Literary and Artistic Works is also called the International Copyright Union, and the revised form of this treaty was ratified in Brussels, Belgium in 1948.

The Berne Convention established two basic principles: first, it abolished the various formalities, such as deposit, copyright notice, and registration, required to secure copyright in each member country; second, each signatory granted foreign authors the same rights as were granted to its own nationals. The United States is not a member of the Berne Convention because of our formalities for registration and our "manufacturing clause." The other important nonmembers of the Berne Convention are the Soviet Union, China, and all Latin American countries except Brazil. Although the Soviet Union does not belong to the Berne Convention this treaty offers copyright protection to the works of Soviet authors first published in a "Berne" country in the original Russian language. This is the protection Solzhenitsyn enjoys because of publication of *August 1914* (in the Russian language) by the YMCA Press in Paris.

The second convention was the treaty signed in Buenos Aires in 1910. All Latin American countries except Brazil signed this treaty. For purposes of our discussion today, details of the Buenos Aires convention are not necessary.

The third treaty on copyrights is the most important. This is the Universal Copyright Convention, a creature of UNESCO, dated September 6, 1952.[1] There were twelve original contracting nations, including the United States. Among the original twelve were such signatories as Andorra and Monaco. During the intervening years between 1952 and early 1973 other states joined, bringing the number of signatory nations to sixty-three.

Under the Universal Copyright Convention, the United States grants full first-term copyright protection to any work of foreign origin first published in a Convention state in English or in a foreign language, provided only that said work carries a Universal Copyright Convention notice from first publication. Copyright notice is a ©. It is not necessary for UCC authors to comply with any of the other formalities, such as registration, fees, or deposits.

237

The USSR Signs Up

On February 14, 1973, Soviet Foreign Minister Andrei A. Gromyko wrote to the Paris headquarters of UNESCO signifying Soviet intention to join the Universal Copyright Convention. The letter was formally received at UNESCO on February 27, 1973. Ninety days later, on May 27, 1973, the Union of Soviet Socialist Republics became the sixty-fourth member of the Universal Copyright Convention.

Before we go into the pros and cons of what Soviet membership in the Universal Copyright Convention may mean to world publishing relations, we should take a look at the publishing scene in the USSR, past and present.

Prior to Soviet acceptance of the UCC we had a relatively uncomplicated situation. Publishers in the Soviet Union, all tools of the state, stole whatever books they wanted and printed them at will. Soviet publication of books in English was tremendous. It was, and is, common practice in the Soviet Union to translate many titles into all Soviet languages. Since there are nearly ninety different languages under the Soviet flag, it should be remembered that all the following statistics are heavily loaded in their favor. Let's look at Soviet publication of popular American authors:

> Unpublished Soviet figures on the publication histories of American authors in the U.S.S.R. from 1918 through July 1, 1959, place Hemingway eighteenth on the "All-Time Best Seller List," with seventeen titles published, a total of 487,000 copies, in seven languages. Another register of best sellers, as of July 1, 1960, places Hemingway tenth on the list, with 1,362,000 copies sold. If both of these lists are correct, then in the year between July, 1959, and July 1960, more than 800,000 copies of Hemingway were sold.[3]

Hemingway appeals very strongly to Soviet readers. His ideological stance and the rugged, earthy style used in his escapist stories are highly admired by Soviet readers. It is interesting to note that there are more critical articles written about Hemingway's works in Russian than in English.

In the twenty-eight year period between 1918 and 1947, more than two and one-half million copies of Mark Twain's works were stolen, translated, and printed into eighty-nine Soviet languages. Upton Sinclair, O. Henry, Bret Harte, and James Oliver Curwood also were immensely popular. Twenty-three million copies of American authors' works were translated and distributed in the USSR during this twenty-nine year period. Over twenty million copies of Jack London's works alone were printed and distributed.

The scope of publishing in the Soviet Union today is still enormous. Alan U. Schwartz, in a definitive article in the January 15, 1973 issue of *Publishers Weekly*, cites some more astonishing figures. Schwartz's figures are based on statistics published in Germany by the Institute for the Study of The USSR. Schwartz states that during the eight-year period between 1959 and 1968 the *annual average* number of new books and pamphlets issued in the Soviet Union was 75, 294; the number of copies printed was over 1,250,000. More significant, for our purposes, is Mr. Schwartz's figures for translated items; a yearly average of 8320 were translated, accounting for 195,754,000 copies.

What Does Soviet Membership in UCC Imply?

What is Soviet participation in the Universal Copyright Convention likely to mean to the Western world and particularly to American publishers and authors? Let us start with the great international common denominator—money. Royalties are the first and, for most publishers and authors, the most important question. Under the new scheme of things the Soviet publishers will now be required to pay any author registered under the Universal Copyright Convention royalties for works published in any or all the Soviet languages. This royalty payment is not retroactive. The many millions of copies of American or English titles already published in the Soviet Union are "lost" as far as royalties are concerned. One of my colleagues, with some real sense of practicality, recently pointed out to me that the Soviets already have most of the good stuff; they can now start paying on the current material because it will not sell in such large quantities.

Boris I. Stukalin of the Soviet Council of Ministers on Publishing Matters, Printing and Bookselling, during his visit to the United States in February (1973), stated, "Royalties will be paid in the currency of the author's choice. This can be negotiated on a case by case basis." To me, as a publisher, the "case by case basis" statement is frightening. If the Soviets have over eight thousand "cases" to be "negotiated" each year, it will be some long time before any bureaucracy can decide what should be done with each case. There will be as many royalty arbitrators in the Soviet Union as there are censors!

Assuming payment, the next most important question will be whether the payments will be in hard currencies or in blocked rubles. If payments are limited to blocked rubles, successful American authors will have to spend their summers on the Black Sea or traveling throughout the Soviet Union. This will not be a handicap for some authors, but it might be very difficult for others. This situation opens up vistas of university professors being able to buy ruble deposits from American authors at very low rates.

I personally doubt that there will be any restriction on Soviet royalty payments, because if these are imposed, the United States can retaliate very easily by blocking payments to Soviet authors. Practically, however, retaliation against Soviet authors may not be too effective, because the balance has been, and will probably continue to be, in favor of the USSR. Dr. Yuri Matveev,

Kiev University, stated that in 1971 only 2500 Russian titles were published abroad.[4] This is a little more than 25 percent of what the Soviets are translating into the various Soviet language.

Stukalin also stated, "Foreign authors will be paid on exactly the same basis as Russian authors." This is within the spirit of the Universal Copyright Convention, which requires that member nations treat authors of other member nations exactly as they treat their own authors. However, since Soviet payments to their own authors have been a wholly whimsical operation in the past, this statement may not be as clear as one would first assume. Susan Wagner, an editor at *Publishers Weekly,* observed:

> Many factors weigh in the decision as to how much a Russian
> author is paid: the length of the book, the press run, the author's
> popularity, his standing with the government, and the kind of book—
> novel, poetry, textbook—all figure in the formula.[5]

Personally, I would be nonplussed to have to use this formula to determine our royalty rates! To my way of thinking, the only defensible royalty policy is to treat everybody the same way.

Scheduling of Soviet royalty payments may be on a considerably longer-term basis than customarily used by American publishers. Most of our houses pay twice a year, but it is perfectly possible that Soviet payments might be on an annual or biannual basis. This is not too serious a problem if the money eventually gets home.

After we solve all these questions of money, we come to the problem of term of copyright. Herein lies a minor problem. Internal Soviet copyright protects the author during his life plus fifteen years after his death. This will have to be extended to life plus twenty-five years to meet minimum UCC standards. Matveev pointed out that domestic Soviet copyright law has already been amended to conform to UCC. He further stated that in those instances where there are still differences, international law would prevail.

On this quesiton I do not anticipate too many problems. Term of copyright is not an important factor in any situation, because publishers can always issue a "revised edition" and start a new term while the author is alive. It is the interests of heirs after the death of the author that may create major legal problems. Abe A. Goldman, acting register of copyrights, said one of the changes in Soviet copyright law that "was very disturbing in this country" involves the description of copyright as owned by authors and their heirs or "legal successors." Goldman pointed out that the Soviet government "may be thinking in terms of becoming the 'legal successors.' "[6]

The third problem that looms large is the Soviet demand for tax relief. In recent talks with Soviet leaders they have demanded that the United States grant tax relief to Soviet authors by waiving the 30 percent withholding tax on royalties earned in the United States. This will have to be subject to a bilateral agreement, because tax matters are not covered in the UCC. George D. Cary, United States register of copyrights, points out that, in his opinion, this is little more than a "bargaining point." I hope he is correct, but I'm not so sure. This could be a major stumbling block in USSR-USA negotiations. If we do not accede to this demand, our recalcitrance could be used by the Soviets to justify lower royalty rates, longer periods between payments, payments in blocked currency, or tax penalties in the Soviet Union.

The final problem, and possibly the most important, is the question of how the Soviets might use membership in the UCC to curb the publication of their dissident writers outside the USSR. Right after the announcement that the Soviet Union had applied for membership in the Universal Copyright Convention, some fears were raised in publishing circles that the whole move was calculated to help the Soviets curb the publication of their dissident writers outside of the USSR. The mechanics of this would be for the Soviets to publish the particular work in Russian and sell a limited number of copies in the Soviet Union, thus meeting the "publication" requirement of the Universal Copyright Convention, and then refusing translation permission. This is, of course, a possibility, but it is pretty farfetched. Even if this did come to pass, what is there to prevent the sort of clandestine publication that has been going on for years? Professors Carl and Elleander Proffer of the University of Michigan sounded several warnings in an open letter to Senator McClellan, chairman of the Senate Judiciary Subcommittee dealing with copyright matters.[7] They raised this question of controlled publication in Russia. They also expressed the fear that all translations would have to follow the original Russian publication, which, of course, would be the *censored* version. In my opinion, this is a much more serious threat than the prospect of controlled publication.

The Proffers are authorities on Russian literature. Elleander Proffer is editor of *Russian Literature Triquarterly,* and together they manage is small publishing house, Ardis Publishing, which specializes in publication of classical Russian literature. They feel that potentially the most serious threat in purely literary terms is that translation rights on the best material simply won't be offered.

Censorship and The Union of Writers

We now come to the item that is of paramount importance in the coming detente between the United States and the USSR on the matter of copyright—domestic Soviet censorship. This is regarded by the Soviets as a purely internal matter which is, essentially, none of our business. However, the entire problem of censorship and curbing of dissidents is looming larger and larger in this affair.

Censorship is not new in Russia. It existed under the tsars before the Revolution. Today, we are told that there are 70,000 censors in the USSR![8] Alan U. Schwartz, in the January 15, 1973 issue of *Publishers Weekly,* described the Soviet censorship procedure as follows:

> Roughly speaking, the censorship procedure works as follows: The first step is to submit two copies of the proposed material for publication to an individual censor. He will then spend up to two weeks reading it, although in certain circumstances it can be much longer. Obviously, long delays hurt magazine publishers and writers most because of strict publishing deadlines. And sometimes the delays are most painful. When the censor is ready he invites the publisher to come in and discuss any "dubious points" with him. According to regulations, only the chief editor of a publication, his deputy or another assistant who may be responsible for the manuscript may deal directly with the censor. The author has no direct role in this process.
>
> The conversations with a censor are generally quite detailed and involve questions of the source material of many references in the proposed work if it is a work of nonfiction, and questions of identification if it is fiction. Copious notes are made by both parties as to answers given and information to be found and later supplied. Behind this dialogue is the presence of a thick green book familiarly referred to as the "Talmud" which lists all the information that it is forbidden to publish at any given time. Everything forbidden by the "Talmud" is marked by the censor in red pencil and is stricken, changed or, in rare instances, published with special permission. The "Talmud" is stamped "secret" and kept in a safe with other secret documents in the censor's office. All references made to factories, industrial sites and other items (and people) which may possibly have been banned are researched in the "Talmud." It is extremely difficult for a writer and editor to meet all the possible censorship requirements in advance of these meetings with the censors. Not only are there different levels of censorship involved (for example, can a particular factory be mentioned? If so, can what it produces be mentioned?, etc.), but also, since the "Talmud" is changed from time to time, it is impossible for a writer or editor to know precisely whether or not a particular factory, person or historical event is listed in any given edition.

Apparently this is not a desk-thumping screaming commissar sort of operation. Schwartz goes on to describe the procedure:

It is important to understand that the dialogue of censorship which
goes on between the censor and publisher or editor is to a large extent
implied rather than explicit. The discourse is often unhurried, courtly,
even wryly amusing, filled with a peculiarly Russian kind of fatalism.
The censor does not suggest particular changes directly. That would
be "censorship." Rather he implies "problems," insinuates changes
and asks the publisher or editor to supply suggested revisions. Needless to say, the perspicacious publisher or editor involved will somehow "divine" from the censor what word, phrase or reference may
well be acceptable. There is a lot of small talk, there is a lot of social-
izing, but beneath it all the fact remains that the censor and the publisher or editor are merely participants in a rigid process which leads
to the dissemination of material which has been boiled and strained
down to a point where it may safely bear the label of the Soviet
Communist Party.

Soviet participation in the UCC will not change one bit of this censorship procedure. It's built into the Soviet system, a system that has not yet learned that
free men perform better than slaves.

The Union of Writers

In addition to state-imposed censorship, there is the stultifying effect of
the Union of Writers. This is the most powerful author's group in the Soviet
Union: its membership is limited to professionals. In July 3 1971, there were
7290 members.[8] Obviously the union does not include all authors, but its
power extends to all writers. Schwartz states:

The most important fact about the Union of Writers is that it is the
gateway to the publishing houses. Officially, members of the Union
are not given any special preference by the publishing houses but in
reality they are much favored.

In his article, Mr. Schwartz goes on to describe the Union of Writers, its membership, its power, and its subservience to the state. Contrary to popular belief,
expulsion from the union does not technically deny the expelled author his
royalties, but it does have serious political and social disadvantages. The most
noteworthy recent expulsions have been Solzhenitsyn, Sakharov, and Maksimov.

The Treatment of Dissidents

All of my comments and discussion have been based on the requirements of the UCC, publishing relations as they exist today, and internal censorship in the Soviet Union. There has been, and will continue to be, much guesswork going on in the United States about the mechanics of future administration of copyright under the UCC and relations between United States and Soviet publishers. These mechanical matters will eventually fall into place, some to the satisfaction of authors and publishers in the West, some to the satisfaction of the Soviets. There are no clear-cut answers now, and there probably will not be any real decisions for some time to come. The door is open, but we are still in the initial bargaining stage.

As a publisher I cannot get too concerned about how these procedural matters will eventually be resolved. However, as an individual, raised in a free society, I am, and will continue to be, very much concerned about Soviet suppression of the works of their creative writers. This is the real nub of the whole matter for me, and it is becoming increasingly obvious that it is the main stumbling block to amiable publishing and copyright relations with the USSR. Our press has been full of items about persecution of what *Time* describes as "the dwindling band of Soviet authors." The United States government is currently very wedded to detente at any price, including publishing deals and information exchanges. However, support of Soviet dissidents in this country grows stronger every day.

Two very important developments have supported the Soviet dissidents recently. The first, the threat by the National Academy of Sciences that "harassment or detention of Sakharov will have severe effects upon the relationships between the scientific communities of the US and USSR and could vitiate our recent efforts towards increasing scientific interchange and cooperation." The second is the recent Jackson amendment designed to bar most-favored-nation economic status to any country restricting emigration. This amendment is pointed directly towards recent Soviet moves to stop emigration of Jews to Israel and the United States.

What is the response in America to Sakharov's appeal for passage of the Jackson amendment? I.F. Stone, writing in the *New York Review of Books* for October 18, 1973, made the following observation:

> For me the decisive argument in favor of the Jackson amendment
> is the consequences of its defeat, now that the issue has been joined.
> If it is defeated, the Soviet bureaucracy and secret police will feel
> they can crack down on the dissidents with impunity. This may
> explain why Sakharov and Solzhenitsyn and twelve leading Jewish
> Soviet scientists waiting for visas to Israel have had the courage to
> risk reprisal by a public appeal to the American Congress just when
> action on the Jackson amendment nears. When they risk so much
> instead of relying on "quiet diplomacy" in the Nixon-Kissinger
> style, we must not only respect their bravery but accept their

judgment—that to hit hard is the best way to deal with the Soviet bureaucracy. The Kremlin needs US technology and credits far more than the US needs its trade—if we're going to give goods away on credit, there are poorer and more deserving places than the Soviet Union. Sooner or later Moscow will have to come to terms. [Reprinted with permission from *The New York Review of Books*. Copyright © 1973 Nyrev, Inc.]

It is obvious that continued pressure by all groups—scientific associations, medical associations, publishers groups, public media, newspapers, magazines, and learned journals—must be exerted if we are to convince the Soviets that we are vitally and unselfishly concerned with the outcome. A recent quotation from *Time* serves as a fitting closing: "Soviet suppression of dissenting opinions is openly challenging the West as to how firmly it is prepared to stand by its humanist beliefs."

Notes

1. The Universal Copyright Convention carries the date September 6, 1952. See Article VIII.
2. Article IX, Part 2, of the UCC reads as follows: "Subsequently, this Convention shall come into force in respect of each State three months after that State has deposited its instrument of ratification, acceptance or accession."
3. Roger Asselineau, (editor). *The Literary Reputation of Hemingway in Europe*. (New York: New York University Press, 1965) pp. 177-95.
4. *Publishers Weekly*, 30 April 1972, p. 37.
5. Susan Wagner, *Publishers Weekly*, 12 March 1973, pp. 32 and 33.
6. Ibid., 23 April 1973, p. 49.
7. *Publishers Weekly*, 14 May 1973, p. 32.
8. Alan U. Schwartz, *Publishers Weekly*, 15 January 1973, pp. 32 *et seq*.

Part VII

War and Peace

12 Soviet Perceptions of Military Sufficiency: 1960-74

Phillip A. Petersen

Soviet perceptions of military sufficiency are of great interest in the context of disarmament dialogue between the Soviet Union and the West. For those perceptions translate into Soviet military capabilities, which, in turn, must be the basis of any discussion of possible US responses to a Soviet threat to actual or perceived US interests. Lack of concern for how these changing Soviet capabilities may affect political and military relationships less ultimate than the destruction of the US as an organized modern society ignores the more immediate political and military impact of the Soviet post-Khrushchev attainment of military flexibility.

The advent of nuclear weapons and jet aircraft, and then ballistic missiles and space technology, created significant discourse within the Soviet Union involving divergent views concerning military strategy and force structure. The military-technological revolution confused the critical issue of sufficiency; it raised questions concerning the nature of a future war and the relationship between deterrence and defense.

The Soviet military establishment was agreed that the Soviet Union must be prepared for a nuclear war, but there was no such agreement concerning specific numbers of strategic weapons sufficient to guarantee deterrence. Certainly, it would be to the advantage of the Soviet Union to halt construction of strategic weapons at as high a number as possible without provoking a US response. In this absence of a Soviet unanimity on "assured destruction"—that is, the absence of a Soviet consensus on what size strategic force would be sufficient, after absorbing the maximum destruction the US strategic force can deliver, to retaliate with enough effectiveness to destroy the US capability to function as an organized society—the Soviets also had to contend with the question of emphasis between strategic nuclear-missile forces and conventional/general purpose forces. For should deterrence fail, would there result a protracted war in which Soviet general purpose forces could prove the decisive factor? Furthermore, might there not arise some conflict in which conventional/general purpose forces would be the major element?

The Emergence of Khrushchev as a Military Authority

The Soviet postwar concept of "hostage Europe" grew out of the incapacity to adopt a strategy of nuclear deterrence. Partly out of necessity, therefore, they emphasized the preparation of their land, air, and naval forces to execute an invasion and occupation of Western Europe.[1] Stalin's public depreciation of the military and political significance of nuclear weapons and vaunting of large conventional forces must be understood within the context of his need to make the Soviet continental strategy credible at least until such time as the Soviet nuclear weapons program achieved success. Thus, the struggle between 1953 and 1960 to free Soviet military thinking from Stalinist doctrine and to adjust to the military-technological revolution was founded in the developing state of Soviet technology and weapons production, credit for which is in no small way due Stalin.[2]

The developing state of Soviet military technology, plus economics, made a military reformer out of Khrushchev and led him to attempt to drag a traditionally conservative military establishment into the nuclear age. As a result of a US-announced post-Korean War reduction in manpower and a US major build-up in strategic delivery forces, Khrushchev proposed nuclear disarmament and fixing the level of conventional forces. Despite Western rejection of several specific proposals, Khrushchev initiated a troop reduction program of his own, indicating that he undoubtedly had hoped to obtain negotiated disarmament benefits from a reduction in force that was already part of his projected military reforms. This troop cut, occurring between 1955 and 1956, reportedly reduced Soviet military manpower from 5,700,000 to 3,860,000 personnel.[3] It was followed by a much smaller troop reduction, which reduced Soviet military manpower to 3,623,000 personnel, during the period 1958 through 1959, when a number of Soviet troops were withdrawn from Eastern Europe, most notably from Rumania.[4]

Khrushchev worked out his ideas of substituting "firepower for manpower," and in January of 1960 laid out his perception of military sufficiency. Had his ideas been fully implemented, there would have been a total transformation of Soviet military strategy and force structure. For in this report to the Supreme Soviet, he proposed cutting the Soviet armed forces from 3,623,000 personnel down to 2,423,000 personnel.[5] Khrushchev stated that he felt that this reduction in force was possible without sacrificing Soviet security because the military-technological revolution had made it possible to increase the firepower of the armed forces by equipping them with "atomic, hydrogen, rocket and other modern weapons."[6] He stressed that these modern weapons would be the principal element in any future war and that the nation's defensive capability was no longer determined by the "number of soldiers it has under arms, the number of men in uniform."[7] Furthermore, he advanced the view that even if the Soviet Union were suddenly attacked, being a territorially large country, it would "always be able to give the aggressor a proper rebuff."[8]

Had the transformation Khrushchev proposed been fully executed, there would have been a sharp reduction in defense expenditures. He himself predicted that his proposed reduction in force would, "yield an annual savings of approximately 16,000,000,000 to 17,000,000,000 rubles."[9] However, he admitted that such a transformation would have caused a "problem of providing jobs for officers and political workers."[10] For although some of the officers and men demobilized from conventional units could be integrated into missile units, a great many others would have to face the complicated task of adjusting to new civilian professions.

When he made his report, Khrushchev claimed to have consulted the military and the general staff concerning his proposed strategy and force structure. Furthermore, he implied that they agreed that Soviet defense would be "quite adequate" under such a strategy and force structure. Yet, in fact, he did not have the concurrence of the Soviet military establishment. For his proposed strategy and force structure set off a tripartite debate within the military involving what has been described as "modernist," "traditionalist," and "centrist" elements. The modernists more or less supported Khrushchev's strategy and force structure proposals, arguing in favor of greater use of modern technology in military science. The traditionalists objected to the relegation of Russia's traditional strategic arm, the ground forces, to a secondary role and felt that reliance on nuclear deterrence should not preclude preparation for a protracted war. The centrists sought to mediate between the other two elements, arguing for a balanced and more flexible strategy and force structure. Thus, the greater part of the military establishment opposed Khrushchev's "one-variant" concept of military sufficiency.

Several developments provided opponents of Khrushchev's concept with the opportunity to prevent the implementation of the ground forces manpower cuts planned for 1961 and 1962. US overflights, culminating in the U-2 incident in May 1960, caused serious doubts among the Soviets concerning a compromise of their true military strength, and the resulting break-up of the Paris summit meeting heightened international tensions. Intensification of the Berlin crisis, to which the US reacted with defense budget increases, expansion of the Polaris and Minuteman programs, and a strengthening of conventional/general purpose forces, required Soviet reappraisal of their own military posture. Furthermore, questions concerning military morale as a result of difficulties many officers were encountering upon return to civilian life had to be dealt with. By the time the reduction in force was finally suspended, however, about 600,000 men had already been demobilized.[11]

The Cuban crisis in October of 1962 only exacerbated the conflict over Soviet military sufficiency. Khrushchev had taken the gamble that the Soviet build-up in Cuba would be presenting the US with a demoralizing *fait accompli*, negating both the US downward reappraisal of Soviet nuclear-missile strength and the US nuclear-missile build-up that had occurred since 1960.[12] In addition to U-2 photos and satellite reconnaissance photos, Western penetration of the Soviet GRU (Military Intelligence) in the person of Oleg Penkovskii undoubtedly played important roles in this reappraisal. At the time of the crisis the US had

approximately a four-to-one edge in ICBMs. In July of 1960 the US had 18
ICBMs and 32 SLBMs, while the Soviets had 35 ICBMs. In July of 1961 the US
had 63 ICBMs and 96 SLBMs, while the Soviets had 50 ICBMs and some SLBMs.
By July of 1962 the US had 294 ICBMs and 144 SLBMs, while the Soviets only
had 75 ICBMs and some SLBMs.[12]

The stiff US resolve caused a party-armed forces divergence over how to
handle the extended Soviet position in the Caribbean. There was little possibility,
with the overwhelming US naval strength in the area, that a Soviet conventional
defense of Cuba would be successful. To be sure, the developing crisis placed
Khrushchev in the position of choosing between a nuclear catastrophe that
might well put the Soviet regime out of business, a conventional "hostage Europe"
gamble, or backing off in an attempt to salvage whatever was possible. However,
with foreign-based US forces ringing the Soviet Union, the armed forces ques-
tioned why the US should be allowed to demand removal of Soviet foreign bases
without a quid pro quo. Thus, they blamed the party for the fiasco of an
embarrassing capitulation to the US.

As a result of the Soviet post-Cuban crisis reappraisal of its strategic position, the strength of the lobby for an increase in the military budget was recognized by Khrushchev in a February 1963 speech.[13] In that speech, he admitted
that in order to keep from falling too far behind the West, a diversion of additional resources from consumption into the strengthening of Soviet military
capabilities would be required. How he felt any increases in defense expenditures
should be apportioned between strategic nuclear and ground forces was suggested
by the elevation of the commander-in-chief of the Strategic Rocket Forces to
the position of chief of the general staff. Furthermore, by December 1963,
Khrushchev had delivered a speech at a Central Committee plenum in which he
proposed that the Soviet defense budget for 1964 be reduced by 600,000,000
rubles (about 4 per cent) and suggested that the reduction be taken in the
strength of ground forces.[14] Before the end of the month the commander of
the Soviet ground forces, Marshal V.I. Chuckov, responded to the proposal by
citing that the West had recognized the danger involved in "one-sided" military
theories and was complimenting strategic nuclear power by steadily developing
its ground forces.[15]

In the spring of 1964 it became evident that Khrushchev did not intend to
stay his planned reduction in the size of the Soviet armed forces. For in a
speech delivered at a Central Committee plenum in mid-February, Khrushchev
stated that although defense requirements would not be slighted, there would
be a reduction in military expenditures and the numerical strength of the
armed forces.[16] This relaxation of the 1963 expansion of the defense budget
rebounded in favor of both investment and consumption.[17] Yet signs of a
mounting countertrend aimed at resisting efforts to economize at the expense
of the ground forces began to appear in April and May with the publication
of two articles by Marshal P.A. Rotmistrov in *Red Star*.[18] Rotmistrov, who

had been a modernist during the early struggle to free Soviet military thinking from Stalinist doctrine, stressed that excessive emphasis on missiles threatened to cripple other forces as well as the development of military theory in general. Similar references to a need for a more flexible concept of military sufficiency began to appear in various publications.

The Post-Khrushchev Military Build-Up

After Khrushchev was removed from the political scene in October, of 1964, the new leadership continued the relaxation of the 1963 defense expansion, and the armed forces debate over force structure subsided. By the spring of 1965. However, the military launched a dialogue with the leadership intended to obtain political acquiescence for a drive to achieve a peacetime "strategic superiority" in order to secure credibility for the Soviet deterrent.[19] Furthermore, the debate over the need for conventional/general purpose forces resurged within the armed forces.

As the debate about military sufficiency moved from the agreed-upon concept that war is possible, reliance on a deterrence in which both sides are vulnerable failed to provide any insurance that the social order could survive should war occur. The debate, therefore, revolved around the question of the strength required to enable the system to survive should deterrence fail. In order to meet perceptions of military sufficiency, there began a military build-up in 1965 that became undeniably evident by the summer of 1966. That this build-up has occurred does not mean, however, that any agreement had been reached. For as Colonel Thomas W. Wolfe stated in his evidence to the United States Senate Subcommittee on Strategic Arms Limitation Talks,

> The Soviet leaders probably embarked on the build-up without a fixed blueprint for the future and without having settled among themselves precisely what sort of strategic posture *vis-à-vis* the United States would prove satisfactory to Soviet policy needs during the next decade. Some segments of the leadership, for example, may have preferred to seek a stable and low-cost strategic relationship with the United States in order to channel more resources to domestic purposes; others perhaps favored parity pegged at a high level in order to keep third parties like Germany and China in their place and to sustain a duopoly of Soviet-American power in international politics; still others may have set their sights on attaining general strategic superiority over the United States in the belief that only thus could military and political freedom of action requisite to Soviet needs be assured.[20]

The post-Khrushchev military build-up seems to have been intended to achieve credibility for the Soviet deterrent and to increase the latitude of Soviet capabilities, for it has increased both strategic nuclear-missile forces and conventional/general purpose forces. The "balance" of emphasis appears to be one of insuring that there is a range of options available to the leadership so as to enable it to avoid taking irresponsible risks, while at the same time possessing a credible nuclear deterrence, which, should it fail, would be backed up by general purpose forces capable of sustaining the Soviet Union in a protracted war. The Soviet Union, then, has adopted a strategy in which the Soviets do not expect the complete destruction of their society should a nuclear exchange occur. They perceive it as possible to survive an exchange as a viable, recuperable national *unity* capable of pursuing an extended war to a successful conclusion. Certainly an impressive example of Soviet hedging against the failure of deterrence is provided by their heavily funded civil defense program. For not only is this program designed to insure the uninterrupted rule of the CPSU, but it is hoped that it would promote a successful war effort. By means of evacuation and shelter, the Soviets would hope to reduce the casualties and shock among the population so as to ensure the personnel necessary for production continuity following a nuclear exchange.

As the Soviets perceive it, "A concrete historical analysis of the contradictions of the modern era leads to the conclusion that it is necessary to be ready to wage various kinds of wars: world and local, swift and protracted, with the use of the nuclear weapon and without it."[21] For they feel that from 1961 onward the US began to turn to conventional and tactical nuclear forces in response to the growth of Soviet nuclear power.[22] That power, as they see it, caused the US to lose its invulnerability and explains the US interest in lesser levels of conflict which would take place on the territories of the allies of the US rather than on the US itself.

> In thinking about the problem of limited nuclear war, the bourgeois
> ideologists do not find their inspiration in the principles of "reason
> and humanism," as asserted by Western propaganda, but in the
> growth of the economic, political and military power of the USSR,
> its scientific and technical achievements, thanks to which the U.S.A.
> lost its monopoly and superiority in the newest types of weaponry,
> lost the former inaccessibility and invulnerability of its territory.[23]

Furthermore, the US restraint from utilizing nuclear weapons over the past twenty-eight years has indicated to the Soviets a deep-seated reluctance to use those weapons. Even the Soviet experiences in Eastern Europe illustrates that nuclear weapons are not always the most suitable military means by which to resolve a conflict.

Although the Soviets find that the changing strategic nuclear balance has forced a change in US strategy, there remains a deep and abiding fear of escalation from local wars limited to conventional weapons, to the use of nuclear weapons in those localized wars, to a general nuclear conflict. Soviets feel that "local wars of imperialists are fraught with the real possibility of escalation into world nuclear war."[24] To them, "the danger of local wars for the cause of peace is connected with their possible escalation to the level of world war if nuclear powers turn out to be drawn into the conflict."[25] Thus, although they feel they must continue to aid "just" national-liberation wars for various reasons, they also recognize that such activities create the very conditions they feel are most likely to increase the chances of escalation. This policy has undoubtedly caused the Kremlin to engage in a delicate and continuous process of calculating the risk in the use of military aid and of the threat of the use of force.

During the course of the build-up the total size of the Soviet armed forces has increased from 3,150,000 personnel in 1965 to 3,525,000 personnel in 1974.[26] In contrast, US manpower has shrunk from a 1968 peak of 3,500,000 personnel down to 2,174,000 personnel, which is significantly below the "pre-Vietnam" level of 2,700,000. It is apparent, therefore, that despite progress towards the mutual regulation of US-Soviet relationships, the post-Khrushchev leadership has not perceived a halt to the military build-up as consistent with the guaranteeing of Soviet military sufficiency. Even a quick look at the build-up suggests that significant changes in the balance of power have occurred.

Strategic Forces

The Soviet expansion of missile forces between 1965 and 1973 has been extremely impressive. The number of ICBM launchers jumped from 270 in 1965 to 1575 in 1974. The structure of this force consists of 288 SS-9 missiles capable of carrying either one twenty-five-megaton warhead or three five-megaton warheads, 1018 SS-11 missiles capable of carrying either a one- to two-megaton warhead or three one-kiloton warheads, sixty SS-13 missiles carrying warheads of approximately one megaton, and 209 older missiles.[27] It is evident at a glance that the SS-9 and SS-11 missiles, the former being designed to be targeted against hard targets and the latter soft targets, have been emplaced on about 1:3:5 ratio.

This, then, indicates the Soviet resource allocation balance between "counter-force" and "second strike" forces. A "counterforce" missile force is one accurate and sophisticated enough to make a discriminating strike against military facilities as opposed to population centers in the hope of altering the strategic balance without provoking a retaliation against population centers for fear of an indis-criminate second strike. This type of capability, of course, will increase the latitude of the Soviet response to a crisis situation. The danger in such a capabi-lity, however, is that should a force become capable of an effective strike, it could very well be perceived as such a danger as to cause the irresponsible behavior of a launch to forestall pre-emption. A "second strike" missile force is one that is large enough to have enough missiles survive a "first strike" as to be capable of retaliating against population centers.

To this impressive array of ICBMs must be added the 720 submarine-launched ballistic missiles carried by the seventy Soviet ballistic-missile submarines.[28] The 1968 introduction of a genuine strategic missile launching system in the "Y-Class" submarine, each carrying sixteen SS-N-6 missiles with a 1500-1750-mile range insured the Soviets of a "post-exchange balance." A "post-exchange" balance is when exchange antagonists still possess enough missiles after an initial nuclear exchange to deter each other from another strike. An example would be if the Soviet Union conducted an all out land-based strategic nuclear strike against the US and the US retaliated with all its surviving land-based strategic nuclear forces, both sides remaining submarine launched missiles would hopefully deter the other from striking again.

More recently, the Soviets have added nine new "D-class" submarines, each carrying twelve SS-N-8 missiles with a 4600-mile range. In addition to the ICBM and SLBM forces, Soviet strategic strength also includes a component, approximately one-fourth the size of its US counterpart, of manned intercontinental bombers.[29] Furthermore, although the six-hundred Soviet medium- and intermediate-range missiles and seven-hundred medium-range bombers cannot strike the US, they too must be considered within the realm of strategic forces because of their utility in reducing the US strategic forces in the proximity of the Soviet Union.[30]

Despite some concern in the US, it is unlikely that the SS-9 was introduced for the purpose of launching a "first strike" against the US. A "first strike" is one that is capable of destroying enough of the enemy's strategic nuclear force as to make whatever retaliation he can muster be acceptable in light of the "victory" obtained. For a Soviet attempt to destroy the US land-based missile system, which consists of 1054 ICBMs, would require some four-hundred more missiles.[31] Even if the Soviets had made the necessary commitment to a strategic missile force weighted that heavily in favor of the SS-9, they would have confronted the US in only one sector of the total strategic forces pircture. Such a Soviet "superiority" would still fail to neutralize US bomber and ballistic-missile submarine forces. In those categories alone the US has 503 intercontinental bombers, each with four thermonuclear weapons, and twenty-one Polaris and twenty Poseidon submarines capable of launching a total of 656 nuclear missiles. To these US forces must be added the nuclear armed tactical aircraft stationed around the periphery of the Soviet Union. Certainly, the geographical spread of such a diverse US strategic force would prohibit what has been called a "synchronized blitz" against these forces, Furthermore, Soviet strategic planners could not guarantee that even all land-based ICBMs would attempt to "ride out" a first strike and not respond to a launch on warning system. It is more likely, then, that the SS-9 was deployed in an attempt to insure the penetration Soviet planners felt they might not be able to get from their more numerous SS-11, particular if the US had decided to build an extensive ABM system.

The Soviet drive to obtain parity with regard to nuclear missiles has involved improvements in quality as well as quantity, for the Soviets have striven to develop several advanced missiles. US Defense Secretary James R. Schlesinger stated in August 1973 that he had "hard evidence" of the successful multi-bomb warhead tests of two of these missiles.[32] The SS-18, carrying at least six bombs in the megaton range, is slated to replace the SS-9. The SS-17, carrying four substantially smaller bombs, is slated to replace the SS-11. Another missile, the SS-19, is believed to be a larger version of the SS-17. Schlesinger added that the first of these new missiles could be deployed by early 1975. Furthermore, in September of 1973 the US Defense Department disclosed that the Soviet Union had developed a new technique for launching missiles.[33] In the normal silo-launching technique the missile must be considerably smaller than the diameter of the silo in order to allow shielding that is required to permit the silo to withstand the high temperatures of expanding gases during hot-launches, but the New Soviet "pop-up" technique allows for the launching of missiles almost the diameter of the silo by utilizing gases to eject the missile from its silo before its engines are ignited. This qualitative breakthrough in launching techniques by the Soviets permits them to place much larger missiles in existing silos. Such a capability is important, because the 1972 Strategic Arms Limitation Agreement between the Soviet Union and the US limited the size and number of missile silos as well as the number of ICBMs, but failed to limit the size of the missiles because of Soviet objections. It is possible, therefore, that the Soviets may attempt to increase the warhead payload of their intercontinental missile force while remaining within the limitations set by the agreement by placing the SS-18 in SS-9 silos that would normally be too small. In the same manner, the SS-17 and/or SS-19 might very well be placed in the SS-11 silos.

Having developed a series of mobile ballistic missiles from SRBM through MRBM to IRBM, it should have been no surprise when the Soviets developed a truck-towed fully mobile ICBM system from a fourth new ICBM, the SS-16. Now, while the 1972 Strategic Arms Limitation Agreement covers fixed land-based ICBMs, it does not mention mobile ICBMs, again because of Soviet objections. Whether or not the Soviets will seek to deploy mobile ICBMs, either within or in addition to the agreed upon figure for land-based ICBMs, or merely seek a concession for a complete ban remains to be seen.

The Soviet decision concerning utilization of their missile developments to drive for a first-strike capability has undoubtedly not been made in the Kremlin yet. The immediate effect of the Soviet strategic missile build-up has been to convince the Soviet leadership that it possesses the nuclear equality perceived as necessary to adequately exercise its coequal role in resolving international political and military problems. The long-term effect of the Soviet build-up, should it continue toward a first-strike capability, would depend upon US domestic support for countermeasures. If the strategic missile build-up continues until the Soviet Union nears such a capability without convincing US budgetary or congressional decision-makers of its significance, the US government would probably los both its self-confidence and its sense of perspective in international affairs. Such a situation conjures up a dire picture of an aggressive Soviet Union that has stalemated US nuclear power and is free to exploit its conventional superiority.

Conventional/General Purpose Forces

With a strength of 1,800,000 men the Soviet ground forces are organized into 110 mechanized divisions, fifty tank divisions, and seven airborne divisions.[34] The deployment of these divisions is: 31 divisions in Central and Eastern Europe, 63 divisions in European USSR, 5 divisions in Central USSR, 23 divisions in southern USSR, and 45 divisions along the Sino-Soviet border area, including two divisions in Mongolia. The divisions stationed in Eastern Europe are maintained at or near combat strength, as are approximately half of those stationed in the Far East. These figures compare with a US army of 782,000, of which about 190,000 are stationed in Europe, and a People's Republic of China army numbering approximately 2,500,000 personnel.

High-speed advance and an extended range of operations are the purpose of Soviet ground force structure and doctrine. The general "profile" is one of a highly mobile force built around armor. The "scenario" is one of tank-heavy divisions striking as deeply as possible into rear areas together with an extensive use of air-dropped, airborne, and helicopter-borne forces to capture "key" objectives and prevent any withdrawal to save forces on the part of the enemy. A Soviet tank division of 8415 officers and men possesses approximately 320 medium tanks, while a US armored division of 16,850 officers and men possesses approximately 324 medium tanks. A Soviet mechanized division would have 190 medium tanks to a US mechanized divisions 216 medium tanks. With two Soviet divisions assigned to cover the same amount of territory as the US division, the Soviets would match their opponents in numbers of personnel but possess approximately twice the number of tanks. The stress on speed and mobility is probably best reflected in Soviet river crossings, which are not perceived as sufficient a concern as to require consolidation of bridgeheads. For in actuality, the Soviets hope to trap and destroy the opposing forces before they can withdraw to the opposite side of a water barrier.

A major area of Western contention concerning the structure of Soviet ground forces is the role of the tank. The Soviets are apparently so convinced of its important role in offensive operations in both nuclear and conventional conflicts that they have produced a new main battle tank.[35] The US army, on the other hand, has been refused funds to build a new main battle tank because of soaring costs. Originally, the US cycle of gradual modification of its main battle tank was to be broken by a joint US-German project. The $1,000,000 per unit cost of the new tank, called the MBT70, was viewed by Congress as too expensive and funding was cut back in 1969. Then the US proceeded to develop on its own the XM803, which was to include most of the major innovations of the joint project except for utilizing a less powerful engine. With inflation, by 1971 the XM803 had almost as high a price sticker as the MBT70 and, therefore, became the first major US army project cancelled by Congress. There is now talk of another new US main battle tank called the XM-1.

The US, therefore, has gone to an interim redesigned M-60, while the West Germans utilize some of the innovations of the original joint project to develop a new tank of their own. Some authorities argue, however, that lightly armored recon tanks like the Soviet PT-76 and the US Sheridan should be the prototype for future tanks anyway. For no tank can withstand a direct hit from an armor-piercing round within the normal engagement distance of 500-2000 meters, so there is no rational reason for producing expensive targets. In the search for an answer to the problem of being overwhelmed by opposing expensive targets, the US has given increasing emphasis to the role of the not inexpensive armed helicopter as a tank destroyer. The US Army's Cobra helicopter, which has been configured in an antitank version, has been procured in its basic form at a unit price of some $520,000. Given the problem of limited manpower resources and the difficulty of containing a tank force breakthrough, a force of antitank helicopters may find an important role in US doctrine.

Two other areas that have caused some Soviet-US comparison discussion in the realm of land forces concerns the lack of protection provided by the US armored personnel carrier and the lack of US multirocket artillery weapons. While the first is most likely due to cost factors involved in going to a new armored personnel carrier that is truly armored, the latter cannot be explained in such terms, because the multirocket system is comparable, or less expensive than, the equivalent tube weapon. Although multirocket artillery weapons lack the precision of tube artillery, they have a considerable advantage in saturation bombardment. Furthermore, the Soviets have found that their multirocket battalion only needs approximately two-thirds the manpower required for a comparable US gun unit.

The Soviet air force has a manpower of 400,000 personnel, and an inventory of about 8000 combat aircraft (if aircraft of the air defense forces are included), which is about 1:1.5 US-Soviet combat aircraft ratio in favor of the Soviets.[36] The revolution in Soviet airlift capability provided by high-speed jet transports and increased logistical and operational mobility provided by helicopters has resulted in a flexibility and mobility that may be the most significant factor after the build-up in strategic forces. Yet another area in which the Soviets have made substantial progress since 1965 is in the competition for tactical air superiority. In this category the US is attempting to play catch-up, while US budgetary decision-makers have been slow to grasp its significance. For the Soviets have deployed the MIG-25 "Foxbat," an air superiority aircraft with a speed of approximately MACH 3.2 and an altitude capability of 80,000 feet, which makes it the world's fastest tactical aircraft as well as an aircraft capable of outclimbing the US F-4 Phantom.[37] Furthermore, a new Soviet air superiority aircraft, the Fearless, is scheduled to be ready for deployment in 1974. All this translates into the fact that unless the US produces the F-14A Tomcat and F-15 Eagle (or adequate substitutes— in sufficient numbers it may lose by default the "keystone" of air power. (Some have argued, however that the more heavily armed Phantom might be able to handle the Foxbat at the lower altitudes at which the aerial engagements are fought.)

Soviet naval strength consists of 448,000 personnel manning 221 major surface combat ships and 245 submarines.[38] Thus, while the US navy's 551,000 personnel make it larger in that category, its 177 major combat surface ships and 73 attack submarines leave it smaller in the category that translates into power.

Traditionally, Soviet naval objectives and strategy have reflected the navy's role of defender of home coastlines and supplementary to ground forces. More recently, however, seapower has been granted an important role in all the major missions of the Soviet armed forces. While the nuclear-missile submarine has a critical strategic role to play in insuring a "post-exchange balance," the Soviet submarine force collectively can support the ground forces in continental campaigns by attempting to "neutralize" enemy naval capabilities in the area of troop movement and support. At the same time, the Soviets have not neglected the role of defense of coastal areas; the navy possesses numerous torpedo boats, fast patrol boats, coastal escorts, and submarine chasers.

The 1958 landing of US marines in Lebanon and the 1962 US naval quarantine of Cuba convinced the Soviets of the value of a seaborne intervention capability. Once having perceived its value, the Soviets embarked upon a program that will give them the capability of bringing highly mobile forces on the scene of an international trouble spot and will, at least to some extent, check American dominance in the area of seaborne intervention. In 1964 the Soviets created an amphibious corps described as naval infantry. Its small size of 17,000 personnel as compared to 196,000 US marines[39] is not as significant as it might seem because Soviet doctrine, unlike US doctrine, calls for the employment of motorized rifle units in the second and all succeeding waves of an amphibious operation. By 1965 the Soviets deployed the first of two helicopter cruisers, each with half a deck used for helicopters, for the dual purposes of antisubmarine warfare and supporting amphibious operations. Then, in 1973, the Soviets built their first true aircraft carrier, though still much smaller than the US attack carriers.[40] The *Kiev*, constructed at Nikolayev on the Black Sea, is about 900 feet long with an angled flight deck of nearly 600 feet. It is in the 45,000-ton class and appears to have sufficient space to accommodate 30 to 40 jet planes and 30 to 40 large helicopter at one time. The ship probably utilizes short-take-off-and-landing aircraft. The

Soviets are expected to have a force of about three aircraft carriers within five years and twelve within ten years. An adequate number of these new carriers would provide the Soviets with the option of seaborne intervention, as they could land troops ashore in helicopters and support them with jet aircraft.

Soviet seapower is a critical part of the Soviet post-Khrushchev military build-up. The Soviet naval chief, Admiral Sergei Georgiecivh Gorshkov, has built, against a power army-dominated military establishment opposition, a Soviet navy capable of applying pressure in places that can cause the US political and military discomfort. The world's largest submarine fleet, the world's largest fleet of small naval craft, a construction program for aircraft carriers, and a highly trained amphibious force all suggest that the Soviets perceived that military sufficiency requires a naval flexibility that has been notably absent in the past.

The Soviet Scenario

As the Soviets view it, they need no longer fear falling victim to US nuclear intimidation. For as they perceive it, the peaceful resolution of any future nuclear confrontation between the Soviet Union and the US will be on the basis of true compromise or by capitulation on the part of the US, no longer by capitulation on their part. Indeed, the credibility of their deterrent requires that in order to avoid nuclear holocaust, any opponent must restrict the level of conflict to less than strategic nuclear exchange.

While Soviet strategic nuclear power provides an essential cover for increasing global activities, the build-up has not yet reached the point where the Soviet Union is confident enough to embark on any dangerous risk taking too distant from her frontiers. One region where the military balance has shifted significantly in her favor, as well as being in geographic proximity, is Europe. In central Europe the Soviet forces alone outnumber the combined NATO forces. The changes reflected in this military imbalance are the result of small and slow changes over a number of years, a general pattern of growth on the part of Soviet forces and reduction on the part of NATO.

Should, for whatever reason, the Soviets feel that it is to their best interests to embark on a military campaign in Central Europe, it can be assumed that they would be anxious to secure a rapid victory so as to prevent NATO's more powerful production capacity from becoming a factor. Whether utilizing only conventional forces or strictly controlled nuclear weapons, the Soviets certainly would attempt to avoid extreme actions that might provoke the US into a nuclear strike against the Soviet Union proper.

As the Soviets see it, the conflict would undoubtedly become nuclear rather quickly because of NATO's inferiority in conventional forces. Therefore, with or without nuclear weapons, the Soviets would upon the initiation of hostilities make NATO's nuclear stockpiles a primary target for their airstrikes. The real question with regards to the destruction of NATO's European nuclear resources is whether or not the Soviet Union will make use of medium- and intermediate-range ballistic missiles, long-range bombers, or seaborne-launched ballistic missiles to attack NATO's military facilities in Great Britain. If such strikes were made against Britain, it is unlikely that the Soviets would fail to attempt to neutralize French strategic nuclear forces also. A justification for the initiation of the use of nuclear weapons might possibly be made of a Soviet nuclear attack on Berlin, which could be blamed on the US. In such a manner, the Soviets would be able to gain justification for the use of nuclear weapons while at the same time eliminating a pocket of resistance behind their lines. Certainly such a charge would find a large number of believers, even in the US.

Once the threshold of nuclear weapons employment has been crossed, it should not be surprising if the Soviets also employ chemical weapons. For while the Soviet Union is a signatory of the Geneva Protocol of 1925 prohibiting the use of such weapons, she has reserved the right to employ them against non-signatories like the US. A justification for their use might conceivably arise from the fact that the US maintains stockpiles of chemical weapons in the Federal Republic of Germany.

In the Soviet scenario, the Rhine bridges are destroyed, and airborne, helicopter-borne, and air-dropped troops would seize "key" objectives to prevent NATO forces from being withdrawn across the Rhine River. In all likelihood, Soviet amphibious landings in Denmark and the Federal Republic of Germany would take place. At the same time, highly mobile ground units capable of rapid concentration during the attack would penetrate NATO resistance in a double envelopment. One breakthrough would take place in the north, sweeping across the German plain. The other, in the south through the Fulda Gap. Upon reaching the Rhine, the Soviet forces would have destroyed a major part of British, German, and US forces. If the Soviet advance to the Rhine has been swift enough to prevent the withdrawal of NATO forces to the west bank and reinforcement by airlift from the US, and before the French could get into action, the Soviets might offer to negotiate on their terms at that time. If these prerequisites are not obtained or if the Soviet moderates do not prevail over the military lobby's desire to complete the thrust, the Soviet forces might continue to drive for the Channel. Either way, the Soviets would hope to present the US with a virtual *fait accompli,* and what US President would dare risk American cities for an already occupied Bonn or Paris when the "Russians are willing to negotiate"?

The massive 1967 Soviet exercise "DNEPR" followed a scenario very similar to the one I relate here. In that exercise, the Soviets fought in a "battle area" resembling Western Europe in size and shape. The exercise also involved an attack against a major river line. Furthermore, the massive 1970 exercise "DVINA" followed a similar scenario.

The Political Implications

For the future, the military and political importance of the Soviet military build-up will be at least to some degree a function of the US and West European political mood. Presently, neither US nor West European public opinion is prepared to support massive increases in military forces. The alternative for the West is accommodation with the Soviet Union. Such an accommodation will require a judgment that the terms are more satisfactory than either allocating the resources to meet the Soviet threat or risking military defeat. If the Soviet objectives are modest enough that they can be satisfied by concessions to which the US and Western Europe can agree, the West will undoubtedly rationalize away their doubts. The concessions sought by the Soviets will depend largely upon how they assess the Western political mood. If the Soviets can discredit the Western non-anti-Soviet critics as they attempted to discredit the Soviet academician Andre Sakharov by fostering the idea that only those opposed to peace would reject the peace the Kremlin proposes, they will undoubtedly succeed in lulling Western concern over the historical record of appeasement.

The Soviet post-Khrushchev leadership has demonstrated that they are as good propagandists as they are good pragmatists. Besides the matter of peace, they have convinced the West that it needs the Soviet Union as much as the Soviet Union needs the West. The more interests in the West recognize the value in accommodation with the Soviet Union, the less Soviet needs become a factor in reaching accommodation. In some ways, this is rather like the maneuvering leading to the 1933 US *de jure* recognition of the Soviet Union. One example of this is the Soviet appeal to the capitalist instincts of the West. As during the 1930s, the Soviets suggest that politics not be allowed to hinder trade. The line is that if the West drops demands for political and/or military concessions on the part of the Soviets, the Soviets will ever so kindly purchase Western technology. For their part, it should be enough that they are aiding in the prolonging of capitalism by making the purchases.

In attempting to arrive at accommodation with the Soviet Union, the West has approached the problem of reducing the Soviet threat in two ways. Specifically, the West has little military strength to bargain away. The only alternative to de facto capitulation necessitates mutual balanced force reductions. Otherwise, the withdrawal of Soviet forces a few hundred miles to the USSR while US forces are flown back three-thousand miles to the US would shift the balance further in the favor of the Soviet Union. The Soviets, of course, have balked at any such proposal, and the Western approach of attempting to "corrupt" the Soviet Union as a means of disarming the Soviet threat has also run into difficulties. For the idea of "freedom of movement of people and ideas" provokes "nightmares" of political contamination for the Soviets. Therefore, they have adopted the tactic of the insisting on the doctrine of noninterference in the domestic affairs of others. This doctrine does not apply, of course, to the individual members of the "socialist community" when the collective perceives some individual member's actions to be something other than in the interest of the "socialist community" as a whole.

The implication of the Soviet military build-up for the US-West European relationship in NATO is that Western Europe may be more likely to disassociate itself from US non-European interests and risk taking. A good example of this tendency is the lack of NATO support for US policy during the October 1973 crisis over the possibility of direct Soviet military intervention in the Middle East. More critical, what might follow is the "neutralization" of Western Europe or, perhaps, even Soviet hegemony in Europe.

Projections for the Future

The Soviet military build-up undoubtedly has been founded on the agreement among Soviet leaders that nothing less than US-Soviet strategic equality was tolerable. It has changed the military balance between the two countries by making the Soviet Union a truly global military power. The era of superior US nuclear power and superiority in Western globally mobile forces has come to a close.

To the Soviets, East-West discussions represent a means by which to validate Soviet gains while obtaining the opportunity to stretch out military programs so as to relieve the heavy burden on Soviet resources. Furthermore, if a US recessional from Europe can be coupled with the strategic arms accord signed on 22 June 1973, the Soviets would be in the position to press Western Europe on coming to terms with the Soviet Union as the best source of security arrangement. In other areas, the improved Soviet capacity to intervene in local situations may also increase the incidence of US-Soviet confrontations. In essence, the Soviets will probably attempt to reinforce their gains with East-West agreements while waiting for new opportunities. When the US demonstrates resolve, which in most cases will now only occur when backed by public opinion, the Soviets will tend to be less militant. In this manner, new gains for the Soviets will be obtained by default rather than conflict. It is highly likely that the Soviets will hope to couple any attempt to make gains on the international scene with a sincere effort to avoid increasing the chances of a rapprochement between the People's Republic of China and the US. However, whatever Brezhnev's personal feeling toward a detente with the West, it must be remembered that there exists a tremendously powerful lobby in the traditional elements of the military, heavy industry, and professional party *apparatchiki* and ideologues that will undoubtedly always be willing to support a more militant group in the Politburo.

Notes

1. See Thomas W. Wolfe, *Soviet Power and Europe 1945-1970* (Baltimore: The John Hopkins Press, 1970), pp. 32-35.

2. Ibid., pp. 35-38.
3. Ibid., p. 164.
4. Ibid., p. 165.
5. See *The Current Digest of The Soviet Press* 12 (January 10, 1960): 3-16.
6. Ibid., p. 10.
7. Ibid.
8. Ibid., p. 11.
9. Ibid., p. 13.
10. Ibid., p. 14.
11. *The Military Balance 1962-1963* (London: The Institute For Strategic Studies, 1962), p. 2.
12. See *The Military Balance 1970-1971* (London: The Institute for Strategic Studies, 1970), p. 106.
13. See Thomas W. Wolfe, *Soviet Strategy At The Crossroads* (Cambridge, Mass.: Harvard University Press, 1964), p. 43.
14. Ibid., pp. 44-46.
15. Ibid., pp. 149-50.
16. Ibid., pp. 151-52.
17. See Stanley H. Cohn, "The Economic Burden of Soviet Defense Outlays," p. 169, in *Economic Performance And The Military Burden In The Soviet Union,* a compendium of papers submitted to the Subcommittee of Foreign Economic Policy of the Joint Economic Committee of the Congress of the United States (Washington, D.C.: US Government Printing Office, 1970).
18. See Wolfe, *Soviet Strategy At The Crossroads,* pp. 168-70. Also see Thomas W. Wolfe, *The Soviet Military Scene: Institutional And Defense Policy Considerations* (Santa Monica, California: The Rand Corporation, June 1969), p. 61.
19. See John Erikson, *Soviet Military Power* (London: Royal United Services Institute For Defense Studies, 1971), pp. 8-9.
20. US Senate Arms Services Committee, Hearing Before The Subcommittee on Strategic Arms Limitation Talks, *The Limitation of Strategic Arms, Part 2,* 20 May 1970 (Washington, D.C.: US Government Printing Office, 1970), pp. 61-62.
21. *Methodological Problems of Military Theory and Practice,* compiled by members of the Marxist Leninist Philosophy Department of the Lenin Military Political Academy, 1966, p. 127.
22. In reality, the Soviet ICBM force was rather limited and vulnerable until the mid-1960s. See *The Military Balance 1971-1972* (London: The International Institute For Strategic Studies, 1971), p. 56.
23. *Methodological Problems,* p. 98.
24. Ibid., p. 41.
25. Col. V.V. Larionov, "The Political Side of Soviet Military Doctrin," *Communist of The Armed Forces,* November 1968, p. 14.

26. *The Military Balance 1965-1966* (London: The Institute For Strategic Studies, 1965), p. 2 and *The Military Balance 1974-1975,* (London: The International Institute For Strategic Studies, 1974, p. 8.

27. *The Military Balance 1974-1975,* p. 73.

28. Ibid., p. 8.

29. Ibid.

30. Ibid., p. 8.

31. See Subcommittee on National Security and International Operations/ Committee on Government Operations. US Senate: Planning Program-ing-Budgeting. Defense Analysis: Two examples (Washington, D.C.: US Government Printing Office, 1969), p. 19.

32. Edward K. Delong, "US Loses Lead on Multi-Bomb Warheads: Soviets Catch Up In N-Missile Race," *Boston Herald American,* 18 August 1973.

33. John W. Finney, "Pentagon Says 'Pop-Up' Missile Gives Soviet Heavier Warhead," *New York Times,* 19 September 1973. The Soviets already have a distinct advantage in "throw weight" because of the larger missiles they employ.

34. *The Military Balance 1974-1975,* p. 9. There have been recent claims that, in fact, the Soviets have increased the number of their airborne divisions to twelve or thirteen divisions. If this is so, it would certainly be a signi-ficant development as regards Soviet intervention capabilities. See Drew Middleton, "Soviet Spending On Europe Troops Hiked by $10B," in the *Boston Herald American,* 8 October 1973. Also, see Drew Middleton, "Big Soviet Airlift and Airborne Capacity Altering Power Balance," in *New York Times,* 26 October 1973.

35. See Trever Cliffe. *Military Technology and the Military Balance,* Adelphi Paper Number Eighty-Nine (London: The International Institute For Strategic Studies, 1972), p. 8. Also see *The Military Balance 1974-1975,* p. 5.

36. *The Military Balance 1974-1975,* pp. 8-10.

37. See Cliffe, p. 47 and 42. Also see Drew Middleton, "F-15 Passes Test in Initial Flights," in *New York Times,* 25 November 1972.

38. *The Military Balance 1974-1975,* p. 9.

39. Ibid., p. 6 and pp. 9-10.

40. See William Beecher, "A Soviet Carrier in '73 Is Indicated," *New York Times,* 17 October 1972 and Beecher, "Soviet Is Said to Build Navy's Second Carrier," New York Times, 27 February 1973, p. 2.

13

Technology in the Prospects for Peace: The View from Another Side

George H. Hampsch

The Marxist-Leninist holds that technological advances have greatly improved the prospects for world peace. The advance of technology, however, also poses actual and potential dangers to world peace in the foreseeable future, especially as viewed from the vantage of a Marxist world view.

The most obvious example of technology serving the cause of peace is in the area of nuclear arms and advanced military technology. Because of nuclear weapons and advanced conventional weapons, the cost in human terms of resolving confrontations between ideological systems by means of full-scale war has become excessive. (Of course, the threat expressed by Secretary Khrushchev at the time of the Suez crisis,[1] and the much graver threat of President Kennedy at the time of the Cuban missile crisis[2] show clearly that advanced weaponry is by no means a foolproof preventative of wars).

Moreover, the possession of nuclear weapons and a high degree of military technology allowed the Soviet Union to assume the position of a military superpower in the post-World War II period, long before it had the wherewithal to be considered an economic power capable of challenging the strength of the United States. The ability of the Soviet Union to play the role of a superpower in this period had important strategic consequences for the future of the world. First of all, it severely limited the options that advanced capitalism had at hand either to undermine existing socialist societies or to prevent the spread of socialism into nonsocialist societies. Few would deny that if the Soviet Union had not been a superpower in the first two decades after World War II, no socialist society would now exist in Eastern Europe (including Albania and Yugoslavia), in East Asia, Cuba, or perhaps even China. Because of the Soviet Union, the socialist nations were able both to consolidate themselves internally and to expand their influence into the nonsocialist world.

These goals have been accomplished while following a foreign policy based upon the principles of peaceful coexistence. These principles are firmly rooted in Marxist-Leninist ideology. They are found consistently and repeatedly in the writings of Lenin.[3] In contemporary times these principles have been stated on numerous occasions.

The principles of peaceful coexistence were stated clearly at the Bandung Conference of 1955, in the statements of the Twentieth and Twenty-first Congresses of the CPSU, as well as in the Moscow Declaration and Peace Manifesto of 1957. They were reemphasized in the important Declaration of

Representatives of the eighty-one Communist Parties Meeting in Moscow in November and December of 1960. More recently the policy of peaceful coexistence has been reiterated in the Report of the Twenty-Fourth Congress of the CPSU and the statement of the Central Committee of the CPSU on the occasion of the Fiftieth anniversary of the USSR. As understood by the Marxist-Leninist, these principles are: mutual respect for territorial integrity and sovereignty; mutual nonaggression; noninterference in the internal affairs of another; equality and mutual benefit; and respect for all peoples freely to choose their socioeconomic and political systems.[4]

The *practical* application of the principles of peaceful coexistence in the form of nuclear pacifism can be traced back at least to the Cuban missile crisis. From 1962, if not sooner, the Soviet Union and the socialist nations of Eastern Europe have consistently followed a foreign policy designed to avoid a major military confrontation between the two ideological power-blocs.[5] The most recent example (at the time of this writing) is the reaction of the socialist nations to the intensive bombing of North Vietnam and the mining of the harbor at Haiphong.

This consistent pursuit of a foreign policy of peaceful coexistence has been eminently successful in bringing about the results for which it was designed. It has significantly lessened the danger of major war between nation-states; it has played a major role in bringing about the conditions of detente between major powers; and it has, in the process, gently but significantly tipped the balance of geopolitical power in favor of the non-Chinese socialist nations. The Soviet Union and the other socialist countries have done this with utmost diplomatic skill, being most careful to bring about this shift in the balance of power without arousing certain "better-dead-than-red" tendencies that lie dormant in the American psyche.

It simply cannot be denied that there has been a significant shift in the geopolitical balance of power. This is manifested by the *Ostpolitik*, the recognition of the GDR, the agreement by the nations of Europe to convene a European security conference, as well as the SALT talks and the agreement of NATO and the Warsaw Treaty Organization to begin talks on mutual balanced force reductions. There have been important shifts of power in the Persian Gulf, on the Indian subcontinent, in Latin America, and in Southeast Asia. There has been an evident shift of naval power in the Mediterranean, the Indian Ocean, and so on.

Because of this shift in the geopolitical balance, the Marxist-Leninist maintains that the United States and, incidentally, the People's Republic of China have been forced to adopt a foregin policy based upon the principles of peaceful coexistence. The United States and the other advanced capitalist powers always have talked in terms of world peace (as Mao continually talked in terms of the "paper tiger" form of peaceful coexistence). But their policies were designed to achieve their political goals at the risk of military confrontation, if necessary.

In fact, US foreign policy became more risky as the consistency of the Soviet policy became evident. Many Americans still feel a sense of pride in recalling the several occasions when the American government was able to call the other side's "bluff" in the "game" of military confrontation. Such events are often interpreted as acts of strength and courage on the part of the US, and as acts of either weakness of crude opportunism on the part of the Soviet Union.[6]

For the Marxist-Leninist, it is indeed fortunate that the present leaders of the advanced capitalist world (and China) are realistic enough to grasp the new situation and not cling to their past tendencies to view their ideology in absolutist terms. Fortunately for Brandt and Bahr, Nixon and Kissinger (as well as Mao and Chou), they have been able to present the shift in foreign policy to their own people, and to a large part of the world, in terms in which *they* appear to be the initiators of a bold new policy. This may prove to be a danger to world peace in the future, however.

At the time of a future world crisis, the American people and their allies may expect the US government to react in its traditionally strong way, yet *suddenly* discover that it is unable to do so. At this juncture, the national pride of the American public, and pressures from foreign governments may very well force the US government to attempt to resolve the crisis by a threat to escalate to strategic weapons.[7] Hopefully the strategists of the socialist world will not overlook this dangerous potentiality.

This shift in the balance of power has many important implications for the socialist world and for the prospects of peace as seen from the socialist world view. First of all, the proletarian states, although they cannot abolish exploitation within the capitalist world, do begin to eliminate the relations of domination and subordination in international affairs. Through peaceful coexistence the antagonism between bourgeois interests and the proletarian states is so modified that the working class in power no longer is able to be exploited by the international bourgeoisie. It confronts them as an independent force.[8]

Second, the shift of power moves the universal need for general and complete disarmament from the realm of moral ideals more and more toward the realm of practical options. One must not overlook, however, the complexities and contradictory aspects of the process of disarmament.

Obviously, every right-thinking person desires an end to the destructive arms race. Yet it must be recognized that the arms race cannot end as long as there is any serious disparity in the quantity or quality of the military forces of the major ideological blocs. As soon as a relative parity in military forces and equipment has been reached in any particular arena, then significant moves toward disarmament can begin immediately, as for example, the SALT Talks I and II, the Mutual Balanced Force Reduction Talks, and the European Security Conference. Disarmament, short of parity, is an utopian dream. The People's Republic of China has indeed recognized this fact. Its position on general disarmament reflects consistently and clearly the realities of the situation.[9] The Chinese will not consent to disarmament short of either nuclear parity with both the United States and the Soviet Union, or else a change in foreign policy by which the goals of the People's Republic and the Soviet Union become unified. Neither appears probable within the foreseeable future; hence, neither does general disarmament.

The Soviet Union also recognizes this principle quite clearly. In those areas in which the United States still has military superiority—for example, in naval power—the Soviet Union feels itself under no moral imperative to stop its military development, short of parity.[10] Still, the prospects for disarmament have greatly improved through the shift in geopolitical power.

A third important implication for the socialist world resulting from the shift in the balance of power is the opportunity that socialism has to vividly demonstrate its advantages in the sphere of economics. Under the conditions of peaceful coexistence, the working class living within advanced capitalism can wage an increasingly effective struggle for better living standards as well as better social and political rights. The bourgeoisie are compelled to make concessions in hopes of either co-opting it or buying off its more radical demands—demands that appear commonplace to workers living under socialism.[11]

In the fourth place, peaceful coexistence holds out to the proletariat the prospect of winning power without an armed struggle. In the past, the international bourgeoisie has been prepared to export counterrevolution, including active military participation. The conditions of peaceful coexistence help create internal conditions as well as world opinion that make military intervention difficult and morally embarrassing. These conditions weaken the most aggressive circles associated with the reactionary military interests and isolated the ultraright.[12]

Finally, the atmosphere of peace and detente provides opportunities to improve relations between the peoples of the capitalist nations and those of the socialist countries. Peaceful coexistence provides a means of expanding the flow of correct information about socialism and its achievements. It makes it harder for antisocialist propaganda, at least in its more blatant forms, to have noticeable effect. An objective basis is created for extending the ideological influence of socialism, especially among the young.[13]

Since the capitalist world has accepted the principles of detente as the basis of its foreign policy, the United States, still very much the leader of the capitalist world, finds itself with three basic options for a future foreign policy.[14] The first option is to continue the game of power politics between the two superpowers, but without the zero-sum implications that existed during the period of the cold war.[15] The second option is to accept the Nixon-Kissinger "five-polar world" model. Here, there is a relinquishing of that type of influence by which the two superpowers hold the political and economic destiny of the world in their hands. This five-polar foreign policy recognizes the interlocking—though unequal—relationships between five power blocs. Through the proper adjustment of these interdependent relationships between the power blocs, a neo-Metternichian or, perhaps better, a neo-Bismarckian world order comes into existence.[16] The United States will still attempt in its own measure to strongly influence the political and economic decisions within this world order, but it will do so in a less visible, more subdued manner.[17]

The third option is that of "neoisolationism" or, perhaps more correctly, "strategic disengagement." Under this foreign policy scheme, the United States voluntarily lessens its political and military influence in the world, and attempts to maintain itself as a world power primarily through its economic presence throughout the world.[18]

For the foreseeable future the Marxist-Leninist perceives that it is the Nixon-Kissinger "five-polar world" policy that will prevail, although the "strategic disengagement" position will have its effect on this multipolar policy. The subdued presence of the United States could be quite marked.

Under the multipolar policy, the United States will engage in three separate sets of relationships with three quite different types of nations.[19] First, it will be in basically a competitive relationship with the Soviet Union and China, designed to keep their power in check by utilizing both their mutual hostility and American military power, and to keep competition under control by cooperating with them on particular measures, especially those necessary to reduce the dangers of war.

Second, the United States will engage in a basically cooperative relationship with the other industrially developed nations, Western Europe, Japan and Canada, in order to deal jointly with the consequences of increasing interdependence, while at the same time allowing the United States to hold its own in the inevitable economic competition with them.

Third, the US government will engage in relationships with the poor nations of the world designed both to help them develop economically, and to mitigate local and regional violence to the extent possible. Thus, it reduces the dangers of both outside involvement and undue dependence on powers that the United States government considers hostile to the national interests of the country.

If this indeed becomes the new foreign policy of the United States, then the goals sought by the policy of peaceful coexistence in the capitalist world and in the socialist world are radically different. The United States views peace primarily in terms of world stability, whereas the Soviet Union and the socialist nations view peaceful coexistence in terms of a successful completion of the class struggle.

For the Marxist-Leninist, this divergent interpretation of peaceful coexistence raises both potential and actual dangers to the future of world peace. Technology will act as a catalyst in precipitating these dangers.

Under the conditions of peaceful coexistence technological advances will tend to undercut the national liberation movements.[20] Advances in military technology nearly always benefit the side of the counterinsurgents. Vietnam provides an excellent example. A solution in Vietnam was postponed at least from 1965 until 1973 through the introduction of massive firepower, sophisticated weapons, and detection devices. It is also obvious that the solution in Cambodia was delayed by the use of identical means.[21]

The advantages advanced weaponry give to the counterinsurgents lessens the need for direct intervention by the major capitalist powers and allows for the greater use of *indigenous* counterinsurgency forces. This changes the sociopsychological character of the struggle as well as removing the more obvious imperialist connotations. It also increases the insurgents' need for military assistance from the socialist nations.

But perhaps the greatest danger to the national liberation movements comes from the effects that economic technology has on the development of nations. The use of sophisticated modernization techniques allows for a rapid development of natural resources in the developing nation with a declining need for imported capital and technical assistance. Direct and obvious intervention into the economy of the developing country by an advanced capitalist power is lessened through the creation of a new educated class of technicians and entrepreneurs. This reduces the stigma of neocolonialism and the stigma attached to the ruling circles. Increased prosperity takes place within the milieu of a strong nationalism. The workers begin to have a vested interest in the status quo. Whatever foreign capital is still needed is primarily in the form of long-term credits funneled into locally owned and controlled enterprises. While these long-term credits can be provided by socialist countries, the vast supply of such available capital is in the hands of the advanced capitalist nations. Granting credits to developing nations slows the internal development of socialist economies, while the exporting of long-term credits is extremely beneficial to the international bourgeoisie.[22]

Since Marxist-Leninists do not perceive their world view in fatalistic terms, it is not inevitable that the developing nations of the world choose the socialist model. They can combine capitalism and nationalist fervor. For example, of the eleven nations comprising the increasingly important Organization of Petroleum Exporting Countries (OPEC), only three (Iraq, Libya, and Algeria) have socioeconomic systems in any way resembling the socialist model. National "liberation" need not go beyond the breaking of colonial-type political ties with the more advanced nations. Exploitation, both internal and external, may continue in a stable, so-called peaceful world.

The conditions of peaceful coexistence opens up new markets for the unused productive capacities of advanced capitalism, especially those of the United States. It also allows the United States to partially convert its resources from large military production to fulfilling the needs, especially the technological hardware and consumer needs of the socialist bloc.[23] This is certainly advantageous for peace and for mankind, and the Marxist-Leninist does not object to increased trade on these grounds alone. However, there is a potential danger. The advantages coming to the economy of the United States as a result of the increased trade with socialist countries will help overcome some of the immediate contradictions within the economy and allow for a bettering of the economic and social conditions of the workers, the farmers, and quite possibly even the poor of the nation. All to the good! Yet the workers may acquire thereby an increased vested interest in the status quo, and especially in the *world stability* that protects the economic status quo. This vested interest may more than offset the increased alienation of the worker in a highly techno-logical society, as well as the disadvantages caused by the economic struggles between the capitalist powers, and the internal monetary and economic crises.

Any Marxist who knows his history is tremendously impressed by the staying power of capitalism, by its ability to co-opt the labor movement, and its ability to use the instinctive nationalist loyalties of the workers to weaken the solidarity of the international worker movement. The socialist world cannot underestimate the potential dangers that peaceful coexistence offers for renewing the economic life of advanced capitalism and renewing the loyalties of the workers to the economies of their respective nation-states.

A second potential danger is to the workers living in the socialist states. Detente creates closer cultural, scientific, economic, and political ties between the capitalist world and the socialist world. These may possibly draw socialist workers toward an acceptance of the basic bourgeois world view, with the con-sequent blurring of class consciousness and the need for class struggle. This danger has been recognized by some of the socialist countries and is reflected in their strong stand during the preliminary talks on the Conference on Security and Cooperation in Europe on those clauses dealing with the free flow of persons and ideas between the two ideological systems.[24]

Another potential danger comes from the economic relationships between the socialist world and the developing nations. Through the help given to these nations, economic relationships can result in which the advanced socialist countries are able to benefit economically more fully than the underdeveloped nations. The danger is that the socialist commonwealth may develop a vested interest in maintaining unequal economic relations. In other words, the socialist nations recognize that they must indeed be on their guard not to fall into "social-imperialism," a relationship of economic hegemony over certain less prosperous nations of the world caused by the need to continually improve the conditions of the workers living under the advanced technology of a developed socialism.

The Marxist-Leninist is convinced that peaceful coexistence does hold high prospects for a world no longer plagued by major armed conflicts. For this man-kind should be grateful. But the danger that this may result in a fraudulent, false peace is also recognized. Active measures will be taken to confront this danger.

The role that technology plays in the ultimate success or failure in reaching the goals of the socialist world view is crucial.

Notes

1. *Khrushchev Remembers,* (Boston: Little, Brown & Co., 1970), pp. 435-36. See also his interview with James Reston, *New York Times,* 10 October 1957, where there is recorded a mild threat against Turkey.

2. Robert F. Kennedy, *Thirteen Days: A Memoir of the Cuban Missile Crisis.* (New York: W.W. Norton & Co., 1969), pp. 108-9, and Jerome H. Kahan and Anne K. Long, "The Cuban Missile Crisis: A Study of Strategic Context," *Political Science Quarterly* 87 (December 1972): 564-90.

3. *Collected Works,* vol. 27, pp. 68-75; vol. 30, pp. 38-39, 50-51, 365-67; vol. 31, pp. 408-15, 487-95; vol. 32, pp. 179-83; vol. 33, pp. 143-55, 162-63, 263-66, 356-57, 383-89; "Interview with Lincoln Eyre", *The World* (N.Y.), 21 February 1920, etc. See also, *History of Soviet Foreign Policy,* ed. by B. Ponomarov, et al. (Moscow: Progress Publishers, 1969), chapters 1-6.

4. The principles of peaceful coexistence were specified quite clearly at the Bandung Conference of 1955, in the statements of the 20th and 21st Congresses of the CPSU, as well as in the Moscow Declaration and Peace Manifesto of 1957. They were emphasized most strongly in the important Declaration of Representatives of the 81 Communist Parties Meeting in Moscow (November–December 1960). More recently the policy of peaceful coexistence has been reiterated in the Report of the 24th Congress of the CPSU and the statement of the CC of the CPSU on the occasion of the fiftieth anniversary of the USSR. The principles of peaceful coexistence as understood by the Marxist-Leninist are as follows: a) mutual respect for territorial integrity and sovereignty, b) mutual nonaggression, c) noninterference in each other's internal affairs d) equality and mutual benefit, e) respect for all peoples freely to choose their socioeconomic and political systems. Cf. Kurt Erlebach, "Peaceful Coexistence—Political Reality, Form of Class Struggle, Revolutionary Factor," *World Marxist Review* (February 1973): 43.

5. See, *History of Soviet Foreign Policy,* chapters 8-13. A European Security Conference was proposed by the Soviet Union as early as 1954. See Paul Seabury, "On Détente," *Survey* 19 (Spring 1973): 70, and Robin Alison Remington, "European Security in the Era of Negotiations," *Current History* 64 (May 1973): 220. For the English text of the Soviet note inviting the U.S. and twenty-three European nations to such a conference, see *New Times* (Moscow) 46 (13 November 1954).

6. On this point see Christopher Leman, "Must We Always Be Tough?", *Foreign Policy,* no. 11 (Summer 1973), pp. 93-101.

7. See, David Watt, "Four More Years—Of What?" *Foreign Policy,* no. 9, (Winter 1972-73), p. 9.

8. Erlebach, p. 43.

9. Chiao Kuan-hua, "Soviet Disarmament Proposal is a Fraud," *Peking Review*

15 (17 November 1972): 5-6; Lin Peng, "Remarks to a Plenary Meeting of the Third United Nations Conference on Trade and Development," quoted in "Chinese Comment on Soviet Foreign Policy," compiled by the Subcommittee on National Security and International Operations of the Committee on Government Operations, U.S. Senate. (Washington: U.S. Government Printing Office, 1972), 7-8.

10. L.I. Brezhnev, Speech of June 1971, as quoted in G. Soyatov and A. Kokoshin, "Naval Power in the U.S. Strategic Plans," *International Affairs* (Moscow) no. 4 (April 1973), p. 62.

11. Erlebach, p. 46; Cf. Peter P. Donker, Address to the Affiliated Industries of Massachusetts, *Worcester Telegram,* 2 May 1973, pp. 12-13. See also Eberhard Mueller, "Humanizing Industrial Society," "*Worldview* 16 (April 1973): 38-43.

12. Erlebach, pp. 46-47.

13. Ibid., p. 47.

14. Cf. Raymond Vernon, "Rogue Elephant in the Forest," *Foreign Affairs.* 51 (April 1973): 573-87.

15. Eugene V. Rostow, *Peace in the Balance,* (New York: Simon & Schuster, 1972), especially chapter 10.

16. See Zbigniew Brezezinski, "U.S. Foregin Policy: The Search For Focus" *Foreign Affairs* 51 (July 1973): 715, and James Chace, *A World Elsewhere* (New York: Charles Scribner's Sons, 1973): 28-35.

17. Seyom Brown, "The Changing Essence of Power," *Foreign Affairs* 51 (January 1973): 286-99; George F. Kennan, "After the Cold War," *Foreign Affairs* 51 (October 1972): 210-27. The five powers are of course the U.S., USSR, Western Europe, China and Japan.

18. Earl C. Ravenal, "The Case for Strategic Disengagement," *Foreign Affairs* 51 (April 1973): 505-21; Robert W. Tucker, *A New Isolationism: Threat or Promise?* (New York: Universe Books, 1972); Richard J. Barnet, *Roots of War,* (New York: Atheneum, 1972); Daniel Yergin, "Fulbright's Circle," *Worldview* 16 (February 1973): 7-13.

19. William J. Barnds, "Nixon's America After Vietnam," *Worldview* 16 (April 1973): 5. See also, "National Security Policy and the Changing World Power Alignment," Report by the Subcomittee of National Security Policy and Scientific Developments, Committee on Foreign Affairs, U.S. House of Representatives (25 October 1972). (Washington: U.S. Government Printing Office, 1972), pp. 3-6.

20. The forces of the ultraleft have clearly recognized this danger. As a result, they have condemned the policy of peaceful coexistence, at least in the manner it has been practiced by the leading socialist countries. See, for example, D. Horowitz, "Nixon's Vietnam Strategy: How It Was Launched With the Aid of Brezhnev and Mao and How the Vietnamese Intend to Defeat It," *Ramparts* 11 (August 1972): 17-20.

21. Cf. William P. Rogers, Secretary of State, Testimony before the U.S. Senate Foreign Relations Committee, *New York Times,* 1 May 1973, p.10.

22. Lynn Turgeon, Address to the *National Conference on American Policy Toward the Two German States,* held at New York City, June 3, 1972. New York: American Society for the Study of the German Democratic Republic, 1972. See, however, G. Skorov, " 'Transfer of Technology' and Neocolonialist Manoeuvres," *International Affairs* (Moscow), no. 5 (May, 1972), pp. 55-62.

23. Turgeon. See also, Seymour Melman, *Pentagon Capitalism,* (New York: McGraw-Hill, 1970), especially pp. 71-96 and pp. 184-205.

24. Joseph Harned, et al., "Congerence on Security and Cooperation in Europe and Negotiations on Mutual and Balanced Force Reductions," *The Atlantic Community Quarterly* 11 (Spring 1973): 11-14, and 43. See also, V. Knyazhinsky, "Détente and the Problems of Ideological Struggle," *International Affairs* (Moscow), no. 4 (April 1973), pp. 17-18, V. Kudinov and V. Pletnikov, "Ideological Confrontation of the Two Systems," ibid., no. 12 (December 1972), pp. 60-61, Jack F. Matlock, "US-Soviet Relations in the 1970's," *Survey* 19 (Spring 1973): 136 and Jean de Madre, Preface to *Impediments to the Free Flow of Information Between East and West,* by Anthony C.A. Dake. (Paris: Atlantic Treaty Association, 1973).

Part VIII

Regional Politics and Influence

14

Pessimism, Convergence, and Soviet
African Relations

Helen Desfosses

The absence of any reference to Africa in the joint Soviet-American com-muniqué issued at the end of Leonid Brezhnev's June 1973 visit to the United States provides yet another indication (if, indeed, more are needed) of the minimal superpower concern with events and developments in this region. In an era when Washington officials are heard to remark that no area ranks lower than Africa as far as American security interests are concerned and Secretary Brezhnev reminds all that Soviet development is the foremost international duty of the USSR, it is surely difficult for African leaders to hope for some significant rise in the flattened curve of great power interest. Of course, a few leaders can derive some optimism from their countries' positions proximity to important raw materials reserves (e.g., Somalia and Ethiopia) or as stages for the last acts of cold war-drama (e.g., Congo-Brazzaville). However, even the leaders of these countries are aware that they are outranked in strategic and/or ideological significance by Southeast Asia and the Middle East and that they, therefore stand in only temporarily sharp relief against the over-all low profile accorded by Brezhnev, Nixon, and now Ford to Tropical Africa.

This low profile for Africa in the seventies is not surprising. Africa's com-parative importance in earlier years stemmed from its position as a potential pawn in a superpower game, a game ruled by a concern with alliance building and winning ideological converts against the day (sometimes deemed inevit-able) when the veneer of peaceful coexistence would crack, exposing a terrible reality beneath. While it is true that Tropical Africa's significance in this game was never overwhelming, the mere fact that the region had not been included in the alliance-building efforts of the Eisenhower administration enhanced its attractiveness to the USSR, while the very logic of the cold war dictated that Soviet interest would have to be parried by the United States. The decisions of Nixon and Brezhnev to change the game from alliance build-ing to bilateral or tripartite agreements among the privileged ranks of the superpowers have reduced the need for pawns, especially in Africa. In Arbatov's words, "In today's world, events are determined not by the arith-metic of a traditional political game of great powers but by the algebra of a complex sociopolitcal struggle embracing our planet."[1]

This continuing emphasis on planetary struggle, albeit differently defined, would seem to point both to a continuing superpower race to stack up mirror-systems and to Africa's utility in this game. However, domestic problems, consumer pressures, intra-alliance difficulties, and the Vietnam imbroglio have combined to bring about great power foreign policies characterized by a mood of cost-benefit analysis. Such analysis, combined with the growing search for avenues of mutually advantageous cooperation, has produced a specialization of both interests and the search for influence by Washington and Moscow. In such an era, Tropical Africa's importance would almost necessarily decrease: most of its states have no sizable energy source reserves; their strategic importance pales in comparison to that of other third world areas.

Finally, the sixties provided neither the US nor the USSR with much success in establishing mirror-systems. In sum, while the sixties demonstrated that the ideological return on superpower financial and diplomatic commitments to Tropical Africa did not justify continued pre-emptive policies of aid giving and influence garnering, the concern in the seventies with strategic pressure points and trade negotiations further diminishes these states' significance. So we approach the midpoint of this decade with the USSR mirroring the American policy toward Tropical Africa: decreasing aid commitments and an over-all low profile with special attention to a few key areas, West Africa and the Horn. Mention should also be made of a (minimal) Soviet concern with guerrilla movements, but significantly, only at a level that would permit deriving political capital from an apparent American commitment to established South African and Portuguese rule. In fact, a survey of potential incentives to increased superpower concern with Tropical Africa reveals few prospects for change.

New Treatment for Old Allies

The Brezhnev-Kosygin regime's response to US willingness to limit the scope of competition and to subject its African aid policy to a cost-benefit analysis has meant many things. Not only did Soviet offers of economic aid decline significantly after 1965 (from 1959 to 1965, new Soviet aid commitments to Africa averaged 30 percent of their annual total commitments, while from 1966-1973, the figure was 11 percent), but there also have been changes in the way this money has been allocated. No longer is aid confined mainly to states of radical political orientation or to prestige projects appraised more for their symbolic value than their economic rationality. Instead, Moscow seems to have concluded that although it might be immoderate to spend time and money in Africa in order to produce revolutionary change, a smaller amount of aid could be used effectively to further Soviet national interests. These include expanding its network of government-to-government relations, developing the Soviet economy, and ensuring stability in Tropical Africa.

This concern with the stability and low economic drain of its African contacts has produced increasingly critical Soviet commentary on progressive states such as Guinea. After all, Brezhnev and Kosygin have viewed the overthrow of Nkrumah, the collapse of Keita, the execution of Communists in the Sudan, and the expulsion of Soviet and East European diplomats from Guinea.[2] In the ideological sphere, they have contended with Ghana's consciencism, Mali's scientific socialism, and various other efforts by Tropical African leaders to blend religion, African socialism, Maoism, and populism with their own interpretations of Marxism-Leninism. Finally, they have watched even the states of national democracy (Ghana, Guinea, and Mali) attempt to play off one great power against another. The concern of African leaders with maximizing their advantage is, of course, understandable to Soviet officials well-schooled in the tactics of *Realpolitik*. However, such understanding will not cause them to overlook the fact that the benefits accruing from a continued adherence to the Khrushchevian policy of investing large amounts of capital and effort in creating mirror-states have been minimal.[3]

Guinea is the only "progressive" Tropical African country whose top leadership has remained the same since the USSR extended diplomatic relations in 1958; it is also the only country of the region where domestic events here not totally invalidated the appelation "state of national democracy,"[4] conferred in the halcyon days of the Khrushchev era. Nevertheless, while the external indicators of current USSR-Guinean relations (military and economic assistance, official visits, etc) do not reveal significant disengagement by Moscow, Guinea is often mentioned in the context of states where "the anti-capitalist slogans of many leaders of the national liberation movement" contributed to "the illusion" that a decisive commitment to socialism would be made.[5] In fact, Guinea is almost invariably listed among countries where transitional difficulties on the road to socialism still loom very large.

These difficulties include the cult of personality, the weak party structure, and an attitude toward economic development whereby "the word is taken for the deed." Regarding "the problem of so-called 'strong personalities,' " Soviet analysts have emphasized their understanding that this is a phenomenon common to all countries where the underdeveloped class structure and general social backwardness result in weak institutions and a power vacuum. They also acknowledge that strong leaders can be progressive. Nevertheless, they fear that a vicious circle may rapidly develop with a leader concentrating power in his own hands because of his doubts about mass activism and dedication, while this very concentration impedes the growth of mass initiative. "Such leaders not only do not attempt to stimulate mass initiative, but rather they act to strictly control it. . . . Paying lip-service to the decisive role of the masses in social life, in practice they assume that progressive political initiative must come from the top, while socioeconomic benefits are 'given' to the masses."[6]

This idea of (possibly) well-meaning leaders hindering the development of mass politization has been a constant theme of Soviet commentary in recent years, largely because of its ramifications for the party structure. Party structures are deemed essential not only to the transition to socialism but also to the continuation of "pro-Soviet" regimes. The overthrow of Nkrumah and Keita is held up as an object lesson to all: leaders must be wary of hurriedly proclaiming "that the developed building of socialism has started," all the while ignoring the preconditions for the program's success: a revolutionary class and its party, developed productive forces, and popular need and respect for democratic institutions.[7]

Soviet theorists find it relatively simple to list the institutional prerequisites for the successful transition to socialism. However, analysis of their writings on individual factors reveals a noticeable uncertainty regarding how institutionalization is to be effected. It is one thing to urge that an activist or vanguard political party be constructed, and quite another to make specific recommendations suitable to African realities. Most Tropical African regimes have constructed mass parties in order to provide a vehicle for socialization and politization of the population in a population where traditionalism and parochialism abound and where there has been little experience with sustained political activity.

It is somewhat surprising that Soviet analysts can acknowledge these barriers to even a mass party, all the while urging African regimes to adopt the more sophisticated vanguard party approach. It is also surprising that the fall of Nkrumah and Keita are attributed to an absence of close links with the masses, while the vanguard party—a rather elitist concept—is recommended to leaders still in power. In theory, the apparent gap could be bridged if the members of the vanguard party were dedicated revolutionaries, capable of, and interested in, forging close links with the general population. However, several writers, including R.A. Ul'ianovskii (deputy head of the International Section of the CPSU Central Committee), have mentioned the bureaucratism and corruption of many party officials—officials united not by a shared commitment to revolutionary ideals, but in defense of their specific group interests and privileged position.[8] The difficulties posed by this phenomenon have been cited as one of the areas to be studied by Soviet scholars in light of the Twenty-Fourth Party Congress.[9]

The problems of economic development were also mentioned in this context, not only because of their obvious implications for the financial health of noncapitalist regimes, but also because of their political ramifications. Ill-founded economic programs could increase popular discontent and also contribute to the continuation of an overwhelmingly parochial, premodern, and tribal orientaton. A proletariat must be created if Tropical African countries are to move eventually from the level of socialist orientation to a higher socialist stage. Although such a transition might not be possible now, progressive leaders must ensure that the conditions for an all-around growth of working-class influence are steadily being established.[10] This is an important aspect of the complexity of creating conditions for socialism in precapitalist societies that third world leaders have underestimated.[11]

Many progressive leaders hastily embarked on industrialization and nationalization, although such radical measures often were unsuited to African realities.

First of all, the overwhelmingly agrarian nature of the economy was ignored, as was the fact that under existing conditions, the development and modernization of agriculture was vital to their economies, both for export and home consumption.[12] Second, progressive leaders sometime failed to keep in mind that socialist aspirations must depend on the level of economic development. Although the "cooperativization of the village on an anticapitalist basis" should be a prominent feature of agrarian programs, the process must be gradual. "A profound study of peasant psychology and daily constructive work, which does not frighten the illiterate peasant with far-reaching aims and political slogans, are the natural and politically justified basis for an organized peasant agrarian movement."[13] Again, the example of Keita's Mali must serve as a warning of the risks of alienating the peasant masses. Progressive leaders must walk a fine line between hampering the development of peasant activism, on the one hand, and making too many political and psychological demands of a still tradition-bound majority, on the other.

African leaders must also take measures to strengthen the proregime orientation of the middle class. While Guinea is praised for having nationalized property belonging to large and medium capitalists, it is also praised for having "bravely exposed" shortcomings of its economy. Such shortcomings have been traceable in Guinea and many other states not only to "objective difficulties in restructuring the economy on fundamentally new principles [but also to the fact that these] are frequently compounded by diverse subjective mistakes which sprang from voluntarism and an inordinate urge to use extra-economic methods to run the economy."[14] Chief among these extra-economic measures are the political repression of the whole medium and small trading and industrial bourgeoisie, and even the bourgeois intelligentsia, in order to proclaim an immediate transition to socialism. This is an erroneous approach, not only because of the shortage of skilled personnel in developing countries, but also because it is an example of "leftist opportunism" to move against middle-class elements that "share common interests with the workers" and strengthen the anti-imperialist front.[15]

African or Soviet Development?

Soviet officials are interested in promoting the stable development of African economies because of a shift in their motivations for giving aid. Thus, whereas, according to the old orthodoxy, the *raison d'être* for giving aid was political, today it is economic, i.e., it represents a search for mutually beneficial cooperation. The USSR will extend aid to countries seeking to develop their raw materials resources or to establish certain industries that might benefit the Soviet trade program (or, in certain cases, its strategic interests). It will no longer act, or insist, upon the claim that economic relations are primarily designed to benefit the development countries and establish mutual trust.[16]

The reasons for this emphasis on economic returns are several. First of all, there is the increasing doubt about the relationship of aid to any type of development. Lack of technical expertise, poor infrastructure, and overextension have impeded the economic success of many programs, not to mention the generation of the substantial good-will toward the USSR that was expected to result. Furthermore, many African countries, such as Guinea, Ghana, Mali and Somalia, have either defaulted on their debt payments, requested long postponements, or disclaimed all responsibility for debts incurred by a previous regime. (It is interesting that the USSR has proven more intransigent on the question of Ghana's debt rescheduling than many Western countries.)

The Soviets have not only objected to the poor economic return from their aid commitment, but also to the absence of political payoff for the USSR. The early expectation that such aid might guarantee support in the United Nations, for example, has been called into question not only by the declining significance of UN notes in the context of superpower relations, but also by the realization that nonalignment had little practical importance for the USSR.

> The policy of nonalignment shows itself, on the one hand . . . in the new states' support for declarations and resolutions on the problems of peace maintenance, disarmament, the rights of man, etc., usually of a broad and general character. On the other hand, the policy of nonalignment constitutes a balancing between the two groups of countries, and an attempt to turn their existing opposition to use and profit.[17]

That nonaligned nations do not necessarily support the USSR vis-à-vis the United States, or worse, China, is indeed galling. However, it is even more upsetting that the developing countries do not appreciate the aid efforts of fraternal socialist countries, but simply accept them as part of the obligation of rich countries to help poor ones. Thus, instead of gratitude, the Soviets receive more and more "one-sided demands" by countries who pay no attention to a state's socioeconomic character, but rather treat all wealthy countries alike.[18]

While it would perhaps be unfair to deny any humanitarian element to recent Soviet aid agreements, it is certainly true that they are increasingly geared to producing what Kosygin calls "mutually advantageous economic relations."[19] Recent agreements with Guinea provide clear examples. For example, in the area of mining, Soviet-Guinean contracts were signed in early 1972 for Soviet aid in the construction of a bauxite mine and in the refurbishing of the ore-handling wharfs at Conakry. In return, the USSR will receive two and one-half million tons of bauxite annually for thirty years, and the port reconstruction project will enable large Soviet ore-carriers (and, possibly, patrol boats) to use it. Similarly, in the general area of trade, many enterprises built in Guinea with Soviet assistance are operated on a cooperative basis.

The increasingly business-like nature of Soviet aid agreements is treated as a boon to developing countries. They can be certain of "stable markets" for their commodities and rest assured that "in no sense" is Soviet economic and technical aid "a matter of charity."[20] If the objection is raised that the USSR seems to be treating the third world as simply a raw materials reserve, Soviet economists can argue, as they have at UNCTAD, that Soviet purchases of manufactures and semimanufactures have been growing (they now constitute about 20 percent of total imports) and will increase even further as quality improves and real incomes in the USSR rise. Furthermore, in many cases, it is in the best interest of the socialist countries to extend aid for the production of a number of labor-intensive industrial products, such as footwear and textiles, to free their own domestic industries for more sophisticated work. Similarly, assisting in the development of chemical and extractive industries could also benefit socialist economies. In sum, the potential for economic relations between socialist nations and

> the developing countries based on the existing division of labor is far from exhausted and continues to expand. However, especially in the more distant future, such new phenomena as the rise in the role of production-oriented forms of collaboration, specialization, and cooperation; joint efforts in the formation of border economic complexes; coordination of effort with the aim of making more complete use of natural resources in the interests of both groups of nations, etc. will become the major directions in the intensification of the division of labor between them.[21]

The USSR is thus very interested in cooperating in certain development efforts that might serve the needs of the Soviet economy. These benefits might be indirect, in that if a "progressive" state were able to generate increased exports, the demand for foreign aid from Moscow might decrease, while the ability to repay debts might increase. In addition, Soviet officials look forward to greater direct benefits from economic development projects that might intensify the existing division of labor between consumer socialist economies (coincidentally searching for export markets) and the raw material producers.

The Horn of Africa in Soviet Strategy

The Horn of Africa can perhaps be cited as one area where some variant of the "classic" pattern of Soviet-Chinese-American competition can be discerned. However, two aspects of this competition are instructive. First, the Horn is strategically important vis-à-vis an area that is of a compelling interest to the three superpowers—the Middle East. Second, each superpower seems to have staked out "its" base in the Horn. The Chinese have Tanzania, the Russians have Somalia, and the United States has Ethiopia. It is interesting that there have been no strong attempts by any power to preempt another's position. While a strategic presence in the Horn is significant, even this region is basically peripheral to the superpowers' larger interests.

Thus, the USSR has not even attempted to "balance" the power and rights that the US has secured in Ethiopia, through the acquisition of base rights in Somalia, for instance. While this may be attributable, in part, to the reluctance of the Somali government to grant such rights, it is instructive that the USSR apparently has not insisted on such an agreement as a precondition of continued relations or of the distribution of huge amounts of aid. The USSR has so far granted almost $90 million in economic aid and $50 million in military aid to Somalia, making the country the largest Soviet aid recipient in Tropical Africa.[22]

It is, of course, true that the USSR has dredged and developed the harbor at Berbera for repair and refueling operations for its ships. It is also true that Soviet military aircraft use Somali airfields and that Soviet personnel have installed a communications facility. However, serveral factors caution against any interpretation of these moves as evidence of a Soviet intention to menace the West or as other than a Soviet attempt to offset an apparently key American pressure point. First of all, there are still over 3500 Americans stationed at the giant US communications facility at Kagnew, compared with the currently accepted estimate of 300 Soviet advisors in Somalia. Second, the 1972 lesson of being expelled from its Egyptian base might have increased the importance of Somalia to the Soviet miitary, but strategists are also wary of any dependence on the facilities of such volatile African and Middle Eastern countries. Third, although naval and air bases can help to compensate for Soviet inferiority in air-craft carriers or sustained air cover, they cannot redress the vulnerability of Soviet supply lines.[23] Fourth, the extremely variegated nature of the states in the Indian Ocean littoral, plus the enormous area concerned, implies the futility of the Soviets even attempting, through base rights, to neutralize NATO's sea-borne strategic missile system.[24] Finally, while the nature of Soviet naval capabilities and the geostrategic environment of the Indian Ocean area mediate against any offensive Soviet posture in subregions such as the Horn, the nature of domestic politics in a country like Somalia also constitutes a hindrance.

For even if one were to accept the debatable point that the Soviets aim at controlling the country, rivalries within the Somali military government repre-sent a constraint of significant proportions. The evidence suggests cleavages between pro-Soviet and pro-Chinese factions, between pro-Western and pro-Communist groups, between those who favor war or detente with Ethiopia, and between those who favor encouraging great power military and economic aid competition and others who fear its effects on Somali sovereignty. President Siad Barre has reacted to these conflicting pressures by opting for the classic zig-zag policy course. For example, 1970 witnessed the expulsion of the Peace Corps and the proclamation of Somalia as a socialist state; 1972 witnessed Siad's visits to both Peking and Moscow,[25] while the friendly reception accorded the new US ambassador indicated some effort at improving Somali-American relations.

The USSR's response to Siad's maneuvers at times suggests Soviet deference to Somali demands rather than Soviet control. For although the Russians retain their dominant position as advisors to the Somali armed forces and as the country's main aid supplier, these positions have not brought proportional influence. References in the Soviet media to Somali "reactionaries"[26] provide some indication of policy disagreements, as do reports by high-level Washington sources that the USSR has been troubled by mounting Somali demands for MIG-21s. In fact, the Soviets face the same dilemmas in planning their military aid program toward Somalia as they do in their economic assistance efforts: how to have leverage without responsibility, how to advise without becoming implicated in Somalia's border disputes, how to give enough assistance to impress Siad (and to some degree, military governments elsewhere) without intensifying the fears of anti-Soviet factions, and how to keep the level of great power competition in the Horn from threatening the general thrust of peaceful coexistence.

The pressure of such multiple dilemmas has produced many situations where the Soviets have reacted to, rather than originated, developments,[27] and where they have assumed an aid burden higher than their apparent "aid for facilities" formula would entail. Furthermore, there is substantial evidence of Soviet vulnerability to increased levels of Somali involvement with the People's Republic of China. For example, the 1971 Chinese loan offer of $110 million elicited a favorable Soviet response a few months later to a previously rejected dam construction project and to the issue of reopening discussions on new arms shipments. In 1971 the USSR also agreed to cancel Somali debts totalling over $2 million and to extend the debt repayment schedule by five years.[28] Informed analysts feel that these offers reflect a Soviet desire to appear responsive without assuming additional commitments to the military. They also reflect a degree of Soviet control over the evolution of its relations with Somalia that is far from all-encompassing.

This minimal control also extends to the matter of Somali disputes with Kenya and, especially, Ethiopia. The extent of the conflict is of significant concern to the USSR. As Somalia's major arms supplier, she could be implicated in violence that might upset the delicate balance in the Horn or threaten the sovereignty of Ethiopia, an important American ally and Western communications center. Thus, even though Somalia confronts the second-largest army in Black Africa (35,000 men) and perhaps the largest air force (2100), ten years of Soviet military assistance have seen the development of only a 17,000-man Somali army and a 350-man air force. Somali requests for sophisticated equipment have frequently been denied, while much of what has been granted seems to be geared more toward promoting an image of Soviet responsiveness than toward developing a viable Somali defense system.[29] Similarly, Moscow's aid policies have aimed at securing port facilities rather than bringing about anything even approaching parity between Somalia and Ethiopia in terms of armed forces, equipment, or volume of military and economic assistance. By its policies and diplomatic efforts, the USSR has attempted to minimize the level of conflict between the two African countries and between the superpowers who are their sponsors.

Another indication of the nonoffensive character of Soviet Indian Ocean policy vis-à-vis the Horn is that while the USSR has attempted to establish itself as Somalia's patron, it has not made the rejection of deals with the United States or the People's Republic a precondition of the relationship's continuance.[30] Nor has the USSR attempted to pre-empt or even challenge America's relationship with the Ethiopian regime or that of China with Nyerere's government. This can, perhaps, be cited as a reflection of the changed character of superpower relations since the Moscow, Peking, and Washington summits and of the muting of cold war postures and the superpower preoccupation with domestic and/or intra-alliance difficulties that the past few years have witnessed.

However, another more compelling explanation derives from strategic considerations. While a strategic presence in the Horn and the Indian Ocean is significant, this region remains somewhat peripheral to the superpowers' larger interests. Naval considerations do not figure prominently in the security efforts of the People's Republic of China; as for the United States, even though it has been far more active in the Indian Ocean region than the USSR in terms of the establishment of bases and port facilities, arms shipments, military advisors and training, and ship visits,[31] most experts argue that the area is not vital to Western or even Soviet nuclear deterrence.

Guerrillas

Soviet involvement with liberation movements in southern Africa is often cited not only as proof of Moscow's enduring dedication to assisting the causes of self-determination, but also as evidence that the USSR remains interested in promoting potentially beneficial instability. However, it can be argued that Soviet support is more verbal than material and that the level of material support is carefully calculated to provide some basis for Soviet rhetorical claims and to offset Chinese aid, while falling short of the levels of aid needed to affect significantly the success prospects of the liberation movements. In fact, the modesty of both Chinese and Soviet aid, combined with their continued support of rival factions within the same territories, suggests that the motivations for this aid are geared more toward the game of superpower relations than toward the needs of the guerrillas. As Christian Potholm remarked, "The USSR and China, with far more modest stakes in the status quo [than the Western powers], have nevertheless regarded its alteration as a tertiary or even marginal goal of their foreign policy."[32]

The USSR cannot, of course, ignore the liberation movements. To do so would, first of all, entail irritating many African governments which, through the Organization of African Unity, provide verbal and monetary support for several liberation groups.[33]   Since the establishment of stable government-to-government relations has replaced the creation of mirror-systems as a key characteristic of Soviet third world policy, the attitudes of governments in power remain important. Second, subjection of proposed guerrilla support policies to the oft-mentioned cost-benefit analysis would demonstrate that it is a relatively low-cost, low-risk method of gaining substantial symbolic gains: it helps the USSR to counterbalance China's claim to being the most sincere friend of third world liberation; it also helps Moscow to express its (at least verbal) distaste for the United States position of support for the status quo. Finally, supporting African guerrillas can help Moscow gain, or at least maintain, influence among the more significant groups in the Middle East.

However, just as there are impetuses to assisting African liberation movements, so there are constraints on the level and nature of that assistance. Host governments, such as Tanzania and Zambia, worry about policing the rebels and maintaining control. The best Western intelligence estimates hold that a real explosion in southern Africa, for example, will not occur for at least thirty years (there is no evidence to suggest that the Soviets are any more hopeful); as a result, the optimism and sense of momentum that often attract superpower commitment are somehow lacking. Similarly, because of internal problems or, in the case of Cabral, alleged Portuguese complicity, the African liberation movements have not been able to produce leaders capable of welding a cohesive organizational structure. Of course, it may be arqued that the Communist rivals' practice of supporting competing factions within the same national movement has only intensified these barriers to success. However, the fact that Moscow and Peking have nonetheless continued these tactics is in itself instructive.

This is not to imply that the Communist powers have any conscious policy of employing "splittist" tactics to decrease the success prospects of the various African liberation movements. Nevertheless, their current methods certainly suggest a greater concern with using these movements as an arena for carrying out the Sino-Soviet dispute than with subordinating this goal to that of ensuring the liberation of another vast segment of the world's oppressed peoples. Similarly, the USSR—and, China specialists would argue, the PRC as well—have further subordinated any ideological commitment to third world revolution to the cause of not jeopardizing detente with the United States. The umbrella of detente has, of course, proved to be rather elastic, able to accommodate superpower meddling in areas within their "own" preserves, or in the Middle East, which seems to have been consciously or unconsciously set aside as an area where the classic cold war competition can continue. However, one suspects that the putative "gentleman's agreement" atmosphere that has allowed for such an exemption has extended to limitations on the degree of rivalry here, as well as to some decision to keep other conflict areas to a minimum. The benefits of supporting the rebels in Portuguese and southern Africa would not offset the instability quotient it would entail for the current state of superpower relations: the rebels' chances of early success are low; the area is not rich in oil or natural gas (the current great power preoccupations), and widespread fighting might impel the United States to strengthen its commitment to the established governments because of direct concern with its existing defense network or with the defense and/or economic well-being of its NATO allies Portugal and, especially, Great Britain. In sum, it is in Moscow's best interests that the guerrillas remain in a no-win, no-lose situation.

Consequently, the USSR has confined its assistance efforts to large doses of rhetoric, modest amounts of military and financial aid, and the training of relatively small numbers of guerrillas in the USSR. On the rhetorical side, we note the promise of one Soviet journalist that "for all the diversity of the existing outstanding international problems, the USSR regards that of eliminating the vestiges of colonialism and eradicating racialism as one of the most pressing."[34] We also note the oft-repeated assurance that the new trends in Soviet-American relations "not only do not run counter to the interests of other peoples, but correspond to these interests."[35] Such concern with rhetoric and symbolic gestures has also conditioned consistently stirring appeals by Soviet United Nations delegates on behalf of Africa's oppressed peoples.

Meanwhile, the level of Soviet material assistance for any African liberation group does not appear to have exceeded 70,000-100,000 dollars per year. Military hardware supplied has been limited both in quantity and in sophistication, with the PAIGC (African Party for the Liberation of Guinea and Cape Verde) receiving the best equipment (gunboats, mortars, and some rockets) as much because of Moscow's commitment to protect Seku Toure's government from another Portuguese invasion as because of a concern with the victory prospects of the PAIGC. Moscow has also provided military training for hundreds of guerrillas who are flown to the USSR.

It has been argued in Moscow's (and China's) defense that the guerrillas have been provided with as much material and military assistance as they can absorb, given their inexperience and small numbers of trained military personnel. However, it can be suggested that such an assertion begs the question of why the Communist powers are not doing more, are/not despatching their own training and support personnel to the area in order to increase the guerrilla movements' absorptive capacities. They have not undertaken such a commitment precisely because, rhetoric to the contrary, the success of the African liberation groups is a low priority that in no way would compensate for the high risks of endangering the flowering of detente.

Sino-Soviet Rivalry

In discussing the prospects for change in the current minimal interest index of Soviet-African relations, the tripolar nature of international politics quite naturally suggests possibly disruptive situations arising from a surge in Tropical African interest by any one of the rivals. While it can quite safely be stated that in the case of the United States, such a development is unlikely, the likelihood of an intensified Chinese concern—and, more important, of a Soviet response—deserves further scrutiny.

A few years ago, there was a belief—and, among some, a hope—that rivalry between the USSR and the People's Republic of China would result in preemptive aid efforts throughout the third world, including Tropical Africa. It was anticipated that this might help the African countries to replace foreign air lost when the cold war atmosphere between the United States and the Soviet Union warmed up considerably (or at least was focused elsewhere). However, the expected degree of rivalry in the third world has not materialized, basically because the USSR has not chosen to react in kind to Chinese assistance offers. In fact, it would seem that the nature of the Sino-Soviet dispute has made it imperative for both sides to concentrate their efforts at winning in Washington or in areas close to home.

Department of State figures can, of course, be cited in support of the argument that China had launched a dramatic aid effort in Tropical Africa; similarly, the case of Somalia can be listed as proof that the anticipated Sino-Soviet rivalry is taking place. However, many aspects of this situation are instructive. Thus, an analysis of Chinese and Soviet cumulative aid extensions from 1954-72 reveals that while the People's Republic of China has accorded Tropical Africa nearly half of its aid extensions, the USSR has directed less than 10 percent of its aid to this area.[36] Furthermore, China allocated at least one-third of its $1.3 billion African aid total to the construction of the Tanzam Railway. While there may have been "revolutionist components" to this decision, such as encouraging national liberation movements and validating Chinese anti-American and revolutionary ideological tenets,[37] it remains a showcase project with a combination of anticipated political and symbolic benefits remarkably similar to those which the Soviet Union expected from the $350 million Aswan Dam project. In fact, it may be argued that Tanzam is to the PRC as Aswan was to the USSR: a one-time project designed to confer prestige upon a donor attempting to exploit third world loyalties in order to further its position vis-à-vis other great powers. Aswan was very helpful to Soviet 1950s plans to assert its right to enter previously exclusively Western preserves; Tanzam was helpful to the PRC in the final stages of its campaign to gain UN membership and superpower status. Similarly, just as the noninclusion of Africa in American alliance-building efforts increased its significance for Moscow's effort in the fifties, so declining America and Soviet interest in this area from the mid-1950s on heightened its attraction for the People's Republic

The validity of the Tanzam/Aswan comparison is heightened by a survey of recent Chinese activities. Thus, while in 1972, sub-Saharan African accounted for $210 million of the total $499 million Chinese aid extensions, these extensions were confined to five states (Burundi, Dahomey, Malagasy Republic, Rwanda, and Togo). These states had never before received economic aid from Communist countries, as much because of Communist criticism of their political complexion as because of the anti-Communist orientation that complexion dictated. That the attitude of the PRC changed in 1972, while the nature of these African regimes remained relatively constant, is suggestive of the transformation in many aspects of China's African policy. In Rwanda and Burundi, for example, the Chinese have shifted from an emphasis on supporting revolutionary opposition to a stress on stable relations with the established governments. Meanwhile, China has learned to reconcile her support for South African guerrilla movements with her support for the government of the Malagasy Republic, a government convinced that trade with the existing South African leadership offers her only hope for survival.

The admission of the People's Republic of China to the United Nations, the improvement in relations with the United States, and the further progress toward detente dictated by the continued military build-up along the Sino-Soviet border have gone far toward promoting "great-power-type" behavior by Peking in the third world arena in the seventies. As one analyst noted recently: "Having failed to achieve dependency relations by revolutionary means—and given a changed international context after 1971—the Chinese turned to a more flexible policy and worked to expand influence through more conventional bilateral trade and aid agreements."[38] Thus, recent Chinese diplomatic and aid activity indicates an awareness of the theory-reality gap in Africa and, more important, a certain willingness to attempt to bridge it. However, like the USSR and the US, the PRC's African efforts have been undertaken in the context of a search for more promising opportunities elsewhere.

The Energy Factor

A survey of current superpower preoccupations reveals only one that might involve Africa, and that is the concern for energy sources, more specifically, oil. However, it has been made implicitly and explicitly clear to all powers that a preemptive competition for petroleum would be highly risky indeed. Officials in Washington seem very hopeful that this will not take place at all; that it would not involve Tropical Africa is accepted as a certainty.

Nigeria is the only sub-Saharan African country with substantial proven petroleum reserves. But a combination of domestic and international factors seem to be operating to remove these reserves from the arena of great power competition. Regarding domestic factors, we find General Gowan's government remaining solidly pro-Western in its trade and political orientation. While the

USSR may have gained gratitude and some trade entree as a result of its significant assistance during the Nigerian civil war, tangible results seem to have been limited. Indeed, the fact that even in 1970, before the war was over, Nigeria ranked as America's largest trading partner in Tropical Africa indicates that the country's pro-Western orientation was sufficiently strong to withstand Washington's noninvolvement policy vis-à-vis the Biafran conflict.[39]

Furthermore, Nigeria is interested in amassing hard currency reserves and in acquiring sophisticated industrial and oil-processing equipment and technological assistance. Oil deals with the West (including the United States, for whom Nigeria is currently the second-largest crude oil supplier) not only can entail advanced technical training and equipment, but also revenues of such magnitude that in 1972, Nigeria joined the "billion-dollars-a-year" club.[40] The USSR, which is now and will remain for the foreseeable future, a net exporter of oil, does not need to participate in the buyers' scramble that made Nigeria's revenue position possible; its general insistence on barter deals with the few countries from whom it does buy energy sources would not be acceptable to Gowan's government. Finally, considerations of its limited tanker capacity plus the costs of transporting oil from Nigeria serve further to reduce Moscow's interest. The USSR is, of course, as willing as any other power to set economic considerations aside if anticipated strategic and/or political benefits would seem to warrant it. However, the persistence of "contradictory factors" in determining Nigeria's socio-economic and political course does not offer substantial grounds for optimism.[41]

Perspective and Prognosis

This survey of current Soviet-African relations and potential incentives to increased involvement has revealed no factor that would significantly disturb the placidity of Moscow's perspective on this area. Soviet interest in Nigerian oil is tempered by an awareness of financial and political realities, as is the level of its dedication to the development of "progressive" states such as Guinea. Similarly, any ideas of increasing its commitment to the African liberation movements or waging any over-all competition with the People's Republic of China in the sub-Saharan region are tempered by a very real awareness of the danger of jeopardizing the relative amicability of Soviet-American relations in exchange for few tangible gains. To the superpowers in the seventies, Tropical Africa's typically low strategic significance has been even further minimzed.

Meanwhile, the prospects of—or, indeed, interest in—securing ideological or cold war allies has been reduced not only by the record of these new states, but also by the changed nature of great power goals. In an era when the minimization of conflict and the search for "mutually advantageous cooperation" have emerged as the prime determinants of Soviet American relations, the general importance of the Third World to either or both superpowers has declined. Tropical Africa apparently has been assigned the lowest value of all. The seventies are witnessing not only reduced aid commitments to this region, but a rather revealing effort by spokesmen in Washington and Moscow to downplay the significance of any lingering commitments that they do have. American officials emphasize their interest in promoting economic stability and debt repayment potential; Soviet commentators echo this view. Furthermore, in contrast to the early sixties, when the nature of superpower relations seemed to impel leaders on both sides to list even the slightest ideological shift or change in foreign visit pattern by an African leader as evidence of a great victory by one system or the other, Soviet analysts now criticize any American perception that the socialist orientation of some African states is communism.[42]

The overt nature of the current pessimism and indifference—and the fact that these attitudes have been building for several years—combine to convince the observer of the minimal prospects for any dramatic, or even significant, increase in superpower interest in Tropical Africa.

Notes

1. G.A. Arbatov, "American Foreign Policy at the Threshold of the 1970s," *SShA,* no. 1 (January 1970), pp. 21-34, trans. *USA* (JPRS 49934, 26 February 1970), p. 18.

2. Recently, the Guinean government expelled a Rumanian official because of his inability to promise the return of Nkrumah's body.

3. Helen Desfosses Cohn, "Soviet-American Relations and the African Arena," *Survey,* no. 1 (186) (Winter 1973), p. 155.

4. R. Alexeyev, "Nigeria on the Road of National Development," *International Affairs,* no. 3 (1972), p. 62; V. Gorodnov and N. Kosukhin, "In the Somali Democratic Republic," *International Affairs,* no. 5 (1972), p. 106.

5. V. Tyagunenko, "Nekotorye problemy natsional 'no-osvoboditel'nikh revoliutsii v svete leninizma" [Certain Problems of the National-Liberation Revolutions in the light of Leninism], *Mirovaya ekonomika i mezhdunarodnye otnosheniia,* no. 11 (1972), p. 114.

6. K. Brutents, "Pravyashchaya revoliutsionnaya democratiya i nekotorye cherty prakticheskoi deyatel'nosti" [Ruling Revolutionary Democracy: Certain Characteristics of Practical Activity], *Mirovaya ekonomika i mezhdunarodnye otnosheniia,* no. 11 (1972), p. 114.

7. M.B. Mitin (ed.), *Leninizm i bor'ba protiv burzhuaznoi ideologii i anti-Kommunizma na sovremennom etape* [Leninism and the Struggle Against Bourgeois Ideology and Anti-Communism in the Present Stage] (Moscow, 1970), pp. 180-97.

8. R.A. Ul'ianovskii, "Leninism, Soviet Experience, and the Newly-Free

Countries II," *New Times,* no. 2 (13 January 1971), p. 23; also Brutents, p. 114.

9. "XXIV s'ezd KPSS i problemy natsional'no-osvoboditel'nogo dvizheniia" [The 24th CPSU Congress and the Problems of the National-Liberation Movement], *Narody Azii i Afriki,* no. 3 (1971), pp. 3-14, especially p. 12.

10. See R.A. Ul'ianovskii, "Sovremennyi etap natsional'no-osvoboditel'nogo dvizheniia i krestyanstvo I" [The Current Epoch of the National-Liberation Movement and the Peasantry], *Mirovaya ekonomika i mezhdunarodnye otnosheniia,* no. 5 (1971), pp. 91-194.

11. *Izvestia,* 28 April 1971.

12. Ul'ianovskii, "Leninism and the Newly-Free Countries," p. 22.

13. R.A. Ul'ianovskii, "Sovremennyi etap natsional'no-osvoboditel'nogo dvizheniia i krestyanstvo II" [The Current Epoch of the National-Liberation Movement and the Peasantry], *Mirovaya ekonomika i mezhdunarodnye otnosheniia,* no. 6 (1971), p. 89.

14. A. Kiva, "Experience of Non-Capitalist Development in Africa," *International Affairs,* no. 7 (1972), p. 29; also *Pravda,* 14 May 1972.

15. R.A. Ul'ianovskii, "Nekotorye voprosy nekapitalisticheskogo razvitiia" [Certain Questions of Non-Capitalist, Development], *Kommunist,* no. 4 (1971), p. 107.

16. Cf. *International Affairs,* no. 10 (1959), p. 71, cited in David Morison, "Tropical Africa: The New Soviet Outlook," *Mizan,* vol. 13, no. 1 (August 1971), p. 53.

17. A.A. Lavrishchev (ed.), *Razvivaiushchiesia strany v mirovoi politike* [The Developing Countries in World Politics], (Moscow 1970), pp. 209-10.

18. V. Smirnov, "An Important Factor in the Developing Countries' Economic Progress," *Foreign Trade,* no. 3 (1971), p. 17.

19. *Pravda,* 7 April 1971.

20. "Interview with V. Sergeyev, Vice-Chairman of the USSR State Committee for Foreign Economic Relations," *New Times,* no. 3 (15 January 1971), p. 18.

21. L. Zevin, "Voprosy povysheniia ustoichivosti i effektivnosti ekonomicheskikh sviazei SSSR s razvivaiushchimisia stranami" [Problems of Increasing the Stability and Effectiveness of Economic Relations between the USSR and the Developing Countries], *Planovoe Khoziaistrvo,* no. 7 (1971), p. 26.

22. Note that in 1971 China completed a number of projects and offered a new loan of $110 million, thereby outstripping Moscow's contribution.

23. Curt Gasteyger, "Moscow and the Mediterranean," *Foreign Affairs* 46 (July, 1968): 680-81.

24. Michael McGwire, "The Mediterranean and Soviet Naval Interests," *International Journal* 27 (Autumn 1972): 527.

25. *The Soviet Analyst* (3 August 1972) reported that the Chinese have been invited to construct the strategic 650-mile Beled Wen-Burao highway and the sports center in Mogadiscio—both projects that Moscow wanted.

26. Moscow Radio Peace and Progress, 26 January 1971.
27. See Uri Ra'anan, *The USSR Arms the Third World: Case Studies in Soviet Foreign Policy* (Cambridge, Mass., 1969), p. 10.
28. Mogadiscio Radio, 4 March 1971.
29. Wynfred Joshua and Stephen P. Gibert, *Arms for the Third World* (Baltimore, 1969), p. 46.
30. The Chinese are reported to have offered Somalia an arms deal in 1973, provided they did not accept similar aid from other powers.
31. *New York Times,* 18 June 1973.
32. Christian Potholm, "After Many a Summer? The Possibilities of Political Change in South Africa," World Politics 24 (July 1972): 634-35.
33. See V.G. Solodovnikov, "Afrika: yedinstvo, nezavisimost', razvitie" [Africa's Unity, Independence, Development], *Azia i Afrika Segodnya,* no. 5 (May 1973), p. 2.
34. V. Katin, "Vo imya spravedlivosti" [In the Name of Justice], *Azia i Afrika Segodnya,* no. 4 (April 1973), p. 12.
35. *Pravda,* 22 July 1973, p. 4.
36. Bureau of Intelligence and Research, Department of State, *Communist States and Developing Countries: Aid and Trade in 1972* (Washington, D.C., 1973), pp. 4-5.
37. Warren Weinstein, "The Evolution of Chinese Policy in Central Africa: 1960-1973." Paper presented to the Conference on Sino-Soviet Aid to Africa (New York, 1973), p. 17 (mimeo).
38. Bruce D. Larkin, *China and Africa, 1949-1970* (Berkeley, California, 1971), pp. 101-2.
39. See *United States Foreign Policy, 1969-1970. A Report of the Secretary of State* (Washington, D.C., 1971), pp. 138-40.
40. "The Billionaire Governments," *Petroleum Press Service* 39 (September 1972): p. 322.
41. N. Kochakova, "Skol'ko rabochikh v Nigerii?" [How Many Workers in Nigeria?], *Azia i Afrika Segodnya,* no. 6 (1973), p. 14.
42. V. Kudryavtsev, "Washington and Africa," *SShA,* no. 4 (April 1970), trans. *USA: Economics, Politics, Ideology* (JPRS 50637), 2 June 1970, p. 109.

15

The Soviet Role in the Middle East
Roger E. Kanet

During the course of the past two decades the Soviet Union has developed from an isolated bastion of Stalinist socialism with virtually no contacts with areas outside its own sphere of domination into a major world power with interests spanning most of the globe. A significant aspect of this increased role of the Soviet Union has been the expansion of Soviet interest and contacts with the developing countries of Africa, Asia, and Latin America. The focus of this chapter will be on the Soviet policy of influence-building in the Middle East during the past two decades. In order to place the Middle East in proper perspective in Soviet foreign policy, however, it will be necessary to survey briefly the development of Soviet policy to the developing world.

At the time of Stalin's death in 1953, Soviet contacts with the newly-independent states of Asia and Africa were virtually nonexistent. The basic Soviet reaction to the establishment of national governments in such countries as India, Burma, and the Philippines in the immediate postwar period was to accuse the new national leaders of continued dependence on the former colonial powers. Even such men as Nehru in India and later Nasser in Egypt and Nkrumah in Ghana were referred to as "lackeys of the imperialists."[1] During the course of the Korean War, however, Soviet views of the developing countries began to moderate as it became obvious that governments such as that of India were not following a policy line determined in London or Washington. By 1952 the Soviets began to speak about the possibilities of expanding their relations—in particular their economic contacts—with some of the developing countries.[2] However, it was not until after the death of Stalin in 1953 that policy toward the developing countries began to shift. By then it had become clear not only that the Stalinist categorization of the new states as appendages of the imperialists was not accurate, but also that the past attempts to influence developments in the colonial and excolonial world by support for violent revolution had not succeeded.

The most dramatic indication of the shift in Soviet policy came in 1954, when Khrushchev and Bulganin made their celebrated tour through several Asian countries emphasizing the friendship of the Soviet Union for the new states. A concrete immediate result of this change in policy was the initiation of the Soviet program of economic assistance, which by the end of 1972 had resulted in the extension of Soviet credits totalling more than $8.2 billion to the developing countries.[3] In addition, by 1956 the Soviets had begun a major reinterpretation of those elements of official Marxism-Leninism that related to decolonization, the role of the developing countries in world politics, and

297

the construction of scientific socialism in agrarian societies.[4] The developing countries were now viewed as an essential element of a worldwide "peace zone" consisting of the socialist countries, the workers in the capitalist West, and the neutralist states of Asia and Africa that had refused to join military blocs.[5]

The initial Soviet reaction to prospects in the developing countries was one of extreme optimism concerning the rapidity with which the new states were likely to introduce foreign policies in line with that of the USSR and to create the domestic conditions conducive to the development of socialism of the Soviet variety. By the mid-sixties, however, even before the political demise of Khrushchev, Soviet commentators began to lament the lack of progress in both of these realms in most developing countries. As they became more familiar with the realities of the developing world, Soviet specialists became much less sanguine concerning the prospects for rapid economic development or the applicability of the Soviet model of development to the vast majority of the countries of Asia and Africa.[6] The coups against some of the major "friends" of the Soviets—Ben Bella in Algeria, Nkrumah in Ghana, and Keita in Mali—and the rise to power of the military in most of the countries of Africa went far to undermine Soviet optimism.

Since the mid-sixties the Soviets have increasingly focused their interest on two specific geographic regions, the Middle East and South Asia, which are geographically and strategically important to the Soviets and in which regional political problems have provided them with opportunities to expand their contacts and influence.[7]

The Soviet Union and the Middle East
Under Lenin and Stalin

Although major Soviet interest in the Middle East has been evidenced only during the past two decades, both tsarist Russia and the Soviet Union had shown indications of concern for the area on several occasions during the past century. Throughout the latter portion of the nineteenth century Russia made efforts to expand its influence into the areas to the south of its empire, where it came into conflict with the British, who were already entrenched there. During World War I the secret treaties entered into by Russia with her Western allies provided for Russian control of the Dardanelles and significant portions of the Ottoman Empire.

Soon after their seizure of power in 1917 the new Bolshevik government, in addition to calling upon the Moslems of the Russian Empire to support the new government, also appealed to the Moslems of the East—among whom the Persians, Turks, Arabs and (by some quirk) Hindus were included—to overthrow their imperialist rulers.[8] In September 1920, at a congress of the peoples of the East called by the Soviets in Baku, a majority of the delegates (excluding those from Russia itself) came from the Middle East, where the Soviets were obviously interested in supporting nationalist uprisings against Western— especially British—colonialism. During the 1920s the Soviets developed political and economic relations with a few of the countries of the Middle East.[9] By the end of the decade, however, even this minimal contact was cut off as the Soviets concentrated on the internal development of their country during the period of forced collectivization and rapid industrialization and, by the mid-thirties, were concerned primarily with the dangers presented by the rise of Nazi Germany.[10]

The next major indication of Soviet interest in the area did not come until the end of the Second World War in 1945, when the Soviets made three attempts to expand their influence into the area. The first of these was the attempt to maintain control over northern Iran, which had been occupied by Soviet troops, in cooperation with the British, early in the war in order to prevent a Facist coup and to keep open the major communications link between the Soviet Union and the West. At the end of the war Soviet troops remained in northern Iran, where Communist regimes were established in the provinces of Kurdistan and Azerbaijan. Not until the US threatened to intervene against the Soviet occupation and the Iranians signed an agreement to provide the Soviets with oil (never ratified by the Iranian parliament), were the troops withdrawn in early 1946.[11]

A second effort to expand Soviet influence into the Middle East occurred in 1945 and 1946 when the Soviets attempted to obtain a trusteeship over the territory that is now Libya. In supporting the Soviet arguments, Foreign Minister Molotov pointed to the losses that the Soviets had suffered in the war (the trust territory was apparently viewed in part as compensation for these losses) and the benefits that Soviet shipping would gain by the acquisition of a naval base in the eastern Mediterranean. Both Britain and the United States opposed the granting of a trust territory in North Africa to the Soviets, and the area was returned to Italy, the former colonial ruler, to administer on behalf of the United Nations.[12]

The major effort of the Soviets to expand their influence into the territories south of the USSR consisted of the pressures on Turkey for a return of Kars and Ardahan (two small areas in eastern Turkey that had been incorporated into the Turkish state at the time of the Russian Revolution, forty years after they had been seized by tsarist Russia) and for participation in control over the Dardanelles. These pressures were resisted by the Turks, and in 1947 the United States, through the Truman Doctrine which promised US support to any country faced with internal or external communist "aggression," came to the assistance of Turkey.[13]

In addition to these efforts to expand their own influence in the Middle East area, the Soviets also supported the creation of an independent Jewish state in Palestine, presumably because this was viewed as a weakening of the influence of the British in the area. In fact, the USSR was the first state to grant formal diplomatic recognition to Israel.[14] Within a short time, however, Soviet-Israeli relations began to sour as it became evident that the leaders of Israel were not likely to follow the lead of the Soviets in foreign policy and when a domestic policy of anti-Semitism was introduced in the Soviet Union.

The Middle East Rediscovered: Soviet Policy After Stalin

Although the Soviet government had maintained some interest in the Middle East in the period prior to Stalin's death, this area had never been high on the list of Soviet priorities. Internal control and development, security in Europe, and a consolidation of Soviet gains in the immediate postwar period were all far more important to the Soviet leadership. However, by 1953-54, when the new Soviet leadership began to reassess its relationships with the emerging states of Asia and Africa, the Middle East exercised an immediate attraction. The primary interest of the Soviets in the post-Stalin period was the reduction of US influence in the area. This influence was most tangibly represented by US military involvement and by the alliance system that the Americans were in the process of forming. Turkey, Iran, Iraq, and Pakistan had already joined the anti-Soviet military pacts that Secretary of State Dulles was creating, and US military power was present along the southern borders of the Soviet Union. In addition, Egypt continued to be under pressure to join the Baghdad Pact and the US alliance system.

The first major opportunity for the Soviets to develop their contacts with the countries of the Middle East arose in 1955, when the United States refused to supply the Egyptians with the military equipment they felt necessary to maintain their security. The Soviets, through Czechoslovakia, provided the Egyptians with approximately $250 million worth of military equipment, including tanks and planes.[15] In the summer of 1956, US Secretary of State John Foster Dulles notified the Egyptians that the earlier US offer of loans to help fund the construction of the Aswan Dam was rescinded. The immediate response of President Nasser was the nationalization of the Suez Canal in order to use the income to finance the dam. In November, when England, France, and Israel attacked Egypt, the Soviets were unable to do more than provide verbal support for the Egyptians. Not until the British, French and Israeli had agreed to withdraw—primarily as a result of US pressure—did Khrushchev issue his threats to rain rockets down on Paris and London and to send Soviet "volunteers" to assist the Arabs. Even though the Soviets did not provide concrete assistance to the Egyptians during the crisis, they have claimed that their intervention on the side of Egypt was the decisive factor in preventing an "imperialist" victory.

Table 15-1
Soviet Economic Assistance to North Africa and Middle East
(In Millions of US dollars)

	1954-72	1971	1972
Afghanistan	826	5	121
Algeria	421	189	–
Egypt	1198	196	–
Iran	562	–	–
Iraq	549	222	–
Morocco	88	–	–
Syria	317	–	84
Tunisia	34	–	–
Turkey	534	–	158
Yemen (Aden)	14	–	–
Yeman (Sana)	92	–	–
Total	4635	612	363

Source: US Department of State, Bureau of Intelligence and Research, *Communist States and Developing Countries: Aid and Trade in 1972.* Research Study, RECS-10, June 15, 1973, appendix, table 1. See also, Charles B. McLane, *Soviet-Middle East Relations* (London: Central Asian Research Centre; distributed by Columbia University Press, 1973), p. 120, where the figures provided differ somewhat (especially for Turkey and Egypt).

In the years immediately following the Suez Crisis, the Soviets initiated a policy of economic assistance to the countries of the Middle East. By the end of 1960 credits totalling more than $800 million had been promised, including $500 million to Egypt.[16] The first of these major projects was a credit of $98 million to Syria in September 1957 for various construction projects, followed the next year by credits to Egypt of $175 and $100 million for the construction of various industrial projects and the first stage of the Aswan Dam. Since that time credits have played an important role in Soviet policy toward the countries of the Middle East. By the early 1960s, for example, the Soviet leadership began to make efforts to wean away from US tutelage those Middle Eastern countries that had tied themselves closely to the United States during the immediate postwar period. All of the countries of the so-called Northern Tier (Turkey, Iraq, Iran, and Pakistan) had initially joined the American alliances, but the overthrow of the pro-Western regime of Nuri-as-Said in Iraq in 1958 resulted in the withdrawal of Iraq from the Baghdad Pact.

In its relations with the other countries the Soviet Union shifted from its past policy of threats and intimidation to one of friendship buttressed by offers

economic and technical assistance (in the case of Iran, Soviet weapons were
even supplied). Obviously the coincidence of Soviet interests with those of
these US allies resulted in a major shift in the relationships between them. By
the early 1960s the Soviet Union was no longer seen as a menace to the
security of Iran and Turkey, as it had been in the years immediately following
World War II. In addition, reliance on the United States for both economic
and military assistance had developed a relationship of dependence which the
leaders of these countries wished to reduce. The new Soviet initiatives were
favorably received by the countries along the southern borders of the USSR;
although they continue to remain within the framework of the US alliance
system, they have improved their relations with the Soviets significantly over
the past decade.[17]

Throughout the remainder of the Middle East during the period between
the Suez Crisis of 1956 and the Arab-Israeli War of 1967 the Soviets concentrated their efforts on a few countries. Most important was the development
of relations between the Soviet Union and Egypt (renamed the United Arab
Republic during this period). However, in spite of the development of cordial
relations between the USSR and Egypt after 1956 and a major commitment
of Soviet resources to the defense of Egypt, the construction of the Aswan
Dam, and the development of industry, a number of issues continued to cloud
this relationship in the early sixties. Most important was the treatment of
Egyptian Communists (and of those in Syria during the short-lived union of
Egypt and Syria) by Nasser's government. During 1958 and 1959, President
Nasser carried out a major propaganda campaign against communism in which
he even accused the Soviets of trying to create a "Red Fertile Crescent."[18]
By 1960, however, this dispute subsided and relations between the two countries developed along favorable lines, in spite of some problems concerning
the continued incarceration of Egyptian Communists and serious lags in the
completion of the first stage of the Aswan Dam.[19]

Until the outbreak of the war between Israel and the Arab states in 1967,
Soviet-Egyptian relations continued to remain cordial. Reforms, especially
in the agrarian sector, and the growth of the state sector of the economy were
viewed by Soviet commentators as indications of the progressive nature of
the regime. One of the major Soviet specialists on developing countries went
so far as to argue that Egypt's leaders were "revolutionary democrats who
understand the necessity of turning the anticolonialist revolution into an
anticapitalist one."[20] In 1965 the Egyptian Communist party was officially
dissolved. This was apparently in response to the recommendations of the
Soviets that Communists need not form independent parties, but should rather
cooperate with the single-party nationalist regimes that had been established
throughout Asia and Africa. Since these regimes were viewed as truly progressive, the recommended policy was to work from within them.[21]

In addition to Egypt, the other major targets of Soviet interest among the

Arab states during the period 1956–67 were Iraq, Syria, and Yemen (San'a).
In Iraq the overthrow of the pro-Western government in 1958 brought to power
a regime viewed by the Soviets as progressive. One of the first acts of the new
government of Kassem was the withdrawal of Iraq from the Baghdad Pact.
The Soviets soon provided the new Iraqi government with a major credit of $139
million for various agricultural and industrial projects, as well as military assistance. However, the relations between the two countries soon soured as Kassem
turned on his domestic Communist supporters and as the Kurdish rebellion,
which was viewed sympathetically by the Soviets, provided a major challenge
to the territorial integrity of Iraq. When Kassem was overthrown by the rightist
Ba'athists in 1963, the local Communists were massacred and Soviet-Iraqi relations deteriorated even more. However, an additional coup in November 1963,
which brought to power a more moderate military junta, brought about an
improvement in the relationship of the two countries. However, the issue of
Soviet sympathy for the Kurdish rebels continued to cloud the development
of cordial relations.[22]

In general, the instability that characterized Iraq's internal politics during
the decade after the overthrow of the monarchy made it extremely difficult
for the Soviets to conduct a long-range foreign policy vis-à-vis the country. In
spite of this, the Soviets continued to provide military and economic assistance
throughout most of this period in an effort to maintain some influence in the
country.

Soviet relations with Syria have tended to follow a pattern similar to that
with Iraq, for Syria also has suffered from endemic political instability during
the past two decades. In spite of the shifts in internal Syrian politics, however,
the Soviets attempted to maintain favorable relations with the successive
regimes.[23] With the coming to power in February 1966, of a regime that has
been able to maintain some semblance of stability, Soviet-Syrian relations
expanded significantly, especially in the area of economic assistance and cultural
exchanges. By the time of the Arab-Israeli War of 1967, Syria had become one
of the focal points of Soviet policy in the Middle East, along with Egypt, and
had come to depend increasingly on Soviet economic and military support.

Soviet relations with Yemen played an unusually important role in over-all
Soviet policy in the Middle East during the 1960s, given the size and backwardness of the country. With the establishment of a republic in 1962 and the outbreak of civil war between the republican government and the royalists, the
Soviets provided significant levels of support to the regime in San'a, including
military assistance, part of which was channeled through Egypt. The major
Soviet interest in the country seems to be related to its geographical location
at the entrance to the Red Sea. Soviet assistance to Yemen during the sixties
included the development of a deep-sea port and an airport, both of which
have subsequently been used by the Soviets.[24]

By 1967 the Soviet Union had become a major actor in the politics of the

Middle East. In a period of less than fifteen years the Soviet leaders had established their country as perhaps the most important outside power in several countries of the area. In particular, Egypt, Syria, and Yemen, and to a lesser extent Iraq, had turned increasingly to the Soviets for military, economic, and political support. In addition, the Soviets had been successful in taking advantage of the dissatisfaction that had developed in Turkey and Iran with a continuation of the virtually total dependence on the US that had characterized the 1950s.

The Arab-Israeli War of 1967 and Its Aftermath

In the Arab-Israeli War of June 1967 the Soviets were presented with a major policy dilemma. On the one hand, they had worked for more than a decade to establish close ties with a number of "revolutionary" Arab countries, especially with the UAR (Egypt), Syria, Iraq, and Algeria, and the prospects for a further improvement of these ties were favorable. On the other hand, there were the broader interests of the Soviet Union as a world power which went far beyond the Middle East—for example, the danger of provoking a direct confrontation with the United States. During the crisis of May 1967 and the June war these two sets of factors came into conflict, and the more general interests of the USSR won out.

Immediately after the war Soviet policy aimed at regaining the prestige and influence that were lost throughout the Arab world as a result of the refusal of the Soviet leadership to grant direct military assistance during the war. Initially, at least, the Soviets were so successful that, in spite of their tarnished image after the military occupation of Czechoslovakia in August 1968, their position in the eastern Mediterranean was much stronger by 1970-71 than it had ever been before the war. Not only was the UAR more dependent on the Soviet Union for both military and political support, but the Soviet fleet had been expanded to the point where it could provide some challenge to the position of US naval supremacy in the eastern Mediterranean.[25] In general, in the years immediately following the Arab-Israeli war, the Soviets were able to continue to expand their contacts with countries in the Arab world.[26]

In the two years preceding the June war, domestic developments in some of the countries of the Arab world had been greeted with satisfaction by the Soviets. In Syria, the UAR, and Algeria, for example, a swing to the left that included the nationalization of foreign investments and programs aimed at government-sponsored industrialization were viewed as the initial steps toward the establishment of socialist governments modeled on that of the Soviet Union. When the beginnings of a new Arab-Israeli crisis appeared in the fall of 1966, with the retaliatory raid of Israel against Jordanian territory, the Soviets interpreted it as a warning to Syria and reaffirmed their complete support for the Arabs against Israel.[27] On May 16, 1967, after Arab troop movements began as a counter to alleged Israeli troop concentrations on the Syrian border, *Pravda* denounced Israel's military build-up and linked it with American efforts to suppress the new Syrian government.[28]

On May 23, at the time that Nasser closed the Gulf of Aqaba, the Soviet government issued a statement assuring the Arabs of support for the just cause of the Arab people in their struggle with the Israeli. However, a note of caution was inserted into the statement that indicated that Soviet "vital interests" had to take precedence over other considerations. The statement referred only to the "all-around assistance" that the Soviets had given the Arabs during the past decade and promised that anyone who tried to unleash aggression in the Middle East would be met by the "strong opposition to aggression from the Soviet Union."[29] In other words, although the Soviets were willing to give verbal support to Nasser's closing of the Gulf of Aqaba, no mention was made of direct military support in case of the outbreak of military hostilities. Apparently the Soviets hoped that their support for the *fait accompli* would enhance their position with the Arabs and that the United States would prevent the Israeli from launching an attack on the Egyptians in order to reopen the Gulf. Soviet calculations proved inaccurate, and the Soviet leadership was eventually forced to choose between Arab defeat and direct Soviet military involvement. Actually the dilemma was not particularly difficult to solve, for whether the Arabs won or lost the war, the Soviets were likely to improve their political position. If the Israeli had been defeated, the Soviets could have claimed that their military and economic assistance had been the decisive factor in the Arab victory. If, on the other hand, as actually did occur, the Arabs were defeated, they would be even more dependent on the Soviet Union in any future attempt to carry on the struggle with Israel.

When the war broke out on June 5, the Soviet government demanded an unconditional cease-fire and the withdrawal of Israeli troops from Arab territory. They took the same position in the Security Council and in the General Assembly of the United Nations, along with demanding that Israel be condemned as the aggressor. However, accounts written by Soviet correspondents in the Arab countries indicated the serious disagreements that existed between the Arabs and the Soviets on the question of the war.[30] On June 10, President Houari Boumedienne of Algeria criticized the Soviets for failing to give direct support to the Arabs. Three days later he arrived in Moscow for talks with Soviet leaders, but returned home without the promises of additional support that he sought.[31]

In the debates on the war in the United Nations the Soviets were eventually forced, in the interests of peace in the area and because of their fear of the outbreak of a major war, to vote against the Arab position. On July 21, against the wishes of the Arabs, the Soviet delegation voted with the United States to return the question to the Security Council.

In the period immediately following the war the major interest of the Soviet

Union in the area was to regain its position of prestige and influence. In order to achieve this goal, the Soviet leaders supported most of the Arab demands, rearmed the UAR and Syria, and stepped up deliveries of economic assistance. They also emphasized their support for the Arabs during the war and attempted to place most of the blame for the Israeli attack on the United States.[32]

Besides providing the Arabs with increased military and economic assistance, the Soviets themselves made a direct show of military power in the area.[33] On December 3, 1967, a group of Soviet TU-16 bombers flew over Cairo and Aswan on a highly publicized "good-will" visit that was clearly designed to indicate the strength of Soviet air power.[34] Soviet military advisors also completely reorganized the Egyptian military, which was purged of officers charged by the Soviets with responsibility for the poor showing of the Egyptian army.[35]

At the same time that they increased their direct involvement in the Middle East, the Soviets also attempted to calm down what *Pravda* called "Arab hotheads" who had reacted too negatively to the compromise resolution of the United Nations.[36] What the Soviet leaders obviously desired in the period immediately after the war was to speed up the process, begun already in the 1950s, of replacing Western influence with their own. Their goals were the

Table 15-2
Soviet Military Assistance to the Countries of the Middle East and North Africa, 1955-72
(In millions of US dollars)

Algeria	$ 400
Cyprus	25
Egypt[a]	2700
Iran	500
Iraq	1000
Lebanon	3
Morocco	15
Syria[a]	715
Yemen (Aden)	25
Yemen (San'a)[a]	75
Total	5458
Total Aid to all Developing Countries	$8475

Source: US Department of State, Bureau of Intelligence and Research, *Communist States and Developing Countries: Aid and Trade in 1972,* Research Study, RECS-10, 15 June 1973, appendix, table 10.

[a]Figures provided by Charles B. McLane in his *Soviet-Middle East Relations* (London: Central Asian Research Centre; distributed by Columbia University New York, 1973, p. 121) differ significantly for Egypt, Syria, and Yemen (San'a). For the period ending with 1970 the figures provided for the three countries are $4500, $900, and $100 respectively.

traditional ones of a great power: prestige, influence, and control. Although
they praised the development of socialism in several Arab countries, the Soviets
realized that the prospects for Soviet-type governments were quite remote in
the near future and they were willing to support any regime that would accept
their support.

By the beginning of the 1970s Soviet successes in the Middle East far sur-
passed what Western observers, or the Soviets themselves, would have predicted
in summer 1967. British influence in the area had almost vanished; the United
States continued to be on the defensive because of its refusal to support the
Arabs in their struggle against Israel. The Soviets seemed to have been able to
move into the area as the only outside power that was both willing and able to
support some of the Arab demands. This position was short-lived, however, for
within the past few years the Soviets have been faced with a number of major
setbacks, most important of which have been the expulsion of the Soviet military
advisors from Egypt in 1972 and the renewed vigor of the US role since the war
of October 1973.

After the apparent height of Soviet involvement and influence in the Middle
East in 1970 and 1971, there was a rather abrupt shift during the period leading
up to the renewed outbreak of war in October 1973. Most important was the
expulsion from Egypt in July 1972 of the approximately 17,000 Soviet military
advisors. In addition, however, in the months preceding the October war Soviet-
Syrian relations were reportedly deteriorating.[37] Since approximately 1972
Soviet policy in the Middle East was increasingly challenged by the rise of a new
self-proclaimed leader of the Arab people: Colonel Khaddafi, the President of
Libya. Khaddafi not only critized the Soviets as atheistic communists who are
uncommitted to the interests of the Arab people, but also began to provide an
alternative source of financial support to those countries primarily engaged in
the conflict with Israel.

Ever since the 1967 war there have been those in the Soviet Union who have
opposed continued Soviet support for the governments of Nasser and Sadat.[38]
By the early 1970s Soviet commentators had become increasingly critical of the
internal developments of Egypt. After the death of Nasser and the rise of
Anwar Sadat to the presidency, a new cause for friction arose. Sadat soon
purged his government of left-wing elements who were known as strong supporters of strengthening the ties of friendship between the Soviet Union and
Egypt. Although the Soviets responded that this was entirely a matter of internal Egyptian politics, it is clear that they were not pleased with this new turn
of events.

In 1971, largely in response to internal political pressures, Sadat indicated
that the year of decision had arrived and that before its end Egypt would regain
the territories lost in the 1967 war. The Soviets, however, in spite of their major
commitment of arms and manpower to the defense of Egypt during the previous

several years,[39] continued to caution against the outbreak of a new war. According to the Soviets, the only path to a solution of the conflict between the Arabs
and Israel was through a political settlement.[40] By mid-1972 President Sadat
was faced with increasing domestic pressure to "resolve" the question of the
occupied territories. In addition, the presence of thousands of Soviet troops in
Egypt resulted in growing friction between Egyptian officers and their Soviet
counterparts. Most important was the direct Soviet control over the most
advanced weapons and the refusal of the Soviets to employ these weapons.[41]

By mid-1972 the Soviets had placed themselves in the position in Egypt of
not being able to permit the Arabs to suffer the type of defeat that they had
suffered in 1967. The presence of Soviet troops (who actually manned much
of the missile defense system) and equipment in the front lines had so committed
Soviet prestige that a defeat of the Egyptian army would have been, in effect, a
defeat of the Soviet Union. Although the Soviets were obviously angered by
the preemptory expulsion of their military forces from Egypt in July 1972, it
would appear that President Sadat did provide them with the means to extricate
themselves from a potentially intolerable situation.

After the withdrawal of most of the Soviet military advisors in mid-1972,
the Soviets increased their criticisms of developments in Egypt. Of major concern was what the Soviets viewed as a retreat from the development of the state
sector of the economy and the revitalization of the role of the bourgeoisie in
the Egyptian economy. According to an article in *Pravda*, the increased activity
of the bourgeoisie and the new privileges that had been granted to them in
Egypt had become "cause for alarm on the part of the progressive public."[42]

Although the Soviets have argued for more than a decade for the creation
of a revolutionary vanguard political party in Egypt as the means to achieving
"scientific socialism," commentary in the Soviet Union prior to the 1973 war
emphasized the necessity of viewing the struggle in the Middle East, not primarily as a war between Arabs and Israeli, but as an integral part of the anti-
imperialist struggle. Only by introducing measures to insure the socioeconomic
transformation of the area could the Arabs succeed in resolving their problems.
According to E. Dmitriev, writing in the ideological journal of the CPSU, "The
future in the Middle East will belong to those genuinely progressive forces,
which view their struggle for the liquidation of the remnants of Israeli aggression
in the context of the broader tasks of the struggle of the Arab peoples against
imperialism."[43]

During the year after the ouster of the Soviet military personnel, the Egyptians made several efforts to improve their relationships with the Soviet Union.
However, the major issue that apparently led to the partial rupture continued to
exist—the Soviet refusal to provide the Egyptian army with the modern military
equipment which the latter demanded. In a speech delivered on the eve of the
twenty-first anniversary of the Egyptian revolution of July 1952, President
Sadat warned that a Soviet-American detente might result in the isolation of
the Soviets from the national liberation movement.[44]

In spite of the deterioration of Soviet-Egyptian relations during 1972 and 1973, however, it was quite clear that neither side was willing to permit the relationship to worsen. From the Soviet point of view, the investments of the past two decades in the military and economic development of Egypt had been far too significant to be written off as a failure. In addition, Egypt provided the Soviets with the equivalent of military bases, in particular naval facilities, for the expanded role of the Soviets in the Mediterranean Sea. In spite of the affront to Soviet prestige, the Soviet Union did continue to provide support to Egypt, including the technicians to man the Soviet-installed radar system.

In other portions of the Arab world the Soviets also suffered new challenges to their role as the major outside power in the early seventies. The rise to power of the anti-communist Colonel Kaddafi as President of Libya presented them with an additional problem. Although the Soviets at first welcomed the anti-Western policies of the Libyan leader, his attacks on communism for "religious, social, economic, political and moral reasons . . . as an invention which does not conform to our customs or national interests . . ."[45] were condemned by the Soviets, who accused him of attempting to seize the mantle of Nasser as leader of the Arab world.[46] In addition, Kaddafi refused to permit the Soviet fleet to use the port facilities that had been used by the U.S. Sixth Fleet prior to the Libyan closing of the U.S. bases. His response was that such permission would merely have meant replacing the U.S. fleet with the Soviet fleet.[47] From the Soviet viewpoint the greatest danger represented by Kaddafi was the possibility of his gaining a following among the more radical elements within the Arab world who are critical of both the West and the Soviet Union.

Relations between the Soviet Union and both Iraq and Syria remained basically cordial prior to the October War. Even here, however, the Soviets were faced with problems. Their failure to provide modern military equipment seems to have been part of the problem, as well as the implications for the Arabs of the detente between the United States and the Soviet Union.[48]

By the time of the outbreak of hostilities between Israel and Syria and Egypt in October 1973, the Soviet position in the Middle East appeared to be significantly weaker than it had been several years earlier. The expulsion of Soviet military advisors from Egypt; the development of a sense of unity among the Arabs in their relations with the West, in particular their newfound position of influence as the result of their increased control over their own oil resources; and the influence of anti-communist Arab leaders such as Kaddafi all resulted in a diminution of the Soviet role in the area.

The War of October 1973 and Its Aftermath

It appears that the Soviets became aware of the Arab plans to initiate military hostilities only a few days before the attack itself. During the three days prior to the outbreak of the war the last Soviet advisors along the west bank of the Suez Canal and Soviet dependents in Syria and Egypt were evacuated.[49]

Once again the Soviets were faced with the decision of either supporting the Arabs in order to maintain what remained of their position in the Arab world, or running the risk of a direct confrontation with the United States. In 1973, as contrasted with 1967, the Soviet leadership opted for the former policy. Within hours the Soviets began replacing the Egyptian and Syrian military arsenals and, as long as the Arabs continued to enjoy military success, they did not intervene in favor of a cease-fire. Only when the Israeli began pushing the Arab armies back and tension between the Soviet Union and the United States increased did Kosygin, during his visit to Cairo in mid-October, apparently urge the Egyptians to settle for the gains that they had achieved and agree to a cease-fire.

How does one explain this reversal of a Soviet policy that had opposed a military solution to the Middle East problem ever since the late sixties? As noted above, the situation of the Soviets had deteriorated significantly during the two years preceding the outbreak of the war. Arab dependence on the Soviets was reduced because of several factors: the ability of the Arabs, for the first time in modern history, to cooperate by using their control over the vital oil resources of the area; the willingness of Saudi Arabia to pay much of the Egyptian military bill; and the newfound self-confidence of the Arabs. The Soviet leaders were faced with the extremely difficult choice between 1) risking the economic and political benefits of the policy of detente with the United States which they had been nurturing for the past few years and the possibility of a major direct confrontation with the United States and 2) writing off two decades of economic, military, and political investments in the Middle East.

In the year that has passed since the October war the Soviets have found that their wartime commitment to the Arabs has not resulted in a major reestablishment of their former position. In fact, one of the most interesting results of the war was the reentry of the United States as a major external actor into the affairs of the area and a renewal of relations between the United States and a number of Arab countries. Throughout the negotiations, which resulted first in the disengagement of Egyptian and Israeli troops in the Sinai (and the withdrawal of the Israeli from the west side of the canal) and later in the disengagement of Israeli and Syrian troops in the north, the United States by far played the dominant role. During the weeks of Kissinger's "shuttle diplomacy" the Soviets were not involved in the negotiations. In fact, during the course of the negotiations they continually warned the Arabs of the deceptiveness of the Israeli and their US backers and, in general, called for an "all or nothing" approach which would hardly have been acceptable to Israel. At a dinner in Moscow honoring President Assad of Syria on April 11, 1974, Soviet party leader Leonid Brezhnev stated: "The aggressor and its patrons may again try to avoid a radical all-embracing solution of the problem . . . 'ersatz plans' for a Middle East settlement were, I must say, put forward lately.

This actually means replacing an overall settlement with 'partial' agreements of a different kind."[50] In spite of Soviet warnings Syria finally accepted the US plan for troop disengagement on May 29.

Although the Soviets did provide massive military assistance to the Arabs during the war, they have found that relations between the United States and Egypt, for example, have expanded significantly in the ensuing year. President Nixon's visit to Egypt in June and the agreements on US-Egyptian economic cooperation; Sadat's efforts to reduce his military dependence on the USSR by finding alternative sources of military equipment; and the generally improved atmosphere in US-Egyptian relations have prevented the redevelopment of the "old" relationship between the Soviets and Egyptians.

As a partial alternative to replacing the close ties with Egypt that characterized the pre-1972 period, the Soviets have expanded their activities elsewhere in the Middle East since the October war. Probably most important has been the changed position on the Palestine Liberation Organization of Yasser Arafat. During the summer of 1974 the Soviets began to support the formation of an Arab Palestine with the obvious hope that a "progressive" Palestinian government established with Soviet support would represent a useful Soviet ally in the Middle East.[51]

In addition, Soviet relations with the Libya of Colonel Kaddafi have made an about-face as both groups of leaders have recognized that developments in the Arab world are not following the path that they have set down. During a visit of Libyan Prime Minister Abd as-Salam Jalloud to Moscow in May 1974, Prime Minister Kosygin noted that what unites the two countries "undoubtedly carries much greater weight" than what divides them.[52] What seems to have brought the Soviet Union and Libya together is their relative isolation. The Soviets have watched as their erstwhile protégé Egypt has turned to the United States, while the Libyans have had their offers of political union with Egypt spurned.

Since the October war and, in particular, after prospects for the reopening of the Suez Canal brightened, the Soviets renewed their efforts to expand their contacts in the areas commanding the approaches to the southern end of the Canal. During a visit to the Soviet Union in July 1974 of a high-level delegation from the People's Democratic Republic of Yemen (Aden), assurances of the "solid ties of friendship" between the two countries were made. Most important, from the point of view of the Soviet Union, is Yemen's (Aden's) continued dependence on the Soviet Union both for military equipment and training and for economic assistance. In return, Yemen has guaranteed the Soviets the use of port facilities for Soviet vessels close to the entrance to the Red Sea and the approaches to the Suez Canal.[53] Across the mouth of the Red Sea from the port of Aden the Soviets have also expanded the harbor facilities of the Somali port of Berbera. The treaty of friendship signed between the USSR and the Somali Republic on July 11 is apparently related to the interest of the Soviet Union in the area.[54]

All of these efforts are part of an attempt by the Soviet leadership to continue to play a major role in the Middle East in spite of the setbacks that they have suffered during the past few years—especially in their relations with Egypt on which they had based most of their Middle East policy during the past wro decades.

The Politics of Influence Building: An Interim Assessment

Prior to the outbreak of hostilities on October 6, 1973, the Soviet Union seemed to be scaling down its support for the Arabs and its overall involvement in the Middle East. The events of 1972 had indicated that in spite of the large-scale investment of development capital, military assistance, and political support in the Middle East during almost two decades, the USSR had failed to acquire significant influence in the area. In addition, by the 1970s the strategic interests of the Soviet Union in the area had been reduced from the situation that had existed twenty years earlier. The development of intercontinental ballistic missiles and the concomitant reduction of the US military presence in Greece, Turkey, and Iran had lessened the military significance of the area for Soviet defense. This does not mean, however, that the Soviets had decided to write off their investment, as their policy during 1974 indicates. In the meantime, other interests of the Soviet leadership—perhaps not as overriding as those of military defense—had surfaced.

By the early seventies the Soviets' prospects for replacing the West as the major power in the entire Middle East and South Asian area had greatly expanded. In South Asia the victory of India and Bangladesh over truncated Pakistan and the resulting loss of US prestige had greatly expanded the role of the USSR. The struggle of the oil-producing states against the West, including the United States, threatened to result in the deterioration of American influence in the few areas where the US continued to play some role—namely, in the more conservative Arab states. The Soviets attempted to facilitate this process by supporting Iraq in its policy of nationalizing Western holdings in the country and providing equipment for the development of Iraqi oil fields.[55]

Even though the Middle East does not represent an area of crucial interest to the Soviets, it is viewed as important for a number of reasons. First, the present Soviet leadership has indicated during the course of the past decade that it shares the goal of its predecessors in maintaining and even expanding the area under Soviet influence. As has already been noted, Russia long ago attempted to expand its imperial interests into the Middle East; Khrushchev revitalized these interests in the 1950s. In addition, the Soviets, and more importantly their East European allies, do have an increasing need for Middle Eastern oil and gas to fill projected needs for the coming years. Presumably the Soviets expect that their support for the Arabs against the West—and against Israel—is likely to insure them of a continuing role in the area. They see in this policy of support the possibility of influencing, at least indirectly, Arab oil policy. This support would also provide them with a possible means of exerting pressure on the West.

It would appear that the major goals of the Soviets in the Middle East are still closely tied to their overall relations with the United States. In spite of the atmosphere of detente that has developed within the past several years, the Soviets have made clear that the struggle against the West still continues. The methods which will be employed to carry on the struggle are primarily ideological, although the Soviets will obviously take advantage of conflicts between the US and other Western powers and third parties—in this case the Arabs—in order to reduce the role of the West in Asia and Africa.[56]

It has become clear, however, that the Soviets have not been successful in controlling developments in the Middle East, even in those countries that have become heavily dependent on them for assistance of all sorts. The Soviet leadership has discovered that the loss of Western influence in the area has not automatically resulted in a corresponding gain in Soviet influence. In many respects they find that their policy in the area is itself influenced, even dictated, by their Arab clients. In order to protect their investment they must do more than provide mere verbal support for the goals of the Arabs. Ever since the 1967 war the Soviets have advocated caution and insisted that the only means to a permanent peaceful solution to the Arab-Israeli conflict was a negotiated settlement. Yet, with the Arab decision to regain the lost territories militarily, the Soviets were forced to decide between 1) supporting the Arabs in order to bolster their role as a defender of the Arab liberation cause and 2) running the risk of a deterioration of relations with the United States.

Another factor has apparently influenced Soviet policy in the Middle East. Ever since the split between the Soviet Union and China in the early 1960s, the latter has attempted to compete with the Soviet Union for the mantle of leadership of the world revolutionary forces. Soviet policy in the Middle East after 1967 was condemned by the Chinese as basically supportive of the Israeli, because the Soviets refused to support a "revolutionary" solution to the problems of the Arabs. In the months immediately preceding the most recent outbreak of violence in the Middle East, the Egyptians began to improve their relations with the Chinese and seemed to be supporting some of China's claims in their struggle with the Soviets.[57] This Chinese condemnation of the Soviets' "no war, no peace" policy in the Middle East and the Soviet fear of expanded Chinese influence in the area[58] apparently influenced the Soviet decision to support the Arabs. In spite of the consequences for their relations with the United States, the Soviets aimed to maintain their revolutionary image.

In twenty years of a policy aimed at influence-building in the Middle East, the Soviets have been extremely successful in accomplishing their first goal:

the reduction of Western involvement. This development, however, has been primarily the result of the dynamics of Arab-Western relations and the Soviets have not been able to determine the direction of that relationship. Rather, they have merely been able to facilitate the process by providing the Arabs with a variety of types of support. On the other hand, the Soviets have been far less successful in expanding their own influence in the area, as the above analysis has indicated. The primary decisions are still made by the Arabs, at times in the face of Soviet opposition. If the Soviets wish to continue to play a role in the Middle East in the future, it will probably have to remain the role of responding to Arab initiatives.

One of the anomalies of the Soviet position in the Middle East is that their present problems are partially the result of their past successes. The Soviet-trained and equippped armies of the Arab states are now far more a match for the Israeli army than they were in the past. Arab self-confidence has risen immeasurably as the result of both the limited military successes of 1973 and the expanded international political role that their control over petroleum resources provides them.

Although the Arabs will remain dependent on the Soviet Union as the ultimate defender against Israel, this dependence is not likely to result in a significant future increase in Soviet influence over Arab domestic or foreign policy. The incongruence of the major interests of the two sides will continue to plague their relations. For the Arabs the primary goal is a solution to the question of relations with Israel and a homeland for the Palestinans. The Soviet Union has been viewed as the only external political actor that has been both willing (to a point, at least) and able to assist in accomplishing this goal. For the Soviets the goal is the reduction of Western influence and the expansion of their own influence. To date none of the Arab states has indicated any interest in becoming a "puppet" of the Soviet Union.

Notes

1. See, for example, V.A. Maslennikov, "Natsional'no-osvoboditel'noe dvizhenie," in V.A. Maslennikov, ed., *Uglublenie krizisa kolonial'noi sistemy imperializma posle Vtoroi Mirovoi Voiny*. Moscow: Gospolitizdat, 1953, pp. 43-44; S.V. Datlin, *Afrika pod gnetom imperializma*. Moscow: Gospolitizdat, 1951, p. 10.
2. See the account of the speech of the president of the Soviet Chamber of Commerce at a conference in April 1952 in Comité de contribution au devéloppement du commerce international, *Rencontre internationale de Moscou*, (Paris, 1952), pp. 67-72; cited in Louis Kawan, *La nouvelle orientation du commerce extérieure soviétique*. Brussels: Centre Nationale pour l'étude des Pays à Regime Communiste, 1958, pp. 61-62.

3. US Department of State, Bureau of Intelligence and Research, *Communist States and the Developing Countries: Aid and Trade in 1972*. Research Study, RECS-10, June 15, 1973, Appendix, Table I. Of this aid the countries of the Middle East and North Africa (from Morocco in the west to Afghanistan in the east) received more than \$4.7 billion in economic credits.

4. For a discussion of the changing Soviet view of the developing countries see Roger E. Kanet, ed., *The Soviet Union and the Developing Countries*. Baltimore: The Johns Hopkins University Press, 1974, pp. 27-50.

5. See Khrushchev's speech at the Twentieth Party Congress in 1956 in Leo Gruliow, ed., *Current Soviet Policies II: The Documentary Record of the 20th Communist Party Congress and Its Aftermath*. New York: Columbia University Press, 1957, pp. 37, 190.

6. See, for example, R. Andreisian and A. El'ianov, "Razvivaiushchiesia strany: diversifikatsiia i strategiia promyshlennogo razvitiia," *Mirovaia ekonomika i mezhdunarodnye otnosheniia*, no. 1 (1968), pp. 29-40 and V. Kondrat'ev, "Gana: Vybor puti i preobrazovanie ekonomiki," ibid., no. 5 (1965), p. 54.

7. One of the best surveys of recent Soviet policy in South Asia can be found in Bhabani Sen Gupta, "The Soviet Union and South Asia," in Kanet, ed., *The Soviet Union and the Developing Countries*, pp. 119-151.

8. See "Appeal of the Council of People's Commissars to the Moslems of Russia and the East," December 3, 1917. Reprinted in Jane Degras, ed., *Soviet Documents on Foreign Policy 1917-1939*. New York: Oxford University Press, 1951, I, 16-17.

9. During the twenties the Soviets signed treaties with Iran and, for a while at least, maintained proper relations with the new nationalist regime of Kemal Attaturk of Turkey. They had even signed a treaty of friendship with Yemen as early as 1928, and maintained a legation in Saudi Arabia from 1926 until 1938. For details of early Soviet contacts with the Middle East see Charles B. McLane, *Soviet-Middle East Relations*. London: Central Asian Research Centre, 1973, distributed by Columbia University Press (New York), *passim*. See also Walter Laqueur, *The Soviet Union and the Middle East*. New York: Praeger, 1959, Part I.

10. In 1940, in discussions between Nazi Germany and the Soviet Union, Ribbentrop, the German foreign minister, proposed a division of British colonial holdings which would have provided the Soviets with the area "in the general direction of the Indian Ocean." The Soviets agreed to discuss the matter but no agreement was ever reached and, in fact, the Soviets were far more interested in delineating German and Soviet spheres of influence in Eastern Europe. For an account of the discussions see R.J. Sontag and J.S. Beddie, eds., *Nazi Soviet Relations 1939-1941*. Washington: U.S. Government Printing Office, 1948, pp. 212-216. See also, Geoffrey Jukes, "The Indian Ocean in Soviet Naval Policy," *Adelphi Papers*, no. 87 (1972), p. 2.

11. For a discussion of the Soviet role in Iran, see George Lenczowski, *Russia and the West in Iran, 1918-1948.* Ithaca, N.Y.: Cornell University Press, 1950.

12. See Herbert Feis, *Between War and Peace: The Potsdam Conference.* Princeton: Princeton University Press, 1960, pp. 306-307, and James F. Byrnes, *Speaking Frankly.* New York: Harper & Row, 1947, pp. 76, 94.

13. For a discussion of the background to the Truman Doctrine see Joseph M. Jones, *The Fifteen Weeks.* New York: Viking Press, 1955.

14. See Laqueur, *The Soviet Union and the Middle East,* pp. 146-150. See also, Karmi Schweitzer, "Soviet Policy Towards Israel, 1946-1956," *Mizan,* XI (1969), pp. 18-30, 174-181.

15. For a detailed discussion of the Egyptian-Soviet arms deal see Uri Ra'anan, *The USSR Arms the Third World: Case Studies in Soviet Foreign Policy.* Cambridge, Mass.-London: The M.I.T. Press, 1969.

16. McLane, *Soviet-Middle East Relations,* p. 120.

17. For a discussion of "The Neutralization of the Northern Tier," see Walter Laqueur, *The Struggle for the Middle East: The Soviet Union in the Mediterranean 1958-1968.* New York: Macmillan, 1969, pp. 14-42. See also, John C. Campbell, "The Communist Powers and the Middle East: Moscow's Purposes," *Problems of Communism,* XXI, no. 5 (1972), pp. 40-54; and the recent study of the benefits to the Soviets that have resulted from improved relations with Turkey in John C. Campbell, "Soviet Strategy in the Balkans," *Problems of Communism,* XXIII, no. 4 (1974), esp. pp. 7-8.

18. *New York Times,* February 22, 1959. This campaign was, in part, the result of Soviet support for the Kassem regime which suppressed an anti-Communist uprising in Iraq.

19. Two excellent discussions of progress on Soviet aid projects through the mid-sixties can be found in Marshall I. Goldman, *Soviet Foreign Aid.* New York: Praeger, 1967, pp. 60-84, and Leo Tansky, *U.S. and U.S.S.R. Aid to Developing Countries: A Comparative Study of India, Turkey, and the U.A.R.* New York: Praeger, 1967, pp. 120-160.

20. Georgii Mirskii, "Tvorcheskii marksizm i problemy natsional'no-osvoboditel'-nykh stran," *Mirovaia ekonomika i mezhdunarodnye otnosheniia* (Hereafter MEIMO), no. 2 (1963), p. 65. Other Soviet commentators challenged this optimistic interpretation and pointed out that Mirskii had presented a one-sided picture. R. Avakov and L. Stepanov, "Sotsial'nye problemy natsional'-no-osvoboditel'noi revoliutsii," ibid., no. 5 (1963), p. 51.

21. See *New York Times,* April 26, 1965, p. 16. For a brief discussion of the Soviet position on nationalist regimes in the mid-sixties see Roger E. Kanet, "The Recent Soviet Reassessment of Developments in the Third World," *The Russian Review,* XXVII (1968), pp. 27-41.

22. For a discussion of these points see Campbell, "Moscow's Purposes," pp. 47-48 and McLane, *Soviet-Middle East Relations,* pp. 55-57.

23. For a survey of Soviet views of developments in Syria during this period see Aryeh Yodfat, *Arab Politics in the Soviet Mirror.* Jerasulem: Israel Universities Press, and New York: Halsted Press, 1973, pp. 103-145.

24. For a discussion of Soviet relations with Yemen, see Oles M. Smolansky, "Khrushchev and the Yemeni Revolution (1962-1964): An Analysis of Soviet Policies and Attitudes," *Soviet Union,* I, no. 1 (1973), pp. 32-53. See also McLane, *Soviet-Middle East Relations,* pp. 111-112.

25. By the summer of 1968, the Soviet fleet in the Eastern Mediterranean included a cruiser, more than five destroyers, a dozen nuclear submarines, as well as landing ships. In September 1968, a helicopter carrier was added to the Soviet fleet, which by then almost equalled in size (though not in firepower) American naval forces in the Mediterranean. See J. Pergent, "La pénétration navale soviétique en Mediterranée," *Est et Quest,* no. 48 (July 1-31, 1968), pp. 24-27; *The Christian Science Monitor,* July 2, 1968, p. 4; and the AP report of September 25, 1968. See also, Carey B. Joynt and Oles M. Smolansky, *Soviet Navel Policy in the Mediterranean.* Bethlehem, Pa.: Department of International Relations, Lehigh University, Research Monograph no. 3, 1972.

26. The Soviets signed agreements with Iraq for the supply of technical assistance and machinery for the latter's oil industry in late 1967; large-scale assistance was provided to South Yemen and, reportedly, Soviet pilots assisted the republican government of Yemen against the Royalists. See *Christian Science Monitor,* December 29, 1972, p. 5; McLane, *Soviet-Middle East Relations,* pp. 87, 112; *The Times* (London), December 13, 1967 and *The New York Times,* December 13, 1967, p. 15.

27. See M. Kremnev, "Centre of Tension in the Arab East," *New Times,* no. 51 (December 20, 1966).

28. *Pravda,* May 16, 1967, p. 1.

29. *Pravda,* May 24, 1967, p. 1.

30. See E. Primakov, "Narod na zashchite svoikh zavevanii," *Pravda,* June 13, 1967, p. 4. See also, the complaint by A. Iskenderov that Arab newspapers misunderstood Soviet policy. "Encounters and Impressions," *Literaturnaia gazeta,* no. 33 (1967), p. 13, translated in *The Current Digest of the Soviet Press,* XIX, no. 34 (September 13, 1967), p. 11.

31. On Algiers Radio, June 10, 1967, Boumedienne stated: "Brothers, you saw during the battle how the whole of Europe, all the European countries, including the progressive, we regret to say, the moderates, the extreme Right wing and the capitalist—took the same attitude . . . which does not differ from that taken by the progressives . . . ." According to the editor of *Al Ahram,* who was considered to be Nasser's mouthpiece, Boumedienne flew to Moscow to inquire why the USSR had not given direct military aid. Boumedienne reportedly complained that the United States was permitted here and elsewhere to suppress national liberation

movements. In reply, Soviet leaders reportedly asked the Algerian president what he thought of an atomic war. *Al Ahram* (Cairo), August 24, 1967. Cited in Süleyman Tekiner, "Soviet Policy Toward the Arab East," *Bulletin,* Institute for the Study of the USSR, XV, no. 3 (1968), p. 37.

32. In an article published in *Izvestiia* in the fall of 1967, a Soviet political commentator argued that the US promoted and encouraged Israel's ventures because they were directed against the nation-liberation movement of the Arab people. He also argued that the West sees the Middle East as a base for a potential attack against the Soviet Union. *Izvestiia,* October 25, 1967, p. 2.

33. According to Israeli intelligence sources, more than 80 percent of the planes, tanks and artillery of the UAR had already been replaced by October 1967. By 1970, approximately 20,000 Soviet military technicians and advisors, see present in the UAR. See McLane, *Soviet-Middle East Relations,* p. 32. See also Laqueur, *The Struggle for the Middle East,* p. 82.

34. Moscow Radio, December 5, 1967; *The New York Times,* December 4, 1967, p. 18.

35. According to the Soviets, "bourgeois" officers were opposed to the social revolution that Nasser had initiated in the UAR and this opposition resulted in a defeatist attitude. See Igor Beliaev and Evgenii Primakov in *Za rubezhom,* no. 27 (1967), pp. 7-8 and their article on "The Situation in the Arab World," *New Times,* no. 39 (1967), pp. 8-11. On the role of Soviet Advisors, see *The Christian Science Monitor,* November 20, 1967, p. 13.

36. *Pravda,* November 27, 1967, p. 5.

37. Both of these problems seem to stem, in part at least, from the same source— Soviet refusals to provide the Arabs with the kind of military support desired and fears of the implications for the Arabs of the detente between the Soviet Union and the United States. See *Strategic Survey, 1972.* London: International Institute for Strategic Studies, 1973, pp. 26-27.

38. For an excellent survey of Soviet attitudes toward the Middle East, and in particular toward Egypt, see Ilana Dimant, "PRAVDA and TRUD—Divergent Attitudes towards the Middle East," *Soviet Union,* 1, No. 1 (1973), pp. 1-31.

39. In addition to the large number of Soviet troops present in Egypt by 1971, and the replacement of the equipment losses suffered by the Egyptian army during the 1967 war, the Soviets supplied the Egyptians with a sophisticated missile defense system along the west bank of the Suez Canal. See J.C. Hurewitz, "Superpower Rivalry and the Arab-Israel Dispute: Involvement or Commitment?" in Michael Confino and Shimon Shamir, eds., *The U.S.S.R. and the Middle East.* Jerusalem: Israel Universities Press, and New York: John Wiley & Sons, Halsted Press, 1973, pp. 155 ff.

40. Recently the Soviet commentator R. Petrov has criticized "those quarters in Israel and the Arab countries who place their own selfish ends above a fair settlement of the Middle East conflict . . ." Among others, this included President Kaddafi of Libya, one of the major Arab advocates of a military

solution to the conflict. See R. Petrov, "The Middle East Needs a Just and Lasting Peace," *New Times,* no. 23 (1973), p. 4.

41. For an excellent discussion of the factors apparently motivating Sadat's decision to expel the Soviet military advisors see Alvin Z. Rubinstein, "Moscow and Cairo: "Currents of Influence," *Problem of Communism* XXIII, no. 4 (1974), esp. pp. 24-26.

42. P. Demchenko, "Ot Kairo do Aleksandrii," *Pravda,* July 23, 1973, p. 3. Several months earlier Demchenko and Iu. Glukhov had written a similar article in which they also noted that increasing numbers of Egyptians were enjoying a level of prosperity unavailable to most Soviet citizens. *Pravda,* February 2, 1973, p. 3.

43. E. Dmitriev, "Problema likvidatsii ochaga voennoi opasnosti na Blizhnem Vostoke," *Kommunist,* no. 4 (1973), p. 107.

44. Several days before this speech, Sadat's national security advisor, Ismail, return from a visit to the Soviet Union, apparently without having achieved his goals, since no final communique was released at the end of Ismail's visit. See Jean Riottel, "Soviet-Egyptian Relations and the National Liberation Movement," *Radio Liberty Dispatch,* August 6, 1973.

45. Kaddafi, quoted in *Le Monde,* May 6, 1971.

46. See the article by K. Borisov, in *Literaturnaia gazeta,* no. 23 (June 6, 1973), p. 14. This article was broadcast by Radio Moscow in Arabic in three parts on June 8, 9, and 10, 1973.

47. Radio Moscow, January 17, 1973.

48. See John K. Cooley, "Syrian-Soviet Strain Perils Kremlin's Power," *The Christian Science Monitor,* September 20, 1973, p. 3.

49. Uri Ra'anan argues that the Soviet Union was not only aware of Egyptian plans, but that it played a major role in preparing them. See his "The USSR and the Middle East: Some Reflections on the Soviet Decision-Making Process," *Orbis,* XVII, (1973), pp. 946-977.

50. See *Pravda,* April 12, 1974.

51. See Leo Gruliow, "Soviets Support PLO in Forming New State," *Christian Science Monitor,* August 5, 1974, p. 2, and "Yasser Arafat on the Problems of the Palestine Movement," *New Times,* no. 20 (1974), pp. 10-11.

52. *Pravda,* May 16, 1974.

53. See *Christian Science Monitor,* September 9, 1974, p. 5.

54. See *Soviet News,* no. 5745, July 16, 1974, p. 1.

55. For a discussion of the Soviet role in the nationalization of the Kirkuk oil fields in July 1972, see Ursula Braun, "Der Irak und die Staaten der Arabishcen Halbinsel in der sowjetischen Aussenpolitik," *Osteuropa,* XXIII (1973), p. 379.

56. Traditional Marxist-Leninist doctrine indicates that an effective means to carry on the struggle against capitalism is to cut the ties of the capitalist

countries with the colonial and neo-colonial areas. This, according to Lenin's theory of imperialism, is the method that the capitalists had developed to stave off the proletarian revolution by finding markets for both manufactured goods and surplus capital and sources of cheap raw materials. Although ideology is not the major determining factor in Soviet foreign policy decision-making, it would appear that the present Soviet leadership still adheres to the belief that Lenin's general interpretation of international relations is correct and that the West would suffer serious economic damage were its economic ties to the third world severed. For a discussion of Soviet policy during the October 1973 war see Foy D. Kohler, Leon Gouré, and Mose L. Harvey, *The Soviet Union and the October 1973 Middle East War: The Implications for Detente.* Coral Gables: Monographs in International Affairs, Center for Advanced International Studies, University of Miami, 1974.

57. See Jean Riollot, "Soviet-Egyptian Relations and the National Liberation Movement," *Radio Liberty Dispatch,* August 6, 1973.

58. The Chinese are already involved in supporting revolutionary movements in the southern parts of the Arabian Peninsula.

Part IX

Detente: The Unity of Opposites

16

An Anti-Anti-Communist Looks at Detente

Alfred G. Meyer

Detente? I have asked myself many times: What detente? True, we have recognized the People's Republic of China and have let Chiang Kai-shek know he no longer is our favorite ally. We have made our peace with the Berlin Wall and the existence of two German states, have abandoned our trade boycott of China, and have bailed the Soviet economy out of its recent difficulties by selling them our not-so-surplus wheat. We have made quite a few concessions. They have yielded little or nothing, and, if anything, become more assertive. No government ever summoned an American secretary of state to a meeting the way Mr. Brezhnev in October 1973 summoned Henry Kissinger to Moscow. No president of the United States ever backed down from a troop alert as quickly as Mr. Nixon did that same month in the face of Soviet threats. If we consider Israel's success in defying UN Security Council resolutions as a barometer of United States strength in the world—and I think it is quite a sensitive barometer— then American strength has declined markedly, while that of the Soviet Union has risen in proportion.

What today is called detente is our own reluctant response to problems and weaknesses we ourselves have helped to create. Among other things, it is an adjustment to new international rivalries, this time between the United States and the partners in anticommunism whom we developed and armed— Japan and Western Europe. Suddenly Moscow and Peking have become desirable trading partners to all these competitors, and all of them, including the United States, have engaged in an undignified scramble for Mao's and Brezhnev's favors and attention. What a nice demonstration that ideological commitments, like anti-imperialism and anticommunism, while useful myths for military and political elites, are scrapped quickly when the profit pinch is felt. When it is convenient, policy-makers in Moscow, Washington, and Peking, like those in other churches, take their dogmas lightly.

What our media and our political leaders call detente is in fact the acknowledgement of massive failure, a declaration of bankruptcy for cold war policies and the cold war ideology. It is ironic that these humiliating concessions had to be made—could only be made—by veterans of the anti-Communist crusade, doubly ironic that these men managed to make all this appear as great acts of statesmanship and made them come just before the 1972 election. What delicious irony to have *Pravda* express an obvious interest in the election and the continued incumbency of Richard Nixon, who thus becomes the candidate of the Communist dictators, while his critics are denounced in Moscow as

323

reactionaries. How quickly old ideological positions can be exchanged for new ones!

We are told that the cold war is over now that bipolarity in world politics has given way to power pluralism. I am not convinced. The cold war goes on quite merrily—as a hot war in Vietnam, where there is neither peace nor honor; as a counterrevolution in Chile; and as a series of confrontations everywhere. The alleged bipolarity of world politics since 1945 is a pervasive myth. At the end of World War II international power was not distributed in bipolar fashion at all. Instead, the globe was dominated clearly and unmistakably by the one power that had emerged undamaged, unbombed, unoccupied, and unimpoverished by the war, the power that had a monopoly in atomic weapons. Beginning in 1944, the United States was supreme in world politics as the single superpower. Her businessmen could operate and profit without control or hindrance almost everywhere in the world. Her armed forces, her police and intelligence agents, her political and ideological representatives were present, active, and powerful everywhere except in the Eurasian heartland. In Iran and Guatemala, in Italy, Indochina and the Dominican Republic, in Europe, Africa, Asia, and South America, we freely intervened in political processes, unmaking governments we distrusted and setting up our own client governments. Practicing a global policy of counterrevolution, the first democracy of the modern age had become what tsarism was in the nineteenth century: the chief bastion of reaction, the world's policeman, the mainstay of all anti-democratic forces. For those who did not appreciate our version of global law and order, our policy was the genocidal one of bombing them back to the Stone Age. *We had assumed the right to decide for the people of the world that they were better off dead than red*, a benevolence that some of them were not sufficiently enlightened to appreciate. Indeed, it seems a ludicrous solution to an equally ludicrous view of what the alternatives really were. Yet, for the sake of this truly mad and crazily arrogant endeavor we committed our national resources. Detente is an acknowledgment that the effort has failed.

Detente, however, cannot repay the price this country has paid for the madness and the arrogance of what George Liska has called America's imperial mission. We are made aware of part of this price every day. The inflationary spiral, the devaluation of the world's most reliable currency, and the deficit in our international trade are, all of them, symptoms of the fact that the United States has wasted its resources recklessly, resources it could have spent for more constructive and humanitarian purposes. The nation has been militarized. The Pentagon and its clients have become parasites on the body politic. The entire world has been militarized. We have rearmed Germany and Japan, thus helping to divide Europe permanently, forever preventing the emergence of a neutral Germany, and making sure that the Soviet Union would remain the foremost European power. We have allied ourselves with some of the most corrupt and oppressive regimes, allowing two-bit dictators to blackmail us by inventing or manufacturing their own red menace. But we have also produced our own domestic usurpers, people to whom William Buckley has attributed a "fascist mentality" and who have spun themselves what Seymour Martin Lipset has called a "web of paranoia." Like the tsarist *Okhrana,* our own so-called security agencies have invented, financed, staffed, and otherwise promoted fake Communist conspiracies of their own; and the general hysteria, the witch hunts, the self-censorship, and other mad manifestations of anticommunism have helped subvert our own political processes. In the end, they have made us so gutless that in the face of the usurpers we act exactly like Soviet citizens: either we are willing to believe anything, or we are ready to believe nothing of what our official leaders tell us.

The tough, unyielding, and indeed menacing stance we have taken in world affairs since 1945, in the name of anticommunism, has produced or reinforced its mirror image in the Communist world. I do not believe in the theory of convergence; but I do see the United States and the Soviet Union as mirror images of each other, down to the reciprocally reinforcing paranoia to which they have succumbed. By their saber-rattling and by their militant rhetoric, the hawks on both sides, the toughs, the Machiavellians, the people of Fascist mentality, have supported each other—men who do not listen to the people but fear them, who do not lead them but manipulate their basest instincts. I, for one, cannot rejoice in their traveling to each other's capitals and shaking hands.

The imperial role of establishing a *pax Americana* with ruthless determination is one to which Americans have never quite become accustomed. It does not sit well with this country. It goes against the grain of all the democratic and liberal ideals we are trained to profess. In fact, it might be described as profoundly un-American. Hence, it requires powerful and insistent arguments to justify such a role.

At the time of World War I the Wilsonian slogans about making the world safe for democracy served this function. But in the peace settlement they were discredited quickly. Since then the ideology of anticommunism has furnished the principal arguments in support of America's role as the counter-revolutionary bastion of the world.

I see this ideology, too, as being in fundamental conflict with the spirit and self-image of the United States, so that, in pursuit of a basically un-American aim, the system has more and more violated its own norms. And today we see it coming apart at the seams. In the name of anticommunism the American democracy has to some extent destroyed itself. The worldwide anti-Communist crusade of the last thirty years may have been for the United States what the Sicilian expedition was for Athens, and the sortie of the mighty Armada for Spain.

What is called detente is to some extent the result of the lifting of the ideological fog. We know today that we have been told many lies and that by grossly misreading reality we have systematically deceived ourselves. Every time the United States has intervened in international affairs with force of arms, from the Spanish-American War through two world wars and the many wars since then, we have seemed, in our own eyes, to be bumbling aimlessly and innocently into these entanglements. One must not underestimate the popularity of many of these entanglements. But we also know today that the presidents who got the country into them always used a good deal of fraud, lies, and mis-representation. American interventionism has been possible only as long as presidents usurped the powers to make war and to conduct foreign policy. The lies we have been told included gross exaggerations of neligible dangers:

1. the nonexistent missile gap of the 1950s and many other attemptes by the Pentagon to alarm Congress with the alleged might of the Soviet Union; including the failure to report that after World War II the Soviet armed forces were demobilized almost as drastically as ours, though for different reasons;

2. the dangers of atomic espionage. No one has made a convincing case for the hypothesis that the Soviet Union profited greatly from the little infor-mation it obtained by this method;

3. the deliberate misinterpretation of the Korean War as alleged proof that Moscow wanted to Bolshevize the world. We know today, from highly respectable sources, that the American government at the time was quite aware that this was a local affair started by the North Koreans; or that at most it was a desperate defensive reaction against our unilateral imposition of a peace treaty on Japan.

We have been told by repentant hawks like Arthur Schlesinger that the war in Indochina was a failure of good intentions, that we misjudged China's strength and aggressiveness and thus got sucked in. The Pentagon Papers show that this, too, is false. They show the Vietnam war, or our role in it, which I consider shameful, to have been deliberate aggression, legitimized by systematic lying to the public and to its representatives in Congress, and with the help of incidents deliberately provoked.

I have never heard one rational and convincing argument in favor of the domino theory, or for the theory that preceded it, which was Dean Acheson's image of the one rotten apple in a barrel of healthy ones. According to this theory, a Communist revolution in Greece would have led to a chain reaction of similar revolutions throughout the Middle East. The defeat of a conservative regime anywhere would cause the fall of conservative regimes everywhere. The withdrawal or reduction of US control would immediately surrender a country to Moscow. This theory, it seems to me, reflects a mad overestimation of Soviet strength, particularly Soviet strength in the first decade after the war, and an equally crazy exaggeration of unity in the Communist camp. In addi-tion, it betrays an incredible lack of confidence, a paranoid feeling of weakness, and a total lack of faith in our own system. It is a theory based on crazy anxieties.

We know today, again from the Pentagon Papers, that many people in the White House and in the defense establishment were quite aware at the time that this rotten apple or domino theory was ideological fog camouflaging the real interests as these people perceived them, that is, securing American power all over the globe, firmly answering every challenge, however puny, maintaining the image of invincibility, demonstrating our *will* to dominate, our *readiness* to fight, and our *ability* to win every war.

The attempts to enlist the public for America's imperial role—again, the term is taken from the works of a conservative political scientist who believes in this role—this attempt was aided always by the ideology of anticommunism, America's mirror image of the stupidities of official Soviet ideology.

Let me make it perfectly clear that my criticism of anticommunism does not deny the useful work its spokesmen have done in calling our attention to the inanities of Marxism-Leninism or the cruelties and failures of Communist systems. Most ideologies, including the maddest ones, contain kernels of truth; indeed, the most dangerous system of self-delusion usually contain a great deal of truth. They are dangerous because they exaggerate and distort this truth and thus delude us.

Anticommunism, precisely because it could adduce obvious facts to back up its fanciful misconceptions, has been a powerful and pervasive influence wherever we sought to understand Soviet behavior or intentions and the activities of Communist movements through the entire world. It has dominated academic work to such an extent that we have often been unaware of how inadequate our understanding was.

Let me adduce some of the myths generated by this ideology, myths that are being challenged only gradually.

1. The myth of the compulsory aggressiveness of the Soviet Union, as expounded clearly by George Kennan, who argued in his famous essay that the Soviet Union needs expansion so badly its system would surely collapse if it were contained.

I regard this as a mindless echoing of Lenin's theory of imperialism, which says similar things about the West. It is based on a capricious, wilful misreading of Soviet intentions, policies, and capabilities. And we know today that Soviet foreign policy has, on the whole, been timid, cautious, conservative, and isolationist. That realization is the main thrust of the books on Soviet foreign policy written in the last few years.

2. The myth of ideological determinism; by this I mean the notion that by reading Marx and Lenin we will understand what makes the people in the Kremlin tick. Behind it is the false assumption that their whole system is but an institutionalization of the ideology, an ideology which then serves as their masterplan for world domination, as a metastrategy so fiendishly effective that it succeeds even when it fails. The theory of the ideological master plan always reminds me of nothing so much as the myth about the *Protocols of the Elders of Zion*.

In fact, Marxist ideology is so ambiguous that it cannot serve as a guide to action, as one brief survey of the many varieties of Marxism in the world today will reveal; and whatever revolutionary implications Leninism may have had fifty years ago, when some of the apostles of anticommunism were members of Communist parties, the words have long ago been drained of all their contents and now constitute one of the most dreary, empty, and conservative litanies.

3. Still, even today some scholars in the field find it possible to assert that this ideology makes it impossible for the USSR to enter into bargains, to make compromises, or to keep international agreements. Even today learned articles depict Moscow as the chief disturber of the international order and as a government with which it is impossible to negotiate in good faith. The Soviet Union, according to such theories, responds only to brute force.

Theories of this kind have been argued on the basis of dubious generalizations about the paranoid national character of the Soviet peasants—I am thinking here about the famous book by Nathan Leites—or on the basis of assumptions made about the force of Leninist ideology. I have in mind several articles in the new encyclopedia comparing Soviet soviety with Western democracy which is now in the process of being published.

Meanwhile we are being told that America has always been naive and gullible, easily conned into suicidal benevolence and softness.

What a transparent pretext these myths have provided for persuading Americans that they, too, must become intransigent, tough, devious, conspiratorial, and ruthless! What I am arguing is that the ideology of anticommunism served as an education for what one can only call a semi-Fascist mentality.

It is clear today that men like Acheson and Dulles, as well as many of their predecessors and successors, did their very best to prevent any conciliatory action on the part of the Soviet Union. They tried systematically to confront Moscow with proposals they knew to be unacceptable. Examples are the Marshall Plan and the Baruch Plan.

Myths about the nature of the Soviet system were matched by myths about the international Communist movement.

Evidence to the contrary, we were asked to take it for granted that Communist parties everywhere were devoted to a revolutionary program, when in fact many of them had become thoroughly reformist.

Evidence to the contrary, their major disagreements were dismissed as devious window dressing, designed to conceal their total coordination by Moscow.

Their strength was grossly exaggerated. And in fact the many recent conspiracy trials in the United States have shown that the subversive threat to a large extent is artificially manufactured by our so-called security agencies and by those supposedly guarding the law.

Paranoia is a self-fulfilling prophesy, not only because the FBI encourages dissident youths to become violent. Whoever arms himself against a weak enemy will put that enemy more on his guard and make him stronger.

Whoever is intransigent forces others to be intransigent.

A black-and-white view that denounces all the many shades of gray, not to speak of green and blue and orange, forces all, neutral greys as well as colorful alternatives, to opt for black and white—as if they were the only alternatives. By telling people they must choose between being red or dead, they are compelled to opt for red.

By taking the toughest possible line, the Western world has, in general, since 1917, forced the Soviet Union and many others into a hard line as well. Thus, according to Bohlen and Kennan, the showdown over the Soviet missiles in Cuba, which could have been handled with greater tact, hastened the downfall of Khrushchev and his replacement by hard-liners.

But then, the sway of anti-Communist ideology made every American leader timid in the face of the public. It tied his hands, making it impossible for him even to *try* more conciliatory moves. To obtain even the illusion of detente, we finally had to elect Mr. Nixon.

Today many of those who stood in the forefront of anticommunism, former diplomats like Kennan and Bohlen, political scientists like Ulam and Schlesinger, are in general agreement that the so-called cold war was an aberration.

But was there ever an alternative?

Many scholars assume that the reciprocal paranoia of the cold war was inevitable, though they differ over the reasons:

1. the expansive, aggressive, and missionary nature of the Soviet regime,
2. a conspiracy of our military and political leaders,
3. the exigencies of imperialism and corporate capitalism,
4. the logic of the power situation, according to which the imperial power must be aggressive in warding off all potential threats, and the underdogs must be aggressive in asserting their autonomy, and
5. the quagmire theory, according to which the whole mess was due to honest mistakes on all sides.

I am reluctant to accept any one of these theories, although all of them make partial sense. I am particularly reluctant to accept theories according to which the mess we are in was inevitable. I would like to think—I have always thought—that there were alternatives to our pressing for total domination and for causing the Soviet Union to arm to the teeth.

If paranoia is a self-fulfilling prophesy, then it seems to me that the alternative might function in similar fashion. Humane behavior, in other words, might also become mutually reinforcing.

The alternative to anticommunism was never communism itself. Those who have been suspicious of the hard-line crusaders in the Western world have not the slightest love for the Soviet system, the Communist movement, or Leninist ideology. It seems to me, instead, that they are the ones who have a deep

commitment to everything that is humane and rational and accommodating in the
democratic tradition we profess, including a healthy distrust of authorities, a
deep suspicion of ideologies, and contempt for the toughs and the bullies of the
world. This frame of mind includes a sociological perspective in which there is
little room for conspiracies, villains, or heroes, and a preoccupation with the
complexities of the world, in which there are no stark blacks and whites and
no brute or simple solutions. It is an ideology that makes the spirit of accommodation a central element of its whole way of life.

The choice is not between red and dead, but between ruthlessness and
decency, between Machiavellian politics and a politics based on respect for the
people; the choice, basically, is that between the fascist and the democratic
mentality. The Machiavellians in our midst have always told us, in so many
words, that we must be oppressive abroad in order to protect our liberties at
home. But this advice, so dear to the Bismarcks and the Metternichs of our
world, has always been the advice of scoundrels. Our democratic tradition
teaches us that one must fight tyranny everywhere and that a nation oppressing
others cannot be free. It also asserts that morality, unlike charity, begins at
home. We know from the history of the last century that the colonial administrators, the many people who oppress others in the name of civilization,
sooner or later come home, when their empire contracts; and, having been
spoiled by their experience for life in a constitutional system, they begin to
treat their own fellow-citizens as if they were natives. I am scared to think of
the counterinsurgency agent, the specialist in "pacification," and other crusad-
ing knights of anticommunism practicing at home what they have learned in
Vietnam.

My fears may be exaggerated; and my vision of the alternative will be dismissed by hard-liners on the left and on the right as dreamy and idealistic. But
if the democratic vision is unrealistic, then the entire thrust of our intellectual
and political heritage has been one big mistake. Must we really come to that
conclusion?

So now we are told we have a detente. And I think much of it is phony.

First, the threat from Moscow has always been exaggerated. If it was real,
then talking to them today changes nothing. If it was unreal but is more real
now, which I think to be the case, then it is we who have done most to make it
more real.

Events in the Near East and in the United Nations show how brittle the
alleged detente is. For the first time the Soviet Union is pushing its weight
around, and we must back down. By the time this essay is published, they
might have demonstrated their growing strength in other areas as well.

Meanwhile the civil war in Southeast Asia goes on merrily. The peace
in Vietnam for which Mr. Kissinger got the Nobel Prize was primarily an election gimmick.

As I said in the beginning of this talk, the so-called detente is primarily the admission of failure and thus the beginning of the end of American world leadership. The scales of power are beginning to tip. *Now*, not twenty years ago, we have a situation of bipolarity.

What are the perspectives for global politics?

Will this evening of the scales maintain peace? Hardly. The Soviet Union and the United States were not very likely, in any case, to wage nuclear warfare. But their first major confrontation, in the Near East, has already taken place.

Will this so-called detente maintain law and order in the world? Perhaps. US-Soviet collaboration might have been an important factor in bringing about the tenuous armistice in the Near East. Both of the major powers are conservative. They do not care for revolution. They might now begin to police the world jointly, a prospect not particularly pleasing to the third world. Conservatism, the Metternichian attempt to hold the line against change, is, of course, self-defeating in the long run.

Meanwhile, the rivalry between the two main powers will go on unabated. There is no prospect that we will scale down our military expenditures. Our present secretary of defense has defined detente as "a mailed fist in a velvet glove," i.e., as phony. He told reporters recently that the hope we might cut the Pentagon budget down and spend the money more usefully was "an enchanting illusion."

Our new secretary of state is a brilliant ideologist, but not a person who believes very much in detente. He is a Machiavellian whose heroes are Metternich and Bismarck. He was the principal theoretician of the arms race in the 1950s, and he is the architect of our secret bombing war in Cambodia. World politics, for him, is a Bismarckian balancing act in a world no longer bipolar, and a Metternichian attempt to hold the line against change. But Metternich grossly misread the signs of the time. He lost power, and his political edifice collapsed, not because of some radical conspiracies, but because it was out of tune with the needs of the time. Meanwhile, Bismarck's balancing act ultimately led to the accumulation of political dynamite that exploded in August 1914. The military and political leaders seem to have learned nothing.

Thus, for anyone with democratic and humanitarian convictions there is no cause for rejoicing. The ideological cold war will continue, abroad as well as at home. Doing business with Mao while denouncing communism may be seen as rank hypocrisy and as a declaration of bankruptcy for the anti-Communist ideology. Khrushchev, when plugging for coexistence, always used to add, "But ideologically we will never coexist," which could be interpreted to mean that life is life and ideology is ideology, and the two have little to do with each other.

But the hypocrisy has consequences. The continued sway of the ideology means the continued dominance of self-delusion and the continued political influence of self-righteous ideologists.

As a result of all these factors, I visualize a further weakening of the domestic political and economic fabric, and a further straining of the legitimacy of the American political system. Meanwhile, the Soviet Union will continue to sit tight and arm to the teeth.

The Soviet policy has for years been a policy of containment. One could well argue that they have been remarkably successful, and that their success is in no small measure due to our own behavior. How many decades will it take them to move from containment to rollback? When will we be forced to realize that the United States, by foolishly launching herself into a global anti-Communist crusade, has begun to transform herself into a second-rate power? As I understand the ideology of anticommunism, it will be one of the most serious obstacles to the development of that realization. It will prevent the American people from gaining a realistic insight into the causes of the decline of our power. The potential consequences of such self-delusion for the American political fabric are likely to be disastrous.

17 Some Problems of the Russo-American Detente

Bertram D. Wolfe

To avoid misunderstanding or misrepresentation, I wish to begin by stating that I am whole-heartedly in favor of a genuine, long-lasting detente with any nation that at present conducts its relations with us on the basis of hostility, strain, or tension. Furthermore, all my life I have been, and I am now, an opponent of war as a means of settling differences between nations. I consider war the cruelest, the most barbarous, the most unsatisfactory way of settling differences between countries. Man mocks his humanity when he resorts to war if any other means are available. Especially in our century, a century of total wars and unparalleled weapons for poisoning the earth and its atmosphere, war is likely to destroy all that civilization has achieved, all that men aspire to.

I was brought up in an age that marked the close of one hundred years of comparative peace and progress. My generation seriously believed that the twentieth century would be too civilized for war. I was shocked beyond belief when on August 1, 1914, I discovered that the Europe I admired as the home of our civilization was not too civilized for war. In 1914 that Europe which was to teach young America how to live and think and dream, began to slip back into barbarism with frightening speed and ferocity, a barbarism armed with the weapons of death and destruction perfected by the technologically magnificent twentieth century.

America, I thought, must stay out of Europe's senseless, bloody, barbarian slaughter, and work for the earliest possible return to sanity, for a negotiated peace, without victory for either side, without a legacy of victors and vanquished, without resentments and rancors and lust for vengeance. I thought America should observe a benevolent neutrality, avoid the shipping of contraband to either side, keep our ships and our citizens out of the war zones, remain at peace, conserve our resources to restore ruined Europe and heal her hatreds.

In the end, America entered Europe's war, entered under two preposterous slogans: that it was "a war to end war" and "a war to make the world safe for democracy."

Our entrance made the war truly total, while the "war to end war" opened our century of total wars. We have experienced two total wars, and we live in terror of a third which may be fought with the most fiendish of weapons.

The war that was "to make the world safe for democracy" killed the nascent shoots of democracy in Russia and Germany and, out of the brutalization that springs from total war, begot the first two totalitarian autocracies.

What thoughtful historian can now doubt that if America had stayed out,

333

had permitted the two sides in Europe to fight to the stalemate and exhaustion that seemed to be shaping up, then had worked for a negotiated peace without victors or vanquished, used its resources to rebuild the devasted continent that was the mother of our civilization—what historian can doubt that we would now live in a better world without a Lenin, without a Stalin, without a Hitler?

The Meaning of Detente

Détente is a French word. Neither we nor the Russians have an exact equivalent. In Russian there is the word *razradit* which means either to unload a weapon or to clear the air. In English, the dictionary definition is simple enough. *Detente* is "an easing of strained relations and political tensions between nations." But when we begin to ask *how* to ease tensions, how far to go in relaxation, what to be relaxed about, how to clear the air of misunderstandings and hostility, then difficulties begin and the problems appear.

A genuine relaxation of tensions must involve at least three prerequisites. The first would seem to be tolerance. If you misrepresent your neighbor's way of life, heap abuse upon it, treat it as an evil way of life that must be eradicated, there can be no genuine and permanent relaxation of tensions. Tolerance of ways of life different from that in your own country requires that you try to speak truthfully and fairly of the other country in question. This requires the not too generous rule of live and let live—you be yourself, let us be ourselves. By virtue of this tolerance, governments may welcome the right of other governments and philosophies to exist, or perhaps reluctantly, perhaps indifferently, perhaps a little contemptuously, suffer each other's presence on the same earth. If, another, a foreign government, seeks to set up a fifth column in your country, supports subversion from abroad, tries to choose the leaders of its agent party from abroad and determine their tactics from abroad, one cannot honestly speak of toleration, nor of "peaceful coexistence of nations with differing systems," nor of "detente."

A second and higher prerequisite is mutual trust. Without mutual trust, a treaty for the mutual reduction of armament is not worth the paper it is written on.

A third, and still more difficult prerequisite is abstention from villifying and misrepresenting the life and the actions and the motives of your neighbors, and permitting them freely to explain their actions and their motives in your land by all the normal means of communication. If *Pravda* and *Izvestia* may be freely sold in our land, and may be subscribed to, as I subscribe to them, but the *Times* and the Chicago *Tribune* and the *Washington Post*, or the *Oklahoman*, may not be sold at all in the Soviet Union, there can neither be mutual trust, nor peaceful coexistence, nor an easing of tensions.

Our Shortness of Memory

As a people, we and our leaders suffer from shortness of memory. The present talk of detente is not the first such episode. For more than five and one-half decades we have waited for the Soviet Union to mellow. The Soviet official hostility to us is permanent and deep, a matter of conviction imbedded in their philosophy. From time to time, however, they have become aware of their weakness compared with the supposed enemy they have sworn to destroy. Thus in the early 1920s they had a great famine. Then it was that Lenin talked peace and trade, while he tried to conciliate his starving country by introducing his New Economic Policy or NEP. That was the moment of our first great illusion.

I remember reading of it in the diary of a noble Englishwoman, Lady Kennet of the Deane. In the summer of 1922, she wrote in her diary, "Our troubles with Russia are over. Fridtjof Nansen came to tea, and brought me the glad tidings that Lenin is returning to capitalism."

Six times since then "our troubles with Russia have been over." From illusions concerning the NEP, we went to illusions concerning Stalin's slogan of "Socialism in one country." Next our spokesmen saw peace in Russia's entry into the League of Nations—until the shock of the Stalin-Hitler Pact to divide the world between the two totalitarian states shattered that illusion. But as soon as Hitler double-crossed his accomplice and invaded Russia, we were relieved again and offered Stalin all-out aid without demanding that he give up his conquest of Poland, Lithuania, Latvia, Estonia, and the other spoils of his alliance with Hitler. After Pearl Harbor we formed the Grand Alliance with Stalin. He, for his part, signed the Atlantic Charter, pledging himself to seek no territorial advantages from the war. But today, the countries still imprisoned behind the Iron Curtain, and the wall across the center of Berlin, show how he kept his promise. Yet that did not prevent us from putting our hopes on Khrushchev's "Thaw," on the "Spirit of Camp David," and now on the "Detente" that Brezhnev offers.

In a half century and more, we still have not learned that Russia's maneuvers go in zig zags according to its own periods of weakness and strength. With every zig, we have proclaimed, "At last!" At every zag, we have muttered, "They really can't mean it." Four decades after Lady Kennet's happy tea with Nansen, the learned Daniel Bell of Harvard sought to prove in his *The End of Ideology* that "no state can live in permanent crisis," therefore "a tendency towards normalization must be at work in Russia as in every crisis state." And now, as we approach the sixth decade of Soviet enmity, we are consoling ourselves with the "detente" that we are here examining.

Lenin The Architect of Peaceful Coexistence

The first thing we must note concerning the "detente" is how insistent

Brezhnev is that his policy of peaceful coexistence was "invented" by Lenin, and that he is not deviating by one iota from Lenin's original policy. He wants his leaders, his party members, and the Communists of Bulgaria, Rumania, Poland, and indeed Communists everywhere, to understand his maneuver by their going back to Lenin's works. Even in his television address to the American people on June 24, 1973, he was careful to stress this idea.

"It is not by mere chance that the very concept of peaceful coexistence. . . was evolved by Vladimir Ilyich Lenin."

Let us take Brezhnev's hint then, and ask: What did Lenin really have to say about peace?

Even before he seized power, Lenin said in October 1915 that, once in power, he would propose to the governments an unacceptable peace and prepare a revolutionary war.

Two short weeks before Lenin seized power, Leon Trotsky declared on behalf of Lenin and himself and the Bolshevik party they were leading: "We desire the speediest possible peace on the principles of honorable coexistence and cooperation of peoples; we desire the speediest overthrow of the rule of capital."

And the day Lenin took power, he himself prepared a decree on peace which contained both these points: a proposal to the governments to make peace, and a proposal to the masses to overthrow those governments to bring peace about.

Now, Brezhnev is offering us a peace plan, conceived he says, in Lenin's spirit. Let us see what Lenin wrote about peace plans:

"Every peace plan is a deception of the people and a piece of hypocrisy, unless its principal object is to explain to the masses the need for a revolution and to support, aid, and develop the revolutionary struggle of the masses. . . ."[1]

And what did Lenin have to say about pacifism?

"No revolutionary class can denounce revolutionary war for it would mean condemnation to a ridiculous pacifism."

And about the attitude of a Socialist country towards the abolition of war, Lenin wrote:

> Socialism, victorious in one country does not exclude the existence of all wars in general. On the contrary, it presupposes them. The development of capitalism proceeds highly unevenly in various countries. . . . From this follows the unavoidable conclusion: Socialism cannot win simultaneously *in all* countries. It will win initially in one or several countries, while the rest will remain for some time either bourgeois or prebourgeois. This should result not only in frictions, but also in the direct striving of the bourgeoisie of other countries to smash the victorious proletariat of the socialist state. In such cases a war on our part would be lawful and just . . . a war for socialism, for the liberation of other peoples from the bourgeoisie. . .

Only after we overthrow, completely defeat, expropriate the bourgeoisie in the entire world, and not only in one country, will wars become impossible.[2]

A little later, as a friendly afterthought, Lenin added: "As soon as we are strong enough to defeat capitalism as a whole, we shall immediately take it by the scruff of the neck."[3]

Thus there are two cherished aims in the minds of the Marxist-Leninist Soviet leaders that they regard as inseparable: to talk peace when tactically advisable, and to aim at our overthrow. And though the Brezhnevs have tried, like Bottom the weaver, to "roar you gentle as any sucking dove," they do not intend to let their shock troops and followers forget for a moment that the gentle roar is only play-acting, while they seek to lull our leaders to sleep in a Midsummer Night's Dream.

Indeed, there is something strikingly unoriginal in Brezhnev's maneuvers. He is quite literally making each of his chess moves by the book that Lenin left him. When he is angling for us to make heavy investments in Siberia, he is guided by Lenin's offers of all the industries of the Peninsula of Kamchatka, and of Siberian timber and oil. Then Lenin told his party cell secretaries of the Moscow Party Organization on November 30, 1920, "Concessions do not mean peace; they too are another kind of war, in another form, one that is to our advantage."

When Brezhnev suddenly cancelled his order to send troops to Suez "to police the cease fire", after Nixon had answered it with a worldwide alert, Brezhnev could be sustained by Lenin's admonition, "We have learned how to attack; we must now learn how to retreat. We must learn how to use peace treaties as a means of gaining strength . . . in order to bring up fresh forces as a respite for another war, a breathing spell."

When Brezhnev maneuvers cleverly to get Nixon and Kissinger to recognize the division of Germany into two with a wall across its capital, the subjugation of Poland, Czechoslovakia, Hungary, Bulgaria, Rumania, Estonia, Latvia, and Lithuania, he can talk peace with a good conscience, and even a single note of Lenin's on the margin of one of the books in Lenin's personal library is enough to sustain him. The book is Clausewitz's *On War*. When Lenin came to the sentence, "A conqueror is always a lover of peace," he laughed with delight and wrote in the margin, "Aha! Clever!" And Brezhnev, who has at last persuaded Nixon and Kissinger, after twenty years of firm American resistance, to recognize the "existing boundaries of states," Brezhnev can truly repeat to himself Lenin's words, "A conquerer is always a lover of peace,—Aha! Clever!" For his roaring gentle as any sucking dove has gotten from us by no more than a dovish coo, the recognition of the control or annexation of Rumania, Estonia, Latvia, Lithuania, Northern East Prussia, Czechoslovakia, Poland, some Finnish territory, Tannu Tuva, Albania (now in the camp of Mao), Bulgaria, Eastern

Germany, Bessarabia, Hungary, Mongolia, over two million square miles of
territory with a population of close to 175,000,000 people. In area and population it is comparable to all Western Europe. Verily, a conqueror is always a
lover of peace. "It is ridiculous," Lenin would add, "not to know the history
of war, not to know that the signing of a treaty is a means of gaining strength."
And then he might whisper yet other words in Brezhnev's ear: "Armistices and
temporary agreements are necessary at times . . . to continue the struggle by
other means for a shorter or longer period." But for the long run, "We should
have but one slogan—seriously to learn the art of war." In these regards, Brezhnev
is a faithful Leninist. And our own leaders are committing the same error that
they committed with Hitler, neither to study, nor to take seriously the words of
Leninism's equivalent of *Mein Kampf.*

I do not know how much knowledge of history I have the right to expect
of our president, but where is Dr. Kissinger's historical knowledge and vaunted
realism? In this wonderland world in which Kissinger and Le Duc Tho can get
the Nobel Prize for Peace for negotiating a pseudo-peace treaty, while an offensive
is building up against South Vietnam, and the Soviet Union is openly supplying
arms to North Vietnam and directing an Arab attack on Israel, the Lenin-
Brezhnev idea of the uses of a peace treaty seems to prevail over that of Kissinger.
To add to the wonderland atmosphere, Le Duc Tho rejects the Nobel Prize until
he has finished, if he can, the conquest of the three Vietnams, leaving both
Dr. Kissinger and the Nobel Committee in the positions of the oysters that
accompanied the Walrus and the Carpenter for a stroll along the sea.

Who Is the Father of the Detente?

Brezhnev is a dull and tedious speaker, and I shall not quote him at length.
In the course of duty, I have had to read Lenin, Stalin, Khrushchev, and Brezhnev.
Stalin was interesting for the demonic in his character; Khrushchev, for his touch
of the mountebank and the clown; but Brezhnev is no more interesting than his
face suggests. If he is interesting at all, it is as the head of a great party and
government that, regardless of our good intentions, has sworn our destruction,
and as one who guides himself by the combination of combativeness and guile
in Lenin's *Works.*

Yet there is one thing about Brezhnev that is exciting indeed. It is not Nixon,
nor Kissinger, but none other than L.I. Brezhnev who thought up the tactical
maneuver of the detente. Back in 1967-1968, Brezhnev discussed the matter
in his Politburo. Why did he not continue with the old Communist slogan of
"peaceful coexistence"? Because it was played out. Because it was bloodstained
by wars in far places, and by the Soviet invasions of Hungary and Czechoslovakia.
The West had to be given a new slogan to lure it into partial disarmament, to
secure from it fresh loans and investments and technology, to induce us to let
our guard down.

Moreover, it was obvious that the West cannot hold too long to any course but soon wearies of it. Was it not a good time to renew the attempt to get the West to recognize the territorial gains Stalin made in Eastern Europe in defiance of his pledge in the Atlantic Charter? Was it not a good time to get America to forget the pledge of all the allies including Russia for the self-determination of Lithuania, Latvia, and Esthonia? A good time to get recognition of the partition of Germany and the infamous wall through Berlin and through the heart of the country? Stalin had tried in vain to get a recognition of the new status quo he had attained first in alliance with Hitler, and then in the generous ill-conceived alliance with the democracies. Khrushchev had tried in vain to bully us out of Berlin, to scare us with missiles in Cuba. Soviet agriculture and Soviet industry were in a mess. Even Soviet arms could use our technology. The country's needs cried for help from the more successful West.

In 1968, Brezhnev canvassed the new detente maneuver and the Conference for the Unity of Europe maneuver in his own Politburo. Then in 1969 Brezhnev called a conference of the representatives of seventy Communist countries to meet in Moscow. It met for thirteen days, had as chairman, Brezhnev, as opening reporter, Brezhnev, as closing speaker, Brezhnev. A thirteen-thousand word policy statement was issued in Brezhnev's name. As usual our leaders failed to study it or try to understand what the Communist bloc was up to, just as they failed to take seriously Hitler's *Mein Kampf.* Yet the whole thing was written out, in terribly dull language to be sure, but plain as the nose on my face for all to see. Next, in April 1971, the Russian Communist party held its Twenty-Fourth Congress, attended by delegates from one-hundred national Communist parties. There once more, the new method of "struggle against imperialism" (that's us) was spelled out complete with a new Popular Front, new forms of struggle, a new peace offensive, new support for wars of liberation, all under the slogan of *the detente.* I shall summarize a few of the decisions, written and published for all to see, if only we bother to watch the plans being made for our undoing.

1. A new "anti-imperialist alliance of the revolutionary working class and broad masses of religious people . . . Joint action of Communists with broad masses of Catholics and followers of other religions in united action against imperialism for democracy and socialism . . . . " The present chaos among priests and nuns and in the Jesuit Order is evidence that this is working out much as the Twenty-Fourth Congress planned it.

2. Cooperation and concerted action with Socialists, Social Democrats, and other democratic parties to establish "advanced democratic regimes." We have seen the consequences in countries as far apart as France and Chile, and in Asia and Africa as well. In France the Communist-Socialist alliance won 45 percent of the vote, the Gaullists only 37 percent.

3. The Congress planned further "wars of liberation" in Asia, Africa, and the Middle East. The Arab-Israeli war is one of the fruits of this so-called "liberation".

4. The recognition of the inviolability of the postwar frontiers that Stalin

had seized in Eastern Europe, that is the legalization of the invasion of Czechoslovakia and Hungary and East Germany, and the legalization of the Iron Curtain. In the detente honeymoon, Nixon and Kissinger and Brandt gave in on
this.

5. The convocation of an All-European Security Conference, which is to
replace NATO and secure the withdrawal of American troops from Europe.

Simultaneously, in less public sessions, plans were laid for loans, investments, technology, whole factories, grain, handouts of every description, and
the most-favored-nation status. American bankers and businessmen are falling
over each other to give Russia the means of overrunning Europe and securing
military superiority over the West. True we are having second thoughts as to
whether there really exists the oil and gas that are offered us in futuristic pipe
dreams, and what it will cost to pipe them across one-sixth of the earth. In this
our government shows no memory of the fact that out of the past twenty-five
agreements reached between Soviet leaders and a succession of seven American
presidents, twenty-four have been broken, just as every Soviet non-aggression
and friendship treaty with her neighbors has been broken by the Russians
except one—that with Hitler's Germany, in which case Hitler did the breaking.

In his radio address to the American people, Leonid Brezhnev said: "To
live in peace, we must trust each other. We must know each other better."
Nice words. But when at Helsinki, Western leaders proposed a freer flow of
men and ideas between Eastern and Western Europe, they were soundly rebuffed
by Gromyko and told that the Soviet Union would tolerate "no interference in
its domestic affairs."

On December 21, 1971, when Brezhnev saw that everything was going
wonderfully in his plans for the detente, when he saw that the West had given
in on "mutual and balanced reductions of forces" (by omitting stress on the
word "balanced"), had given the Soviet Union a three-to-two advantage in land-
and sea-based missiles, and other advantages in submarines and multiple warheads,
that we had ceased to demand the tearing down of the wall through Berlin and
all Germany, that our two leading spokesmen, Nixon and Kissinger, are not
insisting on freedom of immigration, nor the right of Soviet citizens to travel
freely outside their country, nor insisting on the free flow of information from
the West to the Communist world, and that Nixon and Kissinger were fighting
at home, and even in speeches made abroad, against both houses of our Congress
on the most-favored-nation grant, and that the West was going into a state of
euphoria merely because of the rebaptizing of the deceitful "peaceful coexistence" as "the detente"—then Brezhnev chose the Christmas season for this
solemn utterance which none of our papers has commented on: The Communist Party of the Soviet Union has proceeded and still proceeds on the basis of
the continuing class struggle between the two systems— the capitalist and the
socialist—in the spheres of economics, of politics, and of course, of ideology.
It could not be otherwise, since the world outlook and class aims of socialism
and capitalism are opposed and irreconcilable.

That was the Christmas message of the General Secretary of the Communist
Party of the Soviet Union to his people given in Moscow on December 21, 1972.
Or rather the *Dedya Moroz* or Father Frost Message, not so much because the
Soviet Government does not recognize Christmas, but because the meaning of
this message is: We shall continue the Cold War, ideological warfare being merely
a more abstract sounding name for the COLD WAR.

Russian Communism's Twofold War

I do not have to impress upon an informed audience the fact that the dictatorship in Russia is a permanent, state-of-siege dictatorship. Throughout its
existence, the party and the government have waged a twofold war: a war on their
own people to transform them according to a blueprint the party possesses; and a
war on the non-Communist world to remake it according to the same blueprint.
*As long as the Russian government thinks of itself as a cause and not as a country,
this twofold war will continue.*
What is it that gives the Communist Party of the Soviet Union the right to
wage this twofold war? The answer simply is—it's doctrine. It was not the proletariat that seized power in Russia. It was not the masses. It was the armed bands,
or shock troops, the selected stormtroopers of Lenin's party. "Power changed
hands," as Trotsky has written, "while the citizens of Petrograd slept." The
party that seized power was Lenin's party, shaped by Lenin's centralism, by
Lenin's concept of dictatorship from above, by Lenin's doctrinal dogmas.
Leinin was convinced that he possessed an infallibly scientific doctrine, of
which he was the infallible interpreter, a doctrine that told him and his party
what history wanted men to do, to be, and to become. This doctrine provided
him with a blueprint for the remaking of the Russian and of the rest of the world.
Anyone who stood in his path was standing in history's way and had to be swept
into "the dustbin of history."
That is why his party puts so many of the people of Russia into prisons,
concentration camps, insane asylums. To challenge the least of the utterances
of the party leaders who inherit Lenin's power and therefore claim his wisdom
is to stand in history's way. What does it matter to history how the way is
cleared?
The latest figure I have for the concentration camp population at the end of
1972 is something over 1,200,000. I have no figures for prisons, nor for insane
asylums, though I have evidence that the wise and sane who are put into police
psychiatry wards and insane asylums run into the hundreds. My figures for the
latter are sketchy coming from *Samizdat,* as they are for those other intellectuals
who are blacklisted from all intellectual and artistic work, given deliberately
humiliating, back-breaking physical labor, or sent to Siberia for being "social parasites" who want to continue their intellectual or scientific work.
You are all familiar with some of the cases: writers like Solzhenitsyn and

Maksimov, who were not permitted to write, or if they wrote, not permitted to publish. The greatest Russian Cellist Rostropovitch, who was prevented from keeping engagements abroad because he sheltered Solzhenitsyn in his home. Their greatest ballet dancer, Valery Panov, discharged from the ballet, and barbarically given a small room to live in with a ceiling so low that he could no longer practice the leaps necessary to ballet dancing. Vera Panova, his wife, a great ballet dancer, and Prima Donna of her ballet company, also deprived from her lifelong profession for the crime of being his wife. The historians Amalrik and Yakir, the one given three years in a camp where there is no bland diet and no physician to treat his stomach ulcer, and when that did not kill him in three years, given a second three. The other, subjected to pressure and torture for thirteen months, then brought into a trial from which impartial lawyers, foreign reporters, and even his wife, were excluded, and finally, when broken in spirit, made to confess impossible crimes in public. One of their greatest scientists and thinkers, Sakharov, no doubt one of the greatest men of our age, being closed in on, police-written false words being attributed to him in the press, while he is denied the right to refute them, his son denied admission to a university, his daughter thrown out in her senior year.

But why should I torture you by repeating more of these gruesome tales of the deeds wrought by the inner barbarian usurpers who have risen to power over a great nation and now inflict these tortures upon the best of its people?

Rather, I will rejoice your hearts by reading a wise, brave comment of an American spokesman on such tortures.

In a sharply worded telegram to the Chairman of the Soviet Academy of Sciences, the President of our National Academy of Sciences declared:

> This will convey to the Academy of Sciences of the U.S.S.R. the deep concern of the council of the National Academy of Sciences of the U.S.A. for the welfare of our foreign associate member, Academician Andrei Sakharov.
>
> We have warmly supported the growing detente being established by our respective governments. We have done so in the belief that such a course would bring significant social and economic benefits to our peoples and generate opportunity for alleviation of that division of mankind which threatens its destruction by nuclear holocaust . . . .
>
> Implicit in this prominence of scientific cooperation in our recent binational agreements was: 1. The recognition that science itself knows no national boundaries; 2. The awareness that the world scientific community shares a common ethic, a common value system and hence is international; 3. Appreciation that mankind the world over derives deep satisfaction from our ever more profound understanding of the nature of man and the universe in which he finds himself. So true and important are these relationships that the

national scientific communities of the world also share heroes, witness the rosters of foreign members of academies of science, including yours and ours . . . .

Unhappily, as Sakharov and others have noted, application of scientific understanding has also generated the means for deliberate annihilation of human beings on an unprecedented scale . . . .

If the benefits of science are to be realized, if the dangers now recognized are to be averted, and if the full life which can be made possible by science is to be worth living, then in the words of Academician Sakharov, 'intellectual freedom is essential to human society—freedom to obtain and distribute information, freedom for open-minded and unfearing debate, and freedom from pressure by officialdom and prejudice.'

Accordingly, it is with great dismay that we have learned of the heightening campaign of condemnation of Sakharov for having expressed, in a spirit of free scholarly inquiry, social and political views which derive from his scientific understanding. Moreover, it was with consternation and a sense of shame that we learned of the expression of censure of Sakharov's contributions to the cause of continuing human progress that was signed by 40 members of your academy including five of our foreign associate members. . .

The case of Andrei Sakharov, however, is far more painful for the fact that some of our Soviet colleagues and fellow scientists are among the principal attackers when one of the scientific community courageously defends the application of the scientific ethos to human affairs.

Were Sakharov to be deprived of his opportunity to serve the Soviet people and humanity, it would be extremely difficult to imagine successful fulfillment of American pledges of binational scientific cooperation, the implementation of which is entirely dependent upon the voluntary effort and goodwill of our individual scientists and scientific institutions.

It would be calamitous indeed if the spirit of detente were to be damaged by any further action taken against this gifted physicist who has contributed so much to the military security of the Soviet people and now offers his wisdom and insights to that people and to the entire world in the interest of a better tomorrow for all mankind.

Conclusion

And now I wish to conclude with a brief summary of what I have been saying.

We must reject the poisoned semantics of the shabby Communist use of the term "detente." In its place we must spell out patiently and in each separate instance what peace and detente really mean.

We must stand more unequivocally for the freedom which is America's two-hundred year old gift to the world, if we have anything at all important to give. We must couple freedom of trade with human freedom. We must oppose totalitarian tyranny without equivocation and evasion, while making the most of the uneasy armistice brought on by the atomic stalemate.

We must cease to seek false satisfaction in hollow and hypocritical words and spell out their meaning in deeds. We must aim at the modification of Communist dogmas and pseudo-ethics by an appeal to the hearts and minds of the Russian and Chinese people, not excluding their leaders, their parties, their armies, their secret police, their emissaries abroad, not expecting too much all at once and not impatient or afraid to keep up the effort over many, many years. To our words we must add deeds, generous offers safeguarded as to their generosity, deeds which will never aid tyranny but speak to the oppressed in the language of men's hearts. And we must keep things in our own country equal in deed and fact to what we say and try to do with words in our dealings abroad.

Notes

1. Lenin's Central Committee Proposals Submitted to an International Socialist Conference, April 22, 1916. In English in *Selected Works,* Vol. V, p. 237.
2. "Military Program of the Revolution," written in 1916, published in 1917, in English in *Collected Works,* Vol. XIX, pp. 362-66.
3. Speech to Moscow Party Nuclei Secretaries, Nov. 26, 1920, *Sochineniia,* 3rd Edition, Vol. XXV, p. 500.

Index

Index

About the Editor and Contributors

Bernard W. Eissenstat has received degrees from the University of Rochester, the University of Iowa, and the University of Kansas. He has taught at Kansas and Northern Arizona Universities and is presently chairman of the Russian and East European Area Studies Program and Professor of History at Oklahoma State University. He has been organizer, coordinator, and director of a number of television and radio programs, and has contributed articles to such journals as *Slavic Review* and *Soviet Studies*. Professor Eissenstat is the editor of *Lenin and Leninism: State, Law, and Society* (Lexington, Mass.: Lexington Books, D.C. Heath and Company, 1971).

John E. Bowlt is Assistant Professor in the Slavic Department at the University of Texas at Austin. He holds degrees from the University of Birmingham and the University of St. Andrews, and studied for two years at Moscow State University under a British Council Scholarship. Professor Bowlt has taught Russian language and literature at the University of St. Andrews and the University of Birmingham; he was also a Visiting Assistant Professor to the Slavic Department at the University of Kansas. He is the author of *The Russian Avantgarde: Theory and Criticism 1902-1934* (1974) and contributor to *The Slavonic and East European Review, Russian Literature Triquarterly, 20th Century Studies, Apollo, Art in America, Studio International, Forum,* and *Art Journal,* among other scholarly journals.

Helen Desfosses is affiliated with the Russian Research Center at Harvard University. She holds degrees from Newton College of the Sacred Heart, Harvard University, and Boston University. Professor Desfosses is the author of *Soviet Policy Toward Black Africa: The Focus on National Integration* and coauthor of *Socialism in the Third World*. She is the recipient of a Coretta Scott King Fellowship, Chairperson of the Committee on the Status of Women, and a member of the African Studies Association.

Dennis Dunn is Assistant Professor of History and Director of the Institute for the Study of Religion and Communism at Southwest Texas State University. A graduate of John Carroll University and Kent State University, Professor Dunn has taught at John Carroll University, Kent State University, Borremeo Seminary-College, and Cleveland State University.

353

William C. Fletcher is Professor of History and Director of Slavic and Soviet Area Studies at the University of Kansas. He received degrees from the University of California at Los Angeles, California Baptist Theological Seminary, and the University of Southern California. Prior to his present position, Professor Fletcher was Research Associate at the Research Institute on Communist Strategy and Propaganda in the School of International Relations at the University of Southern California, and Director of the Centre de Recherches et d'Etudes des Institutions Religieuses (Geneva). He has published extensively in a number of journals; the latest of his nine books is *Religion and Soviet Foreign Policy, 1945-1970* (London: Oxford University Press, 1973).

George H. Hampsch is Professor of Philosophy at the College of the Holy Cross. He received degrees from Loyola University (Illinois), DePaul University, and the University of Notre Dame. His publications include *The Theory of Communism* (New York: Citadel Press, 1965) and his articles have appeared in *New China, Central Slavic Review, East European Review,* and other professional journals.

W.A. Douglas Jackson has received degrees from the University of Toronto, the University of Maryland, and Columbia University. He is Associate Director of the Russian and East European Institute at the University of Washington (Seattle). Professor Jackson has been editor of a number of journals, and has contributed to such journals as *Soviet Survey, The Slavic Review,* and *The Professional Geographer.* Among his latest books is *Agrarian Problems of Communist and Non-Communist Culture* (Seattle: University of Washington Press, 1971).

Roger E. Kanet is Associate Professor of Political Science at the University of Illinois. He holds degrees from Berchmanskolleg (Pullachi-bei-München, Germany), Xavier University, and Princeton University. Professor Kanet is the author of *The Behavioral Revolution and Communist Studies: Applications of Behaviorally-Oriented Political Research on the Soviet Union and Eastern Europe,* and the coauthor of *The Legal and Political Implications of the Development and Implementation of Remote-Sensing Devices* and *On the Road to Communism: Essays on Soviet Domestic and Foreign Politics.* He has been contributing editor for the *American Bibliography of Russian and East European Studies* (1967-71 issues); book review consultant for the *Slavic Review;* and General Editor of *The Slavic World.*

Wladislaw G. Krasnow was a lieutenant in the Soviet Army and an editor at Moscow Radio's Foreign Broadcast Division until he defected to Sweden in 1962. In 1965, he was invited to become a Fellow of the Slavic Area Studies Committee at the University of Chicago and in 1966 he immigrated to the United States. He holds degrees from the University of Moscow, the University of Gothenburg, and the University of Washington (Seattle). Professor Krasnow has taught Russian language and literature at the University of Lund, the University of Washington, and is currently teaching at the University of Texas at Austin.

Roy D. Laird is Professor of Political Science and a member of the staff of the Slavic and Soviet Area Center at the University of Kansas. He received degrees from Hastings College, the University of Nebraska, and the University of Washington. Professor Laird is a founder of both the Conference on Soviet Agricultural and Peasant Affairs, and the International Symposium of Soviet Agriculture. He is the author of *Collective Farming in Russia, The Rise and Fall of the M.T.S. as an Instrument of Soviet Rule,* and has edited *Soviet Agricultural and Peasant Affairs* and *Soviet Agriculture: The Permanent Crisis.* Professor Laird has also contributed numerous articles to academic journals.

John H. Langley is the Director of the University Press of Kansas. He received degrees from the University of Illinois and Harvard University Graduate School of Business Administration. He has also been Assistant Director of the Duke University Press (1963-70) and held the same position at Prentice-Hall, Inc. (1947-63). Mr. Langley is a noted author and lecturer on publishing.

Alfred G. Meyer received degrees from Harvard University, and has taught at Harvard University, the University of Washington, Michigan State University, and the University of Michigan where he is Collegiate Professor of Political Science. He was previously Assistant Director of the Russian Research Center, Harvard University; Director of the Research Program on the History of the CPSU, Columbia University; and Director of the Center for Russian and East European studies, University of Michigan. Professor Meyer's many publications include: *The Incompatible Allies, Marxism: The Unity of Theory and Practice, Leninism, Communism,* and *The Soviet Political System.*

Phillip A. Petersen is an Extension Specialist in Civil Defense in the University Office of Continuing Education at the University of Illinois. He holds degrees from Central Michigan University, Western Michigan University, and Wayne State University. Professor Petersen has also been an instructor in the Command and Staff Department at the United States Army's Security Agency Training Center and School.

Victor Rashkovsky received his professional training at the Moscow Institute of the Theater Arts. Before coming to the United States he was a Research Associate in the Moscow Institute of Sociological Research, which is attached to the Academy of Sciences of the USSR. Professor Rashkovsky has published over thirty articles in such journals as *The Art of Cinema* and *Soviet Screen and Theater.*

Joseph Schiebel is Director of the Russian and European Program at Georgetown University. He is a special consultant to both the Department of State and the Department of Defense, and his articles have appeared in such journals as *Orbis.*

Charles E. Timberlake is Associate Professor of History at the University of Missouri at Columbia. He has published articles in *Slavic Review, Finnish Historical Review,* and other academic journals. He is the editor of *Essays on Russian Liberalism.*

Richard Ivan Towber has received degrees from the State University of New York at Stony Brook and the University of Minnesota. He has published both in the *Russian Review* and for the United States Government.

Karl A. Wittfogel received the Ph.D. from the University of Frankfurt (Main) in 1928. Since 1925, he has been a member of the Frankfurt Institute for Social Research, which in 1934 was relocated at Columbia University. Professor Wittfogel's many publications include *Oriental Despotism* and *Agriculture, a Key to the Understanding of Chinese Society Past and Present.*

Bertram D. Wolfe is Senior Research Fellow at the Hoover Institution on War, Revolution and Peace at Stanford, California. He holds degrees from City College of New York, the University of Mexico, Columbia University, and the University of California. Professor Wolfe's previous positions include those of Visiting Instructor in Hispanic Culture, Stanford University; Chief of the Ideological Advisory Staff, International Broadcasting Division, Department of State; Distinguished Visiting Professor of Russian History at the University of California; and Townsend Harris Medalist at City College of New York. Professor Wolfe has published extensively; perhaps his most famous volume is *Three Who Made a Revolution.* In 1972 he received the Award for Distinguished Contributions to Slavic Studies from the American Association for the Advancement of Slavic Studies.